Accountable Marketing

Accountable Marketing offers a multi-disciplinary perspective on accountability, based on the work of the Marketing Accountability Standards Board (MASB), a unique forum that facilitates dialog among marketers, financial professionals, and accountants, as well as students and instructors involved in business education. The book covers core marketing issues and topics, including finance, social media, language and metrics standards, and the long-term consequences of marketing decisions. Drawing on the knowledge of expert contributors, editors David Stewart and Craig Gugel offer a complete, internationally-based discussion on marketing accountability.

The book acts as a reference point for the development of standards in marketing reporting by linking marketing activities and their outcomes to the financial performance of a firm. Readers interested in marketing accountability will find its four-part structure easy to navigate. Practicing professionals, faculty, and students will benefit from its practical approach and unique, explanatory diagrams.

David W. Stewart holds the President's Chair in Marketing and Law at Loyola Marymount University, USA. He is a former editor of the *Journal of Marketing* and the *Journal of the Academy of Marketing Science* and is the current editor of the *Journal of Public Policy and Marketing*. He is a co-founder and current chair of MASB and has consulted for a wide array of corporations, government agencies, and not-for-profit organizations.

Craig T. Gugel is Assistant Professor of Advertising & Marketing Communications at Fashion Institute of Technology and President, CEO and Chief Research Officer of Gugelplex TV, Inc., USA. He is an advisory council member of the Marketing Accountability Standards Board and co-manages its Book Project team.

"Marketing science has empirically demonstrated the impact of marketing on business success. By promoting common standards and language, MASB is advancing the dialogue with finance about the value of marketing as an investment. MSI is pleased to be a charter sponsor of this effort. This must-read book provides a roadmap for the future of marketing accountability."

Katherine N. Lemon, Boston College, USA

"After a number of years of hard work, the Marketing Accountability Standards Board has delivered on its promise: to get marketing and CMOs the kinds of measurement tools and empirical evidence that will get them seats at the table at the highest levels of organizations. Dave Stewart and Craig Gugel have curated a book that will be essential reading for all marketing managers and academics as well."

Russ Winer, Stern School of Business, New York University, USA

"There is one group exclusively devoted to marketing measurement . . . predictive of financial return . . . and all marketers who are serious about meeting the accountability mandate should read this book and get involved."

Bob Liodice, President & CEO, Association of National Advertisers, USA

"It is the most complex time in the history of advertising, yet the C-suite questions are simple: (1) 'Do my marketing $ drive growth and sales?' and (2) 'Where do I spend my next marketing $?' MASB's work, focused on the accurate and comparable measurement of marketing efforts, is advancing the industry to respond to these C-suite needs and to drive much needed growth."

Gayle Fuguitt, President & CEO, The Advertising Research Foundation, USA

"This book not only lays the groundwork for new working relations between finance and marketing, it also documents the process of initiating fundamental change in the business community through collaboration across industry lines. Through MASB's efforts, we will soon have the measurement standards necessary for continuous improvement in financial performance."

Rajeev Batra, Ross School of Business, University of Michigan, USA

Accountable Marketing
Linking Marketing Actions to Financial Performance

Edited by David W. Stewart and Craig T. Gugel

NEW YORK AND LONDON

First published 2016
by Routledge
711 Third Avenue, New York, NY 10017

and by Routledge
2 Park Square, Milton Park, Abingdon, Oxon OX14 4RN

Routledge is an imprint of the Taylor & Francis Group, an informa business

© 2016 Taylor & Francis

The right of the editors to be identified as the authors of the editorial material, and of the authors for their individual chapters, has been asserted in accordance with sections 77 and 78 of the Copyright, Designs and Patents Act 1988.

All rights reserved. No part of this book may be reprinted or reproduced or utilized in any form or by any electronic, mechanical, or other means, now known or hereafter invented, including photocopying and recording, or in any information storage or retrieval system, without permission in writing from the publishers.

Trademark notice: Product or corporate names may be trademarks or registered trademarks, and are used only for identification and explanation without intent to infringe.

Library of Congress Cataloging in Publication Data
Names: Stewart, David, 1948- author. | Gugel, Craig, author.
Title: Accountable marketing : linking marketing actions to financial
  performance / David W. Stewart & Craig Gugel.
Description: New York : Routledge, 2016.
Identifiers: LCCN 2015047661| ISBN 9781315639703 (ebk) | ISBN
  9780765647061 (hbk) | ISBN 9780765647078 (pbk)
Subjects: LCSH: Marketing—Management.
Classification: LCC HF5415.13 .S8744 2016 | DDC 658.8—dc23
LC record available at http://lccn.loc.gov/2015047661

ISBN: 978-0-765-64706-1 (hbk)
ISBN: 978-0-765-64707-8 (pbk)
ISBN: 978-1-315-63970-3 (ebk)

Typeset in Times New Roman
by Swales & Willis Ltd, Exeter, Devon, UK

Printed and bound in Great Britain by
TJ International Ltd, Padstow, Cornwall

To my teachers and my students
DWS

To my business colleagues and university professors
CTG

Contents

List of Figures ix
List of Tables xii
List of Contributors xiii
Preface xx
Acknowledgments xxiii

SECTION I
Introduction: Making Marketing Accountable 1

1 **Delivering to the Marketing Accountability Mandate** 3
   MARGARET HENDERSON BLAIR, MITCH BARNS,
   KATE SIRKIN, AND DAVID W. STEWART

2 **Lessons from the Quality Movement** 18
   DAVID W. STEWART

SECTION II
Language, Measures, and Metrics: Establishing Standards 43

3 **Marketing's Search for a Common Language** 45
   PAUL FARRIS, DAVID J. REIBSTEIN, AND KAREN SCHELLER

4 **Measuring Brand Preference** 52
   MICHAEL HESS AND ALLAN R. KUSE

5 **Measuring Return on Brand Investment** 60
   FRANK FINDLEY

6 **Customer Lifetime Value and Its Relevance to the Consumer Packaged Goods Industry** 69
   V. KUMAR AND SARANG SUNDER

7 **Customer Lifetime Value in the Packaged Goods Industry** 83
   RICK ABENS AND DEBRA PARCHETA

8 What Is Known About the Long-Term Impact of Advertising 96
DOMINIQUE M. HANSSENS

9 Long-Term Effects of Marketing Actions 114
MICHAEL HESS

10 Social Media: What Value for Marketing Measurement? 127
KATE SIRKIN

SECTION III
Linking Finance and Marketing 135

11 The Relationship of Marketing and Finance 137
DONALD E. SEXTON

12 Creating a Partnership between Marketing and Finance 149
JAMES MEIER

13 Reporting on Brands 168
ROGER SINCLAIR

14 Brand Valuation in Accordance with GAAP and Legal Requirements 182
MARC FISCHER

15 Measuring the Value of Corporate Brands: Translating Corporate Brand Strategy into Financial Results 201
JAMES R. GREGORY

16 Tax Implications of the Treatment of Marketing Expenses 218
MICHAEL L. MOORE

17 The Marketing Metric Audit Protocol 226
DAVID W. STEWART, MARGARET HENDERSON BLAIR, AND ALLAN R. KUSE

SECTION IV
Organizational Dimensions of Marketing Accountability 233

18 Navigating Barriers, Opportunity, and Change on the Marketing Accountability Journey, or Road to ROMI 235
MARGARET HENDERSON BLAIR AND PAMELA HOOVER FORBUS

19 Marketing Organization and Accountability 243
DAVID W. STEWART AND ROBERT D. WINSOR

20 Epilogue 261
CRAIG T. GUGEL AND DAVID W. STEWART

Index 266

Figures

1.1	Three Classes of Marketing Outcomes	5
1.2	APM Facts: Marketing Activity, Metrics, and Financial Links	9
1.3	MASB: Filling the Need	10
1.4	Organizational Structure	11
3.1	The DuPont Model	47
3.2	Common Language Project	49
4.1	Comparison of ASSESSOR Pre-Test Market and Test Market Shares	55
4.2	Relationship of ARS Persuasion Scores to ASSESSOR Trial	56
4.3	Brand Preference Relates to Quarterly Share Change	57
5.1	Differences in Unit Shares among Brands	61
5.2	Positive Relationship within Each Category	62
5.3	Relationship between Groupings of Brands Based on Their Price Relative to the Category Average	63
5.4	Each Brand's Relative Distribution	64
5.5	Brand Preference Combined with Relative Price and Distribution	64
5.6	Mean and Median Correlations and Corresponding Variances	65
5.7	Average Variance Explained in Unit Share Compared to That of Brand Preference	66
5.8	Perspective on Areas for Improvement	67
6.1	Conceptual Measurement of CLV	71
7.1	Firm Value/Perspective/Intrinsic Value	84
7.2	CLV Target Marketing	85
7.3	Highly Loyal Buyers Who Remain Loyal	86
7.4	Probability of Being an Active Customer	87
7.5	Probability of Being Active Changes	88
7.6a	CE vs. Weekly POS Sales Dollar Trend	89
7.6b	Sales Trend after CLV Study $Y/Y	89
7.7	CE$$$ Trend Shows Customer Equity will Fall and Rise; Panel Sales Fall and Rise in the Future Years	90
7.8	Retain Loyal Buyers/Retain Loyals while Investing in Acquisition	91
7.9a	Price Elasticity of Brand B	92
7.9b	Advertising Elasticity	92
7.10	CE and Advertising for a Pilot Test Brand	93
7.11a	CLV Appears to Be Responsive to Advertising/CE and Advertising for a Pilot Test Brand	94
7.11b	CLV Appears to Be Responsive to Advertising/CE and Advertising for a Pilot Test Brand	94
8.1	Immediate Impact of Oscar Mayer Lunchable Advert	99
8.2	BASES Results for Starkist Tuna in a Pouch	99

8.3	The More Persuasive the Ad, the Higher and Longer the Impact	100
8.4	Explaining Variation in Volume Impacted by TV Quarter-to-Quarter	100
8.5	Ads Work Quickly with Diminishing Returns and Wearout	101
8.6	The Short-Term Impact of Advertising Is Doubled in Years 2 and 3	101
8.7	Wearout (Reversion to the Mean) and Sustained Advertising Activity	102
8.8	Return on Investment for Starkist's Feedback-Based Approach	103
8.9	Citrucel Share Responds to Airing of Persuasive Ads	104
8.10	Citrucel's Success Continues in Year 1, Year 2, and Beyond	104
8.11	Prego's Share Increases with Better Practice Team	105
8.12	ROI for Prego Was over 5,000% for the Five-Year Period	105
8.13	Market Share Declined When Prego Brand Group Turned Over	106
8.14	Duracell Outpaces Eveready in Unit Sales	106
8.15	Duracell's TV Advertising Was More Effective than Eveready's	107
8.16	Sales Soared during the OTC Division's BAP Years	108
8.17	Post-BAP Years Show a Decline in Sales	108
8.18	Correlation Pattern of Marketing Expenditures	109
8.19	Metamucil Loses Share to Citrucel	110
8.20	Prego versus Ragu: Five-Year Overview	111
8.21	Duracell versus Eveready: Eleven-Year Case Study	111
9.1	Pie Chart Comparing Eveready/Trade/Consumer and Advertising	116
9.2a	Duracell's TV Advertising Was More Effective than Eveready's	119
9.2b	Duracell Outpaces Eveready in Unit Sales	119
9.3	Average Incremental Sales Effect of Television Advertising	120
9.4	Results of "Successful" One-Year Advertising Tests	120
9.5	Results of "Non-Successful" One-Year Advertising Tests	121
10.1	Facebook Popularity	127
10.2	How Important Are These Social Media Networks?	128
10.3	Percentage of Time Spent Engaging with Social Media Activities	129
10.4	Facebook Brand Pages—Global Category Norms—March 2015	130
10.5	Automotive Journey Purchase	131
10.6	What is the MOST Important Marketing Metric Your Team Measures and Reports?	133
11.1	ROI Tree	137
11.2	Marketing and Finance Metrics	138
11.3	Perceived Value, and Marketing and Financial Metrics	140
11.4	Perceived Value	140
11.5	How Marketing Works	142
11.6	Competitive Life Cycle	145
13.1	Components of S&P 500 Market Value	169
13.2	External Environment	180
14.1	The Process of Brand Valuation Creation	184
15.1	The Brand Experience	202
15.2	Aflac—Case Study in Building Brand Equity Value. Familiarity and Favorability	208
15.3	Aflac—Case Study in Building Brand Equity Value. Favorability Attributes	209
15.4	Aflac—Case Study in Building Brand Equity Value. CoreBrand Equity Value	210
15.5	The Two Dimensions of Corporate Brand Power	212
15.6	Factors Impacting Corporate Brand Power	215

15.7	Factors Impacting Corporate Stock Price	216
15.8	Communication ROI. Projection of Financial Impact over Time	217
17.1a	Conceptual Basis of the MMAP	227
17.1b	Conceptual Basis of the MMAP	228
17.2	APM Facts: Marketing Activity, Metrics and Financial Links	229
18.1	Reengineered Ad Development and Management Process w/Vendor Tools	240

Tables

4.1	Correlation Relationship between Various Attitudinal Attributes to Changes in Brand Preference	58
6.1	Examples of CLV Implementations in Various Business Settings	73
6.2	Traditional Metrics vs. CLV	75
13.1	Summary of Main Post-Transaction Accounts—P&G's Purchase of The Gillette Company in 2005	171
13.2	Intangible Assets	173
13.3	Relief from Royalty Example	177
13.4	Disparity of Values among the Top Ten Brands	178
14.1	FASB Accounting Qualities and Derived Critical Brand Asset Valuation Criteria	185
14.2	Overview of Measures Used to Compute the Brand Equity Share	190
14.3	Comparison of Choice Model and Heuristic Method Brand Equity Shares across Different Industries	192
14.4	Overview of Variable Definitions and Data Sources for the Calculations of Brand Value in Table 14.5	194
14.5	Financial Value of Selected Brands in the German Market as of 2003	195
15.1	Client's Brand Equity vs. Peer Group Brand Equity	206
17.1	Information in a MMAP Audit Summary	231

Contributors

Rick Abens is founder and President of Foresight ROI, a marketing analytic firm focused on shopper marketing ROI measurement. He developed shopper marketing-specific models to measure ROI and the synergies between shopper marketing and trade merchandising. Foresight published a benchmark study of shopper marketing best practices, performance standards and industry norms from over 13,000 events measured. Rick has been helping CPG companies improve marketing productivity with business insights, applied analytics and practical recommendations for over 25 years. Prior to founding Foresight ROI, he was Director of Global Marketing Analytics at ConAgra Foods, where he built the corporate marketing analytics function and ROI management processes. He has held senior market research positions at Kraft Foods, AC Nielsen, and Kellogg's. Rick also currently serves as Director for MASB. In his work at Foresight ROI and with MASB he is advancing the ability to measure integrated marketing synergies, measure long-term marketing impact and improve shopper marketing effectiveness.

Mitch Barns is Chief Executive Officer of Nielsen. He was appointed to this role in January 2014. Since joining Nielsen in 1997, Mitch has lived and worked on three continents and has held leadership roles across the business, spanning information and insights and the company's segments of Watch and Buy. Throughout 2013, Mitch served as President, Global Client Service, leading the efforts of Nielsen's client service organization worldwide, helping clients manage the performance of their business. Before that, Mitch was President of Nielsen's U.S. Media business from 2011–2013, where he oversaw the development of its analytics practice, integrated its TV and Digital groups, and guided the transformation of the unit's client service model to focus on driving performance improvement and value for Nielsen's clients. From 2008–2011, Mitch served as President of Nielsen's Greater China business where he led its transition to a fast-growing, standalone region. In the early 2000s, he was President of Nielsen's BASES and Analytic Consulting businesses, which have since become the core of the company's growing insights services. He first joined the company as part of Nielsen BASES, where he held various senior positions in the US and Europe. He began his career at Procter & Gamble, where he spent 12 years in marketing research and brand management. Mitch serves on the Board of Trustees for The Paley Center for Media and is a member of the American Heart Association CEO Roundtable. Mitch holds a BS in business administration from Miami University and completed the Stanford Executive Program at the Stanford Graduate School of Business. He joined The Boardroom Project in 2004.

Margaret (Meg) Henderson Blair is founding President and CEO of the Marketing Accountability Foundation. Prior to this position, Meg was founding President of The ARS Group, devoting over three decades to the measurement of advertising and how it impacts behavior in the marketplace. Her passion for measurement development and learning through ongoing research-on-research culminated in extensive knowledge about how advertising works to create consumer brand preference/choice, sales and market share, as well as how empirically-based changes in the advertising processes can lead to dramatic improvement in return. Meg has shared this learning in both spoken and written venues including the *Journal of Advertising Research*, *Business Horizons*, the German publication *Planung und Analyse*, American Academy of Advertising, *Corporate Finance Review*, and Media Post's *Media*. She received the 2005 Distinguished Practitioner Award from the Academy of Marketing Science and the Advertising Research Foundation Lifetime Achievement Award in 2012. Meg attended Sarah Lawrence College, the New School for Social Research, and holds an honorary DSc from the University of Southern Indiana.

Paul Farris is the Landmark Communications Professor of Business at the University of Virginia's Darden School of Business. Previously, he worked in marketing management for Unilever, Germany and the LINTAS advertising agency. Professor Farris is a current or past board member for several international companies and is a past academic trustee of the Marketing Science Institute. He is the co-author of award-winning work in marketing metrics, advertising research, advertising budgeting, and retail power.

Frank Findley is Vice President of Research and Development for MSW•ARS Research. An expert in quantitative measurement, Frank has pioneered numerous improvements to the tracking, media, copy testing, and competitive intelligence techniques used within the industry. In 2006, he designed the first multi-touchpoint holistic campaign testing system and popularized the approach through leading trade conferences and publications. His more recent work has focused on panel quality, non-cognitive measures, gamification, and the sales effectiveness of digital advertising. In 2014, Frank was co-awarded a patent for the outlook® media planning tool used by marketers to optimize and forecast advertising returns. Frank holds a BS in Physics degree from Purdue University and an MS degree from the Krannert Graduate School of Management.

Marc Fischer is the director of the Chair for Marketing and Market Research at the University of Cologne. He is also an affiliated senior faculty member at the marketing discipline group of UTS Business School, Sydney. His expertise includes the measurement and management of marketing performance, brand management, and the optimization of marketing mix. Dr. Fischer studied Business Administration at the University of Mannheim majoring in Marketing, Production and Supply Chain Management, Management Accounting, and Anglistics. He received his PhD from the Faculty of Business at the University of Mannheim and his habilitation from the Faculty of Economics and Social Sciences at the Christian-Albrechts-University at Kiel. His articles have appeared in *Journal of Marketing Research*, *Marketing Science*, *Management Science*, *Quantitative Marketing and Economics*, *International Journal of Research in Marketing*, *Interfaces*, and other academic journals. Dr. Fischer is member of the advisory board of cpi consulting (Berlin), YouGov AG (Cologne), and the Center for Brand Management and Marketing (ZMM) in Hamburg.

Pamela (Pam) Hoover Forbus is Senior Vice President, PepsiCo Global Consumer Demand Insights. In this role, Pam leads the consumer and commercial insights function globally. Her team's mission is to relentlessly pursue decisions that have a material impact on business performance (growth) and advocate for best actions to improve probability of success through advantaged practices in human understanding, demand insights and foresights, and predictive decision science. Pam is an accomplished leader who transformed Frito-Lay North America (FLNA) Insights into a high-impact team. She led a multi-year effort with her team to create industry-leading capabilities in demand science and decision analytics that were foundational to FLNA's growth agenda. Pam serves as a director on the Marketing Accountability Standards

Board, on the board and Executive Committee of the Marketing Science Institute, the advisory board of Yale's Center for Customer Insights, and the advisory board for the Center for Customer Insight and Marketing Solutions, University of Texas. She holds a BBA from Saginaw Valley State University and a professional certification in market research from the University of Georgia.

James R. Gregory is the chairman of Tenet Partners, a global brand innovation and marketing firm based in New York, NY, and Los Angeles, CA. With 40 years of experience in advertising and branding, Jim is a leading expert on brand strategy and is credited with pioneering strategies for measuring the power of corporate brands and their impact on financial performance. Most notable of the tools that Jim developed is the CoreBrand Index® (CBI), a quantitative research vehicle that continuously tracks the reputation and financial performance of over 1,000 publicly traded companies across 50 industries. This study has been continuously fielded since 1990 and is the only database of its kind. Tenet uses the CBI to help clients recognize how their brands compare with industry peers and how communications can impact corporate reputation and financial performance, which includes stock price and revenue growth. Jim is a frequent speaker on the topic of the financial benefits of communications and brand management. Recent speaking engagements include The Conference Board, Association of National Advertisers, National Investor Relations Institute, and the UCLA School of Law. Jim serves on the Board of Directors of Tervis Tumbler Corporation, a privately held consumer products company. Jim is also a founding member of the Marketing Accountability Standards Advisory Council and is the co-chair of the Improving Financial Reporting Committee of MASB. Jim has written four books on creating value with brands: *Marketing Corporate Image*, *Leveraging the Corporate Brand*, *Branding across Borders*, and *The Best of Branding*.

Craig T. Gugel is President/CEO and Chief Research Officer of Gugelplex TV, Inc. He has also served as Chief Research Officer of Merkle, Inc. (LogicLab), President of Telmar Group's North American divisions, as Executive Vice President, Worldwide Analytics & Strategy (IMS) at The Nielsen Company, as EVP, Director of Strategic Insights at Publicis-owned Optimedia International, and as EVP, Director of Media Resources & Research at Bates Worldwide. He began his career as a spot media buyer on automotive accounts and later gravitated to the New York research community working for several agencies including McCann-Erickson Worldwide, Foote Cone & Belding Communications, Bozell Jacobs Kenyon & Eckhardt, Manhattan-Pacific Multimedia (now Gugelplex TV, Inc.), and Organic, Inc. Craig is an advisory council member of MASB, a past board member of both MASB and the Advertising Research Foundation, and a past member of the Editorial Advisory Board of the *Journal of Advertising Research*. He is also an Adjunct Assistant Professor in the Advertising & Marketing Communications Department at Fashion Institute of Technology, a division of the State University of New York. He holds a BA in Communication Studies from the University of Windsor and a BS in International Trade & Marketing from Fashion Institute of Technology.

Dominique M. Hanssens is the Bud Knapp Distinguished Professor of Marketing at the UCLA Anderson School of Management. From 2005 to 2007 he served as Executive Director of the Marketing Science Institute. A Purdue University PhD graduate, Professor Hanssens' research focuses on strategic marketing problems, in particular marketing productivity, to which he applies his expertise in data-analytic methods such as econometrics and time-series analysis. He has served or is serving in various editorial capacities with *Marketing Science*, *Management Science*, *Journal of Marketing Research*, and *International Journal of Research in Marketing*. Six of his articles have won Best Paper awards, in *Marketing Science* (1995, 2001, 2002), *Journal of Marketing Research* (1999, 2007), and *Journal of Marketing* (2010), and eight were award finalists. The second edition of his book with Leonard Parsons and Randall Schultz, entitled *Market Response Models* was published in 2001 and translated into Chinese in 2003. He is a Fellow of the INFORMS Society for Marketing Science and a recipient of the Churchill and Mahajan awards from the American Marketing Association. He is a founding partner of MarketShare, a global marketing analytics firm headquartered in Los Angeles.

Michael Hess previously served as Executive Vice President, Data Fusion and Integration, at The Nielsen Company. He has also held positions in market research at Carat, Omnicom Media Group, Taylor Nelson Sofres, The Clorox Company, Information Resources Inc., and BASES. He has written over 150 articles, conference proceedings, book chapters, etc., on marketing and advertising and co-authored an article for the 50th anniversary issue of the *Journal of Advertising Research* in 2011. Mike holds an MA in experimental psychology from Columbia University, an MBA in marketing research from the University of Pennsylvania's Wharton School, and a BS in psychology from Loyola University.

V. Kumar (VK), the Regents Professor, Lenny Distinguished Chair and Professor in Marketing, and the Executive Director at the Center for Excellence in Brand & Customer Management at Georgia State University. VK is recognized as the Chang Jiang Scholar at HUST, China; Lee Kong Chian Fellow at SMU, Singapore; and has received over 12 lifetime achievement awards in various areas of marketing including the 2015 Distinguished Marketing Educator Award from the AMS and the Paul D. Converse Award. VK has received the Sheth Foundation/JM Award, Robert Buzzell Award, Davidson Award, Paul H. Root Award, Don Lehmann Award, and Gary L. Lilien ISMS-MSI Practice Prize Award. He has published over 200 articles in scholarly journals in marketing as well as book chapters. VK has written over 15 books including *Managing Customers for Profit, Customer Relationship Management, Customer Lifetime Value, Marketing Research, Profitable Customer Engagement, Statistical Methods in CRM*, and *International Marketing Research*. VK spends his "free" time visiting business leaders to identify challenging problems to solve. Recently, VK has been chosen as a *Legend in Marketing* where his work is published in a ten-volume encyclopedia with commentaries from scholars worldwide. Finally, VK is the current Editor-in-Chief of the *Journal of Marketing*.

Allan R. Kuse is Chief Advisor of the MMAP Center, developing and directing the training and advisory services of MASB. The Center includes experienced marketing scientists qualified to train and advise individual organizations with respect to the Marketing Metric Audit Protocol, a formal process for connecting marketing activities to intermediate outcome metrics to the financial performance of the firm. He also assists the MASB Chair and serves as the administrator for all of MASB's project teams. Dr. Kuse has a 35-year track record of applying the science of measurement development, knowledge, and process management to the art of marketing. Prior to his MASB engagement, Dr. Kuse was EVP of Research at rsc The Quality Measurement Company (The ARS Group). He has served on the advisory boards for the Master in Marketing Research Program at Terry School of Business, University of Georgia, and the Master of Marketing Research Program at the University of Texas, Arlington. He began his career on the research faculty at the Institute for Behavioral Genetics, University of Colorado at Boulder. He holds a BA in psychology from Purdue University, and an MA and PhD in quantitative psychology from the University of Colorado.

James (Jim) Meier is the Senior Director, Marketing Finance, at MillerCoors based in Chicago. In this role, Jim reports directly to the MillerCoors CFO and on a dotted-line basis to the CMO. His recurring duties relate to budgeting, reporting, and forecasting. Over recent years, Jim and his function have become more directly involved with annual resource allocation, implementation, and ongoing assessment of marketing mix modeling, and overseeing the application of ROMI (Return on Marketing Investment) principles. He also serves as a liaison to SABMiller's Global

Finance Organization in developing financial competencies and capabilities in areas such as brand financial management. He represents MillerCoors as a trustee of the Marketing Science Institute and has served as a Director for MASB since 2013. Jim graduated from Marquette University in 1984 with an Honors BS degree in Accounting. He initially spent eight years as an auditor with Ernst & Young in Milwaukee. Jim has subsequently spent 23 years with Philip Morris, Miller Brewing Company, and now MillerCoors in a variety of financial support roles across many business functions including internal audit, corporate financial services, sales, integrated supply chain, and marketing.

Michael L. Moore is Professor in Residence of Accounting at Loyola Marymount University in Los Angeles. Moore earned his PhD and MS degrees from Pennsylvania State University and a BA degree from the University of Washington. He has previously served on the faculties of the University of Texas at Austin, the University of Southern California, and the University of California Riverside. He has published extensively on taxation, accounting, and international topics, including articles in *Journal of Accounting Research*, *The Accounting Review*, *Journal of the American Taxation Association*, *The Tax Advisor*, and *Tax Notes*. He is co-author of *U.S. Tax Aspects of Doing Business Abroad*, now in its sixth edition. Professor Moore has served on numerous committees of the American Institute of Certified Public Accountants, the American Accounting Association, and the American Taxation Association. He is past president of the American Taxation Association. He was a practicing CPA for a number of years and had extensive litigation support experience. He currently works with MASB where he serves as MASB Advisor and co-leads the Improving Financial Reporting project.

Debra Parcheta is an engineer, an applied mathematician, and a data scientist. Debra founded Blue Marble Enterprises, Inc. in 1994 to build database systems for measurement and analytics as well as custom data solutions. Her most recent project, BlueHorizon™, is the first forward-looking marketing prediction system for fast-moving consumer goods. Debra holds a BS in Computer Science and Engineering from the University of Colorado with a minor degree in Applied Mathematics. In her spare time, she enjoys volunteering with a local orchestra and the state and local chapters of the American Association for University Women. She also serves as a director on the board of the Community College of Aurora Foundation.

David J. Reibstein is the William S. Woodside Professor and Professor of Marketing at The Wharton School, University of Pennsylvania. Dave has been on the Wharton Faculty for more than two decades. He was the Vice Dean of the Wharton School, and Director of the Wharton Graduate Division. In 1999–2001, Dave took a leave of absence from academia to serve as the executive director of the Marketing Science Institute. He previously taught at Harvard, and was a Visiting Professor at Stanford, INSEAD, and ISB (in India). Dave is currently the Immediate Past Chairman of the American Marketing Association and the host of his very own radio talk show called "Measured Thoughts" on SiriusXM Radio, Channel 111. Dave has authored seven books and dozens of articles in major marketing journals. His most recent book is *Marketing Metrics: The Definitive Guide to Measuring Marketing Performance*. Dave was featured in *Fortune* magazine as one of the eight "favorite business school professors"—the only one in marketing—and in *Business Week* as one of ten "business school professors to watch." He has consulted for companies ranging from Fortune 500 firms to start-ups, including Google, GE, British Airways, and Royal Dutch Shell. Dave has run executive programs in over 300 companies in more than 30 countries. He was a co-founder of Bizrate.com (Shopzilla) and on the founding board of And1, the basketball apparel company. He has also served on the boards of The Fleisher Art Institute, American Marketing Association, MASB, And1, Shopzilla, XMPie, SeniorHomes.com, and several other companies.

Karen Scheller is Project Manager at MASB and is a member of the MASB Common Language Project team. Prior to joining MASB in 2009, Karen spent 19 years in the marketing field, including over 12 years with the ARS Group. Karen holds a BA in international business from the University of Evansville.

Donald E. Sexton is Professor of Marketing and Professor of Decisions, Risk, and Operations, Columbia University. He holds a PhD and MBA from the University of Chicago in Economics and Statistics, and a BA from Wesleyan University in Mathematics and Economics. Professor Sexton has been teaching for more than 45 years at Columbia and received the Business School's Distinguished Teaching Award. Don has taught at several institutions including the University of California-Berkeley, INSEAD, and CEIBS. His numerous articles have appeared in journals such as the *Harvard Business Review*, *Journal of Marketing Research*, *Journal of Marketing*, and *Management Science*. His best-selling books, *Marketing 101* and *Branding 101* (Wiley), have been translated into several languages including Chinese, Russian, Turkish, Polish, and Indonesian. Don's book, *Value above Cost: Driving Superior Financial Performance with CVA®, the Most Important Metric You've Never Used* (Wharton), explains how marketing determines financial performance and is available in Chinese. Don received the 2011 Marketing Trends Award for his work on marketing and branding strategy. He served as President of the Association for International Business Education and Research and President of the New York American Marketing Association. Don is the founder and president of The Arrow Group, Ltd.® an organization that has provided consulting and training services in the areas of marketing and branding to many leading companies such as GE, Pfizer, IBM, Citibank, Unilever, Volkswagen, MetLife, Sony, Verizon, Coca-Cola, and DuPont.

Roger Sinclair has been a MASB Advisory Council member since 2012 and is a specialist in brand valuation and accounting for brands. He was the designer of the globally recognized Brandmetrics valuation tool, which was bought in 2009 by Prophet Brand Strategy. Dr. Sinclair has been an academic partner at Prophet since 2009 and remains a special advisor to the firm and its clients. In 2011, Roger was commissioned by the ANA to draft a set of principles for brand valuation in the US. He writes the financial accounting section of Keller's Strategic Brand Management and wrote the chapter on Trademarks and Brands for *Wiley's Guide to Fair Value under IFRS*. Roger speaks regularly at conferences on brands and brand-related finance. He earned his PhD from the University of the Witwatersrand in Johannesburg, South Africa, where he was Professor of Marketing for a decade. Roger is on the MASB Improving Financial Reporting Project team.

Kate Sirkin serves as Executive Vice President and Global Research Director of Starcom Mediavest Group, where she manages emerging media trends, data, and support for SMG clients, initiates proprietary studies, and acts as its voice on critical media issues. A native of England, she joined Leo Burnett's London office in 1988 as a media researcher and now is recognized as one of the most innovative thinkers in the research industry. Kate is sought out by the trade press for her point of view on the latest media trends and their impact on advertising, and recruited to speak at the most influential industry conferences. Throughout her career, she has spearheaded a number of research initiatives that have helped to expand the field of media research overall, as well as to help her clients grow their brands and their businesses. She brought the elusive "TV optimizers" to the US marketplace in 1997, and has worked with partners in Australia and Argentina to develop SMG's unique TV reach optimization and allocation system. She has also developed TV effectiveness studies based on both single source and aggregate data in the US, Europe and Asia and was one of the first media practitioners to use NASA-based technology to measure brainwave movements to determine viewers' involvement with commercials contained within different TV shows. Kate has also developed parameters to determine the value and effectiveness of advertising in big-ticket TV events (i.e., Super Bowl, Oscars, etc.). Outside her SMG duties, she serves on the Executive Board of the Advertising Research Foundation and the Executive Board of the Coalition for Innovation in Media Measurement. She joined The Boardroom Project in 2004.

David W. (Dave) Stewart is President's Professor of Marketing and Business Law at Loyola Marymount University in Los Angeles. Dave has previously held faculty and administrative appointments at Vanderbilt University, the University of Southern California, and the University of California, Riverside. He currently serves as editor of the *Journal of Public Policy and Marketing* and has previously served as editor of the *Journal of Marketing* and the *Journal of the Academy of Marketing Science*. Dave has authored or co-authored more than 250 publications and 10 books, including the *Handbook of Persuasion and Social Marketing* and *Effective Television Advertising: A Study of 1000 Commercials*. His research has examined a wide range of issues including marketing strategy, the analysis of markets, consumer information search and decision-making, effectiveness of marketing communications, public policy issues related to marketing, and methodological approaches to the analysis of marketing data. Dr. Stewart has been awarded the American Marketing Association's Award for Lifetime Contributions to Marketing and Society, the Elsevier Distinguished Marketing Scholar Award by the Society for Marketing Advances and the Cutco/Vector Distinguished Marketing Educator Award by the Academy of Marketing Science. He has also received the American Academy of Advertising Award for Outstanding Contributions to Advertising Research for his long-term contributions to research in advertising. He earned his BA in Psychology from Northeast Louisiana University and his MA and PhD in Psychology from Baylor University.

Sarang Sunder is a doctoral candidate and researcher at the Center for Excellence in Brand and Customer Management at the J. Mack Robinson College of Business, Georgia State University. His research focuses on applying rigorous statistical methodologies to answer relevant marketing questions. Specifically, he uses state-of-the-art econometric and Bayesian methodologies to address substantive issues in customer relationship management, emerging markets, and salesforce management. His research has been published in premier journals such as the *Journal of Marketing Research*, *Harvard Business Review*, *Journal of Retailing*, and the *Journal of International Marketing*. He has presented his research at various prestigious conferences such as the AMA Winter Educator's Conference, INFORMS Marketing Science Conference, Theory+Practice in Marketing Conference, and the Marketing Dynamics conference to name but a few. Additionally, he was also a doctoral consortium fellow at the INFORMS Society of Marketing Science doctoral consortium in 2014 as well as the AMA-Sheth Foundation doctoral consortium in 2012. He is also the recipient of the 2014 GTA Teaching Excellence Award for outstanding teaching at the Robinson College of Business. Prior to joining the PhD program at GSU, Sarang received his Bachelor's degree in Mechanical Engineering from Anna University, India. He also received his Masters in Marketing degree from GSU in 2015.

Robert D. Winsor is Professor of Marketing at Loyola Marymount University. He earned his PhD in Marketing from the University of Southern California. His research has been published as both book chapters and articles in a large variety of business journals, including the *Journal of Marketing*, *Journal of Business Venturing*, *Journal of Small Business Management*, *Journal of Business Ethics*, *Journal of Business Research*, and *Marketing Theory*.

Preface

In the summer of 2004, Meg Blair and Dave Stewart met for dinner in Marina del Rey, California. Both had a long history of work in the areas of advertising and the measurement of marketing outcomes, Meg as founder and president of Research Systems Corporation (dba ARS Group), an advertising testing company, and Dave as member of the faculties at Vanderbilt University and the University of Southern California. They had collaborated on various research projects and publications over more than two decades. Over dinner they discussed the state of the marketing discipline, the importance of measurement, and the need to make marketing a stronger and more influential business discipline by establishing standards for accountability that linked marketing outcomes to the financial performance of the organization. As a consequence of that meeting they agreed to work together to create an organization dedicated to creating standards and an associated body of knowledge for marketing accountability. Thus, "The Boardroom Project" was born.

Responding to mounting pressure from corporate boardrooms for accountability in marketing, The Boardroom Project was created by a cross-industry/cross-discipline body of marketing scientists.[1] Members recognized that measurement standards (tied to financial performance) are essential for the efficient and effective functioning of a marketing-driven business, because decisions about the allocation of resources and assessment of results rely heavily on credible, valid, transparent, and understandable information.

After comprehensive review of then current practices, needs, and accountability initiatives sponsored by industry organizations, it was determined that while marketing was not ignoring the issues surrounding metrics and accountability, the practices and initiatives underway were narrow in focus, lacking integration, and generally not tied to financial performance in predictable ways. The group also concluded that the absence of well-accepted and uniform definitions of marketing constructs, measures, and processes had hampered the ability of the marketing discipline to be a full partner in the strategic decisions of the firm, much as idiosyncratic processes and the lack of standards had hampered operations prior to the advent of the quality movement.

An early outcome of the project was the drafting of two documents: *Objectives of Marketing Standards* and the *Marketing Metric Audit Protocol (MMAP)* for connecting marketing activities to the financial performance of the firm. The MMAP process included the conceptual linking of marketing activities to intermediate marketing outcome metrics to cash flow drivers of the business, as well as the validation and causality characteristics of an ideal metric. The Boardroom Project team concluded that marketing needed to move from a discretionary business expense to a board-level strategic investment and that this would only happen through an independent standards setting "authority" for measuring (forecasting and improving) the financial return from marketing activities. As was true for manufacturing and product quality (with ANSI and ISO) and for accounting and financial reporting (with FASB and IASB), so it would be true for marketing and consistent growth. This authority became the Marketing Accountability Standards Board (MASB) that is the focus of this book.

Establishing MASB was viewed as the seminal opportunity to approach the measurement foundation of accountability and continuous improvement at the highest level: across industries, disciplines, and domains; with common language, purpose, and financial denominators; and with collaboration and coordinated efforts over all, and over time. Thus, in the fall of 2007, The Boardroom Project launched MASB as part of the Marketing Accountability Foundation (MAF) with ten Charter Members, a one- to three-year plan, and a dozen initial standards' projects.

This book is intended to provide a chronicle of the activities and conceptual thinking of The Boardroom Project and MASB over slightly more than a decade of work. Each of the chapters in the book are based on the work of the participants in The Boardroom Project and MASB: presentations, publications, and project outcomes. Each of the contributors to the book has been actively involved on project teams and has participated in the semi-annual MASB summits. Much of what is reported is a status report on ongoing efforts that are driven by a desire for continuous improvement and ongoing organizational learning. Nevertheless, considerable progress has been made and this book serves as a vehicle for sharing that progress with a broader audience.

The book is divided into four sections. These sections track the MASB journey and the evolution of its work over time. Section 1 focuses on the origins of MASB, its vision, and charter. Chapter 1 offers an overview of MASB, its organization, its operations, and its goals. Chapter 2 anchors the MASB agenda as an important and necessary extension of the quality movement. This chapter also points to the lessons that can be learned from the evolution of the quality movement over time. Among the most important of these lessons for marketing is the need for a common vocabulary, well-accepted and standard measures and metrics, and clearly defined processes.

The early emphasis of The Boardroom Project and MASB was on identification of valid marketing metrics that could be linked to the financial performance of the firm. Section 2 of this book reports on this early work. Chapter 3 focuses on efforts to create a common language for marketing, and the reasons why such a language is important. It is difficult to measure or improve an ill-defined concept. Two broad classes of measures of marketing outcomes have dominated thinking and practice: brand preference and customer lifetime value. Thus, it is fitting that Section 2 includes two chapters on each type of measure. Chapter 4 provides a conceptual and historical review of the brand preference measure, while Chapter 5 reports the results of a MASB project that demonstrates the validity and utility of brand preference. Chapter 6 offers an overview of measures of customer lifetime value and an introduction to the use of these measures. Chapter 7 reports the results of a MASB project that applied customer lifetime value metrics to consumer package goods.

Among the most vexing problems related to measuring the outcomes of marketing actions is the identification of longer-term effects. There is no dispute that many marketing actions have effects that are long lasting, in addition to shorter-term effects. Measuring and quantifying these longer-term effects has been a challenge. Chapter 8 offers a discussion of the long-term impact of advertising and provides empirical data and case studies that illustrate long-term effect. Chapter 9 provides a broader summary of the long-term effect of marketing actions and describes the challenges associated with measuring such effects, as well as approaches for overcoming these challenges.

Finally, Chapter 10 addresses the measurement of the effects of social media. No area in marketing has seen as much growth and change during the period that The Boardroom Project and MASB have existed. Even as social media have become a significant marketing tool and a major expenditure, these media have rapidly evolved as both technology and the creative imaginations using the technology have changed. These changes have presented especially difficult problems for measurement of marketing outcomes.

Section 3 of this book explicitly addresses the linkages between marketing and financial performance. Traditional measures of marketing outcomes are most credible when they can be linked to the financial metrics that senior managers use for decision-making and that they must report to investors. Chapter 11 provides a conceptual discussion of the linkages between financial performance measures and marketing actions, while Chapter 12 offers a discussion of the practical issues associated with aligning the marketing and finance functions in an organization.

No discussion of the relationships between marketing and finance would be complete without addressing the need for reporting and the role of accounting and explicit consideration of taxes. Thus, Chapter 13, 14, and 15 discuss issues related to valuing brands, including accounting requirements and the shortcomings of these requirements as a means for capturing and quantifying the contributions of marketing activities and expenditures.

Furthermore, no discussion of the relationships between marketing and financial performance would be complete without explicit consideration of taxes. There is much misunderstanding about the tax implications of the way(s) marketing expenditures and marketing outcomes are currently treated and how they might change in the future. Chapter 16 provides a non-technical overview of the treatment of marketing expenditures for taxation purposes.

Finally, the identification of the linkages between marketing activities and outcomes and financial performance requires a process for discovering and documenting these linkages. Chapter 17 provides a discussion of such a process, the MMAP, which has been developed and applied by MASB.

As was the case with the quality movement before it, it was inevitable that MASB would eventually need to confront broader organizational and process issues. Even the best of metrics will not be helpful if the organization fails to use them or lacks processes that integrate them. Section 4 addresses these organizational issues. Chapter 18 offers a discussion of organizational barriers, and the means for overcoming such barriers, to making marketing accountable and to making the linkages between marketing actions and financial performance a routine and integral part of the strategic decision process of the firm. Chapter 19 returns to the role of vocabulary introduced in Chapter 3. One impediment to marketing accountability is that the marketing function and its role, responsibilities, and decision rights, vary widely across organizations. In order to create a credible process for accountability it is important to align measures of outcomes with what the marketing function can control and influence. Chapter 19 provides a discussion of the various ways in which the role of marketing may be defined and the implications of such definitions for the measures of accountability. The book closes with a brief review in Chapter 20.

Our goal in creating this book is to stimulate thinking and discussion about the role of marketing. By summarizing and sharing the insights of some of the most notable marketing thinkers in both academic and business settings over more than a decade, we hope to facilitate better marketing and improved financial performance. It is also our hope that the role of marketing and its contributions will be clearer to both those who are marketers and those with whom marketers work.

David W. Stewart
Craig T. Gugel
November 2015

Note

1 Although the intent of the group was to influence decision-making in corporate boardrooms, the project's name was taken from the name of the room in the restaurant where the group held its first meeting.

Acknowledgments

This book is the result of the contributions of many people. As editors we have served as facilitators, motivators, organizers, integrators, and checkers, but the raw material is the work of many others. We thank the authors of the chapters that make up this volume. We also would be remiss if we did not thank the organizations for which these contributors work. These organizations were supportive of the work in many ways: providing time for the work and, in some cases, providing the data and case illustrations that form the basis of individual chapters. This volume is a chronicle of more than a decade of work undertaken with the support and direction of the Marketing Accountability Standards Board (MASB). We thank the directors of MASB and staff members at MASB, including Meg Blair (president), Allen Kuse, Karen Cusco, and Erick Decker-Hoppen. Christina Faulkner, in the College of Business Administration at Loyola Marymount University provided invaluable assistance by gently reminding contributors of deadlines, checking formats and reformatting text, and tracking down copyright permissions and art work. She carried out these tasks with efficiency and good cheer. We thank her for her good efforts. We owe an enormous debt to our publisher. Harry Briggs was the executive editor at M. E. Sharpe who originally saw the potential of this volume and committed to publishing it. While the project was underway M. E. Sharpe was acquired by Routledge/Taylor & Francis, whose staff have been enormously helpful and supportive. Finally, we must acknowledge the many, many individuals who have contributed to MASB and to our own understanding of the role of marketing in organizations. The production of this volume was a genuinely collaborative effort. Any shortcomings or limitations of the volume are our responsibility as editors.

David W. Stewart
Craig T. Gugel

Section I
Introduction
Making Marketing Accountable

1 Delivering to the Marketing Accountability Mandate

*Margaret Henderson Blair, Mitch Barns,
Kate Sirkin, and David W. Stewart*

Introduction

Marketing is one of the last of the wild frontiers in American business today, a place where "cowboys" with wild ideas can literally create fortunes out of thin air. Given access to huge corporate budgets, marketing promises to take (not so) small investments and bring back huge returns. Through the late 1990s, marketing budgets and the organizations that consumed them spent more and more, promising larger market share, higher sales, and greater customer loyalty that would, in theory, generate greater cash flow for the corporation and its shareholders. But like the "wild west" era of American history, the ending of the dot.com boom signaled the close of the old marketing frontier, where marketing practitioners could promise big results without having any real way to quantify them. Sometimes, but all too rarely, they could point to greater market share or higher unit profitability to claim success for the marketing campaign. More often, the returns on marketing expenditures were measured by showing greater awareness, changes in customer beliefs and attitudes, or similar measures. But how efficiently was that money being spent and what is the relationship of these marketing metrics to the financial performance of the firm? What other information could they give the executive suite to prove their value to the company? Though good executives asked these questions in times of plenty, as corporations try to spend their resources more efficiently in the twenty-first century, marketing professionals, like cowboys of old, are having a hard time adapting to this new frontier.

Marketing mix modeling has increasingly found a role in offering managers some insight into the return on marketing expenditures and activities, but such models produce results that are only as good as the data that are available. A central problem is that marketing lacks the kind of accountability and metrics that are common along the value chain of the rest of the corporation. While manufacturing can quantify their costs down to a fraction of a penny and project their return on investments, marketing remains a corporate dark science, where its practitioners can generate desirable results, but cannot tell you how they achieved them. As long as the "wins" outnumbered the "losses," campaigns were thought to be successful. This was the mentality that pervaded industry through the late 1900s, when more and more money flowed into marketing than at any other time in history. Amazingly, marketers had no benchmark against which to measure their campaigns; neither does one exist today.

The problem of measuring marketing's effectiveness and efficiency is profound.[1] Unlike other segments of the corporation, where the language is unequivocally tied to the language of finance, marketing has no common units of measurement. It is not that marketing professionals cannot agree on whether to use yards or meters: they cannot agree whether they are trying to measure volume, distance, or some other third- or fourth-dimensional characteristic.

The Boardroom Project

In 2004, responding to mounting pressure from corporate boardrooms for accountability in the marketing function, a cross-industry body of marketing scientists initiated The Boardroom

Project.[2] Members recognized that measurement standards (tied to financial performance) are essential for the efficient and effective functioning of a marketing-driven business, because decisions about the allocation of resources and assessment of results rely heavily on credible, valid, transparent, and understandable information.

After a three-year comprehensive review of current practices, needs, and accountability initiatives sponsored by industry organizations, it was determined that while marketing was not ignoring the issues surrounding metrics and accountability, the practices and initiatives underway were narrow in focus, lacking integration, and generally not tied to financial performance in predictable ways.

The body then drafted Objectives of Marketing Standards[3] and defined the Marketing Metric Audit Protocol (MMAP)[4] for connecting marketing activities to the financial performance of the firm. This process includes the conceptual linking of marketing activities to intermediate marketing outcome metrics to cash flow drivers of the business, as well as the validation and causality characteristics of an "ideal metric."

Finally, members of The Boardroom Project concluded that marketing will move from discretionary business expense to board-level strategic investment only through an independent standards-setting "authority" for measuring (forecasting and improving) the financial return from marketing activities. As was true for manufacturing and product quality (with ANSI and ISO), and for accounting and financial reporting (with FASB and IASB), so it would be true for marketing and consistent growth (with the Marketing Accountability Standards Board (MASB)).

Establishing MASB was viewed as the seminal opportunity to approach the measurement foundation of accountability and continuous improvement at the highest level: across industries, disciplines, and domains; with common language, purpose, and financial denominators; and with collaboration and coordinated efforts over all, and over time. Thus in the fall of 2007, The Boardroom Project launched MASB of the Marketing Accountability Foundation (MAF) with ten charter members, a one- to three-year plan, and a dozen initial standards' projects.[5]

Marketing Must Be Accountable in Financial Terms[6]

Marketing has a long history of attention to measurement and the creation of metrics, yet most of the metrics used to assess the outcomes of marketing activities are tactical and not directly linked to the overall financial performance of the firm. It is critical that measures of return on marketing investment be firmly grounded in the business model of the firm to provide decision-makers with information and direction regarding economic and financial outcomes. The availability of these measures should also be consistent with the timing of the firm's financial reporting and decision-making processes.

There are several reasons for following this approach. First and most importantly, if marketing is to be a credible contributor to the strategic success of the firm, it must speak the same financial language as the rest of the firm, and it must translate outcomes into economic metrics comprehensible outside the marketing department. Second, economic metrics, or metrics that can be clearly linked to economic outcomes, are the only measures that provide managers with the information necessary for planning, budgeting, and prioritization. Even actions with relatively comparable outcomes, such as scheduling media within the same medium, require a common metric that informs allocation decisions. Most management decisions involve allocation of limited resources among alternative tactical actions that may have non-comparable outcomes. It is impossible to be confident in any decision involving non-comparable alternatives unless their outcomes can be translated to a common scale: the decision to invest more in a firm's website must be weighed against developing and running more television advertising; the cost for exclusive pouring rights at a particular venue for a soft drink manufacturer must be weighed against the alternative of increased advertising in traditional media; investment in one market or product must be weighed against investment in other markets or products. In short, any marketing expenditure must be weighed against alternative marketing and non-marketing investments, and measured against the potential for increasing profitability as a result of marketing in a given quarter and beyond versus not making the expenditure at all.

Three Classes of Marketing Outcomes[7]

Although there are many types of marketing metrics, there are three broad classes of measures that can be identified based on the duration of the measured effect and the extent to which the measured effect is common to all firms. These three classes of measures are: (1) short-term (short-lasting) effects; (2) long-term (effects that persist over time); and (3) real options. Figure 1.1 provides an illustration of these three classes of marketing outcomes.

Short-term effects are well recognized in marketing. They are the focus of much of the marketing mix modeling activity that is carried out by firms. Most often, the economic manifestation of such short-term effects is relatively immediate incremental sales (relative to some baseline). However, it is also important to recognize that there may be opportunity costs associated with not engaging in a particular marketing activity. Thus, loss of sales in the short-term may also provide an economic indicator of marketing decisions (in this case, the decision not to spend on some activity).

Long-term outcomes are effects that also occur rather immediately, but these effects tend to persist over time. Although there have been efforts to estimate such long-term effects, such effects are generally recognized to be difficult to estimate and there is no generally accepted standard for measuring these effects directly. Nevertheless, these longer-term effects have the potential for translation into economic metrics, such as a persistent change in incremental sales relative to a baseline or a price premium for each unit sold. As a result, these longer-term effects are also candidates for standardized measurement, that is, use of a metric comparable across brands and firms.

Finally, there are outcomes of marketing actions that are genuinely idiosyncratic to the firm. In recent years there has been growing interest in what has been called "real options." The concept of real options is of relatively recent origin in finance. At the simplest level it is an approach

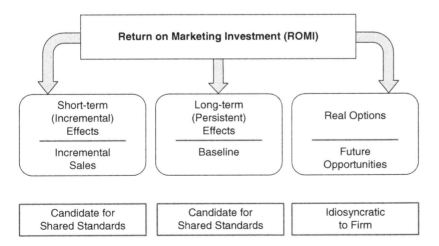

Figure 1.1 Three Classes of Marketing Outcomes.

Source: Stewart, David, *Measuring Marketing's Performance: Lessons from the Quality Movement*, presented to the Marketing Science Institute Conference on Marketing Metrics for the Connected Organization, Dallas, TX, September 2008.

to decision-making that attempts to explicitly recognize the dynamic nature of future decisions where management has the flexibility to adapt given changes in the business environment. Options cost money to create, just as investing in financial options costs real money. However, they also create flexibility and opportunities in the future that would not otherwise be available. Options tend to be highly idiosyncratic to the firm (only a firm that has already invested in a customer relationship system has the option to use this system as part of its marketing to its customers; only Procter & Gamble has the option to develop extensions of its Tide brand). Among the most important options in which firms invest are brands.

Marketing investments are different from financial investments. Many marketing activities are about creating and sustaining real options. These options have value because they afford future opportunities for the firm. The creation of a website creates opportunities for communication with consumers and for product distribution that would not be available but for the creation of the site. Brands represent options because they provide opportunities for brand extensions and for charging a higher price in the future. Indeed, one especially important option open to a firm that has invested in the creation of a brand is to sell the brand. The value of a brand if the option to sell it were exercised is a measure of the potential value of the option. Although firms may not, and most certainly do not, exercise all options available to them, these options have economic value. To the extent that marketing activities create such options they must be considered part of the return on marketing investment: "Manufacturing (and Finance) can construct and maintain an asset, Marketing can create and grow an asset."[8]

Real options are idiosyncratic because they exist only within the context of the individual firm and its unique resources. Although they can certainly be compared with respect to their economic value, both within and across firms, they are not suitable for a shared standard metric in the same way short-term and long-term effects are. Nevertheless, they should be considered in any comprehensive analysis of the return on investment associated with marketing activities.

Measurement Standards Are Imperative[9]

Standard metrics for assessing the outcome of marketing activities have the potential to facilitate and improve a variety of management decisions: (1) optimization of resources in such activities as media planning and design of the marketing mix; (2) forecasting, including both forward forecasting and the analysis of various "what-if" scenarios; and (3) the assessment of financial return and return on investment. One impediment to the identification and adoption of standard metrics is the perception that the effects of marketing activities tend to be highly idiosyncratic with respect to an individual business. This perception appears to be particularly acute with respect to the effects of advertising. The perception of such idiosyncratic effects almost certainly has a basis in reality, but it is less clear that such differences are associated with the actual outcomes of marketing activities. Rather, such idiosyncratic effects may be attributable to the limitations of the marketing mix models employed and the idiosyncratic nature of the data on which such models are constructed. If these are the reasons for such apparent idiosyncratic effects, it is all the more reason for development of standard metrics for directly assessing the impact of marketing activities rather than trying to tease them out of historical data.

It is also important that outcomes arising from marketing activities be clearly identified with respect to their effects over time and the degree to which they may be common to all (or most firms), or are genuinely idiosyncratic to the individual firm. Only those effects that are common across firms are candidates for a shared measurement standard.

Standards are so common that they are often taken for granted. The history of particular standards and how they came into being is often lost. Setting standards has never been easy. There is a rich literature of the economics of standards and standardization that makes it clear that marketing is not unique with respect to the difficulty it has experienced developing generally accepted measurement standards. Standards are important because they provide economic benefits. The availability of a generally accepted standard relieves the individual firm of the costs of developing and maintaining its own unique internal standards. Absent a standard, whether broadly available or unique to an individual firm, there is no efficient means for assessing quality. Standards are an efficient means for discriminating high quality from low quality. If buyers cannot distinguish a high-quality seller from a low-quality seller, the high-quality seller's costs cannot exceed those of the low-quality seller, or the high-quality seller will not survive. This is called *adverse selection* or the *moral hazard problem* in economics. This type of problem currently exists in the areas of marketing measurement, marketing research, and marketing mix modeling.

There are, of course, potential solutions to the adverse selection problem other than the development of a standard. Buyers can carefully screen the quality of measures and models, but this requires significant investment in developing internal expertise, the expenditure of time and resources on the review of alternatives, and an organizational infrastructure to support such activities. Standards reduce such transaction costs because there is less need for buyers to spend time and money evaluating products and services prior to purchase. Alternatively, sellers can build long-term reputation or can guarantee a certain level of quality, but this increases the costs of the seller and creates a moral hazard problem if the buyer does not accept the representation of higher quality and the seller cannot recoup its higher costs. Thus, the presence of generally accepted standards resolves these problems and creates opportunities for the realization of economies of scale by the standards provider, and lower costs to the buyer through cost sharing.

One major impediment to the develop of standard metrics within marketing is the view of some firms that they may be able to achieve competitive advantage if they are able to create a better measurement tool for informing management decisions than is available to their competitors. This issue is not unique to marketing or marketing metrics. Indeed, this issue has been played out in a broad array of contexts. Any potential competitive advantage must not only be weighed against all of the ongoing costs of going it alone but also relative to the opportunity costs and comparative advantages of the firm (that is all of the other ways in which a firm could invest its resources). It is not at all clear that a firm that is very good at product development is better off investing in the development of metrics instead of developing additional products.

History suggests that there are three general approaches by which standards have been developed: (1) government edict; (2) agreement by industry bodies; and (3) market contests. Although it might appear that government edict or agreement by industry bodies are the more efficient means for standard setting, the reality is that most standards are set through market competition. Government standards are usually created only after a long and labor-intensive process, and there are many areas in which government has no interest or where the parties involved are so narrow as to make government intervention inefficient. While agreement by an industry body might appear to offer advantages, it has been observed that:

> Strategies that rely on official acceptance divert effort and alone are unlikely to be effective. Agreement is hard to achieve and is unlikely to be adhered to unless backed up by market pressures. Standards bodies are inherently conservative ... official adoption takes a great deal of precious time. Standards bodies also tend to concentrate on the technical aspects of standards, whereas the most important factors may be on the market side. Standards may be too important to the firms' future to be negotiated in committees and have to be settled in the market-place [sic]. Years of negotiation over DAT [digital audio tape] within standards organizations failed to resolve basic differences between manufacturers and recording companies over copying, and meetings became platforms for dissent.[10]

The empirical reality is that most standards evolve by following the main firm in the market or as the outcome of a standards contest in the market. Generally, the most effective way to establish an efficient standard is not by refining the committee process but by turning over more of the standard setting process to the market. Indeed, within marketing today there are a number of standards that exist by virtue of market competition. Examples of such standards include the media ratings data provided by Nielsen and Nielsen Audio.

Thus, it may be most efficient for marketing organizations to encourage competition among third-party measurement providers in order to facilitate the identification of alternative standards for specific purposes and the emergence of a standard provider. It is, of course, conceivable that such a market competition could produce alternative providers who meet a common standard that is established by some industry body. It is likely that identification of such a common standard will follow from market competition. If common measurement standards are to be developed, there is a need to identify general characteristics of an ideal measurement standard as well as exemplars of measures that might meet these standards in order to inform the market. The next section of this chapter focuses on a process for defining the metrics conceptually, the characteristics of an "ideal metric," and the validation and causality audit applied to a specific exemplar.

Defining the Metrics (Conceptually) and the Marketing Metric Audit Protocol (MMAP)

While marketing does not lack measures, it lacks standard metrics explicitly linked to financial performance in predictable ways. Cash flow both short-term and over time is the ultimate metric to which every business activity, including marketing, should be causally linked through the validation of intermediate marketing metrics. The process of validating the intermediate outcome metrics against short-term and/or long-term cash flow drivers is necessary to facilitate forecasting and improvement in return.

The MMAP is a formal process for connecting marketing activities to the financial performance of the firm. The process includes the conceptual linking of marketing activities to intermediate marketing outcome metrics to cash flow drivers of the business, as well as the validation and causality characteristics of an "ideal metric":

Step 1: Identify cash flow drivers. There will be at least one source of cash and one business model. In many businesses there is a dominant source and a dominant model. For instance, the business model, or how the firm generates cash, might be margin, velocity, or leverage and the source of cash, or customers, might be sales volume, price premium, or market share.

Step 2: Identify intermediate measures of marketing outcomes. Distinguish between measures of efficiency, like cost per thousand and cost per lead, and measures of effectiveness, like redemption rate for coupons and market share. Focus first on measures of effectiveness.

Step 3: Identify the conceptual links. Every marketing action should have an identified outcome metric. If there is no logical link between a marketing outcome and a cash flow driver, you might question the need for the associated marketing activity.

Step 4: Identify the causal links. When there is uncertainty about the causal link between a marketing outcome and one or more cash flow drivers, validation or test is appropriate—especially if the costs of the marketing activity are high (validity and causality audit).[11]

Figure 1.2 shows the conceptual linking of a marketing activity (TV ad) to a specific pre-market measurement (APM facts, or customer brand preference (choice)), to intermediate market outcome measures (sales volume, market share, and price premium) to cash flow drivers (leverage, velocity, and margin) and to cash.[12]

Since every intermediate marketing outcome metric should be validated against short-term and/or long-term cash flow drivers, and ultimately cash flow (or to the drivers of the cash flow

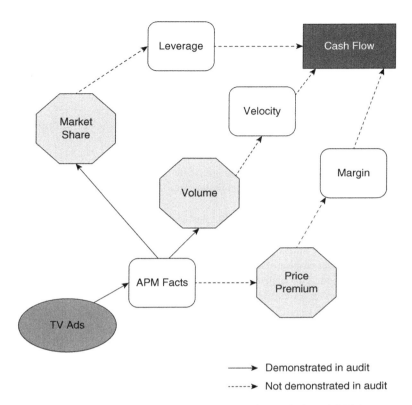

Figure 1.2 APM Facts: Marketing Activity, Metrics, and Financial Links.

Source: MASB, *Metrics Catalogue: APM Facts*, cited April 7, 2015, available at http://www.themasb.org/mmap-metric-profiles/apm-facts/.

drivers), the TV ad pre-market metric was taken through the MMAP validation and causality audit according to the ten characteristics of an "ideal metric":

1 relevant—addresses specific pending action;
2 predictive—accurately predicts outcome of pending action;
3 objective—not subject to personal interpretation;
4 calibrated—means the same across conditions and cultures;
5 reliable—dependable and stable over time;
6 sensitive—identifies meaningful differences in outcomes;
7 simple—uncomplicated meaning and implications clear;
8 causal—course of action leads to improvement;
9 transparent—subject to independent audit;
10 quality assured—formal/ongoing process to assure 1–9.

As well as the overall guidelines for measures of productivity, return on marketing investment is inherently a financial construct. No measure or measurement system is complete without a specific link to financial performance. Thus, measures of return on marketing investment should:

- reflect financial concepts of return, risk, time value of money, and cost of capital;
- provide information for guiding future decisions by predicting future economic outcomes as well as retrospective evidence of the impact of marketing actions;

- recognize both immediate, short-term effects of actions and longer-term outcomes, as well as the fact that short- and long-term effects need not be directionally consistent;
- recognize difference between total return and marginal return on investment;
- recognize that different products and markets produce different rates of return;
- distinguish between measures of outcome and measures of effort;
- provide information meaningful and comparable across products, markets, and firms;
- clearly identify the purpose, form, and scope of measurement;
- be documented in sufficient detail to allow a knowledgeable user to understand utility and make comparisons among alternative measures;
- be assessed relative to generally accepted standards of measurement development and validation;
- be recognized as a necessary investment for assuring sound decision-making, accountability, continuous improvement, and transparency for all stakeholders.

The MMAP audit concluded that the characteristics of this particular measurement of consumer brand preference (choice) would deem it "ideal" for serving as a standard for measuring and forecasting the impact of TV advertising and for managing and improving the return. Application of the metric during the advertising development and management process has enabled improvement in return greater than that needed to offset the rises in TV media costs. While various metrics may be called the same and even look alike in many ways, specific methodologies within classes and types of metrics often yield very different levels of reliability and validity. This specific measurement was identified as an "ideal metric" for use as a standard.[13]

The Standards Body

In 2007, after The Boardroom Project conducted a three-year comprehensive review of current practices, needs, and accountability initiatives sponsored by industry organizations, it was determined that while marketing was not ignoring the issues surrounding metrics and accountability, practices and initiatives underway were narrow in focus, lacking integration and generally not tied to financial performance in predictable ways. Figure 1.3 represents the major industry associations, plotted against the degree to which their focus is on measurement standards tied to

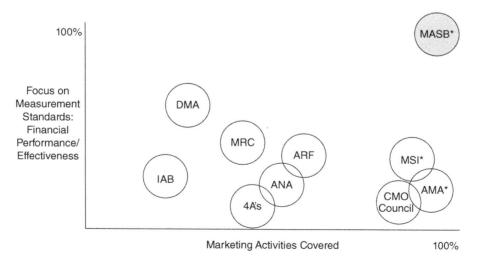

Figure 1.3 MASB: Filling the Need.

Source: MASB, *Establishing Marketing Measurement and Accountability Standards*, November 2009.

* 501 c 3

financial performance (effectiveness) and the marketing activities covered with any marketing accountability initiative or work underway.[14]

There were no other bodies focused on measurement and process standards necessary to deliver to the marketing accountability mandate. Members of The Boardroom Project concluded:

1. Marketing has been relegated to the "default" category (control costs) because it lacks metrics that reliably tie activities and costs to corporate return in a predictable manner.
2. Standards across industry and domain as well as a transparent process by which to develop and select the metrics will be necessary to emerge from the current situation.
3. The market is unlikely to achieve consensus on its own.
4. There is need for an industry level "authority" to establish the standards and to ensure relevancy over time.
5. As was true for manufacturing and product quality (with ANSI and ISO) and for accounting and financial reporting (with FASB and IASB), so it would be true for marketing and profitable growth (with MASB).

The Boardroom Project then recommended, funded, and launched the MASB of the MAF, electing to use the FASB organizational structure as its operating model. Figure 1.4 illustrates the organizational structure of MAF.[15]

MASB is the operating group that was formed first (in 2007) to establish standards for marketing metrics and accountability. The Board is composed of 16–18 directors, plus the chair, who are senior marketing scientists or finance professionals from constituent organizations (including business schools), who collectively represent diverse backgrounds, possess knowledge of marketing and finance, and have concern for the marketing community as a whole. Members

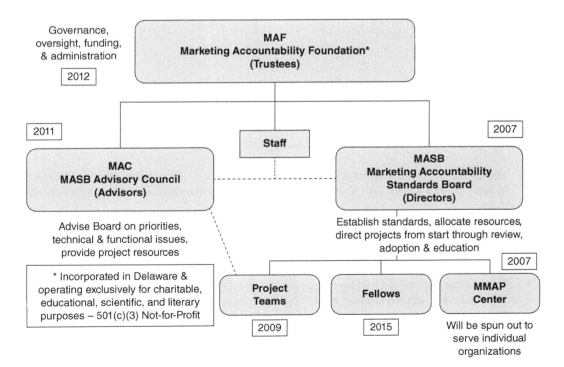

Figure 1.4 Organizational Structure.

Source: MASB, *The Transformation of Marketing from "Discretionary Expense" to "Strategic Investment,"* March 2015.

of the Board guide the standards projects and resolve technical and other issues from project start through adoption. The Board meets monthly with ten virtual meetings and two face-to-face meetings. They are appointed by the MAF trustees for three-year terms, and are eligible for a second term. Members of The Boardroom Project who funded and became charter members of MASB sit on the Founding Board. Their **Precepts in Conduct** of Board activities include:[16]

1 be open and objective in decision-making;
2 weigh carefully the needs and views of constituency;
3 promulgate standards when:

- the logical flow of the argument is tight;
- the empirical support material is convincing;
- conclusions are managerially meaningful;
- scientific evidence pro and con is acknowledged;
- benefits exceed costs.

4 ensure transparency of the standards-setting activity through open due process;
5 bring about needed change while minimizing disruption;
6 review effects of past decisions (interpret, amend, replace).

Prioritization of projects on the MASB agenda is based on:

- pervasiveness of the issue;
- alternative solutions;
- technical feasibility;
- practical consequences;
- convergence possibilities;
- cooperative opportunities;
- resources available.

In the Fall of 2006, The Boardroom Project conducted in-depth interviews with C-level management (CFO, CEO, CSO) of a dozen or so major marketers (including Visa, PepsiCo, Ford, and Novartis), to gain insight into their views regarding the role of marketing in the business process and the value of marketing metrics in the accounting and financial processes. Interviews were completed between December 2006 and January 2008 resulting in the following summary:[17]

- There is a universal need for true marketing ROI metrics . . . valid/predictive performance (return) metrics which can be integrated w/performance metrics from other parts of value chain.
- This need for metrics is especially true for advertising, new product introductions, and in-store/similar "channel" activities as well as competitive moves.
- Metrics related to both short-term and long-term impact are needed . . . with focus on customer outcomes.
- The increased speed of business makes accurate forecasting critical.
- It will take a combined effort of marketing, finance, and sales to find/agree on/work with the "best metrics."
- A self-governing standards body could add real value to meeting these needs.

Initial projects on the MASB agenda were selected and prioritized, in part, based on the results of these interviews, including: the long-term impact of advertising, measuring (forecasting and improving) the return from TV, the brand investment and valuation project, and applying customer lifetime value (CLV) to CPG target segments.

In 2009, a formal structure and process for conducting the work of the MASB through project teams was adopted. Project teams are formed for specific projects on the MASB agenda and include marketing scientists and finance professionals from constituency organizations with skillsets and interests to match the project. Project teams meet virtually on a monthly basis. Team members are appointed by MASB directors with input and support from the MASB Advisory Council (MAC).

The MAC was formed in 2011 to consult with the Board on project priorities, technical issues, and selection and organization of project teams. Advisors are senior managers of constituency organizations who collectively represent diverse backgrounds, possess knowledge of marketing and finance, have concern for the marketing community overall, and are selected to provide the skillsets and expertise necessary to help project teams meet their objectives. They are appointed by MAF trustees for three-year terms, and are eligible for a second term. Formal meetings of MAC are held twice a year when directors meet face-to-face to review all projects, and they meet virtually on a monthly basis with the project teams they advise.

Fellows are an integral part of the research and technical activities of the MASB. They are marketing scientists or finance professionals from academia and/or practice, and appointed by the Board for a specified period of time to help a project team achieve its objectives. The first Fellowship was inaugurated in 2015 to support the *gadfly* Fellows Project. The *gadfly* Fellows will cross academic silos and engineer a MASB recommended structure (accreditation) and curriculum (skillsets) to provide the talent needed by businesses to scale their successful measurement-based accountability processes, all tied to the financial performance of the firm.[18]

During the first five years of the standards-setting work, governance of the body (including its officers) was provided by several founding directors on an interim basis, and in 2012 trustees were recruited to fill the governance roles of MAF. MAF is the independent, private sector, self-governing organization authorized by its membership constituency to establish and improve marketing metrics and accountability standards through transparent and open due process; educate constituents about those standards; provide oversight, administration, and finances of its standards-setting Board (MASB) and Advisory Council (MAC); select the President (staff) and members of the Board and Advisory Council (all volunteers); and protect the independence and integrity of the standards-setting process. As such, trustees are not involved in the operations of the body, including the setting of project priorities or technical issues involved with projects. Trustees are generally C-level managers of constituency organizations who collectively represent diverse backgrounds, possess knowledge of marketing and finance, and have concern for the marketing community overall. Terms are for three-years with eligibility for a second term. Meetings are held quarterly (three virtually, and one face-to-face). Trustees govern according to the MAF by-laws, as well as the body's vision and long-range plan. Trustees are nominated by constituent organizations and by sitting trustees. Directors of the MASB chose its founding President and Chief Executive Officer at the start-up of the body in 2007. MAF is incorporated in the state of Delaware and operates exclusively for charitable, educational, scientific, and literary purposes—a 501(c)(3) not-for-profit corporation.

Funding sources for the MASB include membership dues from constituent organizations, projects, workshops, technical services, publications and training, and advisory and auditing services. Constituent organizations are marketers, measurement, modeling, and software providers, media and advertising agencies, media providers, academic institutions (business schools), industry associations, and independent consultants. Dues vary by constituency and by the size of the organization.

The role of MASB is in setting the standards and processes necessary for evaluating marketing measures in a manner that insures credibility, validity, transparency, and understanding. MASB will not endorse any specific metric, rather it will document, reveal, and highlight how various metrics stack up against MMAP. Belief is that the market will select the specific metrics based on these evaluations. MASB's *Marketing Metrics Catalogue* will be the primary vehicle for documentation and publication. MASB will also exemplify how to evaluate and identify ideal metrics according to MMAP, and delve into the practices underlying the development and management of ideal metrics over time. The body will also delve into the practices utilized to create knowledge, determine causality, and apply to process management for improved return. MASB will serve at the industry level in this fashion and with "open due process" in its work. During the first several years, MASB will also take on a "training, advisory, and audit" capacity to serve individual marketers and/or their agents, much like accounting firms train, advise, and audit individual companies as to how to use/meet the standards. This work will not be conducted with "open due process," but with "confidentiality" on behalf of the marketer and/or their agents (e.g., measurement companies). Once the training, audit, and advisory processes are refined/in sync with the standards, the work will likely be spun out into a separate organization. The MMAP Center umbrella will be used to cover the training, audit, and advisory services to clearly differentiate the industry level "open due process" work of the MASB from the "confidential" work serving individual companies. It is anticipated that marketers and their agents will use the MMAP audit results to justify their practices and to compete in the marketplace.[13]

The Body's Vision, Mission, and Promise[19, 20]

The **Vision** Statement of MAF is:

> Laying the measurement foundations for marketing professionals to realize full accountability and strategic status in the Boardroom as reliable forecasters and achievers of consistent growth in customer revenues, earnings and cash flows quarter-to-quarter and year-to-year.

The **Mission** Statement of MASB is to:

> Establish marketing measurement and accountability standards across industry and domain for continuous improvement in financial performance and for the guidance and education of business decision makers and users of performance and financial information, and Partnering with Finance is the surest way forward.

The ongoing **Promise** of the body is:

> Development of generally accepted and common standards for measurement and accountability processes will significantly enhance the credibility of the marketing discipline, improve the effectiveness and efficiency of marketing activities, and enable continuous improvement in financial return over time.

Delivering to the Promise, achieving the Mission, and realizing the Vision will make a big difference for everyone:

1 Marketing professionals will be accurately forecasting and delivering consistent growth in customer revenues, earnings, and cash flow quarter-to-quarter, year-to-year. Everything they do will be tied to business results, and they will continually improve as demonstrated by financially-linked metrics—even competitive activity will be accounted for in time to make a difference in performance. They will be accountable to both top and bottom lines of

the P&L, making informed decisions about resource allocations between comparable and non-comparable marketing actions to achieve desired business results. In short, they will have earned a permanent seat in the boardroom at the head of the growth table, inspired by creative strategy and guided by reliably predictive metrics.

2 As it was with total quality management and product quality in operations, CEOs who first apply the science of measurement and process management to marketing will gain sustained competitive advantage over those who continue to operate by seat-of-the-pants rules. This has been true for the Japanese in the automobile and electronics industries (first to adopt Deming's principles) and will be true for those first taking the plunge in the marketing arena.

3 CMOs will no longer be concerned about data reliability, predictive validity, causality, or alignment among disparate sources; they will be seeing over dashboards and beyond rearview mirrors, acting quickly and more confidently given the marketing opportunities and threats that lie ahead; they will be out of the black hole of discretionary spending, clearly understanding and able to predict how their work today is impacting the financial results of their brands and businesses tomorrow. The CFO will be their greatest ally by having removed ambiguity and becoming true business partners. Finally, they will be "less disruptive to spouse and the kids" as tenure will be measured in years, not months.

4 CFOs will have great partners and support in the boardroom as marketing eliminates the ambiguity surrounding their role as forecasters and achievers of consistent growth, quarter-to-quarter and year-to-year; they will have sustained credibility with the investment community as their projections and expectations will be in line with performance, consistently—particularly when performance is based on organic growth at the top line; they will understand the true "balance sheet" value of their brands as they can be leveraged across categories, borders and time to produce future revenues, earnings, and cash flows. Company silos will disappear and they will have better communications and performance across discipline and division . . . speaking the same language of accountability . . . tied to financial results. Finally, they will be "home for dinner" at quarter and annual close, because everyone will have met their commitments to the plan and to expectations.

5 Marketing scientists will be measuring everything marketing does with metrics that reliably predict the business results of the planned activities, dumping all those that do not predict along with those not actionable; their metrics and models will be causal for clear understanding of what drives success and for what to do next if part of the plan is in trouble. The CIO will be their greatest ally in delivering relevant metrics, knowledge, and what-if capabilities into the marketing rearview mirrors, onto the marketing dashboards, and out beyond the marketing headlights. The scientists will be doing what they love doing and "valued" for their contributions.

6 Measurement providers will have moved beyond bombardment of requests for more and more information, with more and more confusion and controversy over what it all means, and beyond the adverse selection/moral hazard problem of buyers not being able to distinguish high quality from low quality. They will be focused on providing metrics that are reliable predictors of what will happen to the business given potential marketing actions and how to continually improve results.

7 Modelers will have moved beyond GIGO and beyond the rearview mirrors, validating their models and using them for accurate forecasts of the financial implications of what lies ahead; understanding what drives success and how to improve each and all the marketing activities planned.

8 The value of ad agency work will be determined by contribution to their clients' business performance as measured by high quality, standardized metrics that tie to overall financial analyses; and they will be compensated according to this contribution and thus able to attract and retain top creative talent. Their income will smooth as they learn to improve, and they will "not be tossed aside" at the whim of the once frequently changing CMO.

9   The media agencies will understand the costs and returns for each channel, placing their client messaging across these touch points with fact-based confidence and accurate forecasts of the returns; they will be managing the messages along with the media, knowing how much to spend behind each one for optimal/desired return; and they will be "advising" their ad agency and marketing partners when the messaging should and can be improved.
10 Industry associations will be addressing (through partnership) the top concern of their marketing constituency . . . at its foundation . . . without having to tackle the heretofore stepchild and arduous task of measurement development and process management. The work of accountability is not a one-time event, rather a continuous cycle of metrics development, knowledge creation, and process reengineering (repeat).
11 Business schools will be attracting the brightest to marketing once again; they will be identifying, publicizing, and sustaining standards for relevant measures of marketing performance and business success, making clear the link between marketing actions and financial returns; their structure and curriculum will be engineered with the role of marketing measurement central, integrated with other metrics along the value chain, all tied to overall financial analyses. They will be providing strong grounding in problem definition, critical thinking, and the process of strategic dialog in addition to technical skills . . . formally recognizing the interdisciplinary technical strategic marketing consultant (or demand scientist) in the MBA program, and providing businesses with a cadre of these new marketing professionals to meet the growing demand.
12 Customers will be provided with more new and better solutions for every need and desire, and at a lower price.

Summary and Call to Action

If marketing is to be a credible contributor to the strategic success of the firm, it must work with finance to develop and adopt generally accepted standards for the measurement of marketing outcomes that are explicitly linked to the financial performance of the firm. They must predict and translate outcomes of their activities into economic metrics comprehensible and interchangeable with other economic metrics employed across the value chain. It is not possible to be confident in any strategic decision involving the allocation of resources across comparable or non-comparable alternatives, unless their outcomes can be translated into a common economic scale. Cash flow both short-term and over time is the ultimate metric to which every business activity, including marketing, should be causally linked through the validation of intermediate marketing metrics. While these intermediate metrics might be developed and managed internally, any potential competitive advantage must not only be weighed against all of the ongoing costs of going it alone but also relative to the opportunity costs of the firm. It is doubtful whether a firm that is very good at product development is better off investing in the development of metrics instead of developing additional products or services.

MASB is the independent, cross-industry forum where marketing and finance professionals are working together to establish measurement standards for delivering to the marketing accountability mandate and for creating shareholder value in the twenty-first century.

As the CEO of the Association of National Advertisers (ANA) stated in 2014: "There is one group exclusively devoted to marketing measurement . . . predictive of financial return . . . and all marketers who are serious about meeting the accountability mandate should get involved."[21]

Notes

1 Stewart, David W., 2008, "How Marketing Contributes to the Bottom Line," *Journal of Advertising Research*, March: 94–105.
2 The Boardroom Project, *The Boardroom Project Overview*, February 2006, available at http://www.themasb.org/wp-content/uploads/2009/07/tbpbrochure.pdf.

3 The Boardroom Project, *Objectives of Marketing Standards*, August 2006, available at http://www.themasb.org/wp-content/uploads/themasbvision.pdf.
4 MASB, *Marketing Metric Audit Protocol (MMAP)*, February 2009, available at http://www.themasb.org/marketing-metrics-audit-protocol/.
5 MASB, *About MASB: The Boardroom Project*, available at http://www.themasb.org/about/the-boardroom-project/ (cited April 8, 2015).
6 Stewart, David W., 2006, "Putting Financial Discipline in Marketing: A Call to Action," *Corporate Finance Review*, October.
7 Stewart, David W., 2008, *Measuring Marketing's Performance: Lessons from the Quality Movement*, presented to the Marketing Science Institute Conference on Marketing Metrics for the Connected Organization, Dallas, TX, September.
8 MASB, 2015, "The Transformation of Marketing from 'Discretionary Expense' to 'Strategic Investment'," Islamorada, FL: MASB.
9 Stewart, David W., *Measurement-based Accountability and Standards*, presented at the Annual ARF Convention (*re:think!* 2005), New York, April 19, 2005, available at http://www.themasb.org/wp-content/uploads/2009/04/measurement-based-accountability-standards-stewart-arf-april-2005.pdf.
10 Grindley, Peter, *Standards, Strategy and Policy*, 1995, New York: Oxford University Press.
11 MASB, *Measuring and Improving the Return from TV Advertising (An Example)*, May 2012, available at http://www.themasb.org/wp-content/uploads/2012/04/Measuring-TV-According-to-MMAP-An-Example-2012-Copy.pdf.
12 MASB, *Metrics Catalogue: APM Facts*, available at http://www.themasb.org/mmap-metricprofiles/apm-facts/ (cited April 8, 2015).
13 MASB, *Measuring and Improving the Return from TV Advertising (An Example)*, May 2012, available at http://www.themasb.org/wp-content/uploads/2012/04/Measuring-TV-According-to-MMAP-An-Example-2012-Copy.pdf.
14 MASB, 2015, "The Transformation of Marketing from 'Discretionary Expense' to 'Strategic Investment'," Islamorada, FL: MASB.
15 MASB, 2015, "The Transformation of Marketing from 'Discretionary Expense' to 'Strategic Investment'," Islamorada, FL: MASB.
16 MASB, *Establishing Marketing Measurement & Accountability Standards*, November 2009, available at http://www.themasb.org/wp-content/uploads/2009/07/about-masb-yr-i-review.pdf.
17 Plummer, Joseph and Margaret H. Blair, *C-Level Views on Marketing ROI*, July 2008, available at http://themasb.org/themasb.org/wp-content/uploads/2015/08/Getting-Seat-at-Table-C-Level-Views.pdf.
18 Stewart, David W. and Roger Sinclair, *Gadfly Fellows (GFF) Project*, March 2015, available at http://www.themasb.org/themasb.org/wp-content/uploads/2015/08/H.-Fellowship-Sinclair-8.15F.pdf.
19 Margaret H. Blair, *What Will Be Different? The MASB Vision*, The Boardroom Project, August 16–17, 2007, available at http://www.themasb.org/wp-content/uploads/themasbvision.pdf.
20 MASB, 2015, "The Transformation of Marketing from 'Discretionary Expense' to 'Strategic Investment'," Islamorada, FL: MASB.
21 MASB, 2015, "The Transformation of Marketing from 'Discretionary Expense' to 'Strategic Investment'," Islamorada, FL: MASB.

2 Lessons from the Quality Movement

David W. Stewart

Introduction

Marketing is by now a well-established discipline. With its institution comes the expectation that companies, firms, small startups, and even authors or speakers will devote a portion of their time, energy, money, and personnel to its diktats, namely: attracting and keeping the customer.

The fact that all organizations now rely on marketing as a key tool in their business plans and devote budget to it, however, does not necessarily make it a standardized process or even, in all cases, a particularly useful endeavor. Marketing's often poor organization and haphazard approach stem from a lack of attempts, up until the last decade or so, to analyze marketing efforts using meaningful metrics.

Today, marketing is at a crossroads. Executives have begun to realize that without scrutiny, they cannot determine if marketing is effective, nor can they figure out how to improve it. As stated by Ed Gaskin for C-Suite Insider:

> While the marketing budget may be reduced based on a lower revenue or earnings forecast, it has been hard to look under the hood and see what was and what wasn't working. From a benchmark perspective as long as our sales and marketing dollars seemed to be as productive as the industry average, it was hard to ask for much more.[1]

In other words, both the efforts made by the marketers as well as their results were so hard to quantify that a company's best bet was simply to lower the budget if things were not going well. As long as the organization was doing all right, however, marketing retained its budget. Such an approach lacks the statistics on which to base a firm examination, as well as any link between cause and effect.

Fortunately, marketing's current state has a well-documented predecessor. Its disorganization, in fact, bears a striking resemblance to the state of manufacturing operations in the 1940s. Without statistics-based quality measures, industry suffered due to poorly designed processes and rifts between management and workers that decreased efficiency and limited customer satisfaction. By applying the ideals of total quality management (TQM), however, many companies transformed operations from messy processes with incompletely formulated ideals into neatly streamlined powerhouse manufacturing systems. This transformation can teach us much about where marketing is headed in the coming decades.

Many boardrooms are already knee-deep in efforts to apply the quality movement to marketing. However, the realization that marketing input must be linked to output has come with an accompanying realization that marketing has a long history of neglecting standards and measurement. Furthermore, because these efforts are still in their infancy, it is hard to draw any conclusions about results to this point. Nevertheless, we can predict much of what will happen by examining the similar transition within operations throughout the twentieth century. Marketing now, like operations then, is characterized by a lack of standards and recognizable vocabulary as well as idiosyncratic processes and muddy goals uninformed by financially-based metrics.

A full application of the quality movement's lessons, however, requires an understanding of how it came into existence and how it evolved the methodical, reliable approach it takes today. This examination will begin with an overview of total quality, its history, its leaders, and its relevance to marketing and economics. From there we will proceed to examine the applications of total quality to marketing; the importance of developing standardized approaches, ethics, and vocabulary; and the importance of crisis help and overcoming resistance. Along the way we will also take a look at several key organizations and sets of principles, and conclude with a look at marketing's current state.

What Is Total Quality?

Total quality and TQM are terms often used interchangeably. According to the American Society for Quality, TQM is: "a management approach to long-term success through customer satisfaction. In a TQM effort, all members of an organization participate in improving processes, products, services, and the culture in which they work."[2] A quality management system is a "tool used by management that is designed to ensure product quality and customer satisfaction."[3]

In other words, total quality means improving every step of the process to create the best possible outcome. Typically, this has been applied to productions and operations, where by measuring and assuring quality at every level of production and giving the means for improvement to every worker, no matter his station, the company stands the best chance of producing a beautiful, functional product, which will in turn result in a high degree of product reliability and customer satisfaction.

Total quality carries an important overtone of comprehensiveness. Rather than addressing one specific aspect of an organization's operations or management, TQM processes emphasize improving *every* department, managerial process, and assembly line. The word "total" is key, indicating the need to penetrate every corner of an organization to ensure that nothing is missed.

It is also important to recognize that "quality," while it is often used as an adjective interchangeable with "nice" or "expensive," does not merely indicate that something is well made or has value. Rather, it means that the product meets specific standards and metrics laid out for it ahead of time, based on real quantitative values.

While total quality's specific traits or sub-systems are myriad and may vary depending on the source, it relies heavily on two other methods of ensuring quality. The first is statistical quality control (SQC), a process that uses specific, measurable traits to assess the quality of a product.[4] These might include dimensions, chemical composition, or reflectivity, for example. An organization determines ahead of time what constitutes a quality sample of a particular good, then measures its various traits and records those measurements. It then applies them to all subsequent goods by using the initial sample as the standard. This is an effective way to check products for quality when they are finished, but is not necessarily the most efficient way to determine the causes of poor quality.

A better way to do that is statistical process control (SPC). While SQC monitors the quality of outputs, SPC monitors inputs, according to the American Society for Quality.[5] DataNet Quality Systems, who rely heavily on it, explain SPC another way:

> Statistical Process Control, commonly referred to as SPC, is a method for monitoring, controlling and, ideally, improving a process through statistical analysis. The philosophy states that all processes exhibit intrinsic variation. However, sometimes processes exhibit excessive variation that produces undesirable or unpredictable results. SPC, in a manufacturing process optimization context, is used to reduce variation to achieve the best target value.[6]

This reduction in variation of process leads to consistently better product, inextricably linking SQC and SPC. Total quality, therefore, is a combination of measuring and ensuring the quality of both inputs and outputs. In addition, it takes into account the performance and enfranchisement of all members of a company, so that everyone has a voice and the power to contribute to continual improvement.

According to the American Society for Quality, total quality rests on eight main pillars.[7] If an organization institutes these principles, it stands a much better chance of creating and executing a consistent product that will lead to consumer satisfaction, long-term retention of the customer, business growth, and increased market share. These "primary elements," or values, are as follows:[8]

Customer-focused: Ultimately, the customer is all that matters, because the customer will determine whether or not a product is good enough. An organization must therefore place the customer's opinion about what constitutes "quality" above everything else.

Total employee involvement: All employees must be fully engaged in the process. In order for this to occur, managers must ensure that the work environment is conducive to employee involvement and lacks elements that might make them fearful of sharing their opinions, offering criticisms or pointing out errors.

Process-centered: Process is integral to quality. Each process, and an organization may have many, must transform its inputs into outputs without varying too far from the expected norm. When unexpected variations do occur, this can signal a problem in the process.

Integrated system: Thorough integration is the hallmark of a successful organization, one in which all small processes add up to larger processes which, when taken together, add up to the sum of the business process overall. Communications must be integrated as well as processes, so that everyone understands the larger goals.

Strategic and systematic approach: A solid plan incorporates the mission, vision, and goals of an organization and holds quality paramount.

Continual improvement: Improvement is not a one-shot deal, but rather a continual process. Adherents to quality believe that only by constantly seeking betterment can an organization keep its foothold in the market and continue to grow.

Fact-based decision-making: Decision-making should not be based on hunches, history, or any other metric that lacks actual facts and statistics. Rather, it should be based on data. This requires organizations to institute methods for gathering and analyzing data, and drawing conclusions from it to use in the decision-making process.

Communications: Total quality is impossible without good communication between departments and levels. It is crucial to motivation and morale, and relies on planning and implementing an intentional strategy.

These eight principles shed considerable light on marketing's current shortcomings. Marketing may be closest to achieving the principle of "customer-focused," though as Gaskin points out above, this is only in the sense that marketing efforts are deemed sufficient if the company is "as productive as the industry average." This hardly counts as shooting for excellence, even if marketing departments take their success from whether or not the customer is attracted and satisfied. In other areas, marketing may be even further behind. Only by embracing total quality's importance will companies dedicate enough time and resources to the effort to catch up.

Why Is Total Quality Important?

Total quality does more than simply assure a good product. Although excellent work and customer satisfaction are crucial facets of total quality, one cannot truly understand its value without taking into account the impact it has on a company's mindset.

Total quality recognizes no finishing line. Instead of choosing a target to hit or a stopping point, after which both production and product will be "perfect," total quality contains an inherent emphasis on continuing, everlasting improvement. Companies that embrace this mindset show consistent, long-term return on investment, because they are always the first to take advantage of changes in the market, to implement new techniques, to explore new technologies, and to recognize and capitalize on drifting consumer interest.

If, for instance, a manufactured product were to be tested during the production process and its condition found to be below company standards, then production on that particular product would be halted and an explanation sought for the drop in quality. Such tests take place before the final product is made and released to customers, minimizing the chance that the company will waste resources further developing a faulty product or dealing with expensive refunds or recalls. This approach enables companies to continually check that the quality of their products is up to par and meets their standards for customer satisfaction.

A total quality mindset has other benefits, too. Those that embrace it strengthen their competitive position by portraying an image of excellence. Because their products are rarely faulty (publicly, anyhow), consumers learn to trust the brand as always producing and standing behind an excellent product. This increases profits and builds lifelong customers to the *brand* rather than the *product*, which in turn results in more sales. The emphasis on total quality also relentlessly seeks out defects, areas of waste, and imperfect processes, further reducing unnecessary expenditures and increasing profits.

Employees tend to be happier at institutions that prize total quality, with heightened feelings of agency and morale, as well as increased job security. Company shareholders and stakeholders feel more secure too, sticking with the company over the long haul.

Arguably, most importantly, the organization benefits from a pattern of innovation, in which the belief in a better way drives the relentless pursuit of that way. This type of vision offers organizations elasticity when it comes to governmental or environmental regulations, because rather than chafing against a changed system, they immediately move on to the solution.[9]

The Economic Benefits of Total Quality

To some, the economic benefits of total quality are obvious. To others, who erroneously view quality as a cost, they are not. This misunderstanding owes much to the phrase "cost of quality," which is often interpreted solely to mean the cost of making a quality product: the time, energy, and manpower required to streamline or update systems or otherwise change the status quo.

"Cost of quality," however, also refers to the cost of *not* making a good product. These can include remaking an item or system, rebuilding a tool, correcting a financial statement, or otherwise "paying" for a subpar process that has gone wrong. Add enough of these errors together (which is likely in an organization that does not prize data-based oversight), and the result can be a consistent undermining of a company's bottom line, often without the organization realizing it.[10]

Even considering this, total quality might seem like a cozy ideal that does not account for the short-term economic goals of a company, which are based on getting a product to market and selling it, rather than perfecting the underlying processes . . . a good goal for later, perhaps. Alternatively, one could view it as an idea of great value for operations and production, but inapplicable to creative processes like marketing. Consider this statement by C-Suite Insider:

Before marketing was thought primarily to be a creative process, and seen above the fray of such examination. Sure, there were and are many areas in marketing that are quite quantitative (e.g. market and consumer researcher, price elasticity, etc.). No one wants to minimize the importance of creativity in promotion and branding. We could tell how great our advertising was based on the juried awards we won and the "oohs and aahs" we got from others.[11]

In other words, as long as people were impressed with the product, the processes that got it out there should not matter. This is once again akin to Gaskin's statement, and explains why "it has been hard to look under the hood and see what was and what wasn't working." But ignoring the process by which an accolade-garnering marketing campaign was produced is yet another cost of quality, because that campaign is now irreproducible, or at the very least, difficult to recreate. Economically speaking, therefore, total quality is important, because it ensures that success can be recreated, in marketing as well as in operations. Before making the case that total quality does and should apply to marketing, it is important to offer a brief study in the quality movement as background.

Artisans and Guilds: The Roots of Quality

The quality movement is marked by many transformations over a centuries-long period, but the first real effort toward ensuring consistent quality across a range of different processes and craftsman came in Medieval Europe with the institution of merchant and craft guilds. In the Middle Ages, craftsmen of many trades started to organize into larger collectives based around a single industry, called guilds. Some of them, like the masons, left a legacy that stretches to the present day. Other types of guilds included carpenters, painters, blacksmiths, butchers, and a wide variety of specialty trades. While the guilds served many purposes, chief among them was ensuring quality. According to the Encyclopaedia Britannica:

> Craft guilds were organized through regulations . . . By controlling conditions of entrance into a craft, guilds limited the labour supply. By defining wages, hours, tools, and techniques, they regulated both working conditions and the production process. Quality standards and prices were also set.[12]

In most cities during medieval times, one had to belong to a guild to legally practice a certain trade. Guilds therefore served to protect their members by ensuring that those who were unqualified could not sully the reputations of an entire industry, while at the same time keeping the number of workers to a level that would guarantee consistent employment for all its members, or at least try to. By setting prices, tools, and techniques, they also ensured that customers would always know what they were getting when they hired a worker. Despite the overtly monopolistic practices of these guilds, they were an important first step in instituting a process of quality control in industry.

However, while quality control is often conceived of as a group process, applied to large companies and highly routinized manufacturing processes, it played a considerable role in individual manufacturing as well. Craftsmen who relied on trade with local people to keep their business running would fare poorly if they allowed faulty goods to sully their reputation. They therefore needed to maintain consistent oversight of their own product.

Craftsmen often placed signature marks on their work, at first as a way to track a flawed product back to its source, but later as a means of signifying reputation. Guilds also used marks. Their inspection committees, after checking over the goods, stamped their approval of products for the world to see, an early method of quality control.[13]

The Industrial Revolution and Quality Control

At the dawn of the Industrial Revolution, craftsmen trained in the apprenticeship model still provided their own quality control in an effort to keep business by providing excellent products. With the rise of industry, and the accompanying unprecedented rate of production, however, manufacturers began to see the importance of quality assurance on a larger scale.

Initially, they did so by moving craftsmen and laborers onto the factory floor, with craftsmen composing the workforce and shop owners the supervisors. Nascent efforts at quality control consisted of little more than search and destroy missions to remove subpar product. This early step toward streamlined production actually moved away from the ideals of total quality by disempowering craftsmen and removing their autonomy as individual producers.

The Taylor System, developed in the United States by Frederick W. Taylor, added yet another layer to quality control. Summarized by Joseph M. Juran, a nineteenth-century leader in quality management thinking, his approach dictated that while:

> [t]he methods for doing work should be based on scientific study, not on the empirical judgment of foremen or workmen, the standards of what constitutes a day's work should likewise be based on scientific study, [the] selection and training of workmen should also be based on scientific study, [and] piece work payment should be employed to motivate the selected and trained workmen using the engineered methods and to meet the standards of a day's work.[14]

While Taylor's innovation did aim to maximize output with a minimum of input (in this case, skilled workers), and also advanced the cause of quality by instituting the use of data held dear by systems such as SQC and SPC, it nevertheless had serious drawbacks. Not only did workers suffer a further disenfranchisement in the work process but the pay-per-piece system produced a predictable (in hindsight, at least) drop in the quality of each piece. Quality control still rested on inspecting product and removing flawed pieces. At this point, no one had yet thought to address the underlying systems that produced those pieces, flawed or otherwise.[15]

Adding Process to Quality's Roster

Enter Walter Shewhart, an Illinois-born student of physics who joined Western Electric Company's inspection engineering department in 1918. There he made an instrumental contribution to quality.

Bell Laboratories (for whom Western Electric manufactured parts) had already realized that by controlling manufacturing variation, a company could significantly reduce its repair costs, and therefore introduced a program by which they inspected goods. "Even though this program was somewhat effective, it was very costly to deal with inspecting and sorting of finished goods," says Jim L. Smith.[16]

The answer, according to Shewhart, was to distinguish between assignable cause and chance cause. The former has an explanation and only one or a limited number of individual causes, and when detected can be eliminated from the process. On the other hand, the latter is an anomaly that either cannot be explained, cannot be fixed or consists of too many factors and must simply be accepted. To find assignable causes and eliminate them from the process, he proposed what we today know of as the control chart.

A control chart is very simple. Along the Y-axis are measurement numbers, determined by process being measured. The X-axis shows samples, either of a certain process conducted in different places or a process conducted in the same place over time. A horizontal line dictates the average, or measurement to shoot for, with two more lines indicating the upper control limit above and the lower control limit below. Samples that fall within the control limits are not outside of normal variation, while those that fall outside it warrant inspection. Smith explains that:

Shewhart's principle was that bringing a process into a state of statistical control would allow the distinction between assignable and chance cause variations. By keeping the process in control, it would be possible to predict future output and to economically manage processes. This was the birth of the modern scientific study of process control.[17]

Bell's realization that processes could be monitored, and Shewhart's creation of an incredibly simple, incredibly effective tool by which to do so, had lasting implications for all industries. Where previously the final output of a particular process had been subjected to quality control standards, now inputs were eligible too. Before, a piece of finished lumber might be inspected for knots, cracks, or other flaws and measured to ensure it was within specifications; now the process by which the lumber was cut to size could itself be measured to ensure it functioned properly and reliably turned out good product (i.e., a piece of lumber within specifications).

In the preface to *Economic Control of Quality of Manufactured Product*, Shewhart states that:

> The object of industry is to set up economic ways of satisfying human wants and in so doing to reduce everything possible to routines requiring a minimum amount of human effort. Through the use of the scientific method, extended to take account of modern statistical concepts, it has been found possible to set up limits within which the results of routine efforts must lie if they are to be economical. Deviations in the results of a routine process outside such limits indicate that the routine has broken down and will no longer be economical until the cause of trouble is removed.[18]

While today the idea that reducing variation in process can ensure a higher quality product is almost mundane when it comes to manufacturing, the same is not true of all fields: "By way of contrast [to production], one of the most widely observed phenomena in population health is regional and small area variation in care. Medicine has only started down the road of reducing variation."[19] It is safe to say that marketing is in the same camp. Even as it related to operations, however, total quality was far from a fully fleshed out idea. Its main leaders had yet to emerge, and World War II and its fallout at home and especially abroad, in Japan, would have lasting effects on the movement as a whole.

World War II and SPC

Once they had committed to World War II, the United States exerted inordinate effort to ensuring that a civilian system of production conformed to stringent military standards. Because the safety of military equipment was of paramount importance, the U.S. armed forces were forced to devote huge amounts of time and manpower to the inspection of equipment, often vetting each piece individually.

This, of course, was an enormous time sink, but Shewhart's SQC techniques shone a light on another way: sampling. Instead of inspecting each individual item as it came off the line, inspections officials could now use sampling tables in which representative items were randomly selected for inspection, obviating the need to inspect each piece. Unfortunately, these quality control programs rarely outlasted the government contracts that sponsored them, and the idea of quality for quality's sake had yet to take root.[20]

Total Quality Leaders

Total quality's leaders, however, did not disappear with the end of the war. By the mid-twentieth century, most of them were already in place. While a complete discussion of the many influential thinkers who contributed to TQM is not feasible here, we will address a few notable thinkers as well as total quality's arguable reigning champion, William Edwards Deming.

Joseph M. Juran, a chief quality thinker, joined the new SQC team at Bell Systems in 1926. Although he did not stay with the company, he did use his early education in quality to inform his later thinking about good management, and became a leader in quality management. His course "Managing for Quality" has been taught to more than 100,000 people in over 40 countries, and is counted among the most influential additions to quality management in the world.[21] Juran is credited with a wealth of ideas:

> The process of developing ideas had been a gradual one for Juran. Top management involvement, the Pareto principle, the need for widespread training in quality, the definition of quality as fitness for use, the project-by-project approach to quality improvement—these are the ideas for which Juran was best known, and all emerged gradually.[22]

Another shining star in the field of quality was Philip B. Crosby, who developed Four Absolutes of Quality Management:

1 Quality means conformance to requirements, not goodness.
2 Quality is achieved by prevention, not appraisal.
3 Quality has a performance standard of zero defects, not acceptable quality levels.
4 Quality is measured by the price of nonconformance, not indexes.[23]

His idea of zero defects, arguably the one he is best known for, states that if you reduce your level of defects to zero, then there are no remaining costs associated with quality and it becomes free. It is perhaps no surprise, then, that one of his most widely read books is entitled *Quality is Free*.

More than any other, however, total quality owes its widespread institution to the championing of one man: William Edwards Deming. Born in Iowa, Deming earned a degree in electrical engineering from the University of Wyoming. His first job at the Department of Agriculture's Nitrogen Research Laboratory introduced him to a love of statistics, which would contribute to his later thinking on the subject of quality. Although Deming's contributions to total quality were myriad, he is best known for his application of statistics to the manufacturing process:

> Deming particularly criticized the dominant method of quality control used by U.S. manufacturers. Under this system, products were inspected for defects only after they were made. In contrast, Deming maintained it was better to design the manufacturing process to insure that quality products were created from the start.[24]

He is also known for his insistence that it was generally management, not workers, who were responsible for the ills of manufacturing. That, however, was a theory that developed over time. First, it is necessary to gain an understanding of how Deming applied these theories most successfully. His story, along with Juran's, takes off in a wrecked, post-war Japan, the audience to their ideas a small group of forward thinkers known as the Japanese Union of Scientists and Engineers (JUSE).

The Japanese Experience

Although Deming was a well-known American consultant by the time of his death, he had achieved renown in Japan a half-century earlier. Deming gave a series of lectures there after the end of World War II, to which JUSE, and Japan as a whole, freely attribute the country's astonishing rebound from post-war destruction.

In the mid-nineteenth century, Japan was far from the manufacturing paragon it is today. In fact, for years, Japanese products earned the reputation for shoddy design and cheap construction.

According to the Quality Function Deployment Institute, they had few, if any, systems in place to ensure quality:

> Eizaburo Nishibori, one of the country's post-war quality pioneers, describes in a book the humble initial encounter to modern quality concepts that preceded Deming's historic 8-day seminar. It was during [the] American occupation of Japan (1945–1952) when GHQ (offices of the Allied occupation) placed an order of vacuum tubes to Toshiba. Nishibori recalled the American officers wanted to see a "control chart" from the manufacturing process being used to produce their order. No one at Toshiba knew what it was. "You don't know a control chart? How do you plan to manage quality?" Nishibori remembers replying, "If we don't know it, most likely no one in Japan knows."[25]

This encounter was indicative of the kind that set the stage for Deming's subsequent visit and his famed seminar with the JUSE. His stated purpose was to help with the Japanese census, but Deming ended up having a lasting effect on Japan's entire economy with his innovative ideas.

Critical of the American way of doing business, where management makes all the decisions and workers simply comply, Deming lectured that a greater involvement on the part of ordinary workers would help shape quality throughout the workplace. If workers were given the freedom to note problems on the production line, use statistical tools to track them, and suggest solutions to management, which was not as closely in touch with each part of the process as workers were, then quality overall would improve. As a benefit, workers would regain some of the autonomy they had lost with the institution of the factory and the assembly line.[26]

These ideas were revolutionary and helped ensure that Japan rebuilt its economy from the ground up over a period of several decades. This is also the first hint of *total* quality, an idea that rests on each part of a system being the best it can possibly be. Because management lacks the oversight to ensure top performance in every nook and cranny of a company, worker involvement was instrumental. This, along with a close statistical attention to detail, was Deming's major contribution both to Japan and to total quality as a discipline.

Juran's contributions to the Japanese economy are hardly less storied. He was invited to Japan in the 1950s to lecture on management's role in quality. He gave a two-day lecture to senior executives, and headed a ten-day program geared toward mid-level managers. His lecture to senior management rested on "five primary areas of executive responsibility":

1 responsibility for high policy or doctrine on quality;
2 responsibility for choice of quality of design (grade);
3 responsibility for the plan of organization of the company with respect to quality;
4 responsibility for setting up the measurement of what is actually taking place with respect to quality;
5 responsibility for reviewing results against goals and for taking action on significant variations.[27]

Juran also laid out a "cycle of control," whose steps were to:

- pick an objective;
- develop a plan for achieving it;
- carry out the plan;
- provide the resources;
- assign responsibilities;
- have those responsible execute the plan;
- determine if the plan is being met;
- select control points;

- define measures and a method of measuring;
- select performance standards;
- interpret the difference between actual and standard;
- decide action to take and implement.[28]

His cycle of control, along with his emphasis on the importance of effective, accountable management, set the stage for TQM. It also reinforced the important "Deming cycle" that we will address in the following section.

In recognition of the fact that Japan owed much of its astonishing rebound to these two men, the country established prizes in honor of them and to recognize further developments in the field of quality. Japan's Deming Prize was established in 1951, and is one of the world's most prestigious prizes awarded in recognition of contributions to TQM.[29] Juran's contributions were also lauded, and the JUSE had offered to name their follow-up prize (now called the Japan Quality Award) after Juran, but he declined.[30]

By using these principles, Japan was able to reshape its economy and begin churning out goods that were reliably excellent. Their product quality led to major export success and to them acquiring larger and larger market share, an outcome the United States initially attributed to price competition. In response, Americans initially attempted to cut the costs of production, but this did not increase the competitiveness of their products. It was not until 1980, following the broadcast of "If Japan can . . . why can't we?" that the United States accepted that the remarkable achievements coming out of Japan were anything more than price competition.[31] Deming's ideas had finally caught on at home:

> Ford Motor Co., hemorrhaging money in the 1980s, was among the first to hire Deming to reshape its manufacturing operations. One result of that collaboration was Ford's revolutionary Ford Taurus, which became one of the best-selling cars of all time. Other U.S. firms that turned to Deming for help included Xerox Corp., Procter & Gamble Co., AT&T Inc., and *The New York Times*.[32]

Over the decades succeeding Japan's success, the idea that management bore much of the responsibility for the quality of products as well as the company that made them, began a slow global advance into every industry . . . including, as we shall see, marketing.

Quality and Management

In his book *The Five Pillars of TQM: How to Make Total Quality Management Work for You*, Bill Creech writes:

> When I first started in supervisory positions I was told there are two basic management questions: *What's the plan?* and *Who's in charge?* The more responsibilities I accrued the more I realized the wisdom of that observation. When things went wrong it almost always was because the plan was poor or the execution faulty because of poor leadership, or some combination of the two.[33]

Although managers routinely ascribe plummeting quality to workers, the quality movement holds that most decisions and actions that affect quality are actually related to management decisions. This means that although workers are responsible for implementing the vast majority of actual steps required to make a product (including maintaining machinery, making the actual product, taking quality control measures, packaging, and so forth), it is actually management that must bear the brunt of how well decisions work out. Nothing illustrates this point as simply and succinctly as the red bead experiment.

Devised by Dr. Deming for teaching lessons on quality throughout the world, the red bead experiment demonstrates that if you do not control the process, you cannot control the outcome. It also demonstrates that workers have limited jurisdiction over the environments in which they work. It is an effective tool for teaching sampling in SQC, and for proving the importance of good management.

The red bead experiment, or game, works by giving each "player" a bowl filled with red and white beads. The white beads represent good things, while the red beads represent bad things. Players use a special tool, a small paddle with 50 evenly spaced divots in its metal surface, to draw out 50 beads at a time, some red and some white. No matter how many times you conduct the experiment, if there are red beads mixed in with the white beads, you will always get red beads in your sample.

The implications for SPC are clear: if you do not control what goes into the system, you cannot control what comes out of it. Any system that contains red beads will produce samples that contain them also. The only way to reduce or eliminate the possibility that a sample will contain red beads is to remove them entirely from the system, until only white beads are left.

But the red bead experiment's main purpose was to teach about management principles. Since the total quality movement has come to embrace management principles as well, the game also speaks to the working environment. Workers cannot control which beads they will draw, just as they cannot control the larger circumstances of their working environment. When they pull as many "bad" red beads as "good" white ones, the main variable at work is not the worker's intention, discipline, or level of skill, but rather the distribution of red versus white beads.

Similarly, if a worker produces a product of poor quality, it is more likely that the product is a result of a flimsy or faulty system than it is the worker's fault. In fact, according to redbead.com, the main supplier of products to teach Dr. Deming's red bead experiment, only 4 out of 100 problems are the fault of the worker. The other 96 are products of the working environment and decisions made by management.[34]

The game illustrates the point that, while workers bear *some* responsibility for quality, they do not bear much of it. Therefore, penalizing them for *discovering* lapses in quality (as opposed to causing them) simply makes it more likely that workers will stay quiet, problems will go unremarked, and quality will drop. Managers must therefore bring workers into the fold as trusted advisors who can help facilitate meaningful, lasting change.

One approach, devised by Deming (who credits Shewhart)[35] and still used today, is the "Deming cycle" or PDCA (plan, do, check, act) cycle. The four-part process is simple in theory, as quoted from Mind Tools:

1   *plan*: identifying and analyzing the problem;
2   *do*: developing and testing a potential solution;
3   *check*: measuring how effective the test solution was, and analyzing whether it could be improved in any way;
4   *act*: implementing the improved solution fully.[36]

At no point does an organization guess or assume. Instead, each step is based on careful analysis and use of data. With this concept has come the slow but steady development of management system standards, which are still a far cry from universal, but at least provide a starting point when setting up management system standards. According to the International Organization for Standardization, standards provide benefits such as using resources more efficiently, improving risk management, and increasing customer satisfaction.[37]

Deming also offered 14 key principles for the improvement of an organization's effectiveness. According to the Deming Institute, "Many of the principles are philosophical. Others are more programmatic. All are transformative in nature. The points were first presented in his book *Out of the Crisis*."[38]

While a full recitation of these principles is beyond the scope of this chapter, they include many ideas with which we are now familiar: streamline purpose, reduce dependence on inspections, institute on-the-job training and leadership, reduce fear, give workers autonomy and pride of workmanship, and make quality *everyone's* job.[39]

Total Quality

With the understanding that management plays a huge role in the quality of product and company, we finally arrive at the idea of total quality, or TQM. This is a holistic approach to manufacturing that embraces every aspect of operations, from hiring and business culture to assembly lines and inspection processes, to packaging and distribution. No part of a company's planning, execution, or culture can be ignored if total quality is to be achieved.

According to the Business Performance Improvement Resource (BPIR):[40] "The term 'total quality' was used for the first time in a paper by Feigenbaum at the first international conference on quality control in Tokyo in 1969. The term referred to wider issues within an organization." BPIR distinguishes somewhat between total quality as it relates to Western practice and as it is understood in Japan: "Ishikawa also discussed 'total quality control' in Japan, which is different from the western idea of total quality. According to his explanation, it means 'company-wide quality control' that involves all employees, from top management to the workers, in quality control."[41]

In other words, Japan uses the term to refer to quality control in all sectors of a company. By contrast, Western ideology more commonly associates the idea of total quality with excellence in every aspect of an organization, from its philosophies, to its processes, to its staff. Nevertheless, the term is now widely understood to mean a sweeping emphasis on constant improvement in operations and management.

Today the total quality movement boasts many notable adherents. Among them are the United States Department of Defense. According to the abstract of a report published in *Total Quality Management* entitled "Implementing Total Quality Management at the US Department of Defense":

> The US Department of Defense [DOD] needs to control the stifling of technology caused by the current acquisition policy. This is necessary to maintain a technological edge over its adversaries. Total quality management (TQM) was chosen as the management tool to help the USA curb defense spending. TQM will not only curb defense spending, but at the same time, expand technology, control costs and keep the USA competitive in the world marketplace. TQM is not only to be used for the DOD itself, but for defense contractors, their suppliers and vendors. TQM will then spread throughout the USA economy and create a nation able to provide better quality products and services.[42]

This summary points to several key principles in TQM. First, that it not only helps organizations streamline their processes but also helps reduce unnecessary costs. Second, that it helps to retain or expand market share. Third, that a total quality approach not only pertains to the organization itself *but to everyone from whom it sources its inputs*. The quality of an output, after all, is only as good as the quality of its inputs.

Some note that the angle on total quality taken by its main actors, such as Deming and Juran, is best classified as a "systems approach":

> Both Deming's and Juran's total quality movement construct falls within the systems approach and their models emphasize the study and analysis of organizational processes in order to improve system effectiveness. Deming and Juran, like most systems theorists, believe that the whole system is greater than the sum of its individual sub-systems and the way to improve

the whole system is to improve sub-systems processes ... Thus, both the systems paradigm and Deming's and Juran's total quality movement models focus on viewing the interrelationships between the various sub-system processes in an effort to identify and understand the dependent information, shared knowledge, and symbolic discourse that is occurring within the system to strengthen, improve and enhance these relationships.[43]

This stands in contrast to the analytical approach, which perceives reality as immutable, and the actors approach, which views reality from the vantage point of individual perception. For our purposes, however, the important idea is that a systems approach views all parts of a whole as equally important to that whole's best performance, an idea Deming and Juran loudly espoused and which has become firmly embedded in the annals of total quality as it stands today.

Beyond Total Quality

Total quality is now firmly established. Perhaps not surprisingly, now that its usefulness and validity have been proven beyond doubt, it has engendered a number of offshoot philosophies. While the phrase "total quality management" has lost some of its caché, the basic principles are still very much in evidence.

Six Sigma is one of the most famous of these, adopted and popularized by Motorola and used at GM, among other places. At its core, Six Sigma is a standard that marks companies whose products display near perfection. According to iSixSigma, "to achieve Six Sigma, a process must not produce more than 3.4 defects per million opportunities."[44]

Adherents to Six Sigma strive to hit this high mark through two separate processes: the DMAIC process (define, measure, analyze, improve, control) and the DMADV process (define, measure, analyze, design, verify). Change management and constant striving for perfection are at the core of Six Sigma principles, which in turn has spawned its own spinoffs around the world.[45]

The International Standards Organization, as referenced in the above section, makes management standards global. One of their most well-known and widely used sets of standards is the ISO 9000, which by subsection "sets out the requirements of a quality management system," "covers the basic concepts and language," "focuses on how to make a quality management system more efficient and effective," and "sets out guidance on internal and external audits of quality management systems."[46]

Multiple authors, speakers, coaches, and consultants have also adopted total quality principles to help organizations reach the top. One such notable is Tom Peters, with books such as *In Search of Excellence: Lessons from America's Best-Run Companies* and *Thriving on Chaos: Handbook for a Management Revolution*.

With the wide variety of total quality interpretations available, total quality and its descendants have snaked into every corner of production and operations, and are now making inroads into diverse fields such as law enforcement, medicine and pharmaceuticals, the information sector, and numerous others. Among these new members of the movement sits marketing, which has recently awakened to the necessity of total quality, but has yet to implement a strong, standardized, systematic quality presence.

Total Quality's Applications to Marketing

Marketing is a diverse discipline, hard to quantify in any one way. Its intended results are clear (increase customer base and profits, foster brand recognition, generate product interest), but its methods are diverse, its technologies widespread, and its success not always tied to real metrics. In part, because of marketing's diffuse nature, spread across organizations in dribs and drabs and often monitored poorly throughout, the lessons of total quality as derived from operations apply to it perfectly.

Total quality uses as its bellwether the efficient operation of *all* branches of a process, not just a few easy-to-monitor parts of it. This puts the onus of monitoring marketing's effects on workers as well as simply boards and managers, and requires the input of those who play a day-to-day role in marketing efforts in meeting standards of quality. Of course, that requires that marketing standards must exist in the first place. Once they have:

> [t]hey need to be connected to metrics of firm performance, preferably financial metrics. Metrics that measure return on marketing investment can consider the short-term, long-term, or the often-overlooked 'real options' nature of marketing investments. Real options are simply opportunities for the future that a firm may or may not decide to pursue. The key to improving accountability of marketing, however, is to link marketing metrics to sources of cash flow (like customer acquisition and retention, share of wallet within category, share of wallet across categories).[47]

Applying a total quality approach to marketing also requires that creativity be rolled into marketing standards, so that it is appreciated for the crucial role it plays, but its diktats are not allowed to take over. An "anything goes" approach is valuable when generating ideas, brainstorming, or generally spitballing, but not once an organization has already laid out product development and sales processes and is trying to maintain a consistent level of customer satisfaction and service. Moreover, marketing must successfully merge itself with every branch of an organization, explains Eugene H. Fram:

> Long-term success of total quality management programmes depends on initiatives which form strong partnerships with marketing activities. This is the view of a new generation of TQM practitioners. The objective of partnerships is integrating customer requirements into quality programmes, thus improving business functions, such as manufacturing and human resources management.[48]

The truth is, while Deming receives much of the credit for revolutionizing operations, production and management's approach toward workers and the total system, he did not have the targeted customer focus that many today feel is necessary for a satisfactory product, let alone a fully implemented TQM system. As Fram states:

> Early in the quality movement, marketing and its customer focus were not well recognized. The leaders involved appeared to be interested basically in improving systems and human motivations for manufacturing better products. SPC and quantitative analysis formed the bases of their work. The assumption was that improved products, in themselves, would attract buyers. It was the 'product orientation' common to industry prior to the 1960s. Evidence of this orientation can be found in Deming's Fourteen Principles. Not once is the word 'customer' or a synonym used in this document. His early focus was on the production process and the interpersonal efforts needed to improve quality.[49]

Fram's point is not that Deming's approach was incorrect, only that it was incomplete. Stephen George and Arnold Weimerskirch, in their book *Total Quality Management: Strategies and Techniques Proven at Today's Most Successful Companies*, add the following support: "The design of products and services is the most customer-focused activity your company undertakes, the point where external requirements are translated into internal requirements, where customers 'throw the switch' that activates your business."[50]

In today's world, where customer opinion can make or break a product or company, it is crucial to keep customer satisfaction central to *any* endeavor and *every* stage of the process. Marketing, Fram states, is not a solo endeavor, but rather one that must interweave with all other departments of a company, including manufacturing, customer support services, finance, human resources, professional services, information systems, and higher education.

At this point in time, Fram continues, marketing's integration into these sectors ranges widely. The role of some sectors, such as manufacturing and customer support, in the marketing endeavor is well understood. For others it is less so. To fully marry marketing to total quality, however, it will be necessary to ensure that *all* sectors keep marketing, and therefore the customer on which a company is ultimately founded, at the forefront.[51]

Stewart goes on to list the quality movement's implications for marketing managers: as well as the aforementioned linkage of return on investment (ROI) to cash flow, managers should also use metrics that reliably correlate with the firm's financial performance; should establish standards, metrics, and procedures; and should develop measures of return on investments.[52] If total quality has anything to say about it, developing standards will doubtless prove to be one of the most difficult but one of the most rewarding steps forward.

Creating and Teaching Marketing Standards

A key barrier to measuring the return on marketing investment is the lack of marketing standards. Standards help identify poor quality firms and serve as a baseline to which to compare future endeavors. One need look no further than the quality movement to see the importance of standards: like marketing today, quality was once viewed as a cost. Establishing standards was a monumental step forward in altering that perspective.[53]

In marketing, it is still up to each individual firm to determine its principles, practices, and measures. While this may seem freeing, in fact this lack of standardization makes it extremely difficult to quantify success, compete in the marketplace effectively, and determine where to cut efforts and where to increase them. To combat this, several organizations have stepped up in an attempt to offer standards.

While standards range depending on what type of organization and which departments they are geared toward, the Chartered Quality Institute explains that these standards address five key areas: policy, planning, implementation, measurement, and review. A company can choose any set of standards as laid out by various national and global organizations. The International Standards Organization, for instance, has laid out several sets of standards, some general and some tailored to industry. British Standards Institution has laid out others, such as standards for Information Security Management. Other examples include social accountability systems, environmental management systems, and occupational health and safety management systems. Organizations may choose whichever set (or sets) of principles applies to them and use them as a base for their own management decision-making.[54]

One such offering is the internationally accepted marketing standards *Standards Setting Guide*, put out by the International Institute of Marketing Professionals, in its second draft and still awaiting approval at the time of this writing. According to the introduction:

> The purpose of this guide is to establish a comprehensive framework of the standards setting processes involved in developing Internationally Accepted Marketing Standards ... Once this Guide is approved by the IAMS Board it will be used as a reference for the research, development, implementation and maintenance of internationally accepted practices in the field of marketing.[55]

Another is the *Code of Marketing Research Standards* by the Marketing Research Association. To that end:

The Marketing Research Association's (MRA) Code of Marketing Research Standards (Code) is designed to promote an ethical culture in the marketing research profession where principles of honesty, professionalism, fairness and confidentiality combine to support the profession's success. The Code sets standards of ethical conduct for all MRA members applied against the background of applicable law.[56]

A final example is that of the Chartered Institute of Marketing's *Professional Marketing Standards*, which are:

> [a] framework of marketing abilities which provide a guide to the skills and behaviors that are expected of professional marketers at varying levels of proficiency. Developed from extensive new research with employers and employees in marketing and broader business functions, the Standards give individuals and organizations the basis on which to assess the abilities of a capable and competent marketer.[57]

In contrast to the previous two examples, which address standards an organization would apply to its marketing endeavors and behaviors as a whole, the final example offers standards by which to judge the competency of the marketer themselves. This is a useful development, akin to the realization by thought leaders like Deming and Juran that the quality and capability of a manager had a huge impact on the team under their control. An individual marketer must be worthy, or their efforts and the outcomes that stem from them will not be.

It should be noted that technology further complicates the matter of setting standards. Technology changes incredibly rapidly, but each iteration (radio, television, the internet, email, social media) is eagerly adopted by marketing professionals in an effort to leverage newly opened avenues by which to reach the masses. This creates difficulty when setting standards that do not soon become obsolete.

While technology can aid in the standardization of marketing processes and results, its rapid growth also makes delineating and instituting those processes and results more important than ever before. Walter Shewhart was largely driven to create his quality charts through recognition of how helpful they would be in managing large amounts of data stemming from new technologies. In the same way, marketing is now dealing with an unprecedented explosion of technology that makes streamlining and standardizing the marketing process more important than ever.

It remains to be seen how technology's democratizing aspects, which make new approaches ever more possible, will align with marketing's desire to standardize. It also remains to be seen which set (or sets) of proposed standards will come to dominate the marketing scene. In the meantime, "brand" may offer the closest thing to standardization the marketing world has yet seen.

The Role of "Brand"

Often brand is confused with a company's name or its image, but this is not the case. The brand, rather, is more akin to an *association*. A brand's strength comes not from the product that represents it or even the company it belongs to, but rather what the consumer imagines it can do for them. Marketing-Schools.org, an online repository for information about marketing education, offers as examples the following:

> A movie-going parent will assume that a Disney movie is going to be family-friendly. A growing business purchasing a new mainframe and system from IBM can be confident that the new hardware and software has been proven in many other businesses . . . A coffee customer knows a new offering from Starbucks has gone through several levels of testing and quality control, and that it comes from coffee farms practicing sustainable agriculture.[58]

In other words, a brand clearly and succinctly articulates to the customer what they will get out of purchasing an item made under that brand. In the case of Disney, your kids (probably) will not have nightmares; with Starbucks, you can get your daily cup of Joe along with a hearty dose of environmental self-righteousness. Solid brands offer their value propositions right up front: *If you buy this, you'll get this.*

With all the hubbub in today's marketing world about alignment to standards, the almost automatic desire of organizations to create lasting brands seems to have engendered some natural standards: good triumphs over evil in Disney movies; IBM produces doggedly reliable computer systems. In a sense, companies with solid brands have already achieved their core marketing standards, and have achieved the third of Deming's 14 principles for management: "Cease dependence on inspection to achieve quality. Eliminate the need for inspection on a mass basis by building quality into the product in the first place."[59] In other words, companies with a self-set standard to adhere to eliminate or reduce inspection along the way and thereby benefit from the requirements of meeting their own brands' expectations.

This does leave smaller companies, newer companies, more diversified companies, and others who have not yet defined a brand out in the cold. But only for the time being, and in the meantime, striving toward a brand to represent them offers its own incentives to quality control, excellence, teamwork, and professional management.

Of course, branding (like its big brother, marketing) is a creative endeavor as well and therefore subject to continual change as well as marketing efforts that are based on looser, right-brained approaches rather than more fact-based, standardized ones. The recent explosion of internet marketing may, however, offer a partial solution to this.

Enter A/B testing, also called split testing, a creative process tightly controlled by metrics. In essence, it involves offering consumers two choices, say a red banner or a blue banner in their email newsletter. A company will issue two different versions of their newsletter simultaneously (to prevent the variable of time from contaminating the experiment), and whichever fares better becomes the new baseline for future testing.[60]

Best of all, the metrics involved are measurable and financially based: opens, click-through rates, conversions. All of these are measurements that eventually affect a company's bottom line, and it is just these sorts of measurements that marketing must adopt for both its products and its processes if it is to utilize the lessons of the quality movement.

Defining Marketing Processes

Branding and A/B testing may offer some insight into ways to align marketing results with efforts, but these hints cannot currently fill the gap seen by boards that are increasingly calling for marketing accountability. Unfortunately, marketing standards and accountability will come after, not before, a standardization of marketing process, and this is a difficult concept to pin down.

Marketing "products" come in a dizzyingly wide range: anything from letterhead to conferences to television ads may be considered a marketing product. Accordingly, the processes required to create such products varies widely, from design to advertising to public relations. But an effort to update old marketing models to reflect total quality's ideals must take stock of all of these approaches and respect the intended results of each. Moreover, this effort must be comprehensive. To again quote Ed Gaskin of C-Suite Insider:

> It is a commitment to looking at our entire marketing process from how we develop our strategy, conduct our research, execute our promotions and communications, understand the implications of the analysis and then act on it. How can we use the mountains of data we now have available to improve our marketing operations process? What metrics do we need that we don't have? The learning curve only works when learning takes place.[61]

TQM teaches that organizations must have a firm grasp on what their process is and what the acceptable variations within the process are; this is the entire point of Shewhart's control chart. If either of these is lacking, a firm cannot effectively strive for a quality process, nor can it determine where its process is falling short. Moreover, it is not enough to simply input a few new processes into the old creativity-driven, data-blind model. Rather, the model must change completely so that it accounts for real-world, fact-based, statistic-laden observations. As Gaskin explains:

> If you keep doing things the way you have always done them, you won't increase your effectiveness. The next new breakthrough in marketing science, technology or engineering won't save you because your marketing system is broken. Even the marketing department has to commit to continuous improvement as part of a larger marketing innovation strategy. Not doing it would be like wanting to maintain product parity with competitors, but not wanting to spend any money on product development.[62]

The implementation of a controlled marketing process therefore requires commitment on the part of both the marketing department and the larger organization, and a willingness to change in order to meet the needs of this commitment to effective change and the pursuit of excellence.

Common Ground and Shared Vocabulary

One of the most important steps in creating a comprehensive, streamlined, universal approach to marketing standards will be to ensure that those standards cover the needs of everyone to which they apply. They must speak as eloquently to solo business owners as they do to CEOs of 100,000-person companies. If they do not, the opportunity for common ground is lost and marketing will continue to resemble the quality movement at the beginning of the last century: disorganized, focused on immediate profits and short-term goals, disrespectful to the worker and blind to long-term needs.

Shared vocabulary is necessary in order to work toward common goals. Unfortunately, marketers are sorely lacking in a common lexicon. According to one study, marketing professionals cannot even agree on the meaning of ROI.[63] While they understand the point of the word, they cannot figure out how to implement it meaningfully, a problem that is doubtless stopping many companies from effectively using their metrics.

Instituting a shared vocabulary will also help with communications between organizations. Business to business articles, conventions, workshops, and other forms of communication will all benefit from shared vocabulary that engenders common ground and ensures that the parties taking part in important conversations are all on the same page.

Crisis Help

That crisis offers opportunity for meaningful change is an adage so widespread as to become a cliché. However, total quality has proven the truth of this maxim time and again.

To illustrate this point, we return to the story of Deming and Ford. The beleaguered auto manufacturer, tanking in the early 1980s, reached out to Deming for help before they went under. The result was not a slightly updated version of an old model, but a completely new car: the Taurus. It went on to outsell almost all other cars in history, and all because instead of switching up a few things, Ford overhauled its operations completely.[64]

Marketing now has a similar opportunity: not only to respond to crises when they arise but to minimize the chances that crisis will occur in the first place. A "path of continual improvement,"[65] as the Deming Institute puts it, can ensure that marketing departments play a pivotal role in reducing the amount of crisis help their companies will require in future.

Crisis management is a distinct form of marketing. As described by one expert:

> A crisis is a low probability, high impact event that has the potential to change the course of a company or organization's future. In today's 140 character world, organizations in crisis must immediately take control of their reputation or cede that to others.[66]

Another puts it more bluntly: "A reputation of real value takes a long time to grow—like a tree. And like a tree it takes only a minute to cut it down."[67]

A well-rounded approach to marketing necessitates preparation for crisis. In fact, spending time crafting crisis management plans can even prevent them from happening in the first place.[68] Total quality's mandates in this area are clear: only by building a crisis plan that reaches to every corner of the organization, getting all personnel on board, and relying on standardized responses can a company ensure the soundness of its reputation.

Overcoming Resistance

These days, it is hard to find an argument for ignoring metrics in marketing. Sadly, it is not nearly as hard to find examples of marketing experts who routinely do so. A study conducted by Columbia Business School's Center on Global Brand Leadership in conjunction with the New York American Marketing Association surveyed senior marketing executives from large companies, and determined that these executives routinely have trouble processing data and applying it to their decision-making. Only 19 percent collect customer mobile data, for instance, while only 35 capture social media information; 29 percent say they possess "too little or no customer/consumer data"; 28 percent are still basing their marketing decisions on gut instinct.[69]

This speaks volumes to the state of marketing today: while executives know they *should* be using real data, they have a hard time acquiring it in real time, little idea what to do with it, and trouble agreeing on important vocabulary (such as ROI).[70] But before drawing the conclusion that marketers simply do not care, it is important to distinguish between resistance and ignorance. Whereas the former might require a wrist-slap, the latter calls for good education. Education that, because of the current state of marketing, may take some time to assemble.

Where Does Marketing Stand Today?

Today marketing is at a crossroads. Or perhaps a *bend* in the road might be the more accurate metaphor, considering that marketing has little choice but to continue down the same path it is already on. After all, boardrooms across the nation are demanding similar changes from marketing teams: that they set standards, choose financially-related metrics, use them to measure performance, and act according to their results.

In this sense, marketing is at the same bend in the road at which Bell Laboratories found itself around the time Walter Shewhart joined the company. Marketing, as an industry, is aware of the lack of standards and the problems they are causing, but is not yet confident about its ability to root them out and fix them. What marketing needs is a control chart.

Luckily, if not necessarily easy to use well, control charts are relatively simple to set up to measure any metric. A retail outlet might, for instance, set up a control chart to measure how gift cards effect sales on a daily basis. Setting limits based on a history of sales could help the retailer identify any massive outliers, for good or ill, and therefore determine how marketing efforts are affecting sales. Increasingly, businesses are electing to use simple measurement methods in order to track how effective their marketing strategy is. Even so, data that does not take account of the larger company vision, or represent effective communication between departments, will always be missing something.

So another amendment is perhaps in order. Marketing needs a vast slough of control charts, tightly organized and pertaining to individual processes in order to constrain variation. Marketing inputs must finally, reliably correlate to marketing outputs. While "creativity" is not a bad word, it will soon become one if marketing experts cannot put it in its proper place: as yet another tool in the service of pursuing excellence and increasing profit, instead of as a good in and of itself.

Marketing also needs an educational system that teaches students about more than press releases and brand image. One that offers a clear definition of ROI and a clue about what to do with all that social media data. One that offers enough guidance so that marketing "experts" can stop relying on their gut instincts and start using the data they gather in meaningful ways.

As a discipline, though, marketing is getting there. No one disputes the importance of viable metrics any longer. In fact, as it did in operations, measurement is quickly becoming the paramount good in marketing. This is nowhere as apparent as with the Marketing Accountability Standards Board (MASB).

MASB

The Marketing Accountability Foundation (MAF) offers the following introduction to its MASB:

> As the era of 'financial engineering' for growth winds down, marketing professionals are stepping up, beginning to master and apply the science of measurement and process management to the art of marketing. This fundamental change will usher in a new era of marketing accountability that will drive consistent growth, with improved methods for measuring, forecasting and improving the effectiveness of marketing activities and a narrowing of the gap between marketing efforts and financial outcomes. MASB is enabling this transformation by serving as the independent, private sector, self-governing body, establishing measurement and accountability standards across industry and domain for continuous improvement in financial return . . . *attending to measurement* as the foundation and catalyst for advancement.[71]

The italics (original) provide valuable proof of how seriously the marketing industry is currently taking the implementation of metrics-based decision-making. MASB is the brainchild of The Boardroom Project, formed in 2004 by "a cross-industry/cross-discipline body of marketing scientists . . . responding to mounting pressure from corporate boardrooms for accountability in the marketing function."[72]

The Boardroom Project's members realized that: "while marketing was not ignoring the issues surrounding metrics and accountability, the practices and initiatives underway were narrow in focus, lacking integration and generally not tied to financial performance in predictable ways."[73] This is a dead ringer for the realizations that occurred in the early and mid-twentieth century, when executives and thought leaders concluded that quality was routinely stymied by myopic thinking, fragmentation, and lack of communication, and a divorce of process from measurement.

MASB seeks to provide standards, which will hopefully fix some of these issues. Nor is it silent about what these metrics ought to look like. It offers a metrics catalog, formally determined by the Marketing Metric Audit Protocol. The catalog includes several types of metrics, and:

> [i]ncludes the conceptual linking of marketing activities to intermediate marketing outcome metrics to cash flow drivers of the business, as well as an audit as to how the metrics meet the validation & causality characteristics of an ideal metric. This Catalogue is designed to provide vendors and users of marketing metrics with a systematic way of thinking about specific metrics, the criteria for assessing their usefulness (including predictive validity and sensitivity), their relationships between one another, and their relationships to measures of financial performance.[74]

Financial measurement has not yet taken over as the driver of marketing decision-making, but at this point that may be more due to confusion about *how* to do so than any real argument about the value of metrics. In this sense, TQM has already had its say when it comes to marketing: a fully integrated, well-communicated, metrics-based approach to process and product are necessary and possible. What remains is to put this realization into practice. There, operations has had a 75-year head start, give or take, on marketing . . . but then, an excellent role model is hardly a bad thing.

Conclusion

The total quality movement provides a valuable, world-embracing case study for marketing. Like manufacturing, marketing is global, applicable to every country, city, and business in the world. It therefore benefits greatly from the thoroughly studied, carefully crafted trail that quality blazed in the twentieth century.

Perhaps total quality's most important lesson stems from the word *total*. An organization cannot implement total quality measures without enjoining each member of that organization to help; nor can they do so while ignoring one or more departments within the company.

Quality in marketing, therefore, cannot be achieved simply by trying to improve marketing outcomes alone; nor can a company do well and continue to improve if it exempts its marketing department from structure or measurement, giving the green light to a freeform creative process simply because *it was always this way*. To pursue excellence really does require full commitment.

For a company to be successful in today's fiercely competitive global economy, marketing must be excellent. It must adhere to strict standards that are based not on opinions, hunches, nostalgia, or history, but rather on statistics that pave the way for a control process. Only then can marketing departments guarantee their results, confidently build brand, protect market share, and propel the companies they represent into the future.

References

1 Ed Gaskin, "Why Marketing Needs a TQM Movement," *C-Suite Insider*, accessed November 15, 2014, available at http://www.csuiteinsider.com/marketing-tqm-movement/.
2 "Total Quality Management (TQM)," *American Society for Quality*, accessed November 16, 2014, available at http://asq.org/learn-about-quality/total-quality-management/overview/overview.html.
3 Penelope Przekop, *Six Sigma for Business Excellence*, 2006, New York: McGraw-Hill, p. 8.
4 "Statistical Quality Control," *Encyclopaedia Britannica*, accessed November 16, 2014, available at http://www.britannica.com/EBchecked/topic/564167/statistical-quality-control.
5 "Statistical Quality Control Versus Statistical Process Control (SQC Versus SPC)," *American Society for Quality*, accessed November 15, 2014, available at http://asq.org/learn-about-quality/statistical-process-control/overview/tutorial.html.
6 "Statistical Process Control Explained," *DataNet Quality Systems*, accessed November 16, 2014, available at http://www.winspc.com/what-is-spc/statistical-process-control-explained.
7 "Total Quality Management (TQM)," *American Society for Quality*, accessed November 16, 2014, available at http://asq.org/learn-about-quality/total-quality-management/overview/overview.html.
8 "Total Quality Management (TQM)," *American Society for Quality*, accessed November 16, 2014, available at http://asq.org/learn-about-quality/total-quality-management/overview/overview.html.
9 "Total Quality Management Benefits," *American Society for Quality*, accessed November 16, 2014, available at http://asq.org/learn-about-quality/total-quality-management/overview/tqm-gets-results.html.
10 Arne Buthman, "Cost of Quality: Not Only Failure Costs," *iSixSigma*, accessed November 16, 2014, available at www.isixsigma.com/implementation/financial-analysis/cost-quality-not-only-failure-costs/.
11 Ed Gaskin, "Why Marketing Needs a TQM Movement," *C-Suite Insider*, accessed November 15, 2014, available at http://www.csuiteinsider.com/marketing-tqm-movement/.
12 "History of the Organization of Work," *Encyclopaedia Britannica*, accessed November 17, 2014, available at http://www.britannica.com/EBchecked/topic/648000/history-of-the-organization-of-work/67028/The-craft-guilds.

13 "Guilds of Medieval Europe," *American Society for Quality*, accessed November 17, 2014, available at http://asq.org/learn-about-quality/history-of-quality/overview/guilds.html.
14 Joseph M. Juran, "The Taylor System and Quality Control," *The Juran Institute*, last updated 1994, available at http://www.juran.com/elifeline/elifefiles/2009/11/Taylor-System-and-Quality-Control_JMJuran-94.pdf.
15 "The Industrial Revolution," *American Society for Quality*, accessed November 17, 2014, available at http://asq.org/learn-about-quality/history-of-quality/overview/industrial-revolution.html.
16 Jim L. Smith, "Remembering Walter A. Shewhart's Contribution to the Quality World," *Quality Magazine*, last modified March 2, 2009, available at http://www.qualitymag.com/articles/85973-remembering-walter-a-shewhart-s-contribution-to-the-quality-world.
17 Jim L. Smith, "Remembering Walter A. Shewhart's Contribution to the Quality World," *Quality Magazine*, last modified March 2, 2009, available at http://www.qualitymag.com/articles/85973-remembering-walter-a-shewhart-s-contribution-to-the-quality-world.
18 W. A. Shewhart, *Economic Control of Quality of Manufactured Product*, 1931, New York: Van Nostrand, p. vii.
19 M. Best and D. Neuhauser, "Walter A Shewhart, 1924, and the Hawthorne Factory," *National Center for Biotechnology Information*, last updated April 2006, available at http://www.ncbi.nlm.nih.gov/pmc/articles/PMC2464836/.
20 "World War II," *American Society for Quality*, accessed November 17, 2014, available at http://asq.org/learn-about-quality/history-of-quality/overview/wwii.html.
21 "About ASQ: Joseph M. Juran," *American Society for Quality*, accessed November 17, 2014, available at http://asq.org/about-asq/who-we-are/bio_juran.html.
22 "About ASQ: Joseph M. Juran," *American Society for Quality*, accessed November 17, 2014, available at http://asq.org/about-asq/who-we-are/bio_juran.html.
23 "Biography," *Philip Crosby Associates*, accessed November 17, 2014, available at http://www.philipcrosby.com/25years/crosby.html.
24 Doug McInnis, "W. Edwards Deming of Powell, Wyo.: The Man Who Helped Shape the World," *WyoHistory.org*, accessed November 17, 2014, available at http://www.wyohistory.org/encyclopedia/w-edwards-deming.
25 "Deming Influence on Post-war Japanese Quality Development," *Quality Function Deployment Institute*, accessed November 17, 2014, available at http://www.qfdi.org/newsletters/deming_in_japan.html.
26 "Total Quality Management (TQM)," *Inc.*, accessed November 17, 2014, available at http://www.inc.com/encyclopedia/total-quality-management-tqm.html.
27 Peter J. Kolesar, "Juran's Lectures to Japanese Executives in 1954: A Perspective and Some Contemporary Lessons," *The Juran Institute*, last updated 2008, available at http://www.juran.com/elifeline/elifefiles/2009/11/Jurans-Lectures-to-Japanese-Executives-in-1954.pdf.
28 Peter J. Kolesar, "Juran's Lectures to Japanese Executives in 1954: A Perspective and Some Contemporary Lessons," *The Juran Institute*, last updated 2008, available at http://www.juran.com/elifeline/elifefiles/2009/11/Jurans-Lectures-to-Japanese-Executives-in-1954.pdf.
29 "The Deming Prize," *Union of Japanese Scientists and Engineers*, accessed November 17, 2014, available at http://www.juse.or.jp/e/deming/.
30 Peter J. Kolesar, "Juran's Lectures to Japanese Executives in 1954: A Perspective and Some Contemporary Lessons," *The Juran Institute*, last updated 2008, available at http://www.juran.com/elifeline/elifefiles/2009/11/Jurans-Lectures-to-Japanese-Executives-in-1954.pdf.
31 "Total Quality," *American Society for Quality*, accessed November 17, 2014, available at http://asq.org/learn-about-quality/history-of-quality/overview/total-quality.html.
32 Doug McInnis, "W. Edwards Deming of Powell, Wyo.: The Man Who Helped Shape the World," *WyoHistory.org*, accessed November 17, 2014, available at http://www.wyohistory.org/encyclopedia/w-edwards-deming.
33 Bill Creech, *The Five Pillars of TQM: How to Make Total Quality Management Work for You*, 1994, New York: Truman Tally Books/Plume, p. 312.
34 "What Is the Red Bead Game?," *Concept Point*, accessed November 18, 2014, available at http://www.redbead.com/what/.
35 Peter J. Kolesar, "Juran's Lectures to Japanese Executives in 1954: A Perspective and Some Contemporary Lessons," *The Juran Institute*, last updated 2008, available at http://www.juran.com/elifeline/elifefiles/2009/11/Jurans-Lectures-to-Japanese-Executives-in-1954.pdf.

36 "Plan-Do-Check-Act (PDCA)," *Mind Tools*, accessed November 18, 2014, available at http://www.mindtools.com/pages/article/newPPM_89.htm.
37 "Management System Standards," *International Standards Organization*, accessed November 18, 2014, available at http://www.iso.org/iso/home/standards/management-standards.htm.
38 "The Fourteen Points for the Transformation of Management," *The W. Edwards Deming Institute*, accessed November 18, 2014, available at https://www.deming.org/theman/theories/fourteenpoints.
39 "The Fourteen Points for the Transformation of Management," *The W. Edwards Deming Institute*, accessed November 18, 2014, available at https://www.deming.org/theman/theories/fourteenpoints.
40 See http://www.bpir.com (accessed November 10, 2014).
41 "History of Quality," *Business Performance Improvement Resource*, accessed November 18, 2014, available at http://www.bpir.com/total-quality-management-history-of-tqm-and-business-excellence-bpir.com.html#japan.
42 Ahmad K. Elshennawy and Kimberly M. McCarthy, 1992, "Implementing Total Quality Management at the US Department of Defense," *Total Quality Management*, 3(1): 31.
43 B. Tim Lowder, "An Analysis of the Total Quality Movement: In Search of Quality Enhancement through Structural and Strategic Synthesis," *Academia.edu*, accessed November 19, 2014, available at http://www.academia.edu/948786/An_Analysis_of_the_Total_Quality_Movement_In_Search_of_Quality_Enhancement_through_Structural_and_Strategic_Synthesis.
44 "What Is Six Sigma?," *iSixSigma*, accessed November 19, 2014, available at http://www.isixsigma.com/new-to-six-sigma/getting-started/what-six-sigma/.
45 "What Is Six Sigma?," *iSixSigma*, accessed November 19, 2014, available at http://www.isixsigma.com/new-to-six-sigma/getting-started/what-six-sigma/.
46 "ISO 9000," *International Standards Organization*, accessed November 19, 2014, available at http://www.iso.org/iso/iso_9000.
47 David Stewart, "Measuring Marketing's Performance: Lessons from the Quality Movement," presentation at Marketing Metrics for the Connected Organization, *Marketing Science Institute Conference*, Dallas, Texas, September 10–12, available at http://www.msi.org/conferences/presentations/measuring-marketings-performance-lessons-from-the-quality-movement/.
48 Eugene H. Fram, 1995, "Not So Strange Bedfellows: Marketing and Total Quality Management," *Managing Service Quality: An International Journal*, 5(1): 50.
49 Eugene H. Fram, 1995, "Not So Strange Bedfellows: Marketing and Total Quality Management," *Managing Service Quality: An International Journal*, 5(1): 50.
50 Stephen George and Arnold Weimerskirch, *Total Quality Management: Strategies and Techniques Proven at Today's Most Successful Companies*, 1994, New York: John Wiley and Sons, Inc., p. 149.
51 Eugene H. Fram, 1995, "Not So Strange Bedfellows: Marketing and Total Quality Management," *Managing Service Quality: An International Journal*, 5(1): 50.
52 David Stewart, "Measuring Marketing's Performance: Lessons from the Quality Movement," presentation at Marketing Metrics for the Connected Organization, *Marketing Science Institute Conference*, Dallas, Texas, September 10–12, available at http://www.msi.org/conferences/presentations/measuring-marketings-performance-lessons-from-the-quality-movement/.
53 David Stewart, "Measuring Marketing's Performance: Lessons from the Quality Movement," presentation at Marketing Metrics for the Connected Organization, *Marketing Science Institute Conference*, Dallas, Texas, September 10–12, available at http://www.msi.org/conferences/presentations/measuring-marketings-performance-lessons-from-the-quality-movement/.
54 "Management System Standards," *Chartered Quality Institute*, accessed November 19, 2014, available at http://www.thecqi.org/Knowledge-Hub/Knowledge-portal/Compliance-and-organisations/Management-system-standards/.
55 "Internationally Accepted Marketing Standards Standards Setting Guide," *International Institute of Marketing Professionals*, accessed November 19, 2014, available at http://www.theiimp.org/internationally-accepted-marketing-standards/.
56 "MRA Code of Marketing Research Standards," *Marketing Research Association*, accessed November 20, 2014, available at http://www.marketingresearch.org/code
57 "Professional Marketing Standards," *Chartered Institute of Marketing*, accessed November 20, 2014, available at http://www.cim.co.uk/About/Mktgstandards/Introduction.aspx.

58 "Brand Marketing," *Marketing-Schools.org*, accessed November 20, 2014, available at http://www.marketing-schools.org/types-of-marketing/brand-marketing.html.
59 "The Fourteen Points for the Transformation of Management," *The W. Edwards Deming Institute*, accessed November 18, 2014, available at https://www.deming.org/theman/theories/fourteenpoints.
60 Paras Chopra, "The Ultimate Guide to A/B Testing," *Smashing Magazine*, last updated June 24, 2010, available at http://www.smashingmagazine.com/2010/06/24/the-ultimate-guide-to-a-b-testing/.
61 Ed Gaskin, "Why Marketing Needs a TQM Movement," *C-Suite Insider*, accessed November 15, 2014, available at http://www.csuiteinsider.com/marketing-tqm-movement/.
62 Ed Gaskin, "Why Marketing Needs a TQM Movement," *C-Suite Insider*, accessed November 15, 2014, available at http://www.csuiteinsider.com/marketing-tqm-movement/.
63 "Study Finds Marketers Struggle with the Big Data and Digital Tools of Today," *PR Newswire*, last updated March 12, 2012, available at http://www.prnewswire.com/news-releases/study-finds-marketers-struggle-with-the-big-data-and-digital-tools-of-today-142312475.html.
64 Doug McInnis, "W. Edwards Deming of Powell, Wyo.: The Man Who Helped Shape the World," *WyoHistory.org*, accessed November 17, 2014, available at http://www.wyohistory.org/encyclopedia/w-edwards-deming.
65 "Deming Today," *The Deming Institute*, accessed November 20, 2014, available at https://deming.org/demingtoday.
66 "Crisis Management," *Andrea Obston Marketing Communications, LLC*, accessed November 20, 2014, available at http://aomc.com/services/crisis-management/.
67 "Crisis Marketing and Reputation," *Reputation Management for Online Reputation Experts*, accessed November 20, 2014, available at http://www.reputationmanagementfor.com/crisis-marketing/crisis-marketing-a-reputation.html.
68 "Crisis & Reputation Management," *Stanton Public Relations and Marketing*, accessed November 20, 2014, available at http://www.stantonprm.com/crisis-reputation-management/.
69 "Study Finds Marketers Struggle with the Big Data and Digital Tools of Today," *PR Newswire*, last updated March 12, 2012, available at http://www.prnewswire.com/news-releases/study-finds-marketers-struggle-with-the-big-data-and-digital-tools-of-today-142312475.html.
70 "Study Finds Marketers Struggle with the Big Data and Digital Tools of Today," *PR Newswire*, last updated March 12, 2012, available at http://www.prnewswire.com/news-releases/study-finds-marketers-struggle-with-the-big-data-and-digital-tools-of-today-142312475.html.
71 *Marketing Accountability Standards Board of the Marketing Accountability Foundation*, accessed November 20, 2014, available at http://themasb.org.
72 "The Boardroom Project," *Marketing Accountability Standards Board of the Marketing Accountability Foundation*, accessed November 20, 2014, available at http://www.themasb.org/wp-content/uploads/themasbvision.pdf.
73 "The Boardroom Project," *Marketing Accountability Standards Board of the Marketing Accountability Foundation*, accessed November 20, 2014, available at http://www.themasb.org/wp-content/uploads/themasbvision.pdf.
74 "Metrics Catalogue," *Marketing Accountability Standards Board of the Marketing Accountability Foundation*, accessed November 20, 2014, available at http://themasb.org/marketing-metrics-audit-protocol/marketing-performance-measurement/.

Section II
Language, Measures, and Metrics
Establishing Standards

3 Marketing's Search for a Common Language

Paul Farris, David J. Reibstein, and Karen Scheller

Introduction and Motivation

The starting point for any set of standards is a common vocabulary. The marketing discipline has long been plagued by "fuzzy" terminology—the same words can often mean quite different things even in the same organization.

> "When *I* use a word," Humpty Dumpty said, in rather a scornful tone, "it means just what I choose it to mean—neither more nor less."
>
> "The question is," said Alice, "whether you *can* make words mean so many different things."
>
> "The question is," said Humpty Dumpty, "which is to be master—that's all."
>
> (Lewis Carroll, *Through the Looking-Glass* (1872))[1]

> "Nothing is more usual than for philosophers to encroach on the province of grammarians, and to engage in disputes of words, while they imagine they are handling controversies of the deepest importance and concern."
>
> (David Hume)[2]

> "Scientific controversies constantly resolve themselves into differences about the meaning of words."
>
> (Sir Arthur Schuster)[3]

Somewhere between Humpty Dumpty's disdain for the need to share common meanings and interpretations of words, and Hume's caution to avoid fruitless debate about semantics, lies an important challenge for marketing. In 1892, Sir Arthur Schuster recognized this need for a common language in science, finding that: "one of the principal obstacles to the rapid diffusion of a new idea lies in the difficulty of . . . convey(ing) the essential point to other minds."[4]

Many battles have been fought simply over the meaning of different terms. Larry Silverstein, for example, the new acquirer of the World Trade Centers in New York shortly before the disaster of September 11, 2001, brought suit against the insurers of the building claiming there were two "incidents" on the twin towers and not one, thereby leading to compensation of over $7 billion versus $3.55 billion should it be judged to be one incident.[5] Similar battles have been fought over the meaning of "forecasts" as delivered by market research firms that proved to be wrong.

We believe that there are changes occurring in the marketing profession that make it more important than ever for the field to strive toward establishing a common language. The changes have to do with the ever-growing influence of data-based business analytics.

Like most other business functions, marketing is also becoming more reliant on data to guide decisions and evaluate productivity. For a field that is often considered one of the "softer" and "creative" areas of business, the confrontation with data has not always been comfortable, but the move toward data-based decisions is inexorable, because, as Jim Lecinski of Google remarks often: "data beat opinion."[6] So why the discomfort?

One reason that the shift toward data-based marketing is uncomfortable is that many important concepts in marketing have so many possible interpretations and shades of meaning that they are only partially measurable. Here we are thinking of concepts such as "loyalty" and "product differentiation," both of which have been extensively used, but in a variety of different ways. It seems that the longer concepts have been used in marketing, the more variation in how the terms have been used and the higher the level of confusion that has arisen about what the concepts mean and how they should be defined and measured.

Also, some scholars have argued that when a field of inquiry undergoes significant change—such as the growing importance of digital marketing media—the meaning of terms can also change. Even so, there are a host of marketing concepts that are measurable and, when quantification is possible, it is critical to have clearly defined metrics. Otherwise, it will never be possible to separate true measurement error from the underlying concept being measured.

There is also the time dimension which should be considered. More often than not, what is critical is less what the absolute level is of any metric, but how it changes over time and in response to marketing activities. For example, market share is an important metric, but how the market share changes over time and in response to a marketing program is perhaps even more important. This can only be fairly assessed if the method of market share measurement is consistent from one period to the next. One of the critical measures of economic performance is the unemployment levels. Many presidents have been accused of delivering a good economic performance, low unemployment levels, simply by changing how unemployment is measured. The point is that it is critical to have a common and stable definition of terms that everyone understands.

Beyond the desire of academics to push the marketing field more toward the "hard" sciences, there are other motivations to clean up and clarify marketing's language. Finance is pushing marketing to get better at reporting metrics that will improve forecasts of sales and profits, as well as demonstrating adequate returns on marketing spending. Eventually, these metrics may be reported to external audiences. In those cases a host of marketing metrics will require consistent definitions to enable accurate and consistent measurement and reporting. From the other side, operations will pressure marketing to apply concepts of "kaizen"[7] in order to demonstrate improvements to productivity. Standardization and measurement against benchmarks are central to the continuous improvement that other fields are demonstrating. So what is the problem?

The Problem: Lack of Common Marketing Language

In the 1920s the DuPont Corporation started using a standardized accounting practice, which allowed them to compare their various businesses in terms of financial performance. This led to the creation of the DuPont Model, as shown in Figure 3.1.

This model became commonly used within DuPont and subsequently by other companies. The acceptance of these accounting definitions served a very useful purpose—they allowed for comparisons across companies, businesses within companies, and even specific expenditures since there was now a common language/understanding of what these terms mean. Today, taken from the DuPont Model,[8] we can refer to earnings before interest and taxes, EBITA, and know this means earnings minus operating expenses plus non-operating income. These have become commonplace and are now definitional. The advantage of having widely accepted definitions of accounting terms should be clear—aside from allowing comparisons as noted before, it allows for clear communications in which everyone understands each other.

Unfortunately, marketing still not does have that commonality of terminology. There are many terms in active use by marketing practitioners and academics that either have no clear

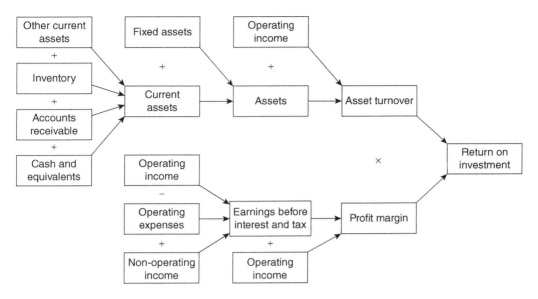

Figure 3.1 The DuPont Model.

Source: Created by the authors from the small figure Groppelli, Angelico A. and Ehsan Nikbakht (2000), *Finance*, 4th edition, 2000, Hauppauge, NY: Barron's Educational Series, Inc., pp. 444–445, available at http://www.myaccountingcourse.com/financial-ratios/dupont-analysis.

definition or are defined very differently across organizations and even within. Ironically, given the focus of the DuPont Model, prominent among these is the term "marketing return on investment" or MROI, also known as return on marketing investment or ROMI. Marketers often refer to the "return" in measures other than profit, be it revenue or even exposures, just to name a few. In a separate chapter we explore the many different ways in which the MROI is used and make some suggestions for adding modifiers that will help readers differentiate among those versions of usage. However, the problem goes much further than this single term. Consider, for example, that "exposures," "impressions," and "opportunities-to-see" are all used to convey the same notion that an advertisement was delivered in a media vehicle and available to an audience of an estimated size. Even notions of reach and frequency, and how they are usually defined, have been confused in articles published by leading marketing journals.

A simple example that should have no ambiguity is the term "market share." When some people report their market share they are reporting so on unit volume, while others are reporting on value, yet it is not always specified. Even when using the same variant, we have seen market shares across firms that have added up to more than 100 percent. This, of course, should never be possible, yet the differences occur in the share of "what?" If one company defines the market as share of carbonated soft drinks and another is reporting share of caffeinated soft drinks (since that is the only domain in which they operate), there is the potential for shares to not be congruent across competitors.

We have often seen differences in definitions and measure of "customer lifetime value (CLV)" within the academic community, as some have defined it as: an "average customer lifetime value," while Fader and Hardie[9] are adamant about only referring to a customer's lifetime value on a cohort level. Perhaps, academics view their job description as working on alternative measurement schemes, yet, within practice, there are wide variations as well. We have heard numerous practitioners refer to their customers' lifetime value as the revenue that a customer generates this year or even more frequently the contribution generated from a customer *this year* with no consideration of likely future purchases.

"Brand equity" is another term that is widely used, but with totally different definitions. Jacobson (2012) and others have suggested rejecting brand equity measurement due to the wide variation in meaning across different measurement services (e.g., Interbrand, Brand Finance, and BAV, to name a few).[10] For example, Apple's brand in 2011 was worth $33.5 billion according to Interbrand, while BrandZ assessed it at $153.3 billion, and Intel was valued at $35.2 billion and $13.9 billion by Interbrand and BrandZ, respectively. Across these services, rankings change over time in different directions. These differences are not the result of measurement error, but rather that different definitions are being used *for the same term*.

We believe most readers will agree that marketing, as a field, needs a common language that rigorously defines important terms and metrics to minimize overlap and confusion. What are the underlying causes of the current state of our language? Part of the problem is that we are a dynamic field, relatively new compared to the "hard" sciences and even some of the other social sciences (psychology, sociology, and economics). Adding to the problem, there are few acknowledged sources of authority for "deciding" what a term should mean.

Concepts, Constructs, and Operational Definitions

Watt and van den Berg distinguish theoretical and operations' definitions in a way that we find useful:

> Concepts represent the 'real world' phenomena being explained by the theory. The scientific method requires that the nature of these concepts be unambiguously communicated to others. This requirement mandates the creation of *theoretical definitions* . . . Concepts must also be objectively observed. This requires that we create *operational definitions*, which translate the verbal concepts into corresponding variables which can be measured.[11]

The same authors differentiate constructs from concepts, arguing that the former are even more abstract than concepts, and cannot be directly observed. They use "source credibility" as an example of a construct that comprises concepts such as expertise, status, and objectivity. Of course, the latter can also be operationalized in a number of ways.

There will continue to be healthy (at least vigorous) debates in marketing on what *should* be meant by various theoretical concepts and constructs. However, at the level of measurement and reporting, the field should be striving for consistency, accuracy, and reliability. None of that can happen without clear operational definitions, and those are the primary focus of the Common Language Project (Figure 3.2).

There is a danger as we go down this endeavor, that we end up defining everything in marketing, and even beyond. We have tried to restrict ourselves to *marketing measures*. This means we are not attempting to define marketing concepts, such as positioning, brand, satisfaction, or other commonly used terms. Indeed, these too need common means of expression. Yet, that is beyond the scope of our efforts. On the other hand, and related, we do define the metrics that are used to measure some of these constructs. For example, we do not define the term "loyalty," yet we will define alternative measures of satisfaction, from direct Likert scales of satisfaction to net promoter score (NPS). As described earlier, we explicitly define measures of CLV, yet we shy away from defining the construct itself.

The Opportunity

The opportunity and need is for a published dictionary in a central, accessible location with the definitions of frequently and commonly used marketing metrics and terms, so that they receive

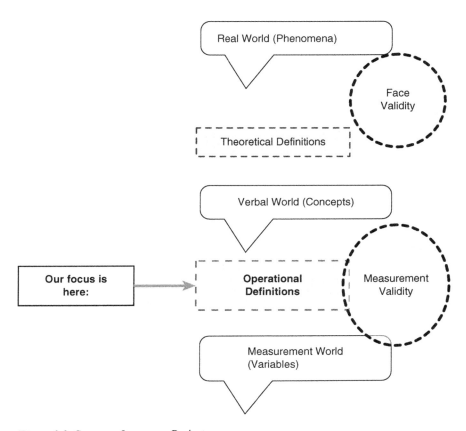

Figure 3.2 Common Language Project.

Source: Created by the authors from Watt, James H. and Sjef van den Berg, *Research Methods for Communication Science*, 1995, Boston, MA: Allyn & Bacon.

wide and general acceptance. For this purpose, the Marketing Accountability Standards Board (MASB) proposed the development of a project team in 2009 called "Common Language in Marketing." From the early stages, two important resources were used to jumpstart this initiative:

1   the second edition of *Marketing Metrics: The Definitive Guide to Marketing Measurement*;[12]
2   the extensive American Marketing Association (AMA) online dictionary, which originated in print in 1995.[13]

From the beginning, it became obvious that a project this ambitious—with the goal of becoming "the global resource for defining marketing terms and metrics"—would require industry-wide support. The project is now jointly funded and run by MASB and three other important marketing associations spanning academia and industry: AMA, the Marketing Science Institute (MSI), and the Association of National Advertisers (ANA). We are looking to add other industry associations to increase the breadth and accuracy of definitions in all fields of marketing.

The next step is to convince editors and reviewers of academic journals and business publications to refer to these "dictionaries" when deciding on an acceptable use and to discourage the publication of new terms in a way that substitutes them for perfectly acceptable existing terms.

It is also incumbent on companies to make sure the terms are used correctly internally. Perhaps the first place to start is with the providers and marketing research terms employed to gather these measures. Similarly, academics need to make sure as they teach the next wave of marketers that they are careful to attend to the definitions in the dictionaries that have become commonly accepted.

The Platform

The first iteration of this project used Wikipedia as a platform. In early 2011, we began adding vetted marketing terms and metrics, primarily from the Farris *et al*. (2010) *Marketing Metrics* book.[14] Some were added as stand-alone entries, while others incorporated the book's definition into an existing Wikipedia definition.

By 2013, the project team became increasingly aware of the shortcomings of the Wikipedia platform for its specific needs. Due to the open nature of the platform, the entries were subject to vandalism, with changes that at times made the entries vile, nonsensical, or meaningless. As an example, the AMA's vetted definition of marketing—*marketing is the activity, set of institutions, and processes for creating, communicating, delivering, and exchanging offerings that have value for customers, clients, partners, and society at large*—was continuously being deleted or changed and at one point the Wikipedia entry for "Marketing" included the statement: "Marketing is the process of beating the innocence of an animal or puppy to death" (sic).

While Wikipedia does an excellent job of removing such vandalism in a timely fashion, the huge volume of user revisions required constant monitoring of each common language entry, and often restoration of the entry to ensure the integrity and consistency of the definitions. The team agreed that, moving forward, we would create an independent wiki-style platform endorsed and financed by multiple industry associations. Maintained by MASB, this new platform would allow comments and suggestions by users, but prevent random editing by visitors to the site. This mobile-friendly site (http://www.marketing-dictionary.org) is accessible from each association's (currently MASB, AMA, ANA, and MSI) webpage. The ongoing vision for the site is for a comprehensive, globally relevant, common language dictionary of marketing terms, activities, metrics, and systems, which are endorsed, owned, and supported by the MASB and major marketing industry associations and accessible by everyone.

Role of Reviewers

We recognize that terms will be added to the dictionary on an ongoing basis, as new constructs need to be measured or as new technologies lead us to new measures, for example, measures that arise in the context of neuroscience and social media. To ensure that the "common language" website remains relevant and universally accepted, MASB is recruiting a group of industry experts—academics and practitioners—to serve as a review panel to vet the definitions. These reviewers will evaluate new terms in their areas of expertise, as well as periodically review existing definitions to ensure they are still valid.

Role of Commercial Suppliers

There is always the challenge that some commercial research providers have developed a new way of capturing a phenomenon worth studying. We are sure that this was the case when the term "same store sales" was developed for capturing retail growth beyond simply an increase in sales that was confounded by the increase in the number of outlets. This should not be curtailed, nor do we aspire to do so.

On the other hand, we do want to caution against the creation of terms to be trade-marked in a way that confuses them with generic terms, for example: "economic value added" (EVA) versus economic profit, or NPS versus satisfaction measures. True innovation in measurement should be rewarded, but simply relabeling may be perceived as an attempt to "own" a concept or a particular measuring process.

Summary

Our goal is clear, but our work is not yet complete. We have chosen to begin with terms that were: (a) commonly used; and (b) less controversial. This was to gain some credibility and general acceptance. As we have continued down this path, we have increased the number of terms, some of which could be debated. As noted earlier, this task will never be complete, but we are hoping this body of work continues to grow. The task, however, should be clear. We are not trying to add complexity, but quite the opposite—clarity to enhance a common understanding and better communications both internally and externally.

References

1 Carroll, Lewis, *Through the Looking-Glass*, 1872, MacMillan and Co., p. 364.
2 Hume, David, *An Enquiry Concerning the Principles of Morals*, 2007, Ann Arbor, MI: University of Michigan Library, p. 106.
3 Schuster, Sir Arthur, *Nature*, 46, August 1892, p. 325.
4 Schuster, Sir Arthur, *Nature*, 46, August 1892, p. 325.
5 Ackman, Dan, "Larry Silverstein's $3.5B Definition," *Forbes*, accessed July 23, 2003, available at http://www.forbes.com/2003/07/23/cx_da_0723topnews.html.
6 Farris, Paul W., Neil T. Bendle, Phillip E. Pfeifer, and David J. Reibstein, *Marketing Metrics: The Definitive Guide to Measuring Marketing Performance*, 2nd edition, 2010, Upper Saddle River, NJ: Pearson Education, p. XV.
7 Kaizen is the practice of continuous improvement. Kaizen was originally introduced to the West by Masaaki Imai in his book *Kaizen*: *The Key to Japan's Competitive Success* in 1986, New York: McGraw-Hill. Today Kaizen is recognized worldwide as an important pillar of an organization's long-term competitive strategy.
8 Groppelli, Angelico A. and Ehsan Nikbakht, *Finance*, 4th edition, 2000, Hauppauge, NY: Barron's Educational Series, Inc., pp. 444–445.
9 Fader, Peter and Bruce Hardie, 2010, "Customer-Base Valuation in a Contractual Setting: The Perils of Ignoring Heterogeneity," *Marketing Science*, 29(1): 85–93.
10 Jacobson, Robert, 2012, "Brands and Branding in Law, Accounting, and Marketing Conference," April, Chapel Hill, NC: University of North Carolina.
11 Watt, James H. and Sjef van den Berg, *Research Methods for Communication Science*, 1995, Boston, MA: Allyn & Bacon, p. 11.
12 Farris, Paul W., Neil T. Bendle, Phillip E. Pfeifer, and David J. Reibstein, *Marketing Metrics: The Definitive Guide to Measuring Marketing Performance*, 2nd edition, 2010, Upper Saddle River, NJ: Pearson FT Press.
13 https://www.ama.org/resources/Pages/Dictionary.aspx.
14 Farris, Paul W., Neil T. Bendle, Phillip E. Pfeifer, and David J. Reibstein, *Marketing Metrics: The Definitive Guide to Measuring Marketing Performance*, 2nd edition, 2010, Upper Saddle River, NJ: Pearson FT Press.

4 Measuring Brand Preference

Michael Hess and Allan R. Kuse

Introduction

Marketers know that some brands in a category are more preferred than others. For some shoppers, Windex is preferred to Glass Plus and to the store brands. For other shoppers, Glass Plus is preferred to Windex and to the store brands. For still others, there is no preference between the two leading brands.

The Marketing Accountability Standards Board (MASB) Common Language Project dictionary (see Chapter 3) provides a good working definition: "One of the indicators of the strength of a brand in the hearts and minds of customers, brand preference, represents which brands are preferred under assumptions of equality in price and availability."[1] This definition takes into account the fact that context is important for brand preference, because it implies that if prices were different, the preference would be affected.

Why Is Brand Preference Important?

Simply put, brand preference is important, because it relates to the cost of doing business and the short- and long-term success of the brand. As the definition itself suggests, brands that are preferred are more likely to win the battle for market share and, in turn, could charge higher prices than less-preferred brands while still retaining a desirable level of share. This implies that brand preference is important, because it can lead to a change in the point of view that advertising is just an "expense of doing business." Blair and Kuse[2] demonstrate that advertisers who understand how brand preference scores predict the effectiveness and efficiency of advertisements no longer consider it an "expense," but a "wise investment." No less a practitioner than David Ogilvy quoted research data which illustrated that:

> My most valuable source of information is the factor analyses I commission at regular intervals from Mapes & Ross. They measure changes in brand preference. People who register a change in brand preference after seeing a commercial subsequently buy the product three times more than people who don't.[3]

From a research perspective, there is another practical benefit because consumers are generally willing to provide information on this topic. As Vincent Lee reported about Millennials born between 1980 and 1995: "In fact, brand preference is the number one identifier that they're willing to share on-line, according to our study."[4]

Marketing mix modeling has also repeatedly demonstrated the importance of brand preference in the pie charts it employs to communicate results. A typical pie chart shows that about two-thirds of the variation in brand sales during a year is driven by the ongoing value of a brand, and not by marketing or advertising activity.[5]

Finally, brand preference is important because advertising and marketing managers have employed some form of the concept for years.[6] It has withstood the "test of time." It is relevant and self-calibrating across geographies (i.e., it is not susceptible to survey bias as are other measures). Furthermore, perhaps even more compelling is how quickly brand preference adjusts to changes in the market. Recognizing its importance, how is brand preference measured?

Attitudinal Measures

Both Jones[7] and Biel[8] agree that brand strength (which drives preference) depends primarily on the development of a "unique, vivid, and meaningful identity for a brand" that differentiates the brand from its competitors. To measure the various aspects of these attributes, research companies have used the following types of measures in tracking studies:

- *Purchase intent.* This is usually based on a 5-point scale ranging from "Definitely would buy this brand" to "Definitely would not buy this brand" on the next occasion shopping for a product in this category.
- *Would recommend this brand to someone.* This also can be a 5-point scale; another scale used in recent years has a 10-point scale and is called the *Net Promoter* score. Those who choose a 9 or 10 response are deemed "Promoters" of the brand; those picking 7 or 8 are "Passives"; and the 0–6 respondents are considered "Detractors" who could actually harm the brand with their comments. The score is calculated by subtracting the percentage of respondents who are detractors from the percentage who are promoters.[9]
- *Share of requirements.* A constant sum question that asks the respondent to indicate which brands will be purchased on the next ten shopping occasions or respondents are asked to allocate 10 chips across brands in their consideration set.
- *Liking.* Using a 5-point scale, possible choices range from "Like very well" to "Not like at all."
- *Price/value.* Typically, a 5-point scale is used that ranges from "Very good value for the money" to "Very poor value for the money."
- *Various specific brand attributes.* These measures refer to functional attributes of the brand, such as the taste of a food product or the ability of a household product to freshen up a room or get a window clean. They may require "yes or no" responses or may use a 5-point scale with the range of responses determined by the specific attribute and how the survey question is worded.

Attitudinal measures are usually tracked at least annually, but some brands, budget permitting, are tracked quarterly. Researchers build descriptive models by correlating these measures to other brand metrics, such as market share and sales. In turn, the correlations might be combined into a full regression model that relates all of the tracking scores simultaneously to sales and market share.

A newer attempt to measure brand preference is in the area of "neuromarketing," a new field of marketing research that studies consumers' sensorimotor, cognitive, and affective responses to marketing stimuli. For example, a special issue of the *Journal of Consumer Behavior* reported a study suggesting that reduction in perceived ambiguity and information costs by providing brand information drives neural representations of brand preference, as promoted by signaling theory in information economics.[10] Further developments in this area as they pertain to brand preference should be monitored closely, since they may provide a new perspective on its biological basis.

Conjoint Approach

A method that is available but not often employed as a direct measure of brand preference comes from "conjoint methodology"[11] in which brand choice situations are simulated with a paired comparison approach. The objective is to determine what combination of a limited number of attributes is most influential on respondent brand choice. By analyzing how respondents make preferences between pairs of products, an implicit valuation of the individual elements making up the product preference can be determined.

If someone is considering an automobile purchase, for example, two different brands of car would be shown to a respondent side by side, with a relevant set of attributes such as gasoline mileage, sound system, time for acceleration from 0–40 mph, air conditioning system, interior upholstery, and, of course, price. This paired comparison process would be repeated, usually about 30–50 times, to allow the statistical determination of which dimensions are weighted more heavily and which are weighted less heavily in respondents' choices between pairs of brands in the category.

As a result, one of the key reporting outcomes from the conjoint process is the relative value of each dimension or attribute in terms of driving the consumer decision process. For example, for a 19-year-old young man, the key drivers might be acceleration and sound system; while for his parents, the decisions might be more heavily driven by price and gas mileage.

Inasmuch as the *brand* (its name, the consumer's experience of it, and all latent consumer associations with it) is an attribute of the product "benefit bundle" in the paired comparison choice task, it too can be assessed in terms of its contribution to the preference decision process. The fact that one brand can have a higher contribution value than another makes this a useful approach to assess brand preference in a more holistic way than in a tracking study of brand attributes.

Behavioral Measures

Perhaps the most powerful technique to assess brand preference is in the area of actual *consumer behavior* toward a brand. These metrics can be divided into actual *purchasing behavior* as part of ongoing category shopping tracking, and "laboratory" approaches to measuring behavior with a purchase or choice from an actual store shelf of a product category. In the latter technique, respondents are asked to select the brand that they prefer if this were a shopping trip. Since these approaches are based on "at-the-shelf," simulated purchase decisions, there is no need to interpret or adjust attitudinal statements, which is an advantage for predicting behavioral action.

The approach based on continuous shopping behavior usually is based on household panel data. From that, a household's share of requirements (SOR) in a category can be calculated. For example, if a household buys 25 boxes of breakfast cereal in a year, and Kellogg's represents 10 of those boxes, then that household's SOR would be 40 percent. A panel-based approach is useful, but the ultimate SOR for a brand depends, of course, not just on that brand's preference but also on its marketing and advertising support before and during the period that the panel is tracked.

For that reason, a more direct measure of behavioral brand preference is obtained by giving the shopper an opportunity to stand in front of a shelf with the category of brands arrayed in a normal fashion. Although today BASES[12] is the most used industry provider for forecasting the success of new packaged goods products, one of the enduring brand preference measures for this purpose is ASSESSOR.[13] The intent of ASSESSOR is to reduce the probability of a new product failure before the expense of a test market or product introduction.

The final ASSESSOR measurement is taken when participants enter a mock store environment where they can purchase (with funds provided as research compensation by the experimenter conducting the simulation) either the new product and/or established products in the category. Each product is presented at the average price it is, or will be, sold in stores. The brands selected by participants are recorded and an estimate of potential market share is derived.[13]

Unlike attitudinal and conjoint measurement approaches, studies of the ability of most behavioral approaches to brand preference estimation for predicting sales or market share have been conducted and published. Figure 4.1 illustrates the relationship (r = .95) between ASSESSOR estimations and actual shares achieved in new product test markets.[14]

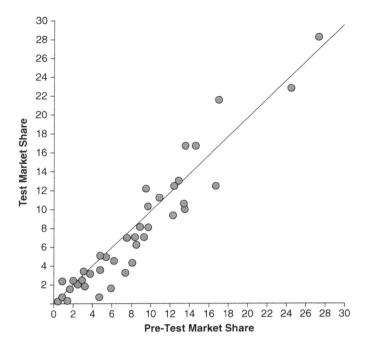

Figure 4.1 Comparison of ASSESSOR Pre-Test Market and Test Market Shares.

Source: Created by the authors from Glen L. Urban and Gerald M. Katz, "Pre-Test-Market Models: Validation and Managerial Implications," *Journal of Marketing Research*, 20(3): 223–234.

A similar but less expensive measure of brand preference, the ARS Persuasion technique correlates highly with ASSESSOR as a predictor of new product share (see Figure 4.2).[15] This metric requires respondents to choose "the brand they truly want" from an array of products shown in a photograph of a simulated store shelf.[16]

Use of Brand Preference Measures

Having defined brand preference, established its importance, and reviewed how to measure it, the next step is to examine how it is actually used by marketers and advertising agencies. Marketers use brand preference measures in a variety of ways, but primarily for comparative and longitudinal assessments.

On a comparative basis, marketers can line up their own brands' preference scores against those of the competitors and assess where they are winning, at parity, or losing. Of course, the same approach can be taken within the firm's product line. For instance, if there are ten brands in a marketer's portfolio, they can be ranked against one another to identify those brands with greater potential return on investment, and those with lesser potential. Marketing implications flow from both comparisons: for stronger brands the marketer might consider the viability of price hikes, while the weaker ones can be strengthened through R&D improvements or with stronger, more effective, advertising.

A substantial portion of marketing research budgets is spent on longitudinal surveys. Though most tracking studies are annual, some critical brands are tracked monthly, or at least quarterly. Scores on key preference-related metrics such as purchase intent or willingness to recommend can increase or decline. These changes, especially declines, often lead to recommendations for

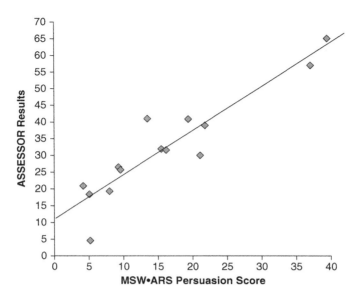

Figure 4.2 Relationship of ARS Persuasion Scores to ASSESSOR Trial.
Source: Created by the authors from MSW•ARS Research Internal Validation Study, 1992.

prompt remedial actions, since the rise or fall of these metrics is believed to be critical to the success of that year's marketing plan and attainment of sales goals. One thoughtful analysis does suggest, though, that most short-term changes in attitudinal metrics are driven in good part by the statistical limitations of performing large numbers of comparisons on quarterly samples of respondents.[17] Such findings can lead to a "last quarter's crisis must be addressed next quarter" mentality. Then, not only are costs of conducting the longitudinal research incurred but also additional costs of trying to reverse the perceived adverse change.

A more compelling concern for marketers, however, is a major decline in scores over a longer period of time, such as two or three years. For example, one marketing VP came back to the US after a two-year assignment in Canada and noticed a substantial decline in a key brand's preference scores during that time period. On a quarterly basis the declines were too small to stand out, while over ten quarters or so the drop was incontrovertible. Analysis of "reasons why" determined that extensive brand cost savings programs during that time led to poorer product performance.[18]

According to Reynolds and Phillips,[19] brand preference scores can also be used to assess how easily a brand can be leveraged by expanding with new items within its category (line extensions) or expanding to other product categories (new products).

Brand Preference and Copy/Touchpoint Testing

It has also been established that brand preference scores are predictive of copy test outcomes. The aforementioned ARS metric, in a pre-stimulus, post-stimulus design, was most widely used to evaluate the sales potential of television advertising.[20] Because of the extensive documentation available, the ARS metric was selected to serve as an example of how to evaluate marketing metrics according to the Marketing Metrics Audit Protocol (MMAP, see Chapter 17). When versions of TV ads that subsequently aired were tested, the metric was able to predict in-market impact, meeting the MMAP protocol for validation and causality to sales volume and market share.[21]

Figure 4.3 shows the relationship between copy test scores of ads tested just prior to airing and quarterly share change for the brands. The correlation between the two is .72 and the chart represents 345 ad cases. It should be noted that the copy test scores represent 100 percent ad reach of one "quality exposure" immediately preceding the preference exercise, hence the higher change in preference relative to what actually plays out in the market.[22] This is not only an important finding in and of itself but also because it suggests that making efforts to improve copy scores can, in turn, have an impact on brand preference.

Such an analysis is summarized in Table 4.1. Of course, the strength of these relationships will vary by category (e.g., brand safety is a big driver in pharma, but not so much in salty snacks), and can vary somewhat over time (e.g., value increased in importance after the "great recession"). Note that these attributes are categorized as either brand attributes or advertisement attributes. Brand attributes deal more with the place the brand holds in the hearts and minds of consumers, while advertisement attributes reflect the effect on the consumer of what the ad communicates about the brand.[23]

Brand Preference and Financial Outcomes

The essence of MASB's mission is to "Establish marketing measurement and accountability standards ... for continuous improvement in financial performance." Recently, there has been a trend among metric providers to link brand preference scores to financial performance. For example, Chattopadhyay and Laborie[24] recommend bringing cost accounting to marketing communications, by using *Brand Experience Points* and *Brand Experience Shares* metrics to provide a forward-looking, customer-centric view of brand contacts. This approach enables impact-based identification, choice, and management of contacts by capturing both efficiency and effectiveness. It is intended to build brand leadership through judicious investments in brand contacts and deliver better brand experiences than competitors.

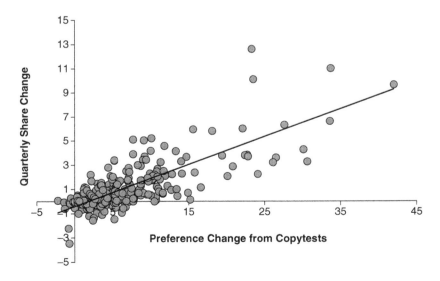

Figure 4.3 Brand Preference Relates to Quarterly Share Change.

Source: Created by the authors from R. L. Polk New Vehicle Registration, IMS HEALTH, IRI Infoscan, Markettrack, Nielsen SCANTRACK, or Nielsen Retail Index, and MSW•ARS Research Persuasion Score.

Table 4.1 Correlation Relationship between Various Attitudinal Attributes to Changes in Brand Preference

Brand Attributes	Correlation to Change in Preference
Value	0.44
Fits lifestyle/needs	0.43
Purchase intent	0.36
Differentiation	0.35
Relevance	0.30
Loyalty	0.27
Convenience	0.25
Safety	0.24
Advocacy	0.21
Believability of claims	0.17

Advertisement Attributes	Correlation to Change in Preference
New information	0.58
Increased interest	0.55
Purchase motivation	0.49
Interesting	0.45
Attention grabbing	0.43
Increased positivity	0.40
Likability	0.39
Ad uniqueness	0.39
Best seen recently	0.39
Watchability	0.37
Relatability	0.34
Commercial believability	0.29
Message importance	0.28
Communication of Brand	0.21
Ease of understanding	0.17
Brand image congruence	0.12

Source: Compiled for the authors by MSW•ARS Research from their database.

In the same vein, Blair and Kuse[25] show how a financially-based approach to television advertising best practices can lead to improved return on investment (ROI) even when specific ads only have a modest impact on sales. MASB has initiated a project using this metric to estimate the "financial value of a brand." The MASB Brand Investment and Valuation Project was defined in 2010 and is the focus of Chapter 5.

Summary and the Future of Brand Preference

It is already clear that most firms employ marketing mix modeling to deconstruct the impact of marketing drivers, brand by brand. The largest slice of any marketing mix pie is inevitably "baseline" sales. Over time, changes from this "brand equity" or "ongoing value" level can be efficiently and effectively assessed with brand preference metrics. They are also valuable for understanding and, when used to identify effective marketing activities, affecting the financial performance of brands. Now, with management emphasis on ROI, we believe the role of brand preference in measuring the outcomes of marketing activities will increase dramatically in the years ahead.

References

1. *Common Language in Marketing, The Global Resource for Defining Marketing Terms and Metrics*, an online compilation of definitions of marketing terms approved and sponsored by a consortium of marketing industry associations including MASB, AMA, ANA and MSI, available at www.marketing-dictionary.org.
2. Margaret H. Blair and Allan R. Kuse, 2004, "Better Practices in Advertising Can Change a *Cost of Doing Business* to *Wise Investments in the Business*," *Journal of Advertising Research*, 44(1): 71–89.
3. David Ogilvy, *Ogilvy on Advertising*, 1983, New York: Random House.
4. Vincent Lee, "8095 Report: For Millennials, Brand Preference is a Form of Self Expression," PSFK. October 2010, about the Edelman 8095 Whitepaper.
5. Mike Hess and Greg Ambach, "Long-Term Effects in Advertising and Promotion," *Marketing Research Magazine*, September 2000.
6. *Dartnell's Advertising Manager's Handbook*, 4th edition, 1997, Chicago, IL: The Dartnell Corporation.
7. John Philip Jones, "How to Use Advertising to Build Strong Brands," *SAGE*, July 13, 1999.
8. Biel, Alexander L., "Exploring Brand Magic," in *How to Use Advertising to Build Strong Brands*, SAGE, July 13, 1999.
9. The Net Promoter Community (website, 2015), available at http://www.netpromoter.com/why-net-promoter/know.
10. Hilke Plassmann, Peter Kenning, Michael Deppe, Harald Kugel, and Wolfram Schwindt, 2008, "How Choice Ambiguity Modulates Activity in Brain Areas Representing Brand Preference: Evidence from Consumer Neuroscience," *Journal of Consumer Behavior, Special Issue: Neuromarketing*, 7(4–5): 360–367.
11. Green, P. and V. Srinivasan, 1978, "Conjoint Analysis in Consumer Research: Issues and Outlook," *Journal of Consumer Research*, 5: 103–123.
12. *Nielsen Fact Sheet for BASES* (2015), available at http://www.nielsen.com/content/dam/nielsen/en_us/documents/pdf/Fact%20Sheets/Nielsen%20BASES%20II.pdf.
13. Alvin J. Silk and Glen L. Urban, 1978, "Pre-Test-Market Evaluation of New Packaged Goods: A Model and Measurement Methodology," *Journal of Marketing Research*, 15(2): 171–191.
14. Glen L. Urban and Gerald M. Katz, 1983, "Pre-Test-Market Models: Validation and Managerial Implications," *Journal of Marketing Research*, 20(3): 223–234.
15. MSW•ARS *Research Internal Validation Study*, 1992, Evansville, IN: Research Systems Corporation.
16. MASB, *Practices & Processes Underlying the Development & Management of an "Ideal Metric,"* 2010, pp. 10–11, available at www.themasb.org.
17. John Seal and Mark Moody, 2008, "Stop Wasting Money by Tracking the Wrong Measures," Burke Marketing Research, available at http://www.burke.com/Library/Articles/Tracking_Research_Seal.pdf.
18. Mike Hess, 1979, personal communication.
19. Tom Reynolds and Carol Phillips, 2005, "In Search of True Brand Equity Metrics: All Market Share Ain't Created Equal," *Journal of Advertising Research*, 45(2): 171–186.
20. Margaret H. Blair and Allan R. Kuse, 2004, "Better Practices in Advertising Can Change a *Cost of Doing Business* to *Wise Investments in the Business*," *Journal of Advertising Research*, 44(1): 71–89.
21. Margaret H. Blair, *Measuring and Improving the Return from TV Advertising—An Example*, 2008, available at www.themasb.org.
22. MSW•ARS Research, 2015, personal communication.
23. MSW•ARS Research, 2015, personal communication.
24. Amitava Chattopadhyay and Jean-Louis Laborie, 2005, "Managing Brand Experience: The Market Contact Audit," *Journal of Advertising Research*, 45(1): 9–16.
25. Margaret H. Blair and Allan R. Kuse, 2004, "Better Practices in Advertising Can Change a *Cost of Doing Business* to *Wise Investments in the Business*," *Journal of Advertising Research*, 44(1): 71–89.

5 Measuring Return on Brand Investment

Frank Findley

Introduction

While prior research strongly suggested that a brand preference metric would be the best candidate for quantifying total brand strength, there was still a hurdle to its widespread use. Specifically, brand preference had to be mathematically linked to both financial outcomes and to the brand awareness and attitude measures commonly used by brand teams. The linkage to financial outcomes would enable brand preference to be translated into accurate estimates of cash flows and thus, ultimately, brand valuation. The linkage to brand awareness and attitude measures would verify the sufficiency of the brand preference concept while simultaneously validating the potential of these other measures as diagnostics to brand preference.

To establish these linkages, the Marketing Accountability Standards Board (MASB) sponsored a multi-year longitudinal study with the cooperation of six blue chip corporations from a variety of industries including fast moving consumer goods, food, beverages, and autos.[1] Each of these participants chose two categories to be included. The resulting 12 categories represent a wide variety of product types and market conditions. Individual unit prices ranged from under $1 to over $30,000. Some of the product categories lent themselves to spontaneous purchase while others required greater deliberation, which could include third-party influencers in the decision-making process. Some of the categories were highly fragmented while others had only a small number of competing brands. Typical consumer purchase cycles could vary from a week to up to a decade.

Each of the participants provided unit sales, pricing, and distribution data for their own and competing brands within their chosen categories. Three of the participants also provided brand awareness and attitude data from their proprietary brand-tracking systems. While each tracking system included category-specific measures, seven common classes were found across at least four of the categories: unaided awareness, aided awareness, advocacy, loyalty, purchase intent, relevance, and value.

The above financial and brand-tracking information was compared to brand preference data provided by MSW•ARS Research. This patented implementation of brand preference was chosen for a variety of reasons. It has undergone the rigorous MASB Marketing Metric Audit Protocol[2] as part of the APM Facts/CCPersuasion copytest measure. As such it has a long established record of meeting the ten characteristics of an ideal metric including being simple, objective, calibrated across categories and geographies, reliable, predictive of business results, and sensitive enough to detect even small changes driven by marketing activities. As deployed in this study it also has the advantage of isolating brand strength from product factors, such as price and distribution.

The data was collected monthly from a United States demographically-representative sample of 400 online panelists. Each of these individuals was given the opportunity to choose the product they truly wanted within each category from among a competitive product set. The competitive product set was defined to include options for all brands with at least one unit share point of the category, and oftentimes even smaller brands were included to ensure comparability to the actual marketplace. The exercise was implemented as a prize drawing to incentivize each respondent to choose the option they most wanted, thereby avoiding cooperation, order, and other cognitive biases inherent within other techniques. Full color images were used to represent the individual products. Brand preference was calculated as the percentage of individuals choosing a product from that particular brand. The analysis presented here is drawn from 15 months of data collection for a total sample size of 6,000 respondents making choices on products representing 120 brands across the 12 categories.

One of the key questions going into the trials was: To what extent does brand strength determine a brand's share of consumer purchases? This is important for two reasons. One is that marketing is primarily focused on creating conscious (cognitive) and unconscious (affective) predispositions to choose the advertised brand over competitors. Therefore, for a measure of brand strength to be relevant, it must explain the percentage of choices allocated to the brand. The second, equally important, reason is that units sold drive financial cash flow models. By combining an estimate of a brand's unit share of market at a given price point and cost of production with assumptions of future category size based on population and category penetration trends, a projection of cash flow can be made. A discounted cash flow calculation can then be used to create a brand valuation. Hence, explaining unit share is fundamental to brand valuation.

Across the trial categories preference alone explains 75 percent of the differences in unit shares among the brands (Figure 5.1). Furthermore, this positive relationship was seen within each of the categories (Figure 5.2). Given the wide variety of category conditions represented, the implication is that brand preference is a powerful indicator of brand strength at any given time for any given brand.

But this begs the questions of what is driving the remaining 25 percent of the variance in unit shares, and how do these factors interact with brand preferences? Previous studies[3] have shown an interaction between brand preferences, product price, and product availability. For example, while an individual may prefer a given product they may choose to purchase a less expensive alternative to save money. This "buy down" phenomenon was especially apparent directly after

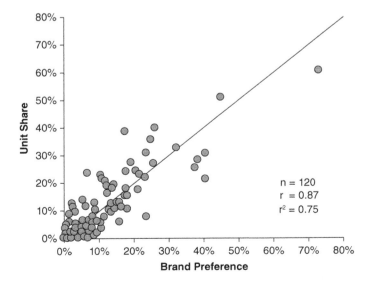

Figure 5.1 Differences in Unit Shares among Brands.

Source: Created by the author from MSW•ARS Research, Nielsen, and other participant-provided data.

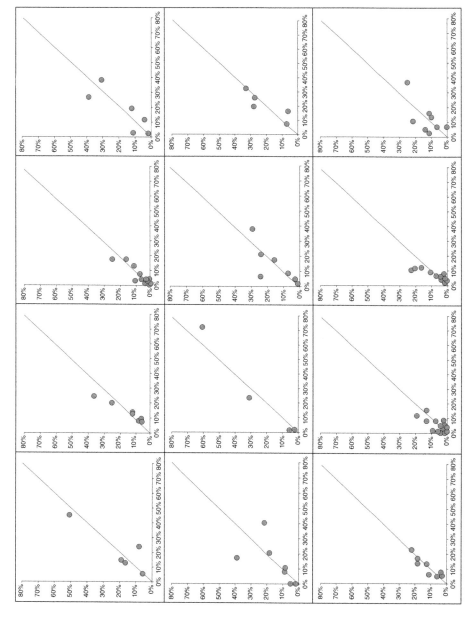

Figure 5.2 Positive Relationship within Each Category.

Source: Created by the author from MSW•ARS Research, Nielsen, and other participant-provided data.

the start of the great recession in 2008.[4, 5] The same effect can be seen in reverse with highly preferred brands gaining more market share with a price decrease, whether that be from a long-term strategic decision or a short-term trade promotion. Similarly, products that are relatively more difficult to acquire can also experience lost sales to more readily available alternatives. This distribution effect can be caused by differences in competing brands' regional footprints, exclusivity to particular retail outlets, and even short-term stock-outs.

A residual analysis was deployed to examine this interaction between brand preferences and price. Brand preference for each case was divided by its corresponding unit share to create an index. This index was then compared to groupings of brands based on their price relative to the category average. A clear relationship is seen (Figure 5.3). Brands with relatively high prices on average have unit shares which underperform their corresponding preferences, as shown by a high index. In contrast, brands with relatively low prices on average have unit shares which overperform their corresponding preferences, as shown by low indices.

A similar analysis was conducted using each brand's relative distribution. However, since the direction of the effect is opposite, in this case an index was created by dividing each brand's unit share by its corresponding preference. Again, a clear relationship is seen, albeit not with as great a difference between groupings as with price (Figure 5.4). Brands with relatively high distribution on average have unit shares that overperform their corresponding preferences, as shown by high indices, while brands with relatively low distribution on average have unit shares which underperform their corresponding preferences, as shown by low indices.

When brand preferences are combined with relative price and distribution the variance explained in unit shares increases to 87 percent across trial categories (Figure 5.5). This level of explanatory power leaves little room for improvement, suggesting that brand preference by itself is a sufficient measure of total brand strength. Consequently, this suggests that it must capture the majority of the predictive power of brand awareness and attitudinal measures.

To directly confirm this hypothesis a correlation analysis was conducted using the participant supplied awareness and attitudinal tracking data. Unlike the brand preference technique, which efficiently provides data for all brands in a category, the realities of "verbally" gathered measures

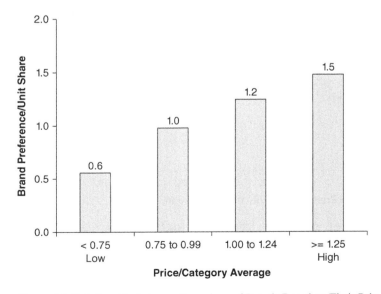

Figure 5.3 Relationship between Groupings of Brands Based on Their Price Relative to the Category Average.

Source: Created by the author from MSW•ARS Research, Nielsen, and other participant-provided data.

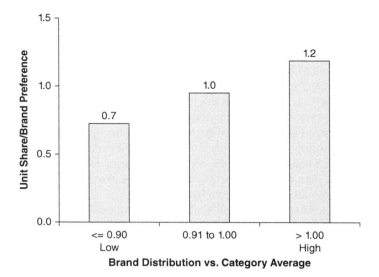

Figure 5.4 Each Brand's Relative Distribution.

Source: Created by the author from MSW•ARS Research, Nielsen, and other participant-provided data.

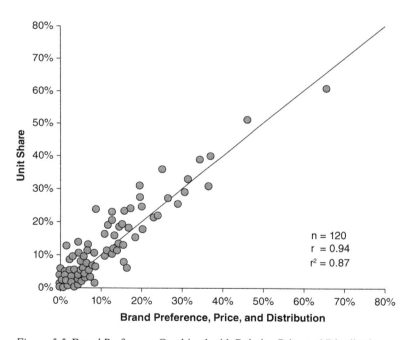

Figure 5.5 Brand Preference Combined with Relative Price and Distribution.

Source: Created by the author from MSW•ARS Research, Nielsen, and other participant-provided data.

restricted the awareness and attitudinal data to only the largest brands within each category. Thirty-three brands were represented across the six categories. To align with this, the brand preference and unit share were recalculated to only include these brands. Another difficulty was that the questions asked varied greatly by category with 70 different questions being asked. But from these 70 questions, 7 broad concepts emerged, which were present in at least 4 categories each:

1   **Awareness Unaided**—report of brand name when prompted with category (no brand list given);
2   **Awareness Aided**—brand name recognized from a list of brands;
3   **Brand Loyalty**—brand is one that they plan to consistently purchase and/or use when need arises;
4   **Value**—brand provides good value for the money;
5   **Purchase Intent**—likelihood to purchase brand in future;
6   **Brand Relevance**—brand fits lifestyle and/or needs;
7   **Advocacy**—brand is one that they would recommend to others.

For each of these seven concepts and brand preferences the correlation and variance explained in unit share was calculated. Since the question wording and scale of these concepts varied by category, it was not possible to directly combine cases across categories. Instead, the variance explained was calculated for each category with the mean and median taken across them. In addition, to provide perspective on the consistency of relationships across categories, the number of categories meeting the common rule-of-thumb correlation of 0.30 was determined.

Unsurprisingly, given their widespread use in managing brands, all of these common concepts show mean and median correlations to unit share above 0.30 and corresponding variances explained above 9 percent (Figure 5.6). But none of these demonstrate an explanatory power greater than brand preference. In fact, the strongest of these, unaided awareness, explains 21 percent less variance in unit share on average and 34 percent less on median. In addition, brand preference and unaided awareness are the only two consistently meeting the 0.30 correlation level within each category for which it is available. So, while the explanatory power of brand preference and unaided awareness transcend categories, the relevance of these other concepts tends to be less universal.

The correlation analysis also supports the contention that brand preference acts as a measure of total brand strength capturing the dynamics of these other measures. Contrasting their average variance explained in unit share to that of brand preference illustrates this (Figure 5.7). In each case, the variance explained in brand preference is greater than that explained in unit share. Therefore, these other metrics are unlikely to add to the explanatory power of brand preference to unit share. In fact, looking across these concepts the ratio in variance explained in unit share to

	Average Share Variance Explained	Median Share Variance Explained	Number of Categories with Correlation > 0.30
Preference (choice)	68%	78%	6/6
Awareness–Unaided	47%	44%	4/4
Brand Loyalty	46%	44%	5/6
Value	32%	44%	3/4
Purchase Intent	27%	26%	3/6
Brand Relevance	19%	19%	2/4
Awareness–Aided	18%	24%	4/6
Advocacy	15%	13%	2/4

Figure 5.6 Mean and Median Correlations and Corresponding Variances.

Source: Created by the author from MSW•ARS Research, Nielsen, IRI, Edmunds.

	Average Variance Explained in	
	Preference (w/Price & Dist.)	Share
Awareness–Unaided	55%	47%
Brand Loyalty	52%	46%
Value	46%	32%
Purchase Intent	36%	27%
Brand Relevance	32%	19%
Awareness–Aided	29%	18%
Advocacy	26%	15%

Figure 5.7 Average Variance Explained in Unit Share Compared to That of Brand Preference.

Source: Created by the author from MSW•ARS Research Data.

that of preference is 75 percent on median (74 percent on average). This is the same level previously seen in the direct relationship between brand preference and unit share (Figure 5.1 above), which lends further credence to this conclusion.

A category-by-category analysis across the 70 available questions also showed little potential for adding to the explanatory power of brand preference. The same pattern was exhibited by 70 percent, with the variance explained in preference being greater than that in unit share. Furthermore, of the 30 percent where the variance to unit share was higher, none was substantially so despite the low sample sizes increasing the probability of seeing such by random chance alone.

These outcomes provide a clear opportunity for brand and marketing teams to improve the sales predictability of their research tools as well as increase the speed at which they identify means of improving brand strength. This has been anticipated since the late 1980s by researchers assessing the predictive capabilities and theoretical underpinnings of the pre-test, post-test, and brand-tracking systems. In 1986, Stewart and Furse posited that:

> Future research efforts would be more insightful if the focus were on measures of persuasion, or behavioral change, rather than exclusively on cognitive measures such as recall or attitude change. This is not to suggest that these other measures are unimportant but that they should be treated as intervening variables influencing the primary measure of consumer choice.[6]

Note the implied suggestion here to use a *behavioral change* form of persuasion measure, specifically one that is based on consumer choice of brands. Furthermore, in 1999, Vakratsas and Ambler made a similar suggestion:

> [w]e have classified and reviewed prior research of intermediate and behavioral effects of advertising using a taxonomy of models . . . Although such models have been actively employed for 100 years, we find them flawed on two grounds: the concept of hierarchy (temporal sequence) on which they are based cannot be empirically supported, and they exclude experience effects . . . We also suggest that behavioral (brand choice, market share) and cognitive and affective (beliefs, attitudes, awareness) measures be compiled in a single-source database to enable researchers . . . to test the interaction of context, intermediate effects, and long- and short-term behavior. In this effort, we also must relieve measures of affective responses from cognitive bias.[7]

Measuring Return on Brand Investment 67

Figure 5.8 Perspective on Areas for Improvement.

Source: Created by the author from MSW•ARS Research, Nielsen, IRI, Edmunds.

Embedding brand preference alongside traditional awareness and attitudinal measures removes the dependency on unverified theoretical models in trying to understand consumer motivations. For example, by contrasting attitudinal measure performance between those who change brand preferences and those who do not after exposure to advertising, it is possible to derive the importance of each factor *for that particular campaign or piece of copy*. Crossing this with overall attribute performance provides a perspective on areas for improvement that traditional norms cannot (Figure 5.8).

The opportunity for enhancing corporate financial stewardship is equally dramatic. As noted by James Gregory, CEO of CoreBrand: "the percentage of a company's market value represented by intangible assets has grown from 17 percent in 1975 to 81 percent in 2009."[8] Yet, despite the increasing shift in enterprise value from tangible to intangible assets, the use of brand valuations has not become commonplace across organizations. This leaves boards and management teams with little guidance as to the long-term financial impact from allocation of resources to brand marketing activities. However, through MASB several organizations have worked together to fill this need. One of their first objectives was to build a prototype "brand valuation model" with corresponding guidelines and recommendations for calculation of brand valuation from brand cash flows. In February 2015, they presented a set of foundational premises of the brand valuation model:

- A discounted cash flow approach is preferable over any other method, such as the "relief from royalty" method.
- "Brand strength" is an important "risk" indicator of the likelihood that future cash flows will be earned and over what period of time.
- "Brand strength" is predominantly driven by marketing effectiveness, competitive factors, and external environmental conditions, and it therefore can be reasonably inferred and factored into the model.

- Brand valuations are not intended to establish amounts to be recorded on the balance sheet (or to specifically test for impairment), nor are they intended to establish or represent a transactional valuation.
- As important as reasonable accuracy at any point in time is the consistency of approach and assumptions over time, which will allow management to see relevant valuation movement to aid in decision-making.
- The model should also enable sensitivity analysis and "what-if" modeling.

The inclusion of brand strength within the model not only serves as a bellwether of future cash flows but also provides a means of highlighting marketing's unique contribution to the financial success of the firm. Jim Meier, MillerCoors Senior Director of Marketing Finance, explained it this way:

> The manufacturing side of the business can purchase and maintain an asset. Marketers can create and grow one... Brands could 'earn' a higher valuation based on improved brand preference which would remove uncertainty relating to future financial assumptions and the longevity of the brand.[9]

Thus, the use of brand preference not only helps companies improve the effectiveness of marketing activities but also informs the corporate resource allocation process. A newly formed sub-team within the MASB Brand Investment and Valuation project is working to integrate these methods and processes for easy adoption by finance and marketing teams.

References

1. MASB Standards Project, *Brand Investment & Valuation (BIV) Project Review & Status*, February 2015, available at http://themasb.org/projects/completed/brand-valuation-project-phase-1/.
2. http://themasb.org/marketing-metrics-audit-protocol.
3. MSW•ARS Research, *Global Validation Summary*, 2008, Evansville, IN: Research Systems Corporation.
4. F. Findley and D. Wilson, *Combating Consumer Buy Down Behavior in Recessionary Times*, 2012, New York: Advertising Research Foundation, available at http://my.thearf.org/source/Events/Event.cfm?EVENT=WEB_021612.
5. D. Crang, *The Effects of the Recession on Brand Loyalty and "Buy Down" Behavior*, 2011, Reston, VA: Comscore, available at https://www.comscore.com/Insights/Presentations-and-Whitepapers/2011/The-Effects-of-the-Recession-on-Brand-Loyalty-and-Buy-Down-Behavior.
6. D. Stewart and D. Furse, *Effective Television Advertising – A Study of 1000 Commercials*, 1986, Lexington, MA: Lexington Books.
7. D. Vakratsas and T. Ambler, 1999, "How Advertising Works: What Do We Really Know?," *Journal of Marketing*, 63(1): 26–43.
8. J. Gregory, *Growing Impact of Companies' Corporate Social Responsibility Initiatives on Brand Value*; PRNewswire, May 22, 2012 available at http://www.prnewswire.com/news-releases/james-gregory-of-corebrand-discusses-the-growing-impact-of-companies-corporate-social-responsibility-initiatives-on-brand-value-152545835.html.
9. J. Meier, *Brand Investment and Valuation Project Review & Status of Finance Sub-Team*, 2015, Islamorada, FL: MASB.

6 Customer Lifetime Value and Its Relevance to the Consumer Packaged Goods Industry

V. Kumar and Sarang Sunder

Introduction

The customer-centricity paradigm has long been documented as being one of the most important tenets of effective marketing in today's dynamic environment (Kumar, 2008, 2009). With the advent of technology and customer relationship management (CRM), there has been an explosion of disaggregate and granular customer data (transactional as well as survey) available to firms. Slowly but surely, organizational perspectives and operations have been modified across various industries from a product-centric view to a customer-centric one. This has led to firms not only focusing on satisfying the customer but also nurturing profitable customer relationships. The next logical step in the area of CRM was to develop the right kind of metric to evaluate the value of a customer.

However, traditional marketing (especially in the consumer packaged goods (CPG) context) has focused on reaching out to consumers through mass marketing and delivering standardized products/services. While this has worked in the past, the importance of individual consumer preferences are largely ignored. Customer-level marketing has become the new paradigm, especially in a digitally interconnected world where firms and consumers interact with one another intimately. As marketers regain respect and power within the board room, the need for businesses to put the customer at the center of decision-making has reached its critical mass.

The explosion of disaggregate customer-level transaction data has spurred a great deal of advancements in CRM, whereby firms are able to leverage data mining techniques, customer transaction data, and the individual consumer data that firms are now able to collect. Implicit in the use of individual customer-level data is the need to assess the value of the customer base. That is, marketers need to answer the questions: How valuable (in terms of profits) is my customer? How can we allocate marketing resources optimally to maximize profits from my customers?

Specifically, in order to optimally allocate marketing resources and efforts to the right customers, marketers need to assess the potential value of the customer base, which is key to achieving customer centricity. But what is the value of a customer? How can it be measured? Also, how does it apply to the CPG industry? In this chapter, we will address the above questions by focusing on: (a) the rise of customer lifetime value (CLV) in marketing applications; (b) the advantages of CLV in today's marketplace; (c) commonly used approaches to measure CLV; and (d) the implementation of CLV in a CPG setting.

CLV

Concept and Definition

Research has proposed several methods and metrics to evaluate the customer, such as recency-frequency-monetary value (RFM) (Cheng and Chen, 2009), share of wallet (SoW) and past customer value (PCV). However, since the mid-2000s, marketing academia and practice have adopted a forward-looking profit-oriented metric called CLV. CRM strategies developed from CLV modeling have led to positive financial gains in business-to-business (B2B) as well as business-to-consumer (B2C) settings (Kumar, 2014). Since the CLV metric is heavily dependent on customer relationships and transaction data, it has mostly been implemented in the relationship-marketing settings, such as financial services and telecommunications. However, the concepts of CLV and customer-centric marketing are applicable in traditionally product-centric industries such as CPG as well.

CLV is an individual-level, customer valuation metric that takes into account the total profit contribution of a customer over their lifetime. It can be formally defined as the sum of the cumulated cash flows, discounted using the weighted average cost of capital, of a customer over their entire lifetime (Kumar, 2014). As is evident from the above definition, CLV measures the net worth of the customer. Since it is measured at the individual level, companies that have computed CLV can now assess the distribution of their customer base according to the potential value that they will achieve. This capability to rank order customers opens the door to the design of customer-specific strategies and eventually optimal marketing spend. In the following section, we elaborate on how firms can use CLV and the consequences of using CLV in marketing decision-making.

Measuring CLV

CLV is a forward-looking (predictive), customer-centric, and profit-oriented metric that allows managers to assess the future potential of the customer base. Intrinsic to the concept of CLV is the power to "predict" customer behaviors. In order to predict those behaviors we need to understand what data needs to be tracked and how to analyze it, and develop insights from the analysis. In this section, we present the conceptual measurement of CLV and motivate what kind of data needs to be collected in order to measure CLV. Next, we discuss the various approaches that could be used to measure CLV, varying from stochastic to deterministic methods. We end the section by motivating how one could choose a specific method based on the data and the context in which CLV is being applied.

Conceptual Measurement of CLV

As we defined earlier, CLV is the net present value of future profits from a customer. This is nothing but the net present value (NPV) of gross contribution margin minus the NPV of marketing cost (dollar spend by the firm toward a specific customer). CLV is usually measured for a period of three years into the future. A three-year window is used for three reasons: (a) the product life cycle; (b) tectonic changes in the marketplace that could influence the CLV model leading to inaccuracies; and (c) the majority of customer profits arise within this period (Gupta and Lehmann, 2005).

In the computation of CLV (see Figure 6.1), we begin by collecting past transaction data at the customer level (products purchased, timing of purchase, and other variables), gross margin/contribution data at the product/brand level, and marketing expenditures by the firm over time. Using past information about customer purchase behavior, a statistical model can be built to predict future behavior. The accuracy of the prediction model is calibrated to satisfaction and then the gross contribution margin, as well as the expected marketing cost, is computed. Finally, the NPV of the difference between the expected gross contribution margin and marketing cost is computed as the CLV.

Figure 6.1 is a pictorial representation of the steps involved in CLV computation. In the following section, we delve into the actual formulation of the CLV metric and some of the common predictive methodologies that are used to measure CLV.

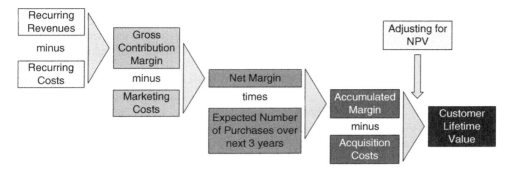

Figure 6.1 Conceptual Measurement of CLV.
Source: Adapted from Kumar (2008).

CLV Formulation

The measurement of CLV depends on two main parameters: (a) the type of data available; and (b) the method being used. Usually, the choice of method for CLV modeling depends on the product category and the industry being considered. In this section, we demonstrate how CLV can be measured and which models can be used in different kinds of situations.

First, we provide a formula to calculate CLV. It is a function of the net present value of the gross contribution margin and the expected marketing resources allocated to the customer. In its general form, CLV can be expressed as:

$$CLV_i = NPV \text{ of } GC_i - NPV \text{ of } MC_i$$
$$= \sum_{t=1}^{T} \frac{(Future\ Gross\ Contribution\ Margins)_{it} - (Future\ Marketing\ Cost)_{it}}{(1+\delta)^t}$$

The calculation of CLV includes determining the future contribution margin and future costs, both of which are adjusted for the time value of money. The usual approach to computing these elements is described below, together with an illustration of their applicability in a CPG setting.

Future gross contribution margin—typically, the calculation of future contribution margin by building two models, the first of which is a probabilistic model to ascertain whether the customer will remain active with the firm (henceforth referred to as P(Alive)). The P(Alive) model describes whether the customer will still be a customer during the prediction time window. There are several approaches that have been suggested to model the probability that a customer will be alive such as "lost for good" stochastic approaches (Fader and Hardie, 2009), or "always a share" approaches (Kumar and Shah, 2009). The choice of an appropriate method depends on the context of the study and the assumptions that the manager is willing to make. While using the P(Alive) approach, an inherent assumption is made that the customer does not return to the firm after choosing to discontinue the relationship. This approach, known as the "lost for good" approach could underestimate CLV (Rust *et al.*, 2004). This can be overcome by using the "always a share" approach, which takes into account the possibility that the customer could return to the firm after a temporary dormancy (Venkatesan and Kumar, 2004). In the "always a share" approach, instead of predicting customer churn (or "death") we are interested in predicting timing/frequency of purchase, thus giving managers a clearer view of customer activity. The "always a share" approach is more appropriate, in a frequently purchased category such as CPG products where customer churn is rare and brand switching is more common. The second part of the gross contribution (GC) model involves a regression-based method to predict the quantity/dollar amount of purchase given that a customer would make a purchase in a given time window. The product of the predicted GC and P(Alive) (or P(Buy) (probability of buying)) makes up the first part of the CLV computation.

Future marketing cost—the second component (expected marketing cost) is much simpler. Marketing costs refer to the costs of campaigns, in store promotions, coupons, deals, and other discounts that are provided to enhance customer relationships and encourage customers to make purchases with the focal brand. These marketing dollars could be spent across various channels, such as direct mail and in store. In today's marketing setting, CPG firms are increasingly engaging with customers across multiple channels, such as social media and loyalty programs. The present value (in dollars) that the firm expects to spend on marketing to the customer during the time window is computed as the future marketing cost in the CLV computation. This could be based on managerial expectations or a predictive model.

CLV Modeling Approaches in Various Business Settings

The choice of an ideal modeling approach for CLV depends on: (a) the type of data available to the marketer; and (b) the assumptions that the manager is willing to make regarding the customer behavior (influenced by purchase context). There are typically two types of broad categories that CLV models tend to fall into, namely deterministic and stochastic CLV models. In this section, we provide a brief description of each approach and some applications in various business settings. While the discussion here is not exhaustive, for a detailed review of methodologies in CLV modeling please refer to Villanueva and Hanssens (2007) who provide a typology of customer equity (CE) models, and Kumar (2008) who provides a detailed review of methods to compute aggregate as well as individual CLV. Table 6.1 provides a summary of some past research implementing deterministic and stochastic methods in various business settings.

Deterministic Approaches

Deterministic models for CLV calculation involve specifying models and inputs for customer behavior and then computing CLV. For example, models describing probability of purchase and the conditional quantity/GC for each purchase could be specified as a function of past behavior as well as marketing activity. Profitable lifetime duration of a customer-firm relationship, a proxy for CLV, depends, differentially, on the exchange characteristics at time t and on customer heterogeneity (Reinartz and Kumar, 2003). The formula is:

$$Profitable\ Lifetime\ Duration_i = f(Exchange\ Characteristics_{it}, Customer\ Heterogeneity)$$

Exchange characteristics broadly include all past behaviors of the customer (such as spending level and cross-buying), and the corresponding marketing activity (such as deals, discounts, rebates and coupons) initiated by the firm. Customer heterogeneity refers to variables that describe how different customers are. For example, some customer heterogeneity variables include demographic variables, such as household composition, size, income, age, etc. In addition to improving the CLV's predictive accuracy, these variables help managers build profiles for high, medium, and low CLV segments.

Several versions of deterministic models have been used in the past to implement CLV in various settings. In the B2B space, there have been implementations of CLV in both the contractual

Table 6.1 Examples of CLV Implementations in Various Business Settings

			APPROACH	
			Deterministic	Stochastic
BUSINESS SETTING AND RELATIONSHIP TYPE	Business-to-Business (B2B)	Contractual	Financial Services *(Shah et al., 2012)*	**Office products** *(Schmittlein and Peterson, 1994)* **Illustrative example** *(Fader and Hardie, 2010)*
		Non-Contractual	**Hi-tech** *(Kumar et al., 2008; Reinartz and Kumar, 2003)*	**Hi-tech** *(Kumar et al., 2011)*[1]
	Business-to-Customer (B2C)	Contractual	**Newspaper** *(Keane and Wang, 1995; Lewis, 2005)*[2] **Insurance** *(Donkers et al., 2007)* **Retail Banking** *(Shah et al., 2012)*	**Newspaper** *(Thomas et al., 2004)* **Magazine/Catalogs** *(Dwyer, 1997)* **Airlines** *(Rust et al., 2004)*
		Non-Contractual	**Catalog Retailer** *(Reinartz and Kumar, 2000)* **Apparel** *(Kumar et al., 2006)*	**Entertainment** *(Dreze and Bonfrer, 2003)* **Internet** *(Fader et al., 2005; Villanueva et al., 2008)*[3] **Retail Banking** *(Haenlien et al., 2007)*

Source: Created by the authors.

Notes
1 Kumar *et al.* (2011) use a hidden Markov model (HMM) framework, which is inherently stochastic and include deterministic components within the model as well.
2 Lewis (2005) uses dynamic programming with deterministic components.
3 Villanueva *et al.* (2008) use a vector auto regressive (VAR) model to study customer equity.

and non-contractual setting. For example, Shah *et al.* (2012) provide a comprehensive evaluation of the effect of cross buy on profitability at the customer level (deterministic approach). They test their hypotheses on five unique datasets varying from B2B (contractual and non-contractual) and B2C (contractual and non-contractual). Further, Kumar *et al.* (2008) showcase a real world implementation of CLV to manage customers at IBM using a deterministic model. In the B2C space too, there have been several implementations of CLV in both the contractual and the non-contractual settings. For example, deterministic models have been used to implement CLV at non-contractual B2C settings, such as catalog retailers (Reinartz and Kumar, 2000; Shah *et al.*, 2012) and apparel retailers (Kumar *et al.*, 2006) to assess both customer-level profitability (CLV) and retailer-level profitability. Similar implementations also exist in the contractual B2C setting. For example, Donkers *et al.* (2007) compare multiple approaches to modeling CLV in the contractual setting (insurance industry) and provide guidance to managers. Similarly, Keane and Wang (1995) apply the CLV concept to a newspaper setting using a deterministic model, and evaluate CLV at the regional level. While deterministic models are used very commonly to study CLV and its drivers in various business settings, past research has also resorted to probabilistic or stochastic approaches to model CLV. In the following section, we briefly discuss some of these implementations.

Stochastic Approaches

The main tenet of stochastic frameworks is that the observed behavior is viewed as the realization of an underlying stochastic process governed by latent (unobservable) behavioral characteristics, which could vary across individuals (Gupta *et al.*, 2006). There are several examples of stochastic models used for customer behavior. One of the earliest forays into building models for CRM was undertaken by Schmittlein *et al.* (1987) who proposed the pareto-NBD model to assess customer behavior. This model was directly applied to study CLV in a B2B non-contractual setting by Reinartz and Kumar (2000), who used it as an input to CLV computation. Advancements and extensions to the pareto-NBD framework have been proposed by several researchers who derive expressions for CLV rather than use the pareto-NBD framework as an input. Examples of such models include Schmittlein and Peterson (1994) who extend the pareto-NBD model to incorporate transaction rate, dropout rate, and average dollar volume, and to estimate a stochastic model in an industrial buying situation (B2B contractual setting). In a B2C non-contractual setting, Fader *et al.* (2010) advance the pareto-NBD framework to a beta-geometric/beta-Bernoulli (BG/BB) model to account for purchasing behavior as well as churn behavior.

Past research has also suggested the use of persistence modeling (Vector Auto Regression (VAR) methods) to assess the long-run dynamic impact of marketing on CE (Villanueva *et al.*, 2008), while controlling for endogeneity of marketing within the framework. Since CLV is itself a long-term metric, persistence modeling is well-suited to this context. While not purely stochastic, researchers have also adopted Markov methods to assess CLV in various settings. For example, in a non-contractual B2B setting (hi-tech hardware and software), Kumar *et al.* (2011) use an inherently stochastic framework (hidden Markov model) to study the role of marketing on the state and profitability of customer relationships. In the airlines setting (B2C non-contractual setting), Rust *et al.* (2004) implemented a stochastic model (Markov switching) while including deterministic components within their framework to measure CLV in an airlines setting. It is also worth noting that they used survey data to arrive at their goals.

Now that we have described the various methodologies/approaches that can be used to measure CLV depending on business context, in the following section we focus on why CLV is extremely applicable to the CPG industry. In fact, we propose that implementing CLV and adopting customer centricity in the CPG industry is no longer a source of competitive advantage, but rather a necessity for survival in today's marketplace.

CLV in the CPG Context

The Need for CLV

CLV Outperforms Traditional Metrics

To evaluate the need and importance of the CLV metric, we should compare it to the traditionally used metrics for customer valuation. First, we assess the need for customer-level metrics over aggregate measures which are commonly used in the CPG industry. Although traditionally used aggregate metrics (such as market share, sales volume, revenue, etc.), which are commonly used in the CPG context to assess brand performance, convey important information about the product/brand and can be readily calculated, they do not provide us with the complete picture. While aggregate metrics give managers an indication of the health of the brand and serve as an "aggregate" proxy for performance, they do not provide any information regarding which customers "grew" and which did not. Further, they do not address the inherent heterogeneity among customer preferences to marketing. For example, in the presence of a coupon or deal at the grocery store, certain price-sensitive customers might be more prone to using a deal than others. An aggregate measure, such as market share, will not be able to capture these differences between customers and their sensitivity to marketing. Finally, with the business world moving from an aggregate view to a disaggregate view, and from a product-centric view to a customer-centric view of decision-making (Shah *et al.*, 2006), it is important for CPG managers to incorporate customer-level metrics in their decision-making.

Traditional customer-level metrics in the marketplace are typically based on simple heuristics, rules of thumb, or require some basic mathematical calculations. While there are over 50 different metrics defined (Farris *et al.*, 2006), we focus on the most popularly used metrics of customer valuation, namely SoW, RFM, PCV, and tenure. In Table 6.2, we outline some basic definitions regarding each of the above metrics and contrast them with the CLV metric.

Table 6.2 describes the strategic customer-based value metrics that are most commonly used in the industry today. While easy to implement, the SoW, RFM, PCV, and tenure metrics have their drawbacks. Since SoW is based on a set of responses from customer samples, it does not provide a clear way to determine future revenue and profits from a customer. The SoW metric suffers heavily from subjectivity bias (because it is survey-based) and sample bias (because it uses responses collected from only a sample of customers). While the RFM value metric addresses the timing and purchase value better than SoW, it fails to consider future profitability. Furthermore, the RFM metric cannot provide managers with the knowledge of why certain customers are more valuable. Similar to the RFM metric, the PCV metric does not account for future profitability or the cost of managing customer relationships. In essence, the traditional metrics are backward-looking and lack the ability to predict the potential value that the customer will bring to the firm.

On the other hand, CLV is a forward-looking, customer-centric and profit-oriented metric that gives managers a holistic view of the customer. The CLV formulation incorporates both the probability of a customer being active in the future and the marketing dollars that need to be

Table 6.2 Traditional Metrics vs. CLV

Metric	Definition	Profit-based	Forward-looking	Account for Marketing cost	Model-driven
Recency-Frequency-Monetary (RFM) value	*Weighted sum of Recency, Frequency and Monetary Value that a customer provides.*	No	No	No	No
Past Customer Value (PCV)	*Present value of a customer as determined by his/her profit contributions in the past*	Yes	No	No	No
Share of Wallet (SoW)	*Degree to which a customer meets his/her needs in the category with the focal brand*	No	No	No	No
Tenure	*Time elapsed since the customer first purchased from the focal brand*	No	No	No	No
Customer Lifetime Value (CLV)	*The sum of the cumulated cash flows—discounted using the weighted average cost of capital (WACC)—of a customer over his/her entire lifetime*	Yes	Yes	Yes	Yes

Source: Created by the authors and is in the public domain.

spent to retain the customer. Further, CLV helps managers evaluate when a customer will buy, how much they will spend and how much it will cost to make the sale. This visibility is greatly useful especially in the CPG setting where firms often resort to aggregate heuristics to allocate marketing dollars. Instead, if firms could understand where and how their marketing dollars were being translated to value, it would be greatly beneficial. CLV also provides managers with a unique view on how and why customers buy, and helps allocate marketing dollars to maximize return on investment.

Implications of Adopting CLV

The adoption of CLV opens the door to proactive customer management and marketing decisions. Specifically, the benefits of a CLV-based approach to marketing outlined by Villanueva and Hanssens (2007) include:

- marketing resource allocation and spending for long-term profitability;
- understanding the relationships between marketing spend, metrics, and financial performance;
- providing a customer-focused approach to measuring firm value;
- providing much needed frameworks, tools, and metrics to enhance productivity of CRM.

Embracing the customer-centricity paradigm in the CPG industry—CLV has been applied and its benefits have been showcased in several industries and business settings. Some examples of CLV implementations in various industries include insurance (Verhoef and Donkers, 2001), catalog mailing (Petersen and Kumar, 2015), B2B hi-tech (Kumar *et al.*, 2008), airlines (Rust *et al.*, 2004), internet retail (Fader *et al.*, 2005), automobile (Yoo and Hanssens, 2005), telecommunications (Kumar *et al.*, 2013), and financial services (Shah *et al.*, 2012). A common theme among the above is that past implementations of CLV have been mostly on "relationship-driven" business settings. In other words, the adoption of CLV and customer-centric concepts have been restricted to industries which have been heavily focused toward building customer relationships. A glaring gap in the above is that the CPG industry is yet to adopt the customer-centric concept. Even today, most CPG managers rely on flow-based and product-centric metrics to evaluate marketing effectiveness. While this has worked in the past, it is no longer sustainable. By relying on flow-based aggregate measures (such as sales, revenue, market share, etc.) CPG managers are leaving the customer at the door. For example, when studying the effectiveness of a promotional campaign, managers would likely state that there is a sales bump during the promotional period, thereby concluding that the promotional campaign has a positive effect on sales. But where are the sales coming from? Which customers are really purchasing the product? Could it be that the promotion only attracted deal-prone, unprofitable customers? Further, did the promotional campaign help the firm cultivate behavioral loyalty (measured as CLV)? Answers to these questions are not obvious using aggregate metrics.

Flow-based metrics that are currently used in CPG industries are very sensitive to extraneous shocks (such as small changes in macroeconomics). The volatility that arises due to this makes marketing decision-making error prone and inaccurate, because managers are unable to assess why a certain phenomenon occurs. Business performance in CPG markets is fast moving and volatile, especially in the presence of heavy promotional spending, thereby leading to short-run, myopic marketing decisions, which are based on reaction rather than strategic focus (Hanssens and Dekimpe, 2008; Yoo *et al.*, 2011). In such environments, it is difficult to assess whether a brand is doing well or not. CLV (or its aggregated counterpart, CE) presents stability based on consumer behavior, which is focused on the long term and forward-looking in nature.

In a digitally connected world, where consumers engage with each other as well as the brand in real time, the customer-centric paradigm (especially in the CPG setting) is no longer a competitive advantage but a necessity. CPG firms are investing heavily in innovations in CRM that would move them closer to a CLV-based approach to decision-making (e.g., Kimberly-Clark's Huggies brand (Nielsen, 2011)). By analyzing customer-level transaction data (obtained through scanner panel studies), managers at Kimberly-Clark were able to not only quantify the dollar value of specific consumer segments but also chart the life cycle of the customer relationships. As a result, Kimberly-Clark was able to garner a clearer picture of its target market as well as the profitable opportunities (consumers) that exist in the marketplace.

A framework to manage customer relationships for profit—a CLV-based marketing approach allows the firm to view the customer as an asset (Srivastava *et al.*, 1998), and assess the impact of marketing spend on customer-level assets. CLV adoption fits very closely within the customer-centricity paradigm where the core philosophy is to "serve the customer" and achieve "customer profitability." Couched within customer centricity are concepts central to marketing such as the need to increase focus on customer satisfaction (Oliver, 1999), customer service (Zeithaml *et al.*, 1993), customer loyalty (Reinartz and Kumar, 2002), and quality perceptions (Rust *et al.*, 2002). CLV represents a path to achieving improvements in the above critical marketing metrics, while maintaining high levels of attention not only among researchers but in practitioner-focused books as well (see Bejou *et al.*, 2012; Kumar, 2014).

The CLV metric opens the door for managers to differentially allocate marketing dollars to specific types of customers or segments of customers based on their profitability. This capability has spurred a great deal of innovation in building marketing strategies to maximize profitability through CLV. By adopting CLV-based marketing strategies, marketers can now not only identify their most valuable customers but also manage the entire customer relationship from acquisition to retention. Some examples of strategic implementations include: managing acquisition and retention (Reinartz *et al.*, 2005), customer churn/defection (Neslin *et al.*, 2006), and product return behavior (Petersen and Kumar, 2015) to name but a few. For a detailed review of the customer management strategies that could be implemented through CLV, please refer to the "Wheel of Fortune" strategies by Kumar (2009). Further, CLV can be flexibly used for making resource allocation decisions in order to achieve financial performance. After implementing a CLV-based paradigm, firms have the capability to vary marketing actions and spend in order to arrive at an optimal marketing mix. Venkatesan (2015) guides managers in this direction by providing a five-step process to optimal resource allocation using CLV. Critically important to the success of the above is the adoption of CLV.

In the following section, we discuss the financial value that CLV presents and how CLV could help marketers in the board room as well as in Wall Street.

Linking marketing to firm value—in today's marketing world, it is not only important to show growth in marketing metrics (such as quality perceptions and satisfaction levels) but also in financial metrics. In fact, Welch (2004) is concerned that marketers are slowly losing ground in the boardroom, because firms and shareholders are demanding that marketing be linked with firm financials.

Taking this challenge head on, researchers have shown that CLV is one of the best paths to creating firm value. Adopting a CLV- or CE-based metric has been shown to have extremely high financial benefits (Bolton, 2004; Gupta and Zeithaml, 2006; Kumar and Shah, 2009). In fact, Gupta and Zeithaml (2006), in their review article on the link between customer metrics and firm performance, make a generalization (based on several years of empirical research) that: "Marketing decisions based on observed customer metrics, such as CLV, improve a firm's financial performance." Customer relationships need to be viewed as investment decisions and, therefore, customers need to be viewed as assets who generate revenue. CLV-based metrics not only improve shareholder value by increasing cash flow but also by reducing retention and switching costs (Stahl *et al.*, 2003). Further, a well-managed CLV paradigm has the ability to accelerate cash flows (through cross selling, for example) by reducing cash flow volatility and vulnerabilities (through the constancy of demand from loyal customers), and to increase the residual value of the firm (through quality, trust, commitment, and reputation). These advantages make customer-centric firms attractive to investors who value these characteristics. To this end, past research encourages firms to report CLV/CE-based measures in their financial reports. Specifically, Wiesel *et al.* (2008) recommend firms report CLV to investors, because such reports align customer management with corporate goals and investor perspectives. CLV signals the health of a firm and, therefore, improves investor perceptions on Wall Street.

Given the operational, managerial, and financial benefits of adopting CLV, firms are investing considerable dollars in tracking customer behaviors and evaluating CLV. In the following section, we elaborate on some of the challenges that CPG managers could face when implementing CLV.

Barriers to Implementing CLV in the CPG Industry

While the expected gains and needs for customer centricity in the CPG context are well documented, the implementation of CLV comes with its challenges. In this section, we discuss some of the barriers and challenges that CPG firms can face when measuring CLV.

Data Availability and Utilization

The first challenge to implementing CLV has to do with the access and availability of reliable customer-level disaggregate data. CPG manufacturers (such as Unilever and Procter & Gamble) rarely have access to individual customer transaction data over a long period of time. This is because the actual data collection happens outside the control of the manufacturer. The data collection (at Point-Of-Sale (POS) systems) happens at the retailer's premises. Thus the ownership of the customer transaction data resides with the retailer. The retailer may or may not want to disaggregate this data since it also represents a competitive advantage to the retailer (due, for example, to store labels). To overcome this problem, manufacturers have two broad options: (a) collaborate closely with the retailer; or (b) purchase data from third-party firms. The first option involves a deep collaboration and negotiation with the retailer and, possibly, entering into a contractual relationship with the retailer. Some opportunities regarding this have been outlined in the supply chain management literature (see, for example, Sari, 2008). The second option for CPG manufacturers is to purchase scanner/panel data from syndicated sources such as A. C. Nielsen or IRI. This method of purchasing secondary panel data is commonly used in marketing research as well as in marketing practice. Several research papers in marketing have leveraged this data to develop insights into the effects of marketing mix on customer behavior (see, for example, Guadagni and Little, 1983; Kamakura and Russell, 1993). In the absence of advanced forms of retailer–manufacturer collaboration (such as vendor managed inventory (VMI) or collaborative planning, forecasting and replenishment (CPFR) systems), our recommendation to manufacturers is to address the data void using syndicated sources.

Customer Relationships are Poorly Defined

The CPG industry is characterized by customer purchases that are frequent, regular and smaller dollar amounts, and lower stated brand loyalty (compared to heavy relationship-focused industries). Product categories such as paper towels and laundry detergent, for example, face almost constant demand with very few fluctuations. This is because customers' interpurchase times are almost constant and they rarely deviate from their purchasing behavior. More problematic is the issue of loyalty. Simply because a customer continuously (and consistently) purchases Brand

A in a specific product category, should we classify them as behaviorally loyal? What is it about the brand that makes them continue to purchase the brand? A robust model-based approach to addressing CLV and its drivers needs to be built very carefully considering these issues. Further, wherever possible, CPG managers need to supplement scanner panel data analyses with primary data (for example, surveys) that would allow them to differentiate between the habitual buyers and the loyal ones.

Heavy Brand Switching and Potential Multi-Brand Purchase Behavior

CPG markets are often plagued by the fact that the cost of brand switching is very low (compared to other industries) (Carpenter and Lehmann, 1985). In other words, consumers perceive very little risk (financial as well as cognitive) in switching from one brand to another for a specific shopping occasion. This problem is further exacerbated given the frequency with which customers make CPG purchases and the number of competitors jostling for power in the market. So a relatively small price promotion in one week could induce customers to switch brands and consume another product (Bell *et al.*, 1999; Sun *et al.*, 2003). Further, this brand switching opens the door to extreme "variety-seeking" behavior among customers, where customers have an affinity to try out new products/brands whenever possible (McAlister and Pessemier, 1982). This variety-seeking behavior could lead to a reduction in brand loyalty, eventually affecting the firm's bottom line. When specifying a CLV model to explain the consumer's future behavior, managers need to explicitly account for potential brand-switching behavior and its heterogeneous effect on CLV.

In addition to brand switching, variety-seeking consumers could actually purchase more than one brand in a specific shopping trip. For example, a household could purchase Brand A and Brand B of laundry detergents in the same month. This leads to a methodological problem known as multiple discreteness (Dubé, 2004; Kim *et al.*, 2007). Existing CLV modeling methodologies (usually reliant on discrete choice methods) are usually focal firm analyses, wherein the assumption is that the customer does not make a concurrent purchase with a competitor. In the CPG setting, this assumption might be an over-simplification. For example, Dubé (2004) shows that multiple discreteness is very much prevalent in the carbonated soft drinks market, and highlights some of the problems that could arise if this issue were ignored.

Some Approaches to Implementing CLV in a CPG Setting

Latest research in the area of incorporating CRM-based analytics (CLV) in the CPG industry is looking toward adopting: (a) a VAR approach (Yoo *et al.*, 2011); and (b) a structural econometric approach (Sunder *et al.*, 2016). Yoo *et al.* (2011) merge a VAR-based framework with a stochastic model for customer behavior (the BG/BB model from Fader *et al.* (2010)) and provide valuable insights describing the evolution of CE in a CPG market. They show that CE is much more stable and a better metric to use in the CPG market.

In their structural approach, Sunder *et al.* (2015) formally address the multiple discreteness issue, relying on utility theory and building a model of budget constrained consumption in a CPG category. They leverage a hybrid Bayesian MCMC technique to infer the consumer's budget constraint for each month and develop insights into future profitability, i.e., CLV.

Conclusion

It is no secret that firms have started to treat customers differentially. The world of marketing is rapidly moving away from a product-centric to a customer-centric paradigm, where the onus is on gaining a 360-degree view of the customer the moment they walk into the store. The need to customize and individually market to consumers is paramount, especially with the growth of the "internet of things" (Wasik, 2013) concept, where appliances, products, brands, and consumers are closely interconnected (Atzori *et al.*, 2010). In such a marketplace reality, CPG industries are mostly being left behind due to several reasons. Being largely product-centric in the past and mostly relying on flow-based aggregate metrics of performance, CPG firms need to move to a customer-centric CLV-based paradigm. The main focus of this chapter has been to introduce CLV as a viable alternative to conventional decision-making metrics in the CPG context. Specifically, we described the CLV domain, some popular methods, and CLV implementations, as well as how CLV could be applied in a CPG setting. We outlined the need for CLV in a CPG setting, and the expected benefits from CLV adoption. Specifically, a CLV-based approach allows marketing to have a stronger voice in the board room by linking marketing spend to firm value, while also providing managers with a holistic view of the customer base. We also briefly described some of the potential issues that could arise when implementing CLV and proposed solutions for the same.

In conclusion, CLV is a metric that is gaining wide acceptance in the marketplace due to its enormous strategic, operational, and financial benefits. Therefore, CPG firms would benefit greatly by including CLV in their decision-making process in order to ensure future growth and sustainable competitive advantage.

References

Atzori, Luigi, Antonio Iera and Giacomo Morabito, 2010, "The Internet of Things: A survey," *Computer Networks*, 54(15): 2787–2805.

Bejou, David, Timothy L. Keiningham, and Lerzan Aksoy, *Customer Lifetime Value: Reshaping the Way We Manage to Maximize Profits*, 2012, New York: Routledge.

Bell, David R., Jeongwen Chiang, and V. Padmanabhan, 1999, "The Decomposition of Promotional Response: An Empirical Generalization," *Marketing Science*, 18(4): 504–526.

Bolton, Ruth N., 2004, "Linking Marketing to Financial Performance and Firm Value," *Journal of Marketing*, 68(4): 73–75.

Carpenter, Gregory S. and Donald R. Lehmann, 1985, "A Model of Marketing Mix, Brand Switching, and Competition," *Journal of Marketing Research*, 22(3): 318–329.

Cheng, Ching-Hsue and You-Shyang Chen, 2009, "Classifying the Segmentation of Customer Value via RFM Model and RS Theory," *Expert Systems with Applications*, 36(3, part 1): 4176–4184.

Donkers, Bas, Peter C. Verhoef, and Martijn G. de Jong, 2007, "Modeling CLV: A Test of Competing Models in the Insurance Industry," *Quantitative Marketing and Economics*, 5(2): 163–190.

Dreze, Xavier and André Bonfrer, 2003, "To Pester or Leave Alone: Lifetime Value Maximization through Optimal Communication Timing," Working paper, Research Collection Lee Kong Chian School Of Business.

Dubé, Jean-Pierre, 2004, "Multiple Discreteness and Product Differentiation: Demand for Carbonated Soft Drinks," *Marketing Science*, 23(1): 66–81.

Dwyer, Robert F., 1997, "Customer Lifetime Valuation to Support Marketing Decision Making," *Journal of Interactive Marketing*, 11 (4), 6–13.

Fader, Peter S. and Bruce G. S. Hardie, 2009, "Probability Models for Customer-Base Analysis," *Journal of Interactive Marketing*, 23(1): 61–69.

Fader, Peter S. and Bruce G. S. Hardie, 2010, "Customer-Base Valuation in a Contractual Setting: The Perils of Ignoring Heterogeneity," *Marketing Science*, 29(1): 85–93.

Fader, Peter S., Bruce G. S. Hardie, and Ka Lok Lee, 2005, "RFM and CLV: Using Iso-Value Curves for Customer Base Analysis," *Journal of Marketing Research*, 42(November): 415–430.

Fader, Peter S., Bruce G. S. Hardie, and Jen Shang, 2010, "Customer-Base Analysis in a Discrete-Time Noncontractual Setting," *Marketing Science*, 29(6): 1086–1108.

Farris, Paul W., Neil. T. Bendle, Phillip. E. Pfeifer, and David J. Reibstein, *Marketing Metrics: 50+ Metrics Every Executive Should Master*, 2006, Upper Saddle River, NJ: Wharton School Publishing.

Guadagni, Peter M. and John D. C. Little, 1983, "A Logit Model of Brand Choice Calibrated on Scanner Data," *Marketing Science*, 2(3): 203–238.

Gupta, Sunil and Donald R. Lehmann, *Managing Customers as Investments: The Strategic Value of Customers in the Long Run*, 2005, Upper Saddle River, NJ: Wharton School Publishing.

Gupta, Sunil and Valarie Zeithaml, 2006, "Customer Metrics and Their Impact on Financial Performance," *Marketing Science*, 25(6): 718–739.

Gupta, Sunil, Dominique Hanssens, Bruce Hardie, Wiliam Kahn, V. Kumar, Nathaniel Lin, Nalini Ravishanker, and S. Sriram, 2006, "Modeling Customer Lifetime Value," *Journal of Service Research*, 9(2): 139–155.

Haenlein, Michael, Andreas M. Kaplan, and Anemone J. Beeser, 2007, "A Model to Determine Customer Lifetime Value in a Retail Banking Context," *European Management Journal*, 25(3), 221–34.

Hanssens, Dominique and Marnik Dekimpe, "Models for the Financial Performance Effects of Marketing," in *Handbook of Marketing Decision Models*, Berend Wierenga, (ed.), 2008, New York: Springer Science+Business Media, LLC.

Kamakura, Wagner A. and Gary J. Russell, 1993, "Measuring Brand Value with Scanner Data," *International Journal of Research in Marketing*, 10(1): 9–22.

Keane, Timothy J. and Paul Wang, 1995, "Applications for the Lifetime Value Model in Modern Newspaper Publishing," *Journal of Direct Marketing*, 9(2): 59–66.

Kim, Jaehwan, Greg M. Allenby, and Peter E. Rossi, 2007, "Product Attributes and Models of Multiple Discreteness," *Journal of Econometrics*, 138(1): 208–230.

Kumar, V., 2008, "Customer Lifetime Value—The Path to Profitability," *Foundations and Trends in Marketing*, 2(1): 1–96.

Kumar, V., *Managing Customers for Profit: Strategies to Increase Profits and Build Loyalty*, 2009, Upper Saddle River, NJ: Wharton School Publishing.

Kumar, V., *Profitable Customer Engagement: Concept, Metrics and Strategies*, 2014, New Delhi, India: SAGE Publications India Pvt Ltd.

Kumar, V. and Denish Shah, 2009, "Expanding the Role of Marketing: From Customer Equity to Market Capitalization," *Journal of Marketing*, 73(6): 119–136.

Kumar, V., Denish Shah, and Rajkumar Venkatesan, 2006, "Managing Retailer Profitability—One Customer at a Time!" *Journal of Retailing*, 82(4): 277–294.

Kumar, V., J. Andrew Petersen, and Robert P. Leone, 2013, "Defining, Measuring, and Managing Business Reference Value," *Journal of Marketing*, 77(1): 68–86.

Kumar, V., Rajkumar Venkatesan, Tim Bohling, and Denise Beckmann, 2008, "The Power of CLV: Managing Customer Lifetime Value at IBM," *Marketing Science*, 27(4): 585–599.

Kumar, V., S. Sriram, Anita Luo, and Pradeep K. Chintagunta, 2011, "Assessing the Effect of Marketing Investments in a Business Marketing Context," *Marketing Science*, 30(5): 924–940.

Lewis, Michael, 2005, "Incorporating Strategic Consumer Behavior into Customer Valuation," *Journal of Marketing*, 69(4), 230–38.

McAlister, Leigh and Edgar Pessemier, 1982, "Variety Seeking Behavior: An Interdisciplinary Review," *Journal of Consumer Research*, 9(3): 311–322.

Neslin, Scott A., Sunil Gupta, Wagner Kamakura, Junxiang Lu, and Charlotte H. Mason, 2006, "Defection Detection: Measuring and Understanding the Predictive Accuracy of Customer Churn Models," *Journal of Marketing Research*, 43(2): 204–211.

Nielsen A. C., 2011, *Nielsen Insights in Action: Determining Consumer Lifetime Value*, accessed April 24, 2015, available at http://www.nielsen.com/content/dam/corporate/us/en/public%20factsheets/Case%20 Studies/CaseStudy-KimberlyClark-ROI.pdf.

Oliver, Richard L., 1999, "Whence Consumer Loyalty?," *Journal of Marketing*, 63(Special Issue): 33–44.

Petersen, J. Andrew and V. Kumar, 2015, "Perceived Risk, Product Returns, and Optimal Resource Allocation: Evidence from a Field Experiment," *Journal of Marketing Research*, 52(2): 268–285.

Reinartz, Werner J. and V. Kumar, 2000, "On the Profitability of Long-Life Customers in a Noncontractual Setting: An Empirical Investigation and Implications for Marketing," *Journal of Marketing*, 64(4): 17–35.

Reinartz, Werner J. and V. Kumar, 2002, "The Mismanagement of Customer Loyalty," *Harvard Business Review*, 80(7), 86–94.

Reinartz, Werner J. and V. Kumar, 2003, "The Impact of Customer Relationship Characteristics on Profitable Lifetime Duration," *The Journal of Marketing*, 67(1): 77–99.

Reinartz, Werner J., Jacquelyn S. Thomas, and V. Kumar, 2005, "Balancing Acquisition and Retention Resources to Maximize Customer Profitability," *Journal of Marketing*, 69(January): 63–79.

Rust, Roland T., Christine Moorman, and Peter R. Dickson, 2002, "Getting Return on Quality: Revenue Expansion, Cost Reduction, or Both?," *Journal of Marketing*, 66(4): 7–24.

Rust, Roland T., Katherine N. Lemon, and Valarie A. Zeithaml, 2004, "Return on Marketing: Using Customer Equity to Focus Marketing Strategy," *Journal of Marketing*, 68(1): 109–127.

Sari, Kazim, 2008, "On the Benefits of CPFR and VMI: A Comparative Simulation Study," *International Journal of Production Economics*, 113(2): 575–586.

Schmittlein, David C. and Robert A. Peterson, 1994, "Customer Base Analysis: An Industrial Purchase Process Application," *Marketing Science*, 13(1): 41–67.

Schmittlein, David C., Donald G. Morrison, and Richard Colombo, 1987, "Counting Your Customers: Who Are They and What Will They Do Next?," *Management Science*, 33(1): 1–24.

Shah, D., R. T. Rust, A. Parasuraman, R. Staelin, and G. S. Day, 2006, "The Path to Customer Centricity," *Journal of Service Research*, 9(2): 113–124.

Shah, D., V. Kumar, Yingge Qu, and Sylia Chen, 2012, "Unprofitable Cross-Buying: Evidence from Consumer and Business Markets," *Journal of Marketing*, 76(3): 78–95.

Srivastava, Rajendra K., Tasadduq A. Shervani, and Liam Fahey, 1998, "Market-Based Assets and Shareholder Value: A Framework for Analysis," *The Journal of Marketing*, 62(1): 2–18.

Stahl, Heinz K., Kurt Matzler, and Hans H. Hinterhuber, 2003, "Linking Customer Lifetime Value with Shareholder Value," *Industrial Marketing Management*, 32(4): 267–279.

Sun, Baohong, Scott A. Neslin, and Kannan Srinivasan, 2003, "Measuring the Impact of Promotions on Brand Switching When Consumers Are Forward Looking," *Journal of Marketing Research*, 40(4): 389–405.

Sunder, Sarang, V. Kumar, and Yi Zhao, 2016, "Measuring the Lifetime Value of a Customer (CLV) in the Consumer Packaged Goods (CPG) Industry," *Journal of Marketing Research*, forthcoming.

Thomas, Jacquelyn S., Robert C. Blattberg, and Edward J. Fox, 2004, "Recapturing Lost Customers," *Journal of Marketing Research*, 41(1), 31–45.

Venkatesan, Rajkumar, 2015, "Customer-Lifetime-Value-Based Resource Allocation," in *Handbook of Research on Customer Equity in Marketing*, V. Kumar and Denish Shah (eds), Northampton, MA: Edward Elgar Publishing, Inc.

Venkatesan, Rajkumar and V. Kumar, 2004, "A Customer Lifetime Value Framework for Customer Selection and Resource Allocation Strategy," *Journal of Marketing*, 68(4): 106–125.

Verhoef, Peter C. and Bas Donkers, 2001, "Predicting Customer Potential Value an Application in the Insurance Industry," *Decision Support Systems*, 32(2): 189–199.

Villanueva, Julian and Dominique M. Hanssens, 2007, "Customer Equity: Measurement, Management and Research Opportunities," *Foundations and Trends in Marketing*, 1(1): 1–95.

Villanueva, Julian, Shijin Yoo, and Dominique M. Hanssens, 2008, "The Impact of Marketing-Induced Versus Word-of-Mouth Customer Acquisition on Customer Equity Growth," *Journal of Marketing Research*, 45(1): 48–59.

Wasik, Bill, 2013, *In the Programmable World, All Our Objects Will Act as One*, accessed March 2, 2015, available at http://www.wired.com/2013/05/internet-of-things-2/.

Welch, Greg, 2004, *CMO Tenure: Slowing Down the Revolving Door*, accessed April 23, 2015, available at http://content.spencerstuart.com/sswebsite/pdf/lib/CMO_brochureU1.pdf.

Wiesel, Thorsten, Bernd Skiera, and Julián Villanueva, 2008, "Customer Equity: An Integral Part of Financial Reporting," *Journal of Marketing*, 72(2): 1–14.

Yoo, Shijin and Dominique M. Hanssens, 2005, "Modeling the Sales and Customer Equity Effects of the Marketing Mix," available at http://www.anderson.ucla.edu/faculty/dominique.hanssens/content/ms_0114-4_manuscript.pdf.

Yoo, Shijin, Dominique M. Hanssens, and Ho Kim, 2011, "Marketing and the Evolution of Customer Equity of Frequently Purchased Brands," available at http://www.anderson.ucla.edu/faculty/dominique.hanssens/CECPG_version_April_11_2011.pdf.

Zeithaml, Valarie, Leonard Berry, and A. Parasuraman, 1993, "The Nature and Determinants of Customer Expectations of Service," *Journal of the Academy of Marketing Science*, 21(1): 1–12.

7 Customer Lifetime Value in the Packaged Goods Industry

Rick Abens and Debra Parcheta

Introduction

Marketing accountability in fast-moving consumer goods (FMCG) businesses has been limited to the measurement of short-term sales and profit returns from marketing. Current metrics for brand success, which remain primarily backward-looking and short-term focused, are not limited to, but include: response elasticity, return on investment (ROI), past sales trends, purchase frequency, and market share. Hence, marketing managers are now more likely to make the "right" tradeoffs to deliver required short-term ROI and market share gains.

However, marketing and financial managers recognize that short-term effects do not necessarily anticipate brand success for the long term. In fact, Yoo et al. (2012)[1] demonstrated that some marketing choices could erode brand success in the long term by causing customers to change their purchasing habits in ways that are not easily changed back. For example, offering sales promotions at frequent and predictable intervals can create "strategic" consumer behavior; that is, consumers wait to purchase until the next promotion cycle, thereby reducing the brand's profit contribution from their purchases.

The purpose of marketing is more about attracting and building relationships with customers than just generating incremental purchases. A brand's success depends on much more than achieving quarterly or weekly sales goals or short-term ROI. If FMCG marketers add future-focused metrics, they would be better able to build brands with foreknowledge of marketing program outcomes and prevent unintentional brand erosion. In 2012, Yoo et al.[2] expanded on the 2005 work of Fader et al.[3] to test the application of customer lifetime value (CLV) and customer equity (CE) on a data set of customer transaction-level data for competing brands of ketchup and yogurt, with encouraging results. From such metrics, the long-term impacts of marketing tactics and tradeoffs can be modeled, allowing marketers to better manage brands for the long term. The promise of CLV for an FMCG brand is to measure current purchasing behavior, household-by-household, and anticipate the brand's future CE trend, which provides a prediction of the net present value (NPV) of cash flows resulting from marketing-driven changes in the brand's relationship with its customers. CLV measurement quantifies this long-term relationship with customers, though it has not been applied to FMCG to date. Consumers exhibit very little loyalty to most FMCG products, with an average customer turnover of 40 percent each year. This dynamic makes it difficult to determine who the customers are and who are the prospects, but also highlights the importance of measuring and managing customer loyalty.

CLV and its effects on marketing were estimated in this study for six FMCG brands. Food, beverage, and personal care brands were included. The methodology for measuring CLV for FMCG brands replicated the method used by Yoo et al. (2012) in a working paper.[4] The number of future purchase transactions and purchase size were estimated for samples of 10,000–40,000 households using Nielsen Homescan national purchase transaction data. These metrics were then used to estimate the NPV of the future purchases for the CLV. The sum of the CLV for all customers is considered to be the total CE for the brand.

We found that the CLV metric is a more stable, slow-moving metric that can be predictive of future business results. The study showed that advertising increases both short-term sales and CLV, while price discounts had a short-term benefit only. These results show that the full impact from marketing can be measured and can help marketers make smarter choices to manage the long-term success of their brands. The study also helped identify additional measures and dimensional detail for improved CLV impact.

Applications for CLV

Direct marketers and marketers who have contractual relationship businesses construct CLVs from customer acquisition, customer retention, and cost of purchase measures to estimate future purchase behavior and derive its NPV. CLV is the standard method for measuring the success of customer relationship management (CRM) programs. Figure 7.1 provides an illustration of how the CLV view of marketing contrasts with the more traditional brand management view.

It is a way of differentiating customers based on value to the company. CLV represents the NPV of the future profits to be received from a given number of newly-acquired or existing customers during a given period of years. The sum of the CLV for all customers of the firm is an estimate of the future profits of the entire firm expressed in the current value of those future profits. Yoo et al. (2012) describe CE as equating to a computation of the CLV for individual customers and then summing the CLV values across acquired and retained customers.[5] Similarly, the price of a stock is essentially based on the current value of a firm's future profits.

While most Consumer Package Goods (CPG) companies are focused on product sales with little effort on measuring their customer "consumer" behavior, it is the changing of customer behavior that drives the change in sales. It is the customer's behavior that you want to understand and monitor. CPG companies also tend to manage short-term results. Managers have pressure from shareholders to deliver results every quarter, so delivering the short-term results sometimes comes at the expense of initiatives that will support the long-term health of the brand. For example, many CPG companies have brand managers who will not advertise in Q4, because budgets are likely to be cut. It is common for management to use marketing budgets as a contingency to cover gaps in profit. By its very nature, CLV focuses both on the customer and the long term.

CLV is a forward-looking metric and can help anticipate future sales trends of the brand. Managers often rely on flow metrics (e.g., units sold, market share) and ignore possibly important stock metrics (e.g., CE). CE is a slow-moving metric, unlike weekly sales, but better captures

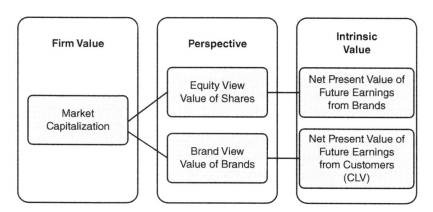

Figure 7.1 Firm Value/Perspective/Intrinsic Value.

Source: Created by Dominique Hanssens.

CLV in the Packaged Goods Industry 85

the brand health and long-term trends. Customer attrition occurs silently, so the impact may not register with normal sales tracking. As customers drop out of active buying, their CLV will plummet and register in the CE metric. In Hanssens and Parcheta's *Application of Customer Lifetime Value (CLV) to Consumer Package Goods (CPG)* paper, they found CE trends to prelude sales trends by six months.[6] They concluded that CE, which is the sum of the CLV for all customers, provides useful information about the direction of future sales, which is a proxy for the trajectory of the brand. Figure 7.2 illustrates the focus of CLV and its emphasis on both the customer and a long-term orientation.

CLV is also used to measure the value of marketing initiatives. Most would say that the purpose of marketing is to acquire, retain, and develop relationships with customers that add value to the firm. Few would say the purpose of marketing is to increase short-term sales even though it is the short-term sales' effects that are most commonly measured. So CLV is a good measure of the long-term impact from marketing if its effects can be isolated from other effects on CLV. Direct marketers do this regularly with test-control experimental design studies.

Common marketing measurement metrics, like marketing mix models or test markets, focus on the product using recent short-term product sales. The long-term effect of marketing is that it builds equity. CLV by definition represents long-term profits, so it can be used to assess the long-term effects of marketing. It also focuses on consumer behavior and can be used to measure the effects of targeted marketing.

Marketers armed with this knowledge can develop targeted marketing campaigns with a specific purpose in mind. The marketing strategy for your most valuable customers would be different than for the least valuable. Powerful customer relationship marketing strategies can be employed to target segments of consumers to optimize long-term marketing ROI.

Marketing Accountability

The current standard for marketing accountability measurement for FMCG brands is econometric time-series regression "marketing mix" models. This method is used to effectively measure the short-term sales and profit returns from marketing. However, marketers and business managers know that there is also a longer-term effect on sales from marketing and want to know the size of this long-term effect. With this knowledge they can make smarter marketing allocation decisions to manage both short-term sales and the long-term health of the brand. The same concepts employed in marketing mix models can be used in "equity mix" models by replacing sales with CE dollars.

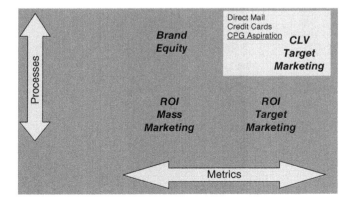

Figure 7.2 CLV Target Marketing.

Source: Created by the author, Rick Abens, of Foresight ROI, Inc.

Finance makes resource allocations for initiatives that have a long payback period based on the NPV of the return. This method accounts for future returns in today's equivalent dollars by reducing future returns by the time cost of capital. For example, if the cost of capital were 10 percent, then $110 one year from now would have an NPV of about $99. A typical decision application for NPV is whether to build a $50m plant, which will return $10m per year for 10 years, or a $50m plant that will return $9m per year for 15 years. The NPV of the 10-year plant is $61.5m, while the NPV of the 15-year plant is $68.5m. Similarly, one could look at the relative return on $50m in trade promotion or advertising, where the short-term increase in profit is $10m for trade and $6m in advertising. If we were to know that the long-term impact from trade is $10m and for advertising is $12m, then we could make a fully informed decision.

Complications with FMCG Brands

Manufacturers of FMCG brands would also like to benefit from the value of measuring CLV so that they can also use CPR strategies, measure the long-term impact from marketing and anticipate changes in sales trends. Consumer purchase transaction data is available from many sources, and some marketers are looking for new ways to glean new insights from these large data sets. The challenge comes from finding a method to distinguish current customers to be retained from non-buyers to be acquired without having a formal relationship between the marketer and its customers. Brand switching is high for FMCG brands due to high purchase frequency, giving buyers many opportunities to switch. The frequency of brand switching complicates separating current from non-buyers.

As illustrated in Figure 7.3 the average FMCG brand loses 40 to 50 percent of their buyers each year. This high brand-switching rate shows the difficulty in maintaining a loyal base of customers, making CRM and CLV important.

Solution for Measuring FMCG Brands

Without a contractual or formal relationship with customers, marketers need an alternative method for categorizing current brand buyers from inactive ones who need to be acquired or

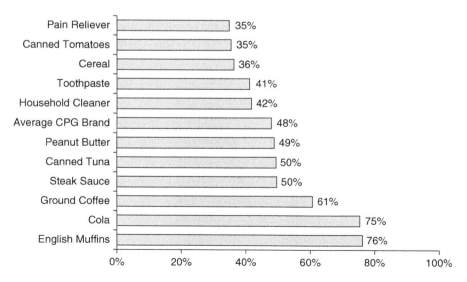

Figure 7.3 Highly Loyal Buyers Who Remain Loyal.

Source: MASB: CMO Council and Pointer Media Network, 2009, Losing Loyalty: The Consumer Defection Dilemma.

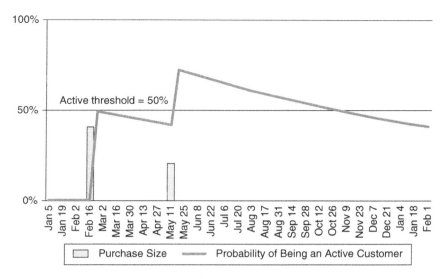

Figure 7.4 Probability of Being an Active Customer.

Source: J. Villanueva, S. Yoo, and D. M. Hanssens, "The Impact of Marketing-Induced vs. Word-of-Mouth Customer Acquisition on Customer Equity," *Journal of Marketing Research*, February 2008.

re-acquired. A common method is to define current brand buyers as those who made a purchase in the past year. The problem with this method is that it is based on an arbitrary time frame that does not account for behavior outside of that window. Some customers may have been loyal buyers and may have a number of reasons why they have not recorded a purchase in the past year, but may still be emotionally loyal to the brand. Other consumers may have purchased once 51 weeks ago.

Current or retained buyers were identified based on the probability of being an active purchaser of the brand. The methodology employed to estimate the probability of being an active buyer was a BG-NBD probability curve developed for this application by Hardie–Fader. The probability estimate is based on the frequency and size of purchases over time. Each brand purchase by a customer increases the probability of being an active brand buyer and conversely, inactivity reduces the probability that the customer is active.

Villanueva *et al.* described a stochastic method in their 2008 paper, which estimates the probability of a consumer being an active brand buyer.[7] This work was an enhancement of the earlier work of Fader *et al.*[8] The result was the estimated probability of a new customer purchasing the brand (acquisition), an existing customer periodically repurchasing the brand (retention), or an existing customer becoming inactive and needing to be re-acquired (acquisition), as illustrated in Figure 7.4.

As can be seen in Figure 7.5, the probability of purchasing varies week by week. If a purchase by a household is made, the probability of a future purchase by that household in coming weeks increases. If a purchase is not made, the probability of a future purchase by that household decreases. Both purchase frequency and purchase size influenced the probability of a buyer being an active brand buyer.

Marketing Accountability Standards Board (MASB) Pilot Test

The CLV estimation methodology was employed for five CPG brands in a pilot test conducted by MASB:

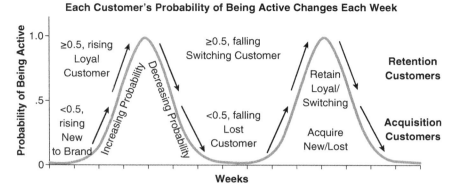

Figure 7.5 Probability of Being Active Changes.

Source: Created by the author, Debra Parcheta, Blue Marble Enterprises.

- one food brand, category leader;
- two beverage brands in separate categories, one is a category leader;
- two personal care brands in separate categories, same umbrella brand.

The methodology employed to estimate the probability of being an active buyer was a BG-NBD probability curve developed for this sort of analytic application by Fader *et al.* (2005) and tested in a paper by Yoo *et al.* (2012).[9] The probability estimate is based on recency, frequency, and size of purchases over time.

For each of the participating brands, a 3-year linked[10] 10/12 static panel was extracted from the Nielsen Homescan panel over the time period August 2008 to July 2010. The number of households in each static panel ranged from 10,500 to just over 40,000 depending on the household penetration for the product categories. Data was analyzed at the household transaction level to derive CLV and CE values.

The results of this pilot study concluded that application of the CLV methodology can help CPG marketers determine the impact their marketing activities have on both the short- and long-term sales trends for their brands. Also, because the metrics are based on projecting each customer's CLV, marketers will be better able to study segments of consumers, identifying which households to target to optimize long-term marketing ROI. This cannot be done with other methods that do not calculate CLV at the household level.

From the CLV and CE metrics, future trends in NPV for different subsets of a brand's business can be projected, thereby assisting with the decisions for optimizing marketing budgets to acquire and retain the most profitable customers. The CLV and CE metrics may identify for CPG marketers which marketing activities to select, and how to manage them, in order to provide greater long-term value.

CLV is a slow-moving metric that preludes long-term trends in sales. Thus, it has value in measuring the health of the brand and is a more stable metric than weekly sales, which vary greatly. These weekly sales fluctuations can distract managers and some overreact. Often, much effort is spent in justifying or explaining these weekly sales variations, which really do not always reflect the true sales trends for the brand. CE is a more stable measure that does reflect the health and true sales trends of the brand, and can help managers to focus on building the brand. It is a forward-looking metric that can be predictive of future sales trends, as illustrated in Figures 7.6a and 7.6b. The decline in CE for one brand predicted the decline in sales one

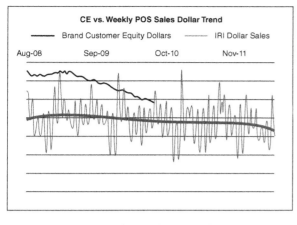

Figure 7.6a CE vs. Weekly POS Sales Dollar Trend (The CE metric seems to have predicted the accelerating sales decline of this CPG).

Source: CE from MASB Model using Nielsen Homescan POS from IRI Infoscan.

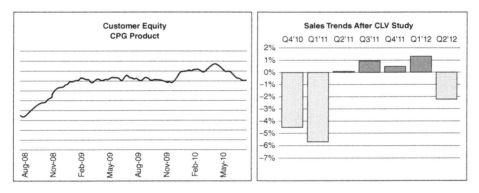

Figure 7.6b Sales Trend after CLV Study $Y/Y (The CE metric seems to have predicted the accelerating sales decline of this CPG).

Source: CE from MASB Model using Nielsen Homescan POS from IRI Infoscan.

quarter later. The increase in CE for another brand predicted sales increases even while weekly sales were declining.

Let us look in more depth at the customer purchasing behavior driving these dynamics. In Figure 7.7 Brand A's weekly sales are increasing though the brand has not been acquiring enough new buyers to sustain the growth; therefore, CE is actually declining. At first the brand was experiencing declines and CE due to not acquiring enough new buyers to sustain future growth: the result was an eight-month sales decline six months later. However, once the brand began acquiring new buyers, CE began rebuilding because these new buyers represented future value. By building CE through acquisition, this resulted in weekly sales increases eight months later. The Ehrenberg-Bass Institute published a study showing the importance of acquiring customers for CPG in their study *How Brands Grow*.[11] In this study they showed the difference between the leading brand in the category and all others is almost completely driven by the number of buyers. The study shows that purchase rate among each brand's buyers are relatively similar for the leading brand and brands with a lower market share.

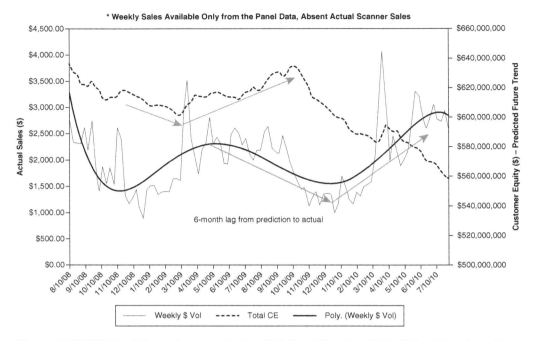

Figure 7.7 CE$$$ Trend Shows Customer Equity will Fall and Rise; Panel Sales Fall and Rise in the Future Years.

Source: Created by Dominique Hanssens.

So you can see the importance of buyer acquisition to growth; however, the health of the brand is driven by how many buyers are retained. It is the loyal customers who build the brand's base and provide a foundation for growth. So you have to balance maintaining your most loyal customers while continually acquiring new customers for growth. One thing that can be misleading about the *How Brands Grow* study is that, while the leading brands have similar average purchasing rates, they maintain that average purchase rate over a larger number of buyers. The new buyers a brand acquires will naturally have a lower purchase rate and are thus driving the average purchase rate of the brand lower. So the larger brands not only have more buyers but they have also been able to increase the purchase rate of all buyers to counteract the influx of these lighter, new buyers (see Figure 7.8).

One good example of this is the success of the DiGiorno rising crust pizza when it was introduced. During the test market, the brand was behind its sales goals by about 40 percent after 6 months. However, further investigation showed that the sales gap was totally driven by the shortage of brand triers. The consumers who did try the brand came back and repurchased at a very high rate. The first repeat rate, which is the percentage of buyers who make a second purchase, was extremely high. The real success of the brand was the high depth of repeat, which is the number of times customers make repeat purchases. These trial and repeat purchase patterns were used to forecast first-year sales in the test market, which showed that actual sales in the next six months would close the gap to the sales goal and exceed it. Based on this information, managers had the confidence to introduce the brand nationwide even though sales were short of its target in the test market. They also used this information to build an introduction marketing plan that focused on attracting trial purchases. DiGiorno pizza quickly became a leading brand in the category, with a high number of triers and very high repurchase rate.

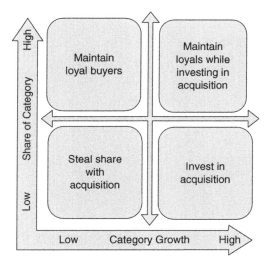

Figure 7.8 Retain Loyal Buyers/Retain Loyals while Investing in Acquisition.

Source: Created by the author, Rick Abens, of Foresight ROI, Inc.

The success of a brand is really about a balance between maintaining your most loyal buyers and continually acquiring new buyers. These purchasing patterns represent ways to manage your customer acquisition and retention strategies to build brand equity. Marketing plans should have strategies and tactics to address the goals of the brand and be reflective of the current CE position of the brand. Your brand could be in a low growth or high growth category, and it could have a high or low market share. Low-share brands should focus on customer acquisition and invest at levels commensurate with the future category growth opportunities. High-share brands should focus on maintaining their loyal buyers with marketing targeted to their heaviest buyers and then investing in acquisition strategies commensurate with the category growth opportunity.

Measuring Marketing Impact on CLV

A regression model was used to measure the media and pricing effects on short-term sales and on CLV. Two models focused on CE for newly-acquired customers vs. retained customers to assess acquisition and retention impacts from marketing. A third similar weekly sales model was used to compare the short-term effects of pricing and marketing to the long-term effects.

For the food brands, price discounts work better than advertising to attract new customers to the brand. We hypothesize that inactive buyers of the brands will screen out messages for the brand and need an incentive to "give the brand a try." Inactive buyers probably buy less frequently than active buyers and thus assign less value to the category or brand and need a lower price to balance the price–value relationship.

Brand B is a leading brand in a dry grocery category. It is fairly responsive to price discounting with a -2.15 price elasticity, which means that a 10 percent discount will increase short-term sales by approximately 22 percent. However, the brand's long-term sales responsiveness to price discounts is not nearly as elastic (Figures 7.9a and 7.9b). The dynamics behind this are that buyers influenced by price discounts are not as likely to be loyal buyers and thus will require further price discounts to be retained.

The TV advertising elasticity shows just the opposite results. The advertising effects to short-term sales effects is about half of the effect advertising has on CE. Managers are misled by

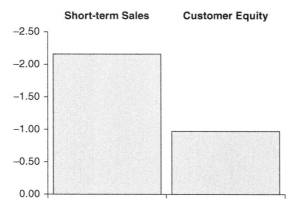

Figure 7.9a Price Elasticity of Brand B.

Source: Created by the author, Debra Parcheta, CEO, Blue Marble Enterprises; and Rick Abens of Foresight ROI, Inc.

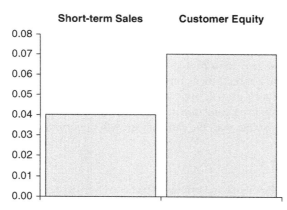

Figure 7.9b Advertising Elasticity.

Source: Created by the author, Debra Parcheta, CEO, Blue Marble Enterprises; and Rick Abens of Foresight ROI, Inc.

short-term effects from marketing and may rely too heavily on price discounting at the expense of the long-term health of the brand. Price discounting can be a useful tool to acquire new buyers. In two of the brands studied we found that new buyers were more price sensitive than retained buyers. In contrast, we found that retained buyers were more responsive to advertising. The implications of these findings are that advertising is important to maintaining the loyalty of your customers with constant reminders of the benefits of your brand and to counteract competitive brand messages. When advertising stops, there is a lagged downward effect on CE, as illustrated in Figure 7.10.

The third brand studied was a personal care brand, which competes in a category dependent on a life stage that has a definite start and end; the marketing effects were different to the

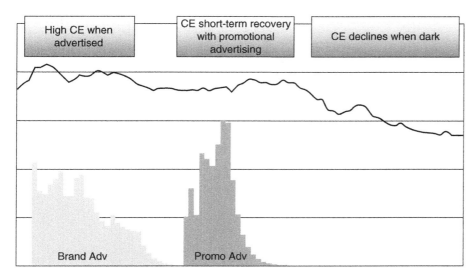

Figure 7.10 CE and Advertising for a Pilot Test Brand.
Source: MASB.

food and beverage brands. Advertising worked better at attracting non-buyers. Consumers do not enter the category until they enter the appropriate life stage, at which time they need and crave information to help them make brand choices about the category and brand advantages in the category.

Current brand buyers become more sensitive to price over time, because they spend a lot of money in the category while in a particular life stage and need to save money. They also may find that the brand performance is less differentiated than expected and that they value price more in the purchase decision. These two dynamics can cause consumers to switch back and forth based on the best price.

New Metrics from Purchase Transaction Data

In the course of calculating CLV and CE for the pilot brands, some exciting new metrics emerged. When CLV is calculated at the household level, CE can be segmented for new insights. In this analysis, brand C finds that 17 percent of households (HH) spend over $500 per year on this brand and generate 87 percent of its future CE. Knowing this, would Brand C choose to focus on one or all three different target groups?

Marketers will also appreciate a metric for expected transactions. Because CLV looks forward, it predicts price, transaction, and size of purchase trends. Traditional models simply report what the average price, number of transactions, or size of purchase has been in the recent history. Product B is expecting fewer transactions from both retention and acquisition households. Knowing this may alert them to competitive or quality concerns that could be mitigated.

At certain points in the calculation of CLV and CE, it is possible to stop and snapshot the CLV of a household in each quadrant of the purchasing curve, as illustrated in Figures 7.11a and 7.11b. What is a customer worth in each model year? Also, when that can be shown, how would targeting or marketing tactics change? A snapshot of the characteristics of the households in each quadrant might also give insights that optimize the selection of future marketing tactics.

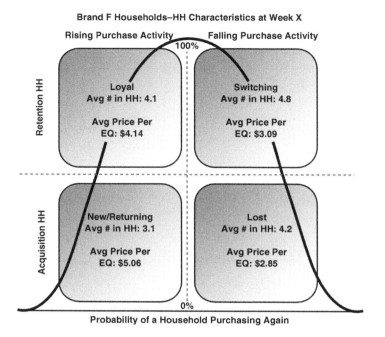

Figure 7.11a CLV Appears to Be Responsive to Advertising/CE and Advertising for a Pilot Test Brand.
Source: MASB, 2011.

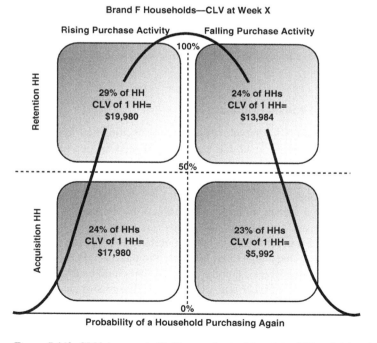

Figure 7.11b CLV Appears to Be Responsive to Advertising/CE and Advertising for a Pilot Test Brand.
Source: MASB, 2011.

Conclusion

The CLV metric and resulting CE forecasts can help marketers manage long-term growth through marketing. It gives them an understanding of how to manage growth with acquisition and retention strategies. Equity mix modeling answers questions about the effectiveness of various marketing efforts for driving CE in the future. Marketers can assess questions such as: How profitable is it in the long run to acquire customers with price deals? What is the long-term health and future CE trend of the brand? What balance of acquisition and retention strategies will produce the best overall performance?

References

1 Shijin Yoo, Dominique M. Hanssens, and Ho Kim, 2012, "Marketing and the Evolution of Customer Equity of Frequently Purchased Brands," Working Paper, UCLA Anderson School of Management, available at http://www.anderson.ucla.edu/faculty/dominique.hanssens/CECPG_version_April_11_2011.pdf.
2 Shijin Yoo, Dominique M. Hanssens, and Ho Kim, 2012, "Marketing and the Evolution of Customer Equity of Frequently Purchased Brands," Working Paper, UCLA Anderson School of Management, available at http://www.anderson.ucla.edu/faculty/dominique.hanssens/CECPG_version_April_11_2011.pdf.
3 Peter S. Fader, Bruce G. S. Hardie, and Ka Lok Lee, 2005, "Counting Your Customers the Easy Way: An Alternative to the Pareto / NBD Model," *Marketing Science*, 24(2): 275–284.
4 Shijin Yoo, Dominique M. Hanssens, and Ho Kim, 2012, "Marketing and the Evolution of Customer Equity of Frequently Purchased Brands," Working Paper, UCLA Anderson School of Management, available at http://www.anderson.ucla.edu/faculty/dominique.hanssens/CECPG_version_April_11_2011.pdf.
5 Shijin Yoo, Dominique M. Hanssens, and Ho Kim, 2012, "Marketing and the Evolution of Customer Equity of Frequently Purchased Brands," Working Paper, UCLA Anderson School of Management, available at http://www.anderson.ucla.edu/faculty/dominique.hanssens/CECPG_version_April_11_2011.pdf.
6 Dominique M. Hanssens, D. and D. Parcheta, forthcoming, "Application of Customer Lifetime Value (CLV) to Fast-Moving Consumer Goods," Working Paper, UCLA Anderson School of Management.
7 Julian Vllanueva, Shijin Yoo, and Dominique M. Hanssens, 2008, "The Impact of Marketing-Induced Versus Word-of-Mouth Customer Acquisition on Customer Equity Growth," *Journal of Marketing Research*, 45(February): 248–259.
8 Peter S. Fader, Bruce G. S. Hardie, and Ka Lok Lee, 2005, "Counting Your Customers the Easy Way: An Alternative to the Pareto/NBD Model," *Marketing Science*, 24(2): 275–284.
9 Shijin Yoo, Dominique M. Hanssens, and Ho Kim, 2012, "Marketing and the Evolution of Customer Equity of Frequently Purchased Brands," Working Paper, UCLA Anderson School of Management, available at http://www.anderson.ucla.edu/faculty/dominique.hanssens/CECPG_version_April_11_2011.pdf.
10 "Linked" panel data requires that a certain customer be reported in a certain number of months throughout the entire panel time frame. For example, in a 10/12 linked static panel set of transactions, a panel member is only included in the data set if they report purchases in 10 out of 12 months in all 3 years of the time frame. An "unlinked" set would not exclude panel members who were less frequent reporters of their purchases, who were new to market after the initial two months of the time frame or who disappeared during the time frame.
11 Byron Sharp, *How Brands Grow: What Marketers Don't Know*, 2010, Oxford, UK: Oxford University Press.

8 What Is Known About the Long-Term Impact of Advertising

Dominique M. Hanssens

Introduction

The focus of most measures of marketing's impact on sales is "short-term." This focus may bias return on investment (ROI) calculations for marketing activities that have both short- and long-term impacts, as it takes into account the complete expenditure but only a portion of the impact. This is an important consideration, as there is evidence that advertising has both short- and long-term impacts while other marketing tactics (such as price promotions) have only short-term effects. Measurement and analyses that consider only short-term impacts may put advertising at an unrealistic disadvantage when allocating marketing resources to maximize long-run profitability.

Pervasiveness of the Issue

The majority of marketing analyses address only short-term impacts, with "short-term" defined as the current budget or planning period (usually a quarter or a year). For the consumer-packaged-goods industry, results of these analyses have caused marketers to shift spending to programs closer and closer to the point of purchase, primarily at retail. This shift in marketing strategy can be seen in the growth of trade promotion budgets at the expense of programs with impact that accrues over time, like advertising.

Objectives

The "Long-Term Project" was undertaken by the Marketing Accountability Standards Board (MASB) to help improve fact-based marketing resource allocation through better understanding of the short- and long-term impacts of advertising. Included in the project and this chapter are:

1   a review of the literature as to what is known about the short- and long-term impacts;
2   an illustration of the findings with practitioner examples;
3   clear direction for business application and improving financial return.

This chapter considers three measures of consumer response and three dimensions of corporate behavior.[1]

Consumer Response

The three measures of consumer response are:

- **immediate effects**—the immediate consumer response to advertising;
- **carryover effects**—delayed buyer response;
- **purchase reinforcement**—repeat buying as a result of the initial, advertising-induced purchase.

Corporate Behavior

The three measures of corporate behavior are:

- **feedback effect**—influence of the initial sales lift on subsequent advertising spending;
- **decision rules**—effect of advertising spending on other parts of the marketing mix;
- **competitive reactions**—can be share stealing or category expanding.

Producing a short-term consumer response to the advertising is important: without it there is no longer-term impact, and with it comes double the effects over a longer period of time.[2, 3] Corporate behavior and business practices are also important and can result in over five times stronger and longer-lasting impact than from consumer response alone.[4] For each of the six factors above, we will provide a definition, look at the key metrics used to assess them, and look at the available analytics and the processes within the marketing area (or across the company) which should be targeted. We will also summarize the key things that have been learned using practitioner examples for illustrative purposes, and conclude with implications for practitioner action.

Consumer Response

Factor 1: Immediate Effects

Immediate consumer response to advertising is the focus of most advertising research. As we will see later in "Key Findings Based on Consumer Response," this factor is a necessary long-term building block, because immediate responses are essential for the creation of long-term impact.

Factor 2: Carryover Effects

Carryover effects reflect a delayed buyer response to advertising. Carryover is not fundamentally different from immediate response; it is simply the result of "letting the dust settle"—a time shift in impact.

Factors 1 and 2 = Short-Term Lift

If you add immediate and carryover effects, you get what we will refer to as total short-term lift. Beyond their definitions, the remainder of the discussion on factors 1 and 2 is combined, because the distinction is simply between immediate effects and those that occur one or two months later. Short-term impact is observed through a lift in a performance metric that is known to be financially relevant (e.g., market share, unit sales, leads, etc.). The analytics used are market-response models and controlled experiments.

The processes targeted for achieving short-term lifts from advertising are pre-market testing and review of advertising activity with tangible action. Process implications involve the effects of the advertising:

- shift resources toward marketing that provides a tangible lift;
- discontinue unproductive marketing.

Factor 3: Purchase Reinforcement

Purchase reinforcement refers to repeat buying as a result of the initial, advertising-induced purchase (i.e., experience with the product or service). It is equivalent to "customer retention" in relationship businesses. It can also build through word of mouth. If customers have a good experience with the product, its long-term potential increases. If the consumer has a negative experience with the brand (that is, there is no purchase reinforcement), the short-term effect of the advertising will not materialize into long-term impact.

The metric used to measure purchase reinforcement is improvement in a reinforcement variable (e.g., repeat-purchase rate, retention rate, customer referrals, or customer satisfaction). Analytics involve monitoring the metric in controlled experiments or dynamic market-response models. The process is simple: periodic monitoring with diagnostic action when needed. For example, you suddenly see your brand's normal repeat rates decline. Why? At this point a red flag should be raised, and the brand group should immediately work to correct the problem.

Key Findings and Examples of Consumer Response Factors

Persuasive advertising produces an immediate impact. Numerous industry studies have shown that persuasive advertising (that is, advertising that causes a positive shift in brand preference/choice) produces an immediate market place impact. In the *Journal of Advertising Research* classic article "An Empirical Investigation of Advertising Wearin and Wearout," Blair[5] wrote: "Effective delivery of advertising occurs much faster . . . than has been indicated through traditional (consumer) tracking measurements."

Based on his short-term advertising strength (STAS) research in the mid-1990s, John Philip Jones found that "advertising can have an immediate and short-term (seven-day) influence on sales."[6] Information Resources Inc. (IRI) has reported similar findings: "When a particular advertising weight or copy is effective, it works relatively rapidly."[7]

Figure 8.1 is an Oscar Mayer Lunchables example of this finding. At the time the Lunchables case study took place, Oscar Mayer tested each of the brand's TV ads before airing (using the ARS brand preference/choice methodology), and then examined its impact after airing. An ad called "Bad Week" achieved an APM Fact above +8.0, the highest score ever achieved by the brand—a huge accomplishment in a category where the brand already dominated the market. Sales volume for the first 12 weeks the ad aired was 48 percent higher than that observed during the previous year. (APM Facts is the **A**RS **P**ersuasion **M**easure for ads that actually air (versus the same methodology used at other stages of the marketing process).)

At the time, Category Information Manager, Bill Bean, stated: "Subsequent sales decomposition modeling revealed that 'Bad Week' accounted for 15 percent of the total Lunchables volume, the largest incremental sales increase Oscar Mayer and A. C. Nielsen had ever seen from television advertising!"[8]

Without this short-term impact, there is no long-term impact. Consistently, it has been found that a short-term impact on consumer purchasing (sales) is a prerequisite for a long-term effect. IRI's "How Advertising Works" study found that: "if advertising [does not] show an effect in six months, then [it] will not have any impact, even if continued for a year."[9] In a follow-up study nearly two decades later, IRI's earlier conclusion was confirmed: "If the . . . advertising does not work the first year, it will not have any long-term impact."[10]

Likewise, Jones's STAS research "rejects the possibility of a 'sleeper' effect—the supposed build-up . . . which does not work immediately and only causes sales to rise after a prolonged period of media exposure."[11]

The size and duration of the impact are determined primarily by the persuasiveness of the ad (message), along with effective delivery (media) and purchase reinforcement (product). The influence of the product on market impact is illustrated by a case study for Starkist: "Tuna in a Pouch." In September 2000, the tuna industry was stagnant and had become a

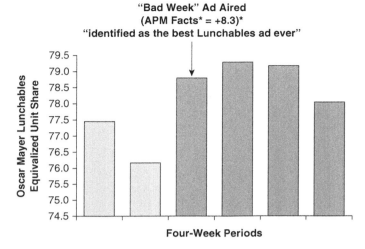

Figure 8.1 Immediate Impact of Oscar Mayer Lunchable Advert.

Source: MASB: Bill Dean (Oscar Mayer), 1995.

* APM Facts = <u>A</u>RS <u>P</u>ersuasion <u>M</u>etric for ads that actually air.

price-based commodity. The "no drain" vacuum-sealed foil pouch was the biggest innovation to the category since canned tuna was introduced in the 1920s.

The product was tested by BASES (Nielsen's new product forecasting service) to determine purchase reinforcement after product use. Results showed a purchase intent of 90 percent after product trial (even higher than the 74 percent interest based on product concept), indicating that consumers were likely to buy the product again (Figure 8.2). The size and duration of advertising's short-term impact is illustrated in a Campbell's Prego Spaghetti Sauce case study (Figure 8.3). The more persuasive the message, the higher and longer the impact.

The relative contribution of media weight and persuasiveness of the message across more than 100 cases and over a business quarter is shown in Figure 8.4. While there would be no impact at all without media delivery, the persuasive power of the ad accounts for most of the overall variation in market impact (as derived independently by marketing mix modelers).

	Concept	After use	Percentile score vs. BASES database
Top two box purchase intent	74%	→ 90%	Top 20%
Liking	4.3	→ 5.0	Top 20%
Uniqueness	3.9	→ 4.0	Top 20%
Value	3.7	→ 4.3	Top 20%

Figure 8.2 BASES Results for Starkist Tuna in a Pouch.

Source: MASB: Barry Shepard (Heinz North America), 2002.

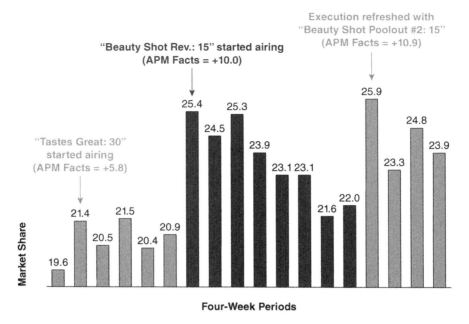

Figure 8.3 The More Persuasive the Ad, the Higher and Longer the Impact.

Source: MASB: Adams (Campbell Soup Company) and Blair, 1992.

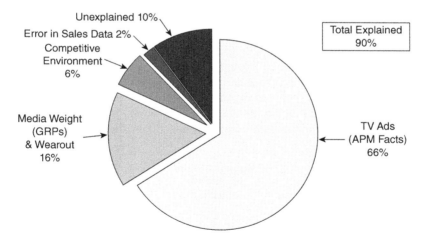

Figure 8.4 Explaining Variation in Volume Impacted by TV Quarter-to-Quarter.

Source: MASB: MASB, 2008.

As shown in Figure 8.5, an ad's persuasive power works quickly, with diminishing returns, wearing out in the process. Both occur in a predictable fashion given gross rating points, indicating how fast effective delivery is achieved, when/where to look for the market impact, and when to refresh with new executions.

The Long-Term Impact of Advertising 101

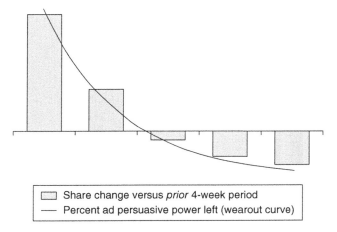

Figure 8.5 Ads Work Quickly with Diminishing Returns and Wearout.

Source: MASB: MASB, 2008.

The Short-Term Impact of Advertising Is Doubled Over the Longer Term

IRI's BehaviorScan Tests highlight the long-term effects of advertising: "[When] advertising works in the short term (year 1), its impacts are doubled over the next 2 years."[12, 13] The results of the 1995 and 2007 studies are combined in Figure 8.6. While the results showed no change in impact for unproductive ads (p > 0.2), persuasive advertising's effects more than doubled in the longer term. Even when all the ads (both productive and unproductive) are considered in total, profit more than triples over the long haul ($0.56m for year 1, versus $1.85m by the end of year 3).

Given competitive markets, reversion to the mean in net positive results is the rule (lift is temporary). In competitive markets, ad wearout and reversion to the mean are the rule, requiring sustained advertising activity to maintain net positive impact, as illustrated by the Campbell's Prego case study in Figure 8.7.[14] Prego's market share increased with the airing of each (fresh) persuasive ad, achieving a net positive trend in share over the 18-month period.

Category	Average elasticity	Short-term (1-year) impact		Long-term (3-year) impact	
		Revenue change ($million)	Profit change ($million)	Revenue change ($million)	Profit change ($million)
(Persuasive) advertising p ≤ 0.2	0.235	4.69	2.05	9.39	5.10
Other p > 0.2	0.036	0.72	−0.53	0.72	−0.53
All	0.120	2.40	0.56	4.38	1.85

Figure 8.6 The Short-Term Impact of Advertising Is Doubled in Years 2 and 3.

Source: MASB: Hu et al., 2007.

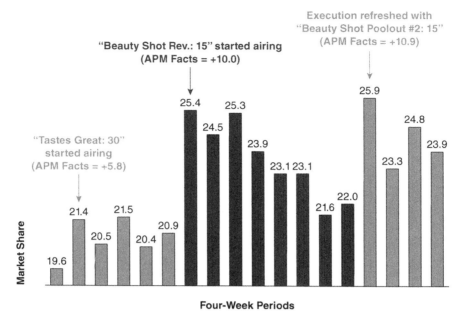

Figure 8.7 Wearout (Reversion to the Mean) and Sustained Advertising Activity.

Source: MASB: Adams (Campbell Soup Company) and Blair, 1992.

Without sustained activity, market share losses are the rule. In a 2004 *Journal of Advertising Research* article, Blair and Kuse[15] reported that airing ads with APM Facts greater than zero has an impact in the marketplace (versus not advertising or airing ads with zero-level APM Facts). The study showed that not advertising (i.e., going dark) results in a loss of 0.4 share points over the next business quarter (in the average market).

Corporate Behavior

Factor 4: Feedback Effect

Feedback effect is the influence of the initial sales lift on subsequent advertising spending (for example, does advertising become "policy" as a result of its initial success?). Reacting properly to advertising's success or failure is key to building long-term impact. Note that feedback effects can result in unproductive escalation of spending if the response effect wanes, and spending alone is considered to achieve the desired effects.

The metric for feedback effect is the evolution of budget allocations as a result of market-response insights—that is, continuing successful campaigns with execution refreshment, and discontinuing or rejuvenating worn-out campaigns. The analytics used for this factor include monitoring the metrics and advertising decision modeling. The process involves a move to response-based marketing.

What is meant by a response-based marketing process? First, it requires that the brand group recognizes past allocation successes and errors and implements any resulting learning that may increase the advertising's—and hence the brand's—chance for success. Ultimately, response-based marketing will result in a conversion to better business practices (process management).

It is important to note that organizations tend to fall back on "tradition-based marketing" when there is turnover in the marketing and/or brand team.

In the following examples, you will see the results of using feedback in decision-making. In some cases, this resulted in a best practice approach to advertising. For "best practice," we will use the following definition: "A documented method of operating behavior that yields a higher level of performance than other operating behaviors."[16]

Starkist Example

In the section on purchase reinforcement, we looked at a case study for Starkist Tuna in a Pouch. In retrospect, the brand team looked at what would have happened if they had used a traditional approach instead of the successful feedback-based approach. For each approach, ROI was based on incremental profits achieved less the costs of the marketing activity (advertising production, media costs, advertising research costs, etc.).

The traditional approach, which was calculated from test market data, shows that the advertising during quarter A resulted in a break-even ROI. The feedback-based approach, on the other hand, resulted in an ROI of 76 percent for the roll-out quarter A. This was achieved by airing only ads with high APM Facts (i.e., ARS Persuasion scores for the ads that actually aired)[17] (Figure 8.8).

The wearout learning indicated that the ads had persuasive power left after the roll-out in quarter A, and so they were aired for an additional quarter (quarter B). When the ROI for the initial quarter was added to the unplanned second quarter, the ROI jumped to 368 percent.

Citrucel Example

Citrucel fiber supplement had observed a gradual decline in sales using a traditional process, with advertising spending at a competitive level. In July 1993, Citrucel began using a feedback-based process that began with testing the brand's selling propositions (using the same measurement methodology applied to the ads). Two propositions were tested: the traditional one, which emphasized "no grit," and a new one that focused on "no gas." The results showed the "no gas" proposition to be significantly more persuasive than the brand's traditional selling proposition (an ARS Persuasion score of +7.8 versus +4.1). Two executions were produced based on the new "no gas" selling proposition, and they achieved scores similar to that of the selling proposition. As shown in Figure 8.9, the persuasive 15- and 30-second advertisements began airing at the beginning of November 1993.

Share responded immediately—increasing over 70 percent from the pre-airing base period—and this was the only marketing activity for Citrucel over that time period. Based on this initial success, the brand team received funding for additional television advertising. Figure 8.10

	Advertising ROI
Traditional approach: Quarter A test-market	–1%
Feedback-based approach: Quarter A roll-out	76%
Feedback-based approach: Quarters A & B roll-out	368%

Figure 8.8 Return on Investment for Starkist's Feedback-Based Approach.

Source: MASB: B. Shepard (Heinz North America), 2002.

104 *Dominique M. Hanssens*

illustrates the outstanding results of using feedback in the first year, the second year, and beyond. Citrucel's brand share continued to increase while price was held steady. Note that the Citrucel success can be traced back to assessing the current advertising selling proposition, testing it against a new one, then following through with the creating, testing, and airing of persuasive advertising. In short, the brand moved from a traditional to a feedback-based process.

Prego "Better Practice" Example

Following the initial success (shown in Figure 8.3), the Prego brand group formed a "better practice team" to monitor advertising feedback effects and to implement learning into better practices. Figure 8.11 shows continuously increasing market share, a result of implementing these practices in years 1, 2, 3, and 4.

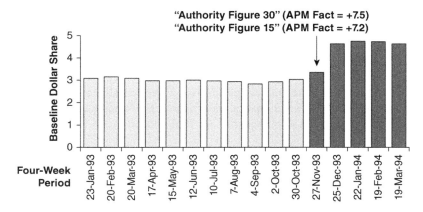

Figure 8.9 Citrucel Share Responds to Airing of Persuasive Ads.

Source: MASB: Shirley (SmithKline Beecham Consumer Healthcare), 1995.

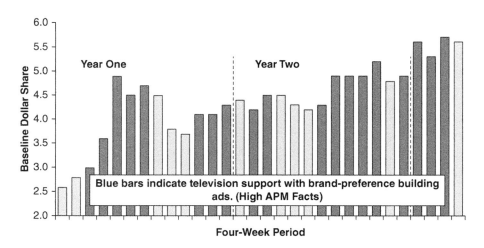

Figure 8.10 Citrucel's Success Continues in Year 1, Year 2, and Beyond.

Source: MASB: Blair, 2004.

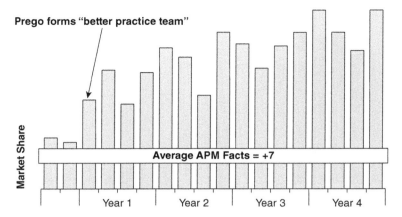

Figure 8.11 Prego's Share Increases with Better Practice Team.

Source: MASB: Adams (Campbell Soup Company), 1997.

Campbell Soup Company's, Dick Nelson, describes the success story:

> What underlies this five-year-long success story? A fundamental change in the advertising strategy and research process. Prego is the only Campbell's brand in the past five years to [test and] consistently stay with the same strong selling proposition, measure every pool out prior to airing (APM Facts), establish hurdles and stick to them, and utilize (wearout learning) to create an awareness of when to "refresh creative."[18]

Over the five-year period, Prego saw an increase of 4.5 points in market share. Taking into account incremental profit as well as the cost of testing and producing additional ads, Prego estimated their return on advertising investment to be over 5,000 percent (Figure 8.12).

Gradually the brand group turned over and drifted away from both the feedback-based process and the strong-selling proposition (Figure 8.13). Over the next five years (year 5 through year 9), the brand's average APM Facts fell to +3, four points below what it had been in the previous period (years 1 to 4). By the end of the nine-year period, share had declined to levels that were close to those before the brand adopted the "better practice" approach.

Average market share increase over baseline	4.5 points
Estimated incremental gross profit	$112,500,000
Incremental cost of testing (15 more)	$225,000
Estimated incremental cost of production	$1,875,000
Payout (ROI)	5,357%

Figure 8.12 ROI for Prego Was over 5,000% for the Five-Year Period.

Source: MASB: Adams (Campbell Soup Company), 1997.

106 *Dominique M. Hanssens*

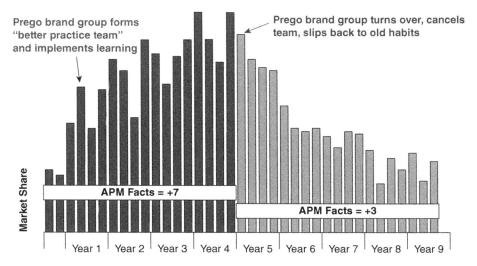

Figure 8.13 Market Share Declined When Prego Brand Group Turned Over.

Source: MASB: Blair and Kuse, 2004.

Duracell "Better Practice" Example

Alkaline battery sales began to take off in the late 1980s, with Duracell and Eveready starting the race at about the same place. Duracell managed to overtake Eveready in the late 1980s and maintained the number one spot in the industry through 1996 (Figure 8.14). By 1996, Duracell's market share had risen to 44 percent, while Eveready held only 32 percent of the market.

They each sold millions of units more every year to meet the electronics demand . . . but why did Duracell sell more? And how did they manage the brand? Duracell tested and used the same strong brand differentiating selling proposition ("lasts longer") over the entire 11-year run.

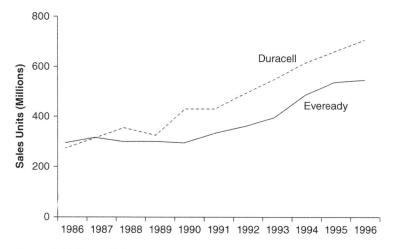

Figure 8.14 Duracell Outpaces Eveready in Unit Sales.

Source: MASB: Blair and Kuse, 2004; Stewart, 2005.

Duracell increased its share of brand preference with 31 percent more effective (brand preference building) television advertising. Eveready's brand preference declined, with less effective advertising. Over the 11-year period, Duracell's APM Facts averaged +5.1 versus +3.9 for Eveready (Figure 8.15). Although the difference in advertising persuasiveness was just over a point, it was enough to make a significant difference in the success of the Duracell brand.

Again, as we observed in the Prego example, a turnover in the brand team ended Duracell's success.

At the end of this successful 11-year run, the Duracell brand was sold to The Gillette Company. The new members of the brand and agency team did not adopt—and may not have even known of—the measurement and research practices that had supported Duracell's success. Subsequently (sales) eroded.[19]

Over-the-Counter (OTC) Division "Better Practice" Example

In the early 1990s, the OTC division of a large pharmaceutical company formed a "better advertising practice" (or BAP) team to improve advertising effectiveness across its brands. The OTC group had experienced success with several individual brands and wanted to extend that success to the rest of its brands.

The team started by defining the process that they would use to gather and implement advertising feedback. The process started with the identification of a persuasive selling proposition (based on ARS Persuasion measurement). Advertising wearout projections were used to plan the number of executions that would be needed as well as refreshment schedules.

An APM Facts hurdle of +4.0 was set, and each subsequent ad was tested for persuasiveness before going to air. To ensure the process was working, the group monitored market response as well as competitive advertising. An "advertising persuasiveness" report went directly to the CEO, showing him the proportion of +4.0 ads going to air for each brand.

Between 1994 and 1998, OTC divisional sales soared as the BAP team was formed, and more and more brands began adopting this "better advertising" feedback-based process. By 1998, sales had reached over $1.1bn, up about $400m compared to 1993 and 1994 (Figure 8.16).

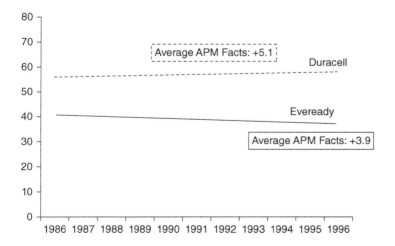

Figure 8.15 Duracell's TV Advertising Was More Effective than Eveready's.

Source: MASB: Blair and Kuse, 2004; Stewart, 2005.

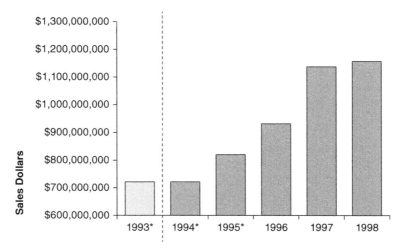

Figure 8.16 Sales Soared during the OTC Division's BAP Years.

Source: MASB: Blair, 2004.

* Includes sales from Wal-Mart.

As we observed in the Prego case study (Figure 8.13), turnover in personnel can be a huge detriment to maintaining a stable feedback-based process. In 1999, the company was bought by a larger one, the CEO moved up, the team and the practices were cancelled, the marketing scientists were eased out, and sales began to decline (Figure 8.17).

Factor 5: Decision Rules

Decision rules refer to the effect of advertising spending on the other parts of the brand's marketing mix (for example, reductions in trade promotions to offset ad spending, or increases in

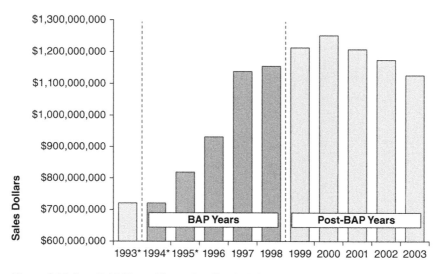

Figure 8.17 Post-BAP Years Show a Decline in Sales.

Source: MASB: Blair, 2004.

* Includes sales from Wal-Mart.

sales calls or retail price to capitalize on positive consumer response to advertising). Decision rules— including both inertia in decision-making and the opportunity to create synergy—shape the firm's overall marketing strategy.

The metric for decision rules is improvement in a reinforcement variable (for example, the correlation between sales calls and advertising support, which should be positive if the two areas are synergistic). Analytics for decision rules include market-response models with interaction effects and marketing decision models.

The process? Development of cross-functional decision teams to ensure coordination when there is synergy, as well as clutter avoidance when there is competition. In our OTC example (Figures 8.16 and 8.17), this was accomplished by the establishment of airing hurdles (an ARS Persuasion/APM Facts level of +4.0 as the action standard across its 22 OTC brands):

- A score of 4 or higher for the "selling proposition" was required to allocate creative/production dollars.
- Only ads scoring 4+ were allocated media dollars.

The CEO received systematic reports showing scores for the ads being aired by brand to determine how well the decision rules (in this case airing hurdles) were being followed.

Multi-Firm Pharmaceutical Example

In a current study of multiple pharmaceutical firms (large companies with multiple global brands), each of the brands has their own marketing budgets. "In theory, a multi-division firm can deploy volatile marketing tactics that do not affect portfolio volatility by strategically coordinating marketing campaigns across brands and regions . . . In that case, we would expect marketing expenditures to be predominantly negatively correlated."[20]

But in practice, they are not. For the three large pharmaceutical companies shown in Figure 8.18, the correlation for marketing spending across brands is predominantly zero. Although spending for individual brands may have been effective, there was no coordination across brands or divisions.

Factor 6: Competitive Reactions

None of a brand's actions takes place in a vacuum. If you take your competitors seriously, you will examine their competitive reaction to your marketing actions and vice versa. Interestingly enough,

		Expenditures in levels		
		Significant (p<.05)		Insignificant
	Number of products	$\rho<0$	$\rho>0$	$\rho=0$
Firm 1	13	5%	37%	58%
Firm 2	9	8%	25%	67%
Firm 3	7	5%	14%	81%

Figure 8.18 Correlation Pattern of Marketing Expenditures.
Source: MASB: Fischer *et al.*, 2015.

in the case of advertising and promotion, the predominant form of reaction is actually no reaction at all.[21] Category-enhancing reactions are also quite prevalent (i.e., competitors help each other out rather than hurt each other). When there are competitive reactions, the intensity of these reactions determines the ultimate level of marketing rivalry in an industry.

What do you do from a data analytic and process perspective? You measure cross elasticities (that is, in addition to measuring the effectiveness of your own marketing, you measure the impact of your competitor's marketing on yourself). The analytics are controlled experiments and competitive market-response models, both with competitive effects and reaction functions.

Assuming good measurement, an organization can develop a process and decision rules for optimal competitive behavior. It is often fairly simple: if there is no negative cross-sales effect, do not react. But if there is a cross-sales effect and it is negative, react (but only with marketing elements that will be effective as determined by pre-market or lead/test market experiments). Note that it is difficult to effectively react to a competitor who has persuasive advertising.

Citrucel versus Metamucil

In the Citrucel example we examined in Figures 8.9 and 8.10, the brand was competing against Metamucil, which enjoyed about 25 percent of the market at the beginning of the case study (Figure 8.19).

Metamucil continued losing share to Citrucel, despite spending more media dollars, cutting the retail price by 15 percent, promoting more heavily (retailer displays and feature ads), and airing more ads. Citrucel's success can be traced back to their feedback-based process, the monitoring of competitive activity, and the testing for and airing of persuasive advertising.

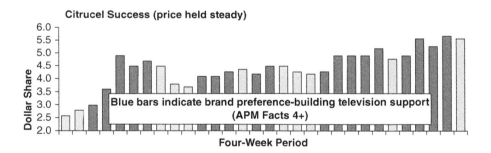

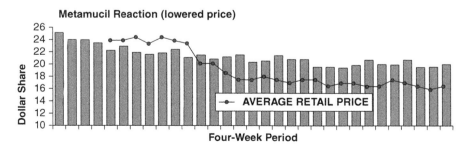

Figure 8.19 Metamucil Loses Share to Citrucel.

Source: MASB: Blair, 2004.

Prego versus Ragu

During Prego's five-year success period (Figures 8.11 and 8.12), they were competing against category leader, Ragu (Figure 8.20).

"Looking at the entire five year [sic] period, Prego's advertising managed to overcome Ragu's heavier spending, retailer support, and lower price. The estimated five-year return-on-investment [sic] associated with Prego's process change was over 5,000 percent."[22] Again, the brand's enhanced performance was due to persuasive advertising and monitoring of competitive reactions.

Duracell versus Eveready

Following up with the Duracell 11-year case study, we see that—corresponding to brand preference trends—Duracell's market share trended upward while Eveready's declined (see Figures 8.14 and 8.15). While both brands began the alkaline race at the same unit sales starting level, Duracell built the brand by continually building consumer brand preference, sales, and market share, while charging a premium price. The end prize was a nearly 3-to-1 market value of the Duracell Company over Eveready (Figure 8.21).

	Prego		**Ragu**
Total GRPs	15,034	←	20,400
Average displays	22	←	43
Average retailer ads	29	←	37
Average selling price	$1.80	←	$1.64
Total TV power (PPDs)*	679	→	448
Sales gains (units)	+22%	→	−19%

Figure 8.20 Prego versus Ragu: Five-Year Overview.
Source: MASB: Adams, 1997.

* <u>P</u>ersuasive <u>P</u>oints <u>D</u>elivered (calculated from APM Facts and media spending).

	Duracell		**Eveready**
Sales (units)	715M	→	568M
Brand Preference	57%	→	37%
Market share	44%	→	35%
Price per unit	$1.02	→	$.86
Profit	$609M	→	$275M
Market value*	$8B+	→	$3B

Figure 8.21 Duracell versus Eveready: Eleven-Year Case Study.
Source: MASB: Stewart, 2005.

* The companies were sold for approximately these prices at about a year after the end of the study.

Summary and Conclusions

Long-term advertising impact develops as a result of six main factors. The first three—immediate effects, carryover effects, and purchase reinforcement—are primarily a result of consumers' response to advertising and the product. The remaining three—feedback effect, decision rules, and competitive reactions— depend on corporate behavior, specifically organizational learning and the development of better advertising and marketing practices.

Consumer Response

Numerous industry studies have demonstrated that productive advertising produces an immediate impact on sales. It has also been demonstrated that without this short-term impact, there is no long-term impact. The size and duration of the impact are determined primarily by the persuasiveness of the ad (the message), together with effective delivery (the media), and purchase reinforcement (the product). Advertising's short-term impact is double to triple over the longer term. Studies conducted by IRI in 1995 and 2007 demonstrated that, on average, the advertising-to-sales impact over three years is double the impact of year one, and the advertising-to-profit impact is triple the impact of year one. Given competitive markets, however, advertisers cannot rely on these "residual effects" to sustain advertising impact. Sustained activity is necessary, because reversion to the mean in net positive results is the rule. In competitive markets, without sustained activity, losses are the rule.

Corporate Behavior

Change in an organization's processes and behaviors can result in over five times stronger and longer-lasting impact.[23] To produce these results, the organization must use advertising consumer response metrics that are predictive of transactional and financial returns; spend on activities that create the short-term effects necessary for long-term build-up; repeat the (successful) behavior; and turn this feedback loop into better business practices (i.e., process management) for both the brand and for the company as a whole.

Implications for Practitioner Action

This chapter suggests several actions that an organization can take to increase the long-term impact of its advertising and other marketing activities:

- select pre-market methods that are proven to be predictive of consumer behavior and market impact tied to financial results (ARS Persuasion/APM Facts and bases are used as examples in this chapter);
- spend on the activities that will create the desirable short-term lifts (and necessary for the long-term build-up);
- continually monitor consumer response and market impact;
- learn from the feedback, document the behavior, repeat the behavior, and turn this into better business practice for the brand and for the enterprise;
- stick with the better practices, even after personnel changes.

References

1 M. Dekimpe and D. Hanssens, 1995, "The Persistence of Marketing Effects on Sales," *Marketing Science*, 14(1): 1–21.
2 L. Lodish, M. Abraham, S. Kalmenson, J. Livelsberger, B. Lubetkin, B. Richardson, and M. Stevens, 1995, "How T.V. Advertising Works: A Meta-Analysis of 389 Real World Split Cable T.V. Advertising Experiments," *Journal of Marketing Research*, 32(2): 125–139.

3 Y. Hu, L. Lodish and A. Krieger, 2007, "An Analysis of Real World TV Advertising Tests: A 15-Year Update," *Journal of Advertising Research*, 47(3): 341–353.
4 K. Pauwels, 2004, "How Dynamic Consumer Response, Competitor Response, Company Support, and Company Inertia Shape Long-Term Marketing Effectiveness," *Marketing Science*, 23(4): 596–610.
5 M. Blair, 1987, "An Empirical Investigation of Advertising Wearin and Wearout," *Journal of Advertising Research*, 27(6): 45–50.
6 J. Jones, 1995. *When Ads Work. New Proof That Advertising Triggers Sales*, New York: Simon & Schuster–Lexington Books.
7 M. Abraham and L. Lodish, 1990, "Getting the Most Out of Advertising and Promotion," *Harvard Business Review*, 68(3): 50–60.
8 B. Bean, 1995, "Oscar Mayer Lunchables: The In-Market Effects of Advertising," in Transcript *Proceedings of the T.Q. Advertising Success Forum*.
9 M. Abraham and L. Lodish, 1990, "Getting the Most Out of Advertising and Promotion," *Harvard Business Review*, 68(3): 50–60.
10 Y. Hu, L. Lodish and A. Krieger, 2007, "An Analysis of Real World TV Advertising Tests: A 15- Year Update," *Journal of Advertising Research*, 47(3): 341–353.
11 J. Jones, 1995, "Does Advertising Produce Sales Today or Sales Tomorrow?," *Journal of Marketing Communications*, 1(1): 1–11.
12 L. Lodish, M. Abraham, S. Kalmenson, J. Livelsberger, B. Lubetkin, B. Richardson, and M. Stevens, 1995, "How T.V. Advertising Works: A Meta-Analysis of 389 Real World Split Cable T.V. Advertising Experiments," *Journal of Marketing Research*, 32(2): 125–139.
13 Y. Hu, L. Lodish and A. Krieger, 2007, "An Analysis of Real World TV Advertising Tests: A 15-Year Update," *Journal of Advertising Research*, 47(3): 341–353.
14 A. Adams and M. Blair, 1992, "Persuasive Advertising and Sales Accountability: Past Experience and Forward Validation," *Journal of Advertising Research*, 32(2): 20–25.
15 M. Blair and A. Kuse, 2004, "Better Practices in Advertising Can Change a *Cost of Doing Business* to *Wise Investments in the Business*," *Journal of Advertising Research*, 44(1): 71–89.
16 ESOMAR & ARF, 2003, Global Research Leaders' Summits, Geneva, Switzerland.
17 Shepard, 2002, *Developing and Managing Advertising with a More Positive Return on Investment: A Success Case for Starkist Tuna in a Pouch* (a publication of the ARS Group).
18 A. Adams. "Chapter Two: Advertising Research," in David Bushko (ed.), *Dartnell's Advertising Manager's Handbook,* 4th edition, 1997, Chicago, IL: The Dartnell Corporation.
19 M. Blair and A. Kuse, 2004, "Better Practices in Advertising Can Change a *Cost of Doing Business* to *Wise Investments in the Business*," *Journal of Advertising Research*, 44(1): 71–89.
20 M. Fischer, H. Shin, and D. Hanssens, 2015, "Brand Performance Volatility from Marketing Spending," *Management Science*, Articles in Advance, February.
21 J. Steenkamp, V. Nijs, D. Hanssens, and M. Dekimpe, 2005, "Competitive Reactions and the Cross-Sales Effects of Advertising and Promotion," *Marketing Science*, 24(1): 35–54.
22 A. Adams, "Chapter Two: Advertising Research," in David Bushko (ed.), *Dartnell's Advertising Manager's Handbook*, 4th edition, 1997, Chicago, IL: The Dartnell Corporation.
23 K. Pauwels, 2004, "How Dynamic Consumer Response, Competitor Response, Company Support, and Company Inertia Shape Long-Term Marketing Effectiveness," *Marketing Science*, 23(4): 596–610.

9 Long-Term Effects of Marketing Actions

Michael Hess

Why Long-Term Marketing? And a Definition

Long-term is the focus on building brands across periods that are longer than the next investor report, quarterly fiscal report or the current budget or planning period. Long-term is about growing a brand for the future. Long-term effects are generally measured through increased brand awareness, brand equity, increased loyalty, or higher price elasticity. For a company to sustain long-term growth and profitability, it is important that it effectively executes both short-term and long-term marketing strategies.

Most marketing variables are primarily measured within the short term, either from marketing mix models, tracking studies, or single source analyses. The focus on short-term is primarily due to the relative ease in determining changes in the market when the influences are fresh—as opposed to the extremely complex task of measuring effects of one set of changes within a constantly changing sea of changes across a long period of time. It is also driven by the interest in moving the brand within the current financial period. Most brand managers and marketers are evaluated on the short-term gains for their brands.

Why a Longer-Term View Is Important

When marketing variables are measured in the short term, the impact of those variables is only focused on the short-term shifts in sales, without a true understanding of how those marketing variables are influencing the future equity or price elasticity of the brand. This is particularly true in the comparisons between marketing spending on advertising versus promotions. We have heard anecdotally of cases of brands that have driven short-term sales with deep price cuts and promotions, only to discover that consumers learn to pantry-load during those promotions and never again are willing to pay full price. Promotions and temporary price reductions, if used too heavily, can turn into permanent price reductions due to reducing the consumer's perception of the value of the brand. Advertising that is designed to build the equity of the brand in the consumer's mind can drive up the equity of the brand, and therefore build stronger loyalty, brand equity, and future brand strength and growth.

Contrast to Short-Term Effects

Within a marketing framework, "short-term" is defined as the current budget or planning period, often a quarterly or annual interval, but sometimes shorter. Short-term marketing activities are those which incentivize purchases in the current period in order to create an immediate but temporary revenue increase. In contrast, "long-term" applies to the perpetual business periods beyond the current planning period. Long-term marketing activities are those which build lasting brand awareness and loyalty. For a company to sustain long-term growth and profitability, it is important that it effectively executes both short-term strategies (because of the need to "make the numbers" for the quarter or year) and long-term marketing strategies.

Long-Term Effects Apply to: Advertising, Promotion, Brand Equity

There are three areas in which the impacts of long-term marketing are especially significant: advertising, price promotion, and brand equity.

Advertising encompasses communications to both current and prospective customers that influence their consumer behavior. It is used to drive product awareness, differentiate the brand image, and create customer loyalty by reducing price sensitivity. Advertising can potentially affect long-term consumer behavior in two ways: (1) advertising memory, whereby consumers remember past advertising independently of their purchase history; and (2) purchase reinforcement by which consumers who purchase a product because of advertising decide to purchase again. In addition to the consumer effects, advertising has latent long-term influences on corporate behavior through organization learning and competitive responses. Advertising outcomes impact other parts of the brand's marketing mix and external competitors' reactions.

Price promotion involves temporary price reductions designed to boost sales. It can take the form of price cuts, coupons, or rebates. Price promotion can be an effective short-term tactical tool to increase both trial (initial purchase) and repeat. However, the long-term effects of price reductions are more tenuous. Research indicates that the revenue increases from price promotions are temporary and that customers quickly return to their prior buying patterns at the end of the promotion period. Some buyers even become accustomed to recurrent promotion patterns and consequently develop more sensitivity to price. Such consumers tend to buy primarily "on deal," and therefore lower baseline sale levels are attained. This, in turn, may negatively affect long-term brand margins and profitability.

Brand equity is value created from having a well-known brand name that can influence consumer behavior decisions. An established brand is often perceived as better than comparable products with less familiar names. Brand equity creation is a gradual, long-term process, which involves strategic marketing investments. Although brand equity is fundamentally important, it can be difficult to quantify. There remains no universally accepted way to measure it. Studies generally indicate that advertising has a long-run positive influence on brand equity, whereas promotions can have a long-term negative effect. In any event, one of the key goals of the Marketing Accountability and Standards Board (MASB) is to better quantify the value of a brand and, importantly, to get agreement between marketing and finance on the ultimate method of valuation.

Measurement of Long-Term Effects

"Long-term effects are complicated, first, by our inability to understand how advertising builds goodwill which can persist into future periods, and, second, by our inability to understand how to model competitive response which dampens the long-term effect."[1] Long-term impacts of marketing have traditionally been difficult to operationalize, quantify, and measure. There is little consensus of what constitutes the long-run and it is difficult to relate future outcomes to current actions, given continuously changing market conditions. Therefore, most measurements of marketing impacts have focused only on the immediate consumer response, which is readily observable. This limitation biases marketing return on investment (ROI) calculations by underestimating long-term effects of marketing activities, and can lead to a suboptimal allocation of marketing resources.

There are several main challenges involved in measuring and evaluating the effectiveness of long-term marketing. First, the evaluation of the effect of advertising communications is difficult to disentangle from other long-term competitive factors. Practitioners are confronted with issues about what to test, how to implement testing in real-world environments, and how to control for different external variables. This is exacerbated when marketing campaigns span across prolonged time periods and multiple platforms. Furthermore, the path not taken can rarely be assessed for a comparison. Marketers are left to guess what would have been the impact if a marketing campaign had been modified or stopped prematurely, or whether it was possible that a program, which tested poorly at first, could have performed better over time.

Measurement and evaluation of long-term marketing is further confounded by the separation between the investment and measurement periods of the marketing life cycle. Marketing ROI measurements can be divided into three distinct time periods, each with different objectives: (1) before the investment decisions—where questions involve whether to invest and which marketing channels to use; (2) during the investment—where questions focus on whether to continue and how to improve the impact; and (3) after the investment—where evaluations can be undertaken to understand the impact and ROI of the marketing campaign. The first time period is the most vital to impact decisions, yet at that point there is the least context for formulating measurements. Conversely, the last period offers the greatest opportunity for measurement possibilities; however, at this point, there is less impact on spending decisions.

It is no surprise, therefore, that advertising has historically been the most challenging marketing variable to measure accurately. However, aided by the use of large transaction-level databases, marketers have been able to accurately evaluate short-term effects of advertising. For example, supermarket scanner data has been used to create data sets for sales of specific brands and stock-keeping units. This sales data, along with information about features, displays, trade deals, coupons, and marketing media plan in terms of gross rating points' levels, allows short-term advertising effects to be assessed with good accuracy using sophisticated marketing analyses called "marketing mix" models. Ambach and Hess demonstrate how this approach can be used to assess the different short-term influencers of sales.[2] They found that, on average, a brand's in-store trade activity drives about 25 percent of sales volume, coupons are responsible for 10 percent and advertising for about 5 percent. "Everyday" volume, which is not directly attributable to other specific marketing activities, accounts for the remaining 60 percent of brand volume. Their findings are illustrated in Figure 9.1 below.

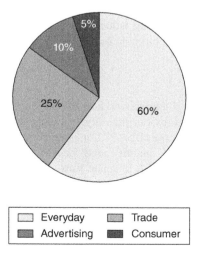

Figure 9.1 Pie Chart Comparing Eveready/Trade/Consumer and Advertising.

Source: Created by Mike Hess and Leslie Wood.

Yet scanner data alone cannot explain where "everyday" base volume comes from. Advertising's incremental short-term effect of only about 5 percent does not account for its potentially substantial (but less easily quantifiable) long-term impact on base volume. Ambach and Hess suggest that household-level transaction data may help address this shortcoming, because by accessing data at the household level, specific purchases can be linked to a specific buying context.[3]

Persistence modeling, a statistical approach introduced by Dekimpe and Hanssens,[4] also has offered some potential to statistically disentangle the long-term effect of marketing investments from other long-term factors. It addresses the problem of measuring long-run marketing impacts by combining into one measure: "the chain reaction of consumer response, firm feedback and competitor response that emerges following the initial marketing action."[5] The approach evaluates whether a time series of sales is stable or evolving over time. If there is a trend, subsequent analysis determines to what extent it can be related to marketing activity.

Measurement of Long-Term Effects: Example

Aflac's advertising campaign with the quacking duck is illustrative of the complexities of long-term marketing measurement and ROI decisions. The campaign started in 2000 and was extremely successful at creating awareness of the company with U.S. consumers, with recognition of the company increasing from under 10 percent to about 90 percent. However, unlike consumer purchase categories, practically none of those aware of the brand can buy the product directly, as it is sold to business representatives who require supplementary coverage. Furthermore, Aflac's internal research indicated that, despite the increased name recognition, there remained widespread lack of understanding about its product. Awareness measures looked great, but linking the campaign directly to sales figures remained problematic. The marketing may have increased confidence and receptivity to the sales force over the long term, but measurement efforts could not separate out, measure, and attribute the marketing effectiveness.[6]

Long-Term Effects and Advertising

Advertising in General

"[t]here is evidence that advertising has both short- and long-term impacts while other marketing tactics ... have only short-term effects."[7] "Measurement and analyses that consider only short-term impact may put advertising at an unrealistic disadvantage when allocating marketing resources to maximize long-run profitability."[8] According to Hanssens, there are six main impacts of advertising:

1 immediate effects: immediate consumer response;
2 carryover effects: delayed buyer response;
3 purchase reinforcement: repeat buying as a result of the initial purchase;
4 feedback effect: influence of the initial sales lift on subsequent advertising;
5 decision rules: effect on other parts of the marketing mix;
6 competitive reactions: share stealing or category expanding.[9]

The first two effects, immediate and carryover consumer responses, form the short-term response to advertising. The immediate consumer response is the focus of most advertising research, and for good reason—it is the driver of all subsequent actions. A strong immediate response is essential for the creation of a long-term impact. IRI's "How Advertising Works" study found that: "if advertising (does not) show an effect in six months, then [it] will not have any impact, even if continued for a year." Conversely, "when advertising works in the short-term [sic] [year 1], its impacts are doubled over the next two years."[10] An advertising campaign that has no measurable short-term impact will inevitably have no lasting impact in the long term.

The carryover effect reflects a time shift in impact to include the delayed buyer response. Taken together, the immediate effect and carryover effect form the complete short-term lift of the advertising campaign. This lift is observed by measuring changes in relevant short-term financial performance metrics using market-response models and controlled experiments. Often this involves comparing pre-market testing with tangible changes during the advertising period.

Purchase reinforcement is equivalent to customer retention. If a customer has a positive purchase experience, then the long-term potential for repeat buying increases; if the customer has a negative experience, the short-term impact of the advertising will not extend into the long term. Purchase reinforcement is measured in controlled experiments or market-response models by examining variables such as repeat purchase rate, customer referrals, or customer satisfaction. The magnitude and duration of the impact of advertising is primarily determined by three factors: (1) the persuasiveness of the message; (2) the effectiveness of the delivery; and (3) the reinforcement from the purchase. The message persuasiveness works immediately, but with quickly diminishing returns, but only if the message is effectively delivered to the target audience. In competitive markets, sustained advertising activity is often required to maintain and reinforce the net positive impact of advertising and prevent reversion to the mean.

The remaining three effects: feedback effect, decision rules, and competitive actions depend on corporate behavior. In particular, the long-term advertising impact will depend on organizational learning and development of better advertising practices. The feedback effect recognizes the influence of the initial sales lift on subsequent advertising budget allocations. This requires that the brand managers learn from past allocation successes and errors to implement changes that may increase their advertising's chance for success. The corporate reaction to the success or failure of advertising is key to building long-term impact.

Advertising actions also will affect other marketing mix decisions, both directly for the brand itself and indirectly for competitors' reactions. Decision rules refer to the impact of advertising spending on the other parts of the brand's marketing mix. Competitive reactions involve competitors' responses to the advertising. The measurement analytics for these impacts are controlled experiments and competitive market-response models. In general, it can be difficult to effectively react to a competitor who has persuasive advertising.

Advertising Example: Duracell and Eveready

These two companies held about the same market share as the alkaline battery market grew quickly in the 1980s. By committing to implementing a long-term brand-differentiating advertising campaign ("lasts longer") over the following decade, Duracell managed to increase its share to 44 percent, while Eveready held only 32 percent of the market. Duracell focused its advertising on the long-term objective of building consumer brand preference, while charging a premium price. Its television advertising persuasiveness was more effective, earning an average APM Facts score of +5.1 compared to Eveready's +3.9. The consequence after a decade was a nearly 3-to-1 market value of Duracell compared to Eveready. Figures 9.2a and 9.2b illustrate the brand preference trends and sales trends for the two battery manufacturers.

TV Advertising Specifically

Since the 1950s, U.S. television advertising has generally been considered the most effective mass-market advertising format. TV advertising campaigns aim to build brand recognition, differentiate the product, and increase loyalty by decreasing customers' sensitivity to price.

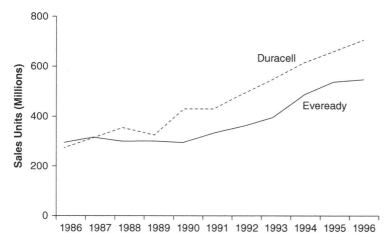

Figure 9.2a Duracell's TV Advertising Was More Effective than Eveready's.
Source: MASB: Blair and Kuse, 2004; Stewart, 2005.

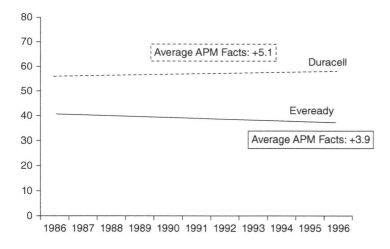

Figure 9.2b Duracell Outpaces Eveready in Unit Sales.
Source: MASB: Blair and Kuse, 2004; Stewart, 2005.

In a pioneering article, Lodish *et al.* (1995) report on in-market experimentally based measurement of long-term TV advertising effects for 55 BehaviorScan tests over 4 years.[11] They assessed average incremental sales effect over three years of television advertising that had been increased only during the first year. Figure 9.3 depicts the experimental design.

Results from analysis of the successful TV advertising campaigns suggested that the average initial first-year sales impact is approximately doubled when the sales impacts over the next two years are added. On average, there was a significant carryover from the first-year increase to the second year, and a smaller but still significant carryover to the third year. Additionally, an average of 106 percent of the initial year's sales volume increase carried over into the next two years. There also was significant carryover effect of advertising on market

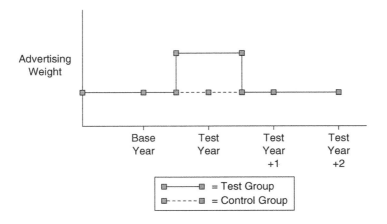

Figure 9.3 Average Incremental Sales Effect of Television Advertising.

Source: Created by Mike Hess and Leslie Wood.

expansion, with 100 percent of the market-share increases persisting for the next two years. Figure 9.4 shows the results of "successful" one-year advertising tests when the sales impact was measured over the next two years.

Unsuccessful TV advertising campaigns were also evaluated after one and two years using the same methodology. On average, for unsuccessful TV advertising campaigns that have no initial first-year sales impact, there was no long-term effect in the subsequent years either. Therefore, if advertising is not initially effective, it does not seem to have any subsequent efficacy in the following periods. Figure 9.5 shows the results of "non-successful" one-year, established advertising tests when the sales impact was measured over the next two years.

The empirical result that successful advertising persisted two years after the advertising weight change is somewhat longer than many econometric studies project. It implies the value of choosing a successful campaign is even higher when the multi-year horizon is considered. Analysis was undertaken to understand whether the reason for the successful test was due to changes in brand penetration or buying rates. On average, buying rates tend to carry over to the second year, while brand penetration did not. The implication is that successful advertising brings in more fringe category users into the brand franchise, while simultaneously causing current users to increase their purchase frequency even after the advertising increase ends. A related implication is that this increase in

	Covariate Adjusted % Increase in Sales Volume			**Covariate Adjusted % Increase in Market Share**		
	Test Year	Test Yr. +1	Test Yr. +2	Test Year	Test Yr. +1	Test Yr. +2
Mean	20.9**	14.3**	8.0**	13.8**	9.5**	4.2*
Standard Deviation of the Mean	4.8	5.6	3.5	3.6	3.4	2.4

Figure 9.4 Results of "Successful" One-Year Advertising Tests.

Source: Created by Mike Hess and Leslie Wood.

** = Significant at better than the .05 level.
 * = Significant at better than the .10 level.

	Covariate Adjusted % Increase in Sales Volume			Covariate Adjusted % Increase in Market Share		
	Test Year	Test Yr. +1	Test Yr. +2	Test Year	Test Yr. +1	Test Yr. +2
Mean	0.7	2.2	5.8	0.3	5.9	2.0
Standard Deviation of the Mean	6.44	8.32	6.7	2.04	7.53	3.47

Figure 9.5 Results of "Non-Successful" One-Year Advertising Tests.
Source: Created by Mike Hess and Leslie Wood.

purchase frequency is correlated to an increase in that brand's share of requirements (SOR), also referred to as "share of wallet." This, in turn, means that the enhancement in SOR is coming from the volume for competitive brands more so than from an overall increase in category demand. As such, improvements in a brand's long-term advertising values are reflected in share increases as well.

Long-Term Effects and Price Promotion

The key questions here are: Are there long-term effects from promotion? If so, how large are they relative to advertising? "While the net short-term effect of sales promotions is positive, their long-term impact on a brand's market share and profitability can be negative due to their adverse impact on brand equity."[12] Consumers become more price sensitive over time, because of reduced advertising and increased promotions.[13] Marketers have to manage trade-offs between the short-term benefits of promotions and their potentially adverse long-term consequences. The short-term impact of price promotions can be divided into two components: (1) a positive effect that encourages consumers to switch to the promoted brand; and (2) a negative effect on brand equity. It is important to consider the long-term consequences of temporary price cuts and promotional deals.

Firms often increase promotion spending to meet short-term revenue and market-share objectives, while neglecting to recognize the potentially negative impact on long-term effects. A number of factors tend to influence this shortsightedness. First, the abundance of short-term data makes it easy to link an increase in sales to a price promotion. The proliferation of easily-available real-time sales has given managers an indisputable link between discounting and sales. Marketers compare the immediate profitability of promotions with baseline sales models using estimates extrapolated from periods when there are no price reductions. The observable sales increases give the impression that promotions are highly profitable. However, this effect is often short lived and, in fact, can be eroding profit margins. Shoppers who encounter regular promotions learn to wait for the next sale rather than purchase a product at full price. This leads to decreased sales when the product is not discounted, which eventually reduces baseline sales. This further magnifies lift over baseline from promotions, creating a spiraling outcome that inevitability makes promotions look profitable when they may be decreasing profit margins.

Competitive responses can also substantially diminish the success of price promotions. When one company discounts its price point, others often react competitively and follow suit. Studies have found that price sensitivity is considerably higher when measured weekly than when measured quarterly. In part, this is because weekly data takes into account increases in purchases, but ignores subsequent competitive price reactions and changes in consumer behavior.

The long-term effects of price promotion are more difficult to gauge than the immediate short-term effects, which can be easily attributed. Practitioner research on the long-term effects has proceeded along a number of different streams. Studies have used a distributed-lag response model to examine how promotions change consumers' price and promotional sensitivity over time. For example, key findings from one major study demonstrated that repeated promotional activity increases purchase quantity, but decreases category incidence.[14] Persistence modeling has also been used to capture the potential for permanent effects of promotion. The findings have generally suggested that permanent results of promotions are largely absent, implying that promotions do not induce structural changes in sales over time.

Sriram and Kalwani present methodology for evaluating the optimal level of advertising and sales promotion expenditures when these instruments have a long-term effect on brand equity.[15] This research develops a state-space model that captures the dynamics of brand equity, as influenced by drivers such as a brand's advertising and sales promotion expenditures. It identifies and compares optimal allocations for advertising and promotion strategies when decision-makers consider only the short-term consequences of marketing versus when the consequences being considered are long-term oriented. Using empirical results based on store-level scanner data for two major brands in the orange juice category, the short-term effect of sales promotions is positive. However, for both brands, sales promotions have a negative effect on own-brand equity. The results of the study demonstrate that the optimum forward-looking promotion levels are significantly lower than the myopic ones. Overall, although price promotions have a net positive impact (both short-term and long-term), the implied total profit elasticity including the long-term effect is smaller than the short-term profit elasticity.

Pauwels *et al.* (2002) use persistence modeling on weekly sales data to examine the extent to which price promotions have a long-term impact on three components of brand sales: category incidence, brand choice, and purchase quantity.[16] For each component, they tested permanent changes in the time series to determine whether such changes are due to price shocks. The results suggest that time series for all three sale components are stationary for 80+ percent of the brand-store combinations. This implies no permanent promotional effects are present. Also, brand choice is found to be the dominant factor in the immediate elasticity breakdown. Total promotional effects are higher for category incidence than for brand choice or purchase quantity.

Mela *et al.* (1997) examined price promotion over an eight-year period for a frequently purchased packaged good.[17] The findings indicate that consumers become more price and promotion sensitive over time as promotions increased within the market studied. As might be expected, non-loyal consumers were more price sensitive than loyal consumers. However, both loyal and non-loyal consumers became more sensitive to pricing after promotions.

Brand Equity

How Brand Equity Reflects the Long-Term Value of Brand

The American Marketing Association defines brand equity as: "the value of a brand based on consumer attitudes about positive brand attributes and favorable consequences of brand use."[18] Brand equity encompasses the collection of attributes that the consumer comes to expect from a product, such as high quality or low cost. The brand can include individual products or the company as a whole. Often an established brand name is fundamental to a product's success, and may be considered the most valuable intangible asset of the business. It is especially important in markets with substantial repeat purchases, so that marketers can differentiate their products from competitors and build additional value. Increases in brand equity shift the demand curve to the right, increasing the buying rate across all price points.

The fundamental purpose of the brand is differentiation and this brand identity persists exclusively in consumers' minds with their perceptions of the product. The brand strengthens a product's long-term competitive position by retaining a positive perception in the minds of consumers. For branding to be successful, consumers must be convinced that there exist meaningful differences between products or services within the same category.

Building brand equity requires a long-term perspective and investment. Four stages of consumer experience eventually lead to positive brand equity: (1) the consumer becomes aware of the brand and learns what it offers versus competitors; (2) the consumer tries the product; (3) consumers who like the brand become repeat purchasers and develop emotional connections to the brand; and (4) brand loyalty increases so that no adequate substitute for the brand exists in the consumer's mind. For these steps to be accomplished, long-term analysis and planning on brand positioning in the marketplace is required.

An example illustrates these stages. Lacoste is a high-end French clothing manufacturer known for its shirts by a signature crocodile logo. The company became popular in the US when it entered the market in the 1950s. General Mills acquired the crocodile brand in 1969 and it continued to increase in popularity throughout the 1970s. Yet in the mid-1980s, in order to further grow sales, General Mills lowered prices and expanded the distribution from strictly high-end stores to discount outlets. The short-term outcome was predictably an immediate revenue increase. However, within a number of years, the brand lost its prestige image and profit margins flattened. By 1990, sales were slumping and Lacoste was facing a brand management crisis. General Mills decided to sell the brand and the change in leadership refocused the marketing strategy by raising prices, using celebrity endorsements, and limiting distribution to high-end retailers. The change in marketing efforts initially had minimal effect on revenue. Nonetheless, Lacoste had the long-term insight to stick with the reversal in marketing strategy, and it gradually restored the high-status image. Since that time, sales have increased 800 percent. Had the leadership stuck with its short-term focus, it would likely not have revived the brand.[19]

How Brand Equity "Bleeds through" the Other Marketing Variables Like Advertising, and Influences Them

Advertising works better if brand equity is higher. The influence of brand equity "bleeds through" into the other important marketing variables. High brand loyalty and awareness can reduce marketing costs because of the credibility already associated with the brand. This can influence buying decisions, protect market share, and support pricing premiums. Strong brand equity can help achieve success for new products introduced as brand extensions. It can also enhance consumer confidence and reduce consumer perceptions of risk in new product categories. A long-term marketing strategy should be continually aware of the brand perceptions and work to preserve and develop them through thoughtful use of advertising and promotions.

The role of advertising is significantly shaped by the level of brand equity. For a new brand, the goal is often to build recognition. Consumers must become aware of the product and develop an interest to try it for the first time. At this early stage in the brand equity development, the aim will be to develop awareness within the target segment. This often will require more focus on the product attributes and properties. In contrast, well-recognized brands use advertising to maintain and strengthen their position within the minds of consumers who are already familiar with the brand. The function of advertising for these brands is more focused on influencing the emotional associations with the brand experience. For example, Coca Cola does not need to focus on developing recognition of their product through advertising. However, it still maintains an enormous advertising footprint to shape consumer perception and emotional associations. In practice, these perceptions and emotional connections, in turn, help maintain/improve the brand's SOR in its category.

Price is often perceived as distinct from brand equity, as a factor that consumers evaluate in light of their feelings about a brand. This can be misleading, because price is just as integral to forming a brand's equity as advertising. Price is a source of brand identity and not just a separate counterbalancing variable. For luxury brands, the status of the brand is underpinned by the high price.

The pricing adds to exclusivity and creates a symbol of value that customers enjoy. However, it is not only luxury products that can provide emotional benefit from pricing. Mid-price brands that offer a satisfactory experience and good value can similarly evoke a positive emotion. Increased promotion runs the risk of leading to the perception that the key differentiating feature of the brand is the price. Consumers who buy a product because of a promotion are likely to attribute their purchase to the promotion and not to personal preference for the brand. Promotions can help a brand develop increased familiarity and experience. However, this effect is likely to be small for mature product categories where consumers are already familiar with the brand.

How Long-Term Effects of Marketing, Especially Advertising, Actually Build Up the Equity of a Brand

Marketers rely on advertising as the primary tool to develop and maintain brand equity. Along with product performance and packaging, advertising is an essential driver of brand equity. The basis of brand advertising is to connect with consumers emotionally, rather than rationally, to generate positive responses toward the brand. In particular, "fame" campaigns have been found to be both efficient and effective at building brand equity. A fame campaign refers to advertising that is designed to inspire consumers to a point where they want to share their passion with others, which in turn creates buzz for that brand and increases brand equity. Fame campaigns also increase the brand's profitability as consumers are willing to spend more for a brand that people are talking about. Advertising affects the price elasticity of a brand in two ways: (1) it can increase price elasticity by increasing the number of brands considered; and (2) it can decrease price elasticity by increasing the relative strength of brand preference. If the advertising message is price oriented, it can increase consumer price sensitivity. An increase in volume occurs as well; however, that increase is seen only for the short term. Conversely, if the advertising message is non-price oriented and brand-building, then it lowers consumer price sensitivity. Profits are greater when there is a reduction in price sensitivity rather than an increase in volume, and it has a long-term impact.

The Future of Estimation of Long-Term Marketing Effects

How much is it being used now and will it be higher in the future? Mounting evidence suggests that a brand's ability to compete in the marketplace will be best supported by including a long-term orientation. The potential impact of a marketing campaign on sales and profits extends well beyond the current spending period. Growing empirical verification suggests that only a fraction of the financial return from a marketing investment occurs in the year of the expenditure, with the vast majority of the benefits carrying over into future years.

One recent promising area has emerged in an analysis of long-term effects for a Kellogg's cereal brand, reported by CBS and Nielsen Catalina Services at the April, 2014 Advertising Research Foundation (ARF) conference. In that analysis, a multiplier of about 3.5 was found for the long-term effect as opposed to the 2.0 average that has long been used as an industry placeholder for the "average" effect of long-term versus short-term. Future analyses will shed light on whether or not this new approach to long-term calculations will continue to report 3+ multipliers or will revert back to the 2.0 average.[20] An updated, expanded analysis in this area supported the dynamic that indirect increases on future purchases are driven through a combination of trial as well as increases in loyalty and brand equity.[21] While they repeat support for the general applicability of the 2x multiplier as an industry average, the follow-up paper to the ARF-reported study in *Journal of Advertising Research* also makes the important point that we should move beyond just a simple catch-all multiplier because: "Learning how to increase the long-term effect, therefore, will have a direct impact on how well an advertising campaign will perform now and in the future."[22]

It is also interesting to note that long-term effects can even be extended well beyond consumer packaged goods to include areas such as album purchase. Moe and Fader[23] differentiated, for example, between those sales effects that were due to contemporaneous radio airplay from those attributed to longer-term effects in that industry.

Investor Pressures

Despite the evidence that marketing strategies can yield better long-term returns, many companies still manage brands with a short-term perspective. This shortsightedness is incentivized by Wall Street analysts who use quarterly sales figures to value firms. As investors focus on each quarter's current sales increases, management can feel pressure to rely on effective short-term promotional strategies. This is exacerbated since brand managers generally have short tenures. Any investments that they make in long-term strategies are likely to benefit the performance of subsequent managers, decreasing the motivation for individual managers to take a long-term perspective. Again, one of the objectives of MASB is to properly quantify the value of a brand, and taking into account long-term marketing effects is part of that effort.

Measurement Issues

The issue of measurement remains the most significant limitation for adopting a long-term perspective. In this chapter we have seen that marketing strategies with longer-term impacts are more difficult to measure and attribute. As long as such long-term marketing strategies as advertising, new product introductions, and increased distribution have effects that span over a number of years, it will be difficult to directly accredit the results to the marketing activities themselves.

In this chapter, we have tried to provide an overview of what "long-term" means and why it is so important. However, practitioners continue to lack consensus on the long-term effects even in their most basic constructs: What are they? How does one measure them? The industry could be advanced if there was some established currency-type metrics to measure the carryover effect of advertising over long periods of time. Developments in this area would certainly alter the way companies view marketing expenditures, from being expensed in the current period as a cost, to being considered a longer-term "investment." We can even foresee in the future, given an adequate measurement framework, that it would be possible for certain marketing expenditures to be capitalized and amortized in a manner similar to how R&D investments are accounted for today. The ideal combination would include a blend of capitalization and expensing that is proportional to the longer- versus shorter-term impacts of the marketing activities.

MASB and the Shift toward Quantifiable Methods

With an increasing emphasis on corporate business accountability, organizations today seek new approaches to measure and evaluate the long-term effectiveness of marketing activities. As groups such as MASB advocate measurable standards for marketing research, there may be a gradual shift away from measures based on assumptions to ones which are more quantifiable. With continued advances in database and measurement systems, marketers will be aided by more analytical capabilities to quantitatively measure consumer attitudes, purchase patterns, and rate of return on marketing investments. In this chapter, we have tried to make the case for insuring that such quantification extends to long-term effects of marketing as well.

References

1 David A. Aaker and James M. Carman, 1982, "Are You Overadvertising?," *Journal of Advertising Research*, 22(August): 57–70.
2 Greg Ambach and Mike Hess, 2000, "Measuring Long-Term Effects in Marketing," *Marketing Research Magazine*, Summer: 23–27.

3 Greg Ambach and Mike Hess, 2000, "Measuring Long-Term Effects in Marketing," *Marketing Research Magazine*, Summer: 23–27.
4 Marnik G. Dekimpe and Dominique Hanssens, 1995, "The Persistence of Marketing Effects on Sales," *Marketing Science*, 14(1): 1–21.
5 Marnik G. Dekimpe and Dominique Hanssens, "Persistence Modeling for Assessing Marketing Strategy Performance," in *Assessing Marketing Strategy Performance*, 2004, Cambridge, MA: Marketing Science Institute, pp. 69–93.
6 Daniel P. Amos, 2010, "How I Did It: Aflac's CEO Explains How He Fell for the Duck," *Harvard Business Review*, January–February, available at http://hbr.org/2010/01/how-i-did-it-aflacs-ceo-explains-how-he-fell-for-the-duck/ar/1.
7 Dominique Hanssens (forthcoming), "What is Known about the Long-Term Impact of Advertising," published in this book as Chapter 8, pp. 96–113.
8 Dominique Hanssens (forthcoming), "What is Known about the Long-Term Impact of Advertising," published in this book as Chapter 8, pp. 96–113.
9 Dominique Hanssens (forthcoming), "What is Known about the Long-Term Impact of Advertising," published in this book as Chapter 8, pp. 96–113.
10 Leonard M. Lodish, Magid Abraham, Stuart Kalmenson, Jeanne Livelsberger, Beth Lubetkin, Bruce Richardson, and Mary Ellen Stevens, 1995, "How T.V. Advertising Works: A Meta-Analysis of 389 Real World Split Cable T.V. Advertising Experiments," *Journal of Marketing Research*, 32(2): 125–139.
11 Leonard M. Lodish, Magid Abraham, Stuart Kalmenson, Jeanne Livelsberger, Beth Lubetkin, Bruce Richardson, and Mary Ellen Stevens, 1995, "How T.V. Advertising Works: A Meta-Analysis of 389 Real World Split Cable T.V. Advertising Experiments," *Journal of Marketing Research*, 32(2): 125–139.
12 S. Sriram and M. U. Kalwani, 2007, "Optimal Advertising and Promotion Budgets in Dynamic Markets with Brand Equity as a Mediating Variable," *Management Science*, 53(1): 46–60.
13 Leonard M. Lodish and Carl Mela, 2007, "If Brands Are Built over Years, Why Are They Managed over Quarters?," *Harvard Business Review*, 85(7/8): 104–112.
14 Mela, Carl F., Sunil Gupta, and Donald R. Lehmann, 1997, "The Long Term Impact of Promotion and Advertising on Consumer Brand Choice," *Journal of Marketing Research*, 34(2): 248–261.
15 S. Sriram and M. U. Kalwani, 2007, "Optimal Advertising and Promotion Budgets in Dynamic Markets with Brand Equity as a Mediating Variable," *Management Science*, 53(1): 46–60.
16 Keon Pauwels, Dominique Hanssens, and S. Siddarth, 2002, "The Long-Term Effects of Price Promotions on Category Incidence, Brand Choice, and Purchase Quantity," *Journal of Marketing Research*, 39(4): 421–439.
17 Mela, Carl F., Sunil Gupta, and Donald R. Lehmann, 1997, "The Long Term Impact of Promotion and Advertising on Consumer Brand Choice," *Journal of Marketing Research*, 34(2): 248–261.
18 Available at https://www.ama.org/resources/pages/dictionary.aspx?dLetter=B.
19 Leonard M. Lodish and Carl F. Mela, 2007, "If Brands Are Built over Years, Why Are They Managed over Quarters?," *Harvard Business Review*, 85(7/8): 104–112.
20 Jack Neff, 2014, "Study: Long-Term Sales Lift from Advertising Stronger than Ever," *Advertising Age*, June 10, available at http://adage.com/article/cmo-strategy/study-finds-long-term-ad-effects-strong/293636/.
21 Leslie Wood and David Poltrack, 2015, "Long-Term Ad Effectiveness Measurement—Phase 2," presentation at the 2015 Advertising Research Foundation *Re:Think* Conference, New York: March 17.
22 Leslie Wood and David Poltrack, 2015, "Measuring the Long-Term Effects of Television Advertising," *Journal of Advertising Research*, 55(2): 123–131.
23 Wendy W. Moe and Peter S. Fader, 2001, "A Joint Segmentation Model of Consumers and Products Applied to the Sales of Music Albums," *Journal of Marketing Research*, 38(3): 376–385.

10 Social Media

What Value for Marketing Measurement?

Kate Sirkin

Introduction

Social media, as defined by today's marketing industry, began life in February 2004 with the start of Facebook in the dorms of Harvard University. At that time, no one could have predicted the enormous impact that Facebook, Twitter, Sina Weibo of China and VK of Russia (along with LinkedIn, Instagram, SnapChat, and many other players) would have on both consumer behavior and the business of marketing.

Facebook now has 1.44 billion monthly active users (see Figure 10.1)[1] and Twitter has exceeded 300 million.[2] Weibo has more than 143.8 million[3] and VK more than 80 million.[4]

Consumers use social media mainly to connect with their social network of friends via "following" and "reading" what their "friends" are doing, as well as posting status updates, photos, and videos of what they themselves are doing.

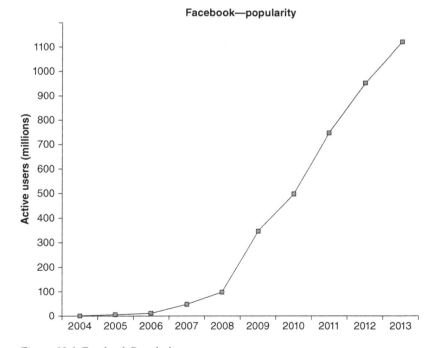

Figure 10.1 Facebook Popularity.

Source: Wikimedia.org.

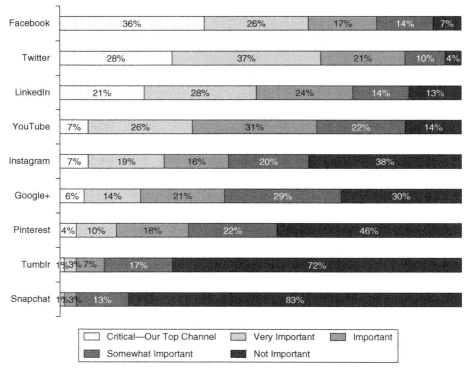

Figure 10.2 How Important Are These Social Media Networks?
Source: Social media trends 2015 research, Rival IQ.

Direct messaging has become more popular now as it is integrated into the functionality of the platforms along with the contact lists for all friends (see Figure 10.5).[5] Gaming only accounts for 4 percent overall of social time spent, but is likely a significantly higher percentage for heavy gamers.

Brand, personalities, and cause-related marketing activities account for less than 10 percent of all activity on social channels right now (see Figure 10.3).[6] As all of the social platforms aggressively look for ways to monetize their audiences via brand marketing, we expect this to grow. At the same time, the platforms need to balance the impact of higher brand presence with time spent and engagement rates.

Paid, Owned, and Earned: Definition and Opportunity

The current media landscape is divided into three core sectors in terms of using media to drive sales for marketers. We think of *paid media* as traditional advertising vehicles that consumers use, watch, listen to, or read—with advertisers paying a publisher for a chance to be exposed to that media vehicle's audience. We think of *owned media* as content or information that a brand owns and controls and can be used to push messages to its current or prospective targets, such as a brand website, a retail location, a sales person, or a piece of content specifically developed for the brand.

We think of *earned media* as additional exposures often connected to some kind of endorsement that one viewer has "shared" with another. Social platforms provide an ideal infrastructure for users to "share" items with their networks (such as videos, messages, competitions,

% time spent engaging with activities	Interacting with cause-driven organizations	IM or chatting	Posting	Engaging with status updates	Checking in	Reading others peoples status updates	Gaming	Interacting with brands, products or services	Interacting with celebs, personalities or fan pages
Male	1.2	7.4	17.9	23.7	1.0	40.7	3.7	2.9	1.5
Female	0.8	8.0	17.4	24.8	0.5	40.7	4.9	2.0	1.0

Figure 10.3 Percentage of Time Spent Engaging with Social Media Activities.

Source: Created by the author from SMG PACE PANEL, USA, Touchpoints 2014, All Adults.

and images). Generally these items have more power to persuade people than paid media, because they come from someone you know and trust, and not a corporation. Marketers now are trying to optimize the balance of *paid, owned*, and *earned* media to reach their objectives at the least cost.

Social Media's Role in Marketing Process: Listening, Measurement, Amplification

Due to the huge sizes of these social platforms and the open nature of the data collected on them, there is significant opportunity in the analysis of that data with specific reference to marketing metrics. The data sets can be thought of as a gigantic focus group or ethnographic study of the pulse of the world. Facebook measures emotion, location, social situation, media consumption, eating habits, vacation logistics, relationship status, and many more personal habits and preferences of many of its users (Figure 10.4).[7]

Clearly, it does not measure everybody on everything, but simply due to its scale and people's willingness to share so much about their lives and habits, we can gain insight and perspective from studying this data. We call this "social listening." Social data also is able to pick up brand sentiment very well for some categories—travel, finance, media, auto, to name but a few. Clever analytics around this data can show where in the consumer journey a brand prospect is and what are the marketing communications most likely to push them to the next stage of that journey. We call this "social measurement."

Social platforms also provide the perfect vehicle to precisely target consumers with very relevant messaging, and give them "packets" of information and content that are easy to "share" with their networks, thereby activating them to influence others on behalf of the brand. We call this "amplification."

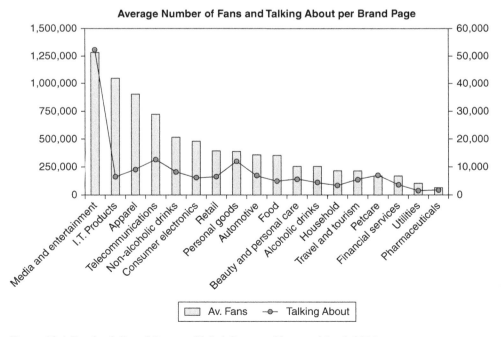

Figure 10.4 Facebook Brand Pages—Global Category Norms—March 2015.

Source: Publicis Group Socialtools.

Social Measurement of the New Automotive Journey

A recent analysis of social media data commissioned by Starcom MediaVest Group found that social media and mobile access have an overwhelming influence over the consumer decision journey associated with an automobile purchase, resulting in a new Automotive Purchasing Model. The updated model unlocks new and expanded opportunities to conventional funnel marketing strategies for auto marketers.

The study used advanced social listening and conversation segmentation to analyze more than ten million automotive conversations and other consumer engagements. Over a 12-month period, data was collected from social media platforms including Twitter, YouTube, public Facebook posts, forums, blogs, and blog comments. Starcom MediaVest Group's Big Fuel partnered with Mashwork for the analysis.

By identifying the data points and quantifying the conversations, the study produced insights that can help marketers better engage with in-market shoppers on social media and measure the impact (Figure 10.5).

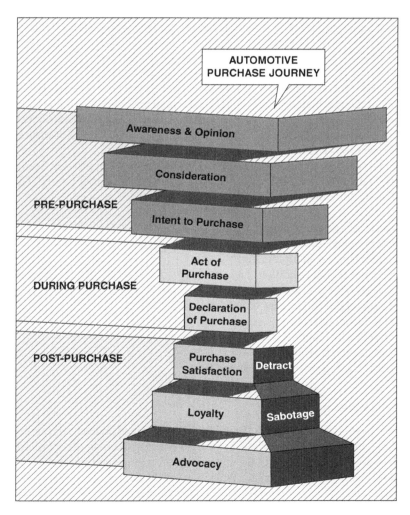

Figure 10.5 Automotive Journey Purchase.

Source: Created by the author.

- **Social media has dramatically and permanently altered the auto purchase journey.** The journey now includes an expanded "during purchase" phase that reflects the rise of social check-ins and status updates via mobile devices and the addition of a "post purchase satisfaction and dissatisfaction" stage.
- **People in the US are having conversations about their auto purchase journey on average 30,000 times per day, 1250 times per hour and 21 times per minute on social media.** Twitter alone generated 184 million potential impressions per day.
- **The single largest type of conversation in the new journey resides in the "consideration" phase at 29 percent.** Brands not included in this phase rarely make it to the final stage of the auto purchase journey.
- **"Declaration of purchase" represents 19 percent of total conversation.** People feel compelled to show off their new cars to their social networks and express how excited they are to have taken ownership. When declaring their car purchases, many new owners choose to attach a photo of their new car to add visual appeal to the excitement.
- **"Post purchase satisfaction" conversation occurs three times more often than post purchase dissatisfaction conversation.** When discussing dissatisfaction, conversation tends to be more passionate and has higher levels of emotion than in positive conversation.

Initial Metrics

Digital platforms clearly offer a myriad of metrics for marketers to gauge how their marketing is working. User engagement metrics include shares, likes, and comments. Behavioral platform-based metrics include page views, time spent, frequency, daily or weekly unique users, as well as outcome metrics based upon actions taken either directly within the digital device or offline, in-store or simply in the consumer's conversations with others.

It is critical to understand what the metrics are needed for and what they can provide from a Marketing Accountability Standards Board (MASB) perspective, and then choose wisely. The MASB characteristics of an ideal metric are listed below.

1. relevant—addresses specific (pending) action;
2. predictive—accurately predicts outcome of (pending) action;
3. objective—not subject to personal interpretation;
4. calibrated—means the same across conditions and cultures;
5. reliable—dependable and stable over time;
6. sensitive—identifies meaningful differences in outcomes;
7. simple—uncomplicated meaning and implications clear;
8. causal—course of action leads to improvement;
9. transparent—subject to independent audit;
10. quality assured—formal/ongoing processes to assure 1–9.

Direct Social Measures (Value and Use)

Direct user base measures have been available to brand and agencies and indeed consumers, based upon every post, share, like, or comment. While helpful for ongoing tracking of the volume of social engagement, they do not clearly link to the financial performance and in many cases only have a size dimension—showing nothing about the quality of the engagement. Many conference and academic papers claim to have figured out the value of a like or a fan[8] and these help us understand how and why social engagement is working for brands.

Though in its infancy, marketers rank social media engagement metrics as a top-ranking metric that marketing teams provide to the CMO (see Figure 10.6).[9] This industry is in a state

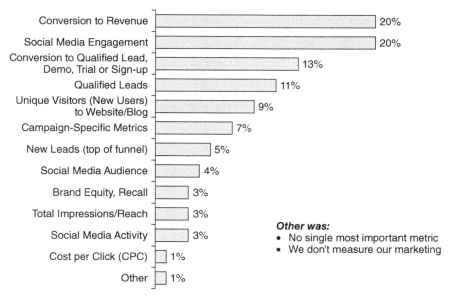

Figure 10.6 What is the MOST Important Marketing Metric Your Team Measures and Reports?
Source: Social Media Trends 2015 Research, Rival IQ.

of rapid growth and change, and any deeper understanding of why something works or does not work provides valuable help for marketers who cannot wait for standard metrics to be validated and calibrated.

Conclusion

Social media is still in considerable flux, with at least 15 promising new companies entering the arena in 2015.[10] As cross-screen media expands, marketing measurement needs to encompass viewing on televisions, desktop, and laptop computers, as well as mobile devices. A fundamental rethink of the traditional purchase funnel is needed if marketers want to effectively target media and messaging. Marketing metrics must be more integrated into workflow.

While advancements have been made in understanding, it is still a "Wild West" in terms of accepted and trusted metrics. As new ones emerge, MASB's Marketing Metric Audit Protocol process will evaluate their usefulness and their relationships to measures of financial performance. By identifying ideal metrics for social media marketing, future investment in this rapidly growing industry will yield much higher returns on investment.

References

1 *Facebook Popularity*, originally uploaded on en.wikipedia. Licensed under CC BY-SA 3.0 via Wikimedia Commons, http://commons.wikimedia.org/wiki/File:Facebook_popularity.PNG#/media/File:Facebook_popularity.PNG.
2 *Number of Monthly Active Facebook Users Worldwide as of 1st Quarter 2015 (in Millions)*, Statista, http://www.statista.com/statistics/264810/number-of-monthly-active-facebook-users-worldwide/.
3 "Sina Weibo News, Trends, Stats & Insights," *China Internet Watch*, http://chinainternetwatch.com/tag/sina-weibo/.
4 "Vkontake Company News," *Crunch Base*, http://crunchbase.com/organization/vk.

5 *Social Media Trends 2015 Research*, Rival IQ, available at https://www.rivaliq.com/blog/wp-content/uploads/2015/02/Social-Media-Trends-2015-Research-Report-Feb-2015.pdf.
6 SMG Pace Panel, USA Touchpoints 2014. (Proprietary database of SMG.)
7 Publicis Groupe Social Tools. (Proprietary database of Publicis.)
8 "Value of a Facebook Fan," *Syncapse*, http://syncapse.com/value-of-a-facebook-fan-2013/#.VZLjFE05BD8.
9 *Social Media Trends 2015 Research*, Rival IQ.
10 "Social Media Companies to Watch in 2015," *Forbes*, http://www.forbes.com/sites/ilyapozin/2014/12/17/15-social-media-companies-to-watch-in-2015/.

Section III
Linking Finance and Marketing

11 The Relationship of Marketing and Finance

Donald E. Sexton

Introduction

A major goal of most businesses is to increase the value of the business. The value of a business consists of the present value of its cash flow over time. In turn, cash flow depends on profit after taxes, depreciation, and changes in various items on the balance sheet such as accounts receivable, accounts payable, inventories, and plant and equipment.

All of these financial metrics are summarized in the return on investment (ROI) Tree shown in Figure 11.1. The relationships among these financial metrics are well-defined and well-understood. For example, turnover is equal to the amount of money taken in by a business from sales in a particular period. What is less well-defined and less well-understood are the relationships between these financial metrics and the marketing activities that fall under the general heading "selling expense."

Finance managers focus much of their attention on the financial metrics in the ROI Tree. Marketing managers focus much of their attention on the marketing activities and corresponding expenditures summarized as selling expense.[11]

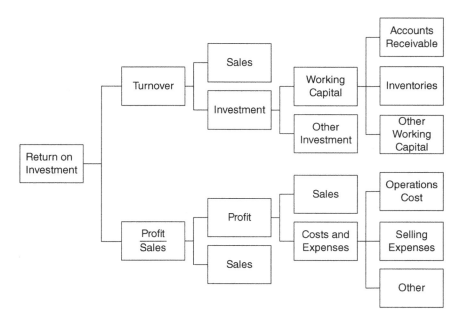

Figure 11.1 ROI Tree.

Source: Created by the author.

Marketing Metrics		Financial Metrics	
Awareness	Satisfaction	Sales	EVA
Knowledge	Reach	Turnover	Cost of capital
Liking	Frequency	Cost of goods sold	Return on sales
Preference	Engagement	Selling expense	Return on investment
Conviction	Price premium	Overhead	Accounts receivable
Trial	Website visits	Contribution	Debt
Purchase	Cost per click	Gross margin	Quarterly earnings
Usage	Life-time customer value	Depreciation	Share price
Loyalty		Profit	
Recommend	Market share	Cash flow	
Complaints	Sales		

Figure 11.2 Marketing and Finance Metrics.

Source: Created by the author.

These differing viewpoints often result in debates between finance and marketing about how to set marketing budgets and how to allocate marketing resources or, worse, create silos where finance and marketing managers do not talk to each other. Often there is little overlap between the metrics commonly used by marketing managers and those commonly used by finance managers (Figure 11.2).

Compounding this communication gap is the use by marketers of measures, such as awareness, that may be informative when managing and monitoring marketing activities, but may not have a clear relationship with financial results.

How Finance Views Marketing

Several surveys have been conducted by the Association of National Advertisers and others investigating how finance managers view marketers.[5, 6, 7, 8, 9, 10, 21] In general, these studies suggest that finance managers do not think marketing managers understand the financial impact of their actions.

In one survey of finance managers, approximately 60 percent of respondents said they did not believe the numbers in the financial forecasts of marketers, and over 70 percent stated that they did not use marketing inputs in their financial analyses.[21] Eighty percent of senior managers expressed a lack of confidence in marketing's ability to forecast the impact of marketing activities on financial outcomes.[9, 10]

Interestingly, many marketing managers seem to agree with the finance managers. In several studies, no more than 30 percent of marketing managers surveyed had confidence that they could forecast the impact of a 10 percent cut in their budgets.[5, 6, 7, 8, 9, 10] One major study found that approximately 60 percent of marketing managers were not using any information about marketing ROI when determining their budgets, and 22 percent of those surveyed stated that the *only* metric they used for their decisions was awareness.[24]

The result is that in only about one-quarter of companies do marketing and finance appear to cooperate fully and use common metrics.[7, 8, 9, 10] Consequently, in the majority of companies, marketing budgets are frequently determined by history, not by use of forward-looking metrics.[6, 21]

How Marketing Views Finance

While many finance managers seem to distrust marketers' metrics and forecasts, marketing managers have complaints about finance managers. They view finance managers as being short-term oriented. Research has corroborated that belief—in a study of hundreds of managers from around the world, spanning 30 years, the financial objectives of United States' companies were consistently found to be far more short-term oriented than companies in the rest of the world.[30, 32]

Marketers understand that customers represent relationships which generate cash flows over time (lifetime customer value), and these relationships can be created with effective branding and communications actions. Many marketers believe that finance managers focus primarily on individual transactions—a short-term outcome—rather than on the long-term relationship with the customer and therefore treat any marketing outlay as an expense instead of an investment.

Implications of the Relationship between Marketing and Finance

If marketing and finance approach strategy from differing viewpoints, then that can impact organizations in many ways, including: developing strategy, determining marketing activities, and evaluating the marketing budget.

Developing Strategy

Some marketing activities, such as price changes, promotions, and certain kinds of communications, such as reminder ads, can be expected to deliver results in the short run. However, other marketing activities, such as new product introductions and brand-building communications, may require long periods of time to achieve an acceptable financial return. Imposition of short-run financial objectives limits the marketing strategies that might be considered.[20] During the 1980s, the decline of the United States' consumer electronics and automotive industries was due in part to the quarterly earnings focus of U.S. managers versus the longer-run view of Japanese managers.[39]

Determining Marketing Activities

Use of short-run financial objectives may result in focus on marketing activities that can be expected to result in quick financial returns, but which may steal revenue or profits from future time periods. A variety of studies over many years have shown that advertising leads to long-term financial results by building brand loyalty, while promotion leads to short-term financial results by encouraging price-searching behavior.[22, 31]

Evaluating Marketing Budget

Marketing success occurs in most industries when a relationship is developed with a customer and that relationship generates cash flow over time—the lifetime value of a customer, which will always be greater than the value of an individual transaction with that customer. Ignoring lifetime customer value means that marketing efforts are evaluated in the short term. Often those short-term results may be insufficient to justify a marketing expenditure and may lead to sub-optimal marketing budgets.

How Marketing Drives Financial Results

To unite marketing and finance, what is needed is a conceptual framework and metrics that show how marketing efforts lead to financial results and, therefore, how marketing metrics are related to financial metrics. Marketing improves the financial performance of organizations—either through increasing demand in units or increasing the ability to charge a higher price, or both. The key metric that unites marketing and finance is *perceived value* (Figure 11.3).[38]

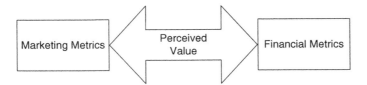

Figure 11.3 Perceived Value, and Marketing and Financial Metrics.

Source: Created by the author.

Perceived value links marketing metrics to financial metrics so that marketing managers have a common basis for discussion with finance managers. Perceived value has been shown in several studies to have a strong relationship with financial metrics such as revenue, contribution, and stock price.[1, 2, 4, 12, 16, 17, 23] The relationships these researchers found between perceived value and financial outcomes are strong and, perhaps, are arguably stronger than the relationships between metrics such as awareness and knowledge (from the purchase funnel model,[13, 19] although there are empirical weaknesses in this model[3, 37, 40, 41]) and financial outcomes.

Perceived Value

Perceived value is the maximum that a customer will pay for a unit of the product or service (Figure 11.4). Perceived value is *not* price but the ceiling on price. Sometimes perceived value is referred to as "willingness to pay." When a price is set, the difference between perceived value and the price represents the *incentive* for the customer to purchase the product or service. The difference between the price and variable cost per unit is the *margin* or *contribution* per unit.

For example, if a customer is comparing a system offered by Huawei to a system offered by one of Huawei's competitors, such as Alcatel-Lucent, the customer will have in mind the maximum they might be willing to pay for each offering. That perceived value will depend on the benefits each company offers, but also on the reputation or brand of each company providing those benefits. In making their choice of suppliers, the customer will have in mind the perceived value for each

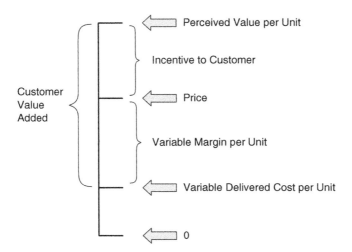

Figure 11.4 Perceived Value.

Source: Created by the author.

offering as well as the price. The larger the difference between that perceived value and the price, the more likely is the customer to purchase from that supplier, other things being equal.

Perceived value varies by customer since different customers may have different priorities regarding benefits, and different customers may have different perceptions as to how successfully a particular brand of a product or service might satisfy their needs. Customers who regard a brand as having approximately the same perceived value are typically members of the same market segment.

Perceived value does not remain constant over time. It depends on customer preferences and knowledge, which may change, and competitors, which may change. For example, perceived value can be expected to be highest in the rapid growth stage of the competitive life cycle when customers are expert and direct competitors are few. During the later stages of the life cycle, such as the mature stage, perceived value per unit will be lower and, finally, in the decline stage perceived value may fall below the unit cost of the product or service due to the emergence of a new product or service in the marketplace—as, for example, the perceived value of film fell markedly in comparison with digital imaging in most applications.

Perceived value can vary with the customer use situation. If an operations manager needs a specific part to keep a production line running, the perceived value of that part will be higher than if the purchase is a routine purchase made to restock inventory.

The impact of brand on perceived value varies by product or service. As one might expect, brand as a percentage of perceived value is highest for luxury products and lowest for industrial commodity products.[18] Nonetheless, the brand does play a role in determining the perceived value of the product or service in both consumer and industrial buying situations. When Huawei was becoming a global brand, their initial challenge was to communicate their performance to prospective customers who were not familiar with them, so that customers would associate their performance with their brand.

What Is Marketing?

Marketing is the management of perceived value. All the decisions and actions of a marketer—including the famous four Ps (product, price, place, promotion), as well as strategic choices such as targeting markets and positioning products or services and building brands—affect the perceived value or willingness to pay of a customer.[34] Perceived value has been selected by brand managers to be the most important single metric to employ in managing their brands.[28] Perceived value is both measurable and actionable and is used by many well-known companies to guide their marketing decisions.[14, 25, 29]

Estimating Perceived Value

Some customers perform elaborate cost–benefit analyses to determine their perceived value in a given situation. Others use judgment. Most customers likely use a mixture of quantitative analyses and judgment to arrive at their perceived value, but all customers know the value—as perceived by them—of any product or service they are considering: it is the maximum that they are willing to pay. Organizations need to know the perceived values of their customers. There are many ways to estimate perceived value.[35, 38]

In industrial purchase situations, often the "value-in-use" approach is used. For example, costs to the customer of using different brands of routers are compared. Then a "price" is found, which would make the operating cost of the selling organization's router equal to that of the most attractive alternative router from a competitor. That "price" would be the maximum the customer might pay for the selling organization's router and, together with the brand impact, would be the perceived value of their router. The price the selling organization quotes would need to be below that perceived value to provide an incentive for the customer to purchase.

For consumer products and services, often constrained choice models are employed to estimate perceived value. The two most common forms of constrained choice models are conjoint analysis and discrete choice modeling. With conjoint analysis, for example, a refrigerator manufacturer might ask a respondent to choose among offerings of refrigerators of different size, price, and brand name. If there were 3 sizes, 2 prices, and 2 brand names, then the respondent would be faced with 12 choices. The respondent would be asked to rank these choices from the one they like most to the one they like least. From such information, it is possible to estimate not only the perceived value in monetary terms of any of the offerings but also how much each cubic foot of storage space is worth and how much each brand name is worth.

If quantitative analyses are unavailable, judgment can be used to estimate perceived value. In fact, sales representatives use judgment all the time in their negotiations with customers in order to arrive at the appropriate price. For more information on methods for estimating perceived value, see Sexton and Gaber[14] and Sexton.[38]

Perceived Value Drives Revenue

One can predict revenue with perceived value, because perceived value is the customer's financial evaluation of a product or service. A customer will not consider purchasing a product or service unless the price is equal to or below its perceived value. The prices of competing products and services are also considered by the customer. The customer will likely purchase the product or service with the highest incentive per unit—perceived value per unit less price. For example, if two brands of bottled water have the same price, but brand A has a higher perceived value than brand B, then the customer will likely purchase brand A since it has a higher incentive per unit.

Perceived value predicts revenue through the demand curve. A demand curve shows the quantity of a product or service that will be purchased depending on the price of a product or service. The height of a demand curve is perceived value. Demand curves show the distribution of perceived value among all the customers in a market. Customers who value a product or service highly are willing to pay a high price and are on the left side of the demand curve. Customers who are very price sensitive are on the right side of the demand curve. The height of the demand curve at any point represents the perceived value of customers in a specific group.

Marketing activities change perceived value. Changes in perceived value shift the demand curve for the product or service (Figure 11.5). If the change in perceived value is positive,

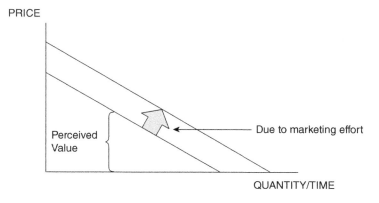

Figure 11.5 How Marketing Works.

Source: Created by the author.

the demand curve shifts to the right.[26] However, sometimes a company takes an action which negatively affects perceived value. Then, the demand curve shifts to the left.

Sexton's Revenue Law

The impact of changes in perceived value on revenue are exponential. Based on microeconomics, assuming that price is determined optimally, one can show the following relationship between relative change in perceived value and relative change in revenue:[38]

Relative change in revenue = (Relative change in perceived value)^2

For example, if perceived value is expected to increase by 20 percent (relative change equal to 1.2), then revenue for the next time period can be expected to increase 44 percent (since 1.2^2 is equal to 1.44). If perceived value is expected to decrease by 20 percent (relative change equal to 0.8), then revenue for the next time period can be expected to decrease 36 percent (since 0.8^2 is equal to 0.64).

Sexton's Revenue Law has been utilized by companies as part of their regular planning process. One large consumer products company used it to evaluate all their pricing in Asia as well as to forecast revenue. Perceived value was found to predict next year's revenue for several products with R-squared values greater than 0.9.[25]

Customer Value Added Drives Contribution

Customer Value Added or CVA® is the difference between perceived value per unit of the product or service and the *variable cost per unit* of the product or service (as per Figure 11.4 above). CVA® represents the net amount of value—as perceived by customers—which the organization is providing to society. The CVA® concept is similar to that of consumer surplus in economics. Microeconomics can be employed to determine the specific relationship between changes in contribution and changes in CVA®—again assuming that price is determined optimally.

Products or services fail if their perceived value per unit is allowed to fall below variable cost per unit, causing CVA® to become negative. In those circumstances, the cost of producing a unit of the product or service is greater than the price anyone will be willing to pay for it, so the organization is wasting society's resources and, if the organization is not subsidized in some way, the organization will fail.

On the other hand, the higher the CVA® of an organization's product or service, the more perceived value per unit it is providing to society in excess of costs and the more success the organization will enjoy—either through high unit sales, high variable margin per unit, or both. CVA® predicts contribution in the same way as perceived value predicts revenue—through the mechanism of the demand curve. Contribution (also known as variable margin) is equal to revenue less variable costs. If a demand curve shifts to the right and up due to an increase in perceived value, then contribution will increase.

Sexton's Contribution Law

Relative change in contribution = (Relative change in CVA®)^2

For example, if CVA® is expected to increase by 10 percent due to a marketing action, then contribution can be expected to increase 21 percent (since 1.1^2 is equal to 1.21). If CVA® is expected to decrease by 10 percent, then contribution can be expected to decrease by 19 percent (since 0.9^2 is equal to 0.81).

Profit, Cash Flow, and Share Price

Perceived value predicts revenue directly. CVA® predicts contribution directly. Since contribution is an important component of profits and cash flow, CVA® also indirectly predicts profit and cash flow. To the extent that predicted profit and cash flow influence shareholder value, CVA® also predicts shareholder value. These relationships between perceived value, CVA®, and financial results have been empirically verified by the author[25] as well as by many other researchers working with a variety of data sets.[1, 2, 12, 16, 17, 23]

In summary, maximizing perceived value and maximizing CVA® maximizes most financial result metrics. Therefore, perceived value and CVA® can be employed to predict the financial return from *any* type of marketing action that affects perceived value or CVA® per unit.[29] These include both strategic decisions and tactical decisions such as:

- media spending;
- message content;
- message creative expression;
- social media;
- logos;
- public relations;
- endorsements;
- customer service;
- pricing;
- distribution;
- modification of product or service;
- new product or service;
- product or brand repositioning;
- brand extension;
- targeting markets.

To illustrate the process of evaluating the financial impact of a marketing decision, suppose naming a stadium is predicted by analysis of CVA® to add $200m to the present value of total contribution over time. If the naming cost exceeds $200m, based on financial criteria, one would not want to proceed since the net contribution of the action would be negative. On the other hand, if the naming cost is $180m, one would consider going ahead with the naming since the net increase in contribution would be $20m. However, one would compare the net contribution return due to the naming to the net contribution return from other marketing alternatives under consideration. Perhaps that same $180m invested in social media might return more than $200m in total contribution for a net contribution in excess of $20m. If so, then perhaps the social media option should be chosen.[37]

Marketing's Impact on Financial Results over Time

As customers and resellers become more knowledgeable regarding the product or service, and as more competitors enter the market, the competitive environment changes. These changes are shown in four metrics that define the competitive life cycle: unit sales, margin per unit, cost per unit, and perceived value per unit (Figure 11.6).

Competitive Life Cycle

The competitive life cycle consists of five stages: introduction, rapid growth, competitive turbulence, maturity, and decline.[33, 34] The first entrant into a product or service category is known

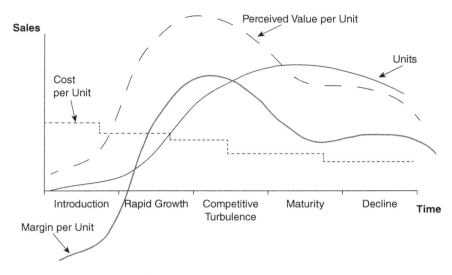

Figure 11.6 Competitive Life Cycle.
Source: Created by the author.

as the pioneer. During this introduction stage, the competing products or services are usually from old technologies. In the second stage, rapid growth, a few direct competitors—the "fast followers"—enter to challenge the pioneer. The competitive turbulence stage is characterized by many competitors, most of whom are imitators of the products or services introduced by the pioneer and the fast followers. Frequently, price competition occurs during the competitive turbulence stage, since that is how the imitators try to differentiate their offerings. In turn, price wars may result in "shakeout"—none of the producers may survive. Those producers that survive move to the maturity stage when market growth is relatively slow and steady and brands provide protection for share positions.[27] During the decline stage, new products or services based on a new technology are being introduced, which leads to falling prices for the old products or services. (For an example of the dynamics of the competitive life cycle, see Gillette and Winter,[15] for an account of Blackberry over time.) Of course, stages can repeat if, for example, new uses or new markets are found for a product or service.

Changes in Customer Value versus Changes in Cost

Initially, perceived value per unit starts low during the introduction stage. The exception would be brand extensions where the perceived value of a new product or service is enhanced by an already existing positive brand image. Perceived value per unit increases during the introduction stage as marketing communications and customer experience build knowledge of the benefits of the product or service.[36]

Perceived value per unit may reach a peak during the rapid growth stage, but then falls as imitators enter during the competitive turbulence stage. Perceived value is always *relative* to other offerings available in the marketplace so decreases as copycats become competitors.

During the maturity stage, perceived value per unit is relatively stable, as most of the benefits of the product or service are known by customers and resellers. Perceived value per unit then falls during the decline stage as products or services based on new technologies enter the market.

Cost per unit is high at the start of the competitive life cycle, due to production costs and marketing expense. Over time, if managed well, cost per unit should fall as scale of production increases and as value-engineering leads to savings in production costs per unit.

CVA® can be expected to be highest during the rapid growth stage and margin per unit can also be expected to be at a maximum then. Shakeout—when producers fail—typically happens during the competitive turbulence stage. During that stage, perceived value per unit is falling due to the imitators and, if a producer cannot reduce their costs sufficiently, their margin will be crushed between the falling perceived value curve and the cost curve.

Companies can survive shakeout if they manage their perceived value and costs competently. Those that do survive move to the maturity stage and may enjoy steady profits *until* new products or services enter the market. Then they survive only if they are among those introducing the new product or service. If the perceived value of the old product (e.g., cassette tapes) is zero, then customers will not purchase the old product at any price.

Toward a New Relationship between Marketing and Finance

Marketing and finance should have a common goal—the financial success of their organization. However, the metrics they need to track those goals need to be the same, otherwise they may try to follow different paths.

Mutual Understanding

Mutual understanding begins with understanding how each side makes decisions and how those decisions will affect their common goal—the financial success of their organization. Perceived value is a concept that is based on both marketing and economic theory, so it should be understandable to managers from the marketing side and from the finance side. Once, the author was conducting a marketing course and a finance manager happened to attend the lecture on the competitive life cycle where perceived value per unit, cost per unit, and CVA® per unit were explained. His after-class comment as he left the lecture room was: "Now I finally understand what marketing does."

Employing Mutual Metrics

Perceived value and CVA® are metrics that can be understood and employed by both marketing managers and finance managers. They have been proven in theory and in practice, and are endorsed by many managers. A common metric can significantly increase the understanding and the cooperation between marketing and finance. In particular, perceived value links marketing efforts, such as building brand attributes, to pricing.[35] Otherwise, these two decisions tend to become separated between marketing and finance.[25] Perceived value brings marketing and finance together by relating investments in branding (marketing) to future pricing power and future revenue and profits (finance).

Summary and Conclusions

The metrics perceived value and CVA® provide the needed link between marketing metrics and finance metrics.[38] These metrics give managers steering control over marketing decisions, because perceived value predicts future demand for a product or service—the ability to predict financial outcomes before marketing actions are implemented—and operational guidance as to what marketing must do to achieve desired financial objectives. Perceived value and CVA®

should be monitored regularly and should be included among the key performance indicators on *both* marketing and finance dashboards.

References

1. Aaker, David and Robert Jacobson, 1994, "The Financial Information Content of Perceived Quality," *Journal of Marketing Research*, 31: 191–201.
2. Aaker, David and Robert Jacobson, 2001, "The Value Relevance of Brand Attitudes in High-Technology Markets," *Journal of Marketing Research*, 38(4): 485–493.
3. Agres, Stuart, *Brand Asset Valuator® Presentation*, 1996, New York: Columbia Business School.
4. Aksoy, Lerzan, Bruce Cooil, Christopher Groening, Timothy L. Keiningham, and Atakan Yalcin, 2008, "The Long-Term Stock Market Valuation of Customer Satisfaction," *Journal of Marketing*, 72(4): 105–122.
5. Association of National Advertisers, *The State of Marketing Accountability Study*, 2004, New York: ANA.
6. Association of National Advertisers, *The Path to Marketing Accountability Study*, 2005, New York: ANA.
7. Association of National Advertisers, *The Path to Marketing Accountability Study*, 2006, New York: ANA.
8. Association of National Advertisers, *Marketing Accountability Study*, 2007, New York: ANA.
9. Association of National Advertisers, *Marketing Accountability Study*, 2008, New York: ANA.
10. Association of National Advertisers, *Marketing Accountability Study*, 2009, New York: ANA.
11. Beaman, Karen, Gregory R. Guy, and Donald E. Sexton, *Managing and Measuring Return on Marketing Investment, Research Report 1435–08-RR*, 2008, New York: The Conference Board.
12. Robert D. Buzzell and Bradley T. Gale, *The PIMS* Principles*, 1987, New York: Free Press.
13. Colley, Russell, *Defined Advertising Goals for Measured Advertising Results*, 1961, New York: ANA.
14. Gaber, Sabrina, Donald E. Sexton, Kamal Sen, and Alfred Lin, 2009, "Customer Input: Incorporate Perceived Value into Marketing Strategy," *Business Digest*, (October): 3–9.
15. Gillette, F., Brad, D. and Winter, C., 2013, "The Rise and Fall of BlackBerry," *Bloomberg Business Week*, (December): 54–61.
16. James R. Gregory, *Driving Brand Equity*, 2005, New York: ANA.
17. James R. Gregory, *The Best of Branding*, 2003, New York: McGraw-Hill.
18. Interbrand, *Presentation on Brand Valuation*, 2000, New York: Columbia University.
19. Lavidge, Robert and Gary Steiner, 1961, "A Model for Predictive Measurements of Advertising Effectiveness," *Journal of Marketing*, (October): 137–169.
20. Lodish, Leonard and Carl Mela, 2007, "If Brands Are Built Over Years, Why Are They Managed Over Quarters?," *Harvard Business Review*, (July/August).
21. Marshall, Jeffrey, 2008, "Finance: Friend or Foe?," Paper presented at the 2008 ANA Marketing Conference, July.
22. Mela, Carl, Sunil Gupta, and Donald R. Lehmann, 1997, "The Long-Term Impact of Promotion and Advertising on Consumer Brand Choice," *Journal of Marketing Research*, 34(2): 248–264.
23. Mizik, Natalie and Robert Jacobson, 2008, "The Financial Value Impact Perceptual Brand Attributes," *Journal of Marketing Research*, 45: 15–32.
24. Rogers, David and Donald E. Sexton, *Marketing ROI in the Era of Big Data*, 2012, New York: BRITE and NY AMA.
25. Sen, Kamal, 2015, "Why PV Models Are Necessary for Complete Understanding," Working paper.
26. Sexton, D. E., 1972, "A Microeconomic Model of the Effects of Advertising," *Journal of Business*, (January): 29–41.
27. Sexton, D. E., *Branding 101*, 2008, Hoboken, NJ: John Wiley & Sons, Inc.
28. Sexton, D. E., 2005, "Building the Brand Scorecard," *The Advertiser*, (February): 54–58.
29. Sexton, D. E., 2010, "Competing with Customer Value Added," *Effective Executive*, (February): 44–47.
30. Sexton, D. E. and Susan Burke, *ANA Global Brand Equity Report*, 2013, New York: ANA.
31. Sexton, D. E., 1970, "Estimation of Marketing Policy Effects on Sales," *Journal of Marketing Research*, (August): 338–347.

32 Sexton, D. E., 2015, "International Marketing Strategy—Does Country Nationality Matter?," *Journal of Marketing Trends*, (January): 47–54.
33 Sexton, D. E., 2004, "Managing Brand Equity over Time," *Quarterly Review of Canada China Business Council*, (Summer): 9–11.
34 Sexton, D. E., *Marketing 101*, 2nd edition, 2009, Hoboken, NJ: John Wiley & Sons, Inc.
35 Sexton, D. E., 2006, "Pricing, Perceived Value, and Communications," *The Advertiser*, (April): 56–58.
36 Sexton, D. E., 2006, "Principles for Building Strong Brands," *Effective Executive*, (August): 12–15.
37 Sexton, D. E., 2014, "Using Metrics to Achieve 'Steering Control' of Your Marketing Actions," *Effective Executive*, 17(1): 7–19.
38 Sexton, D. E., *Value above Cost: How CVA® Drives Financial Performance, the Most Important Metric You've Never Used*, 2009, Upper Saddle River, NJ: Wharton School Publishing.
39 Toyo Keizai, 1981, "Corporate Objectives of US and Japanese Firms," August 20.
40 Vakratsas, Demetrios and Tim Ambler, 2009, "Advertising Effects," *Journal of Marketing*, (January): 26–43.
41 Vaughn, R., 1980, "How Advertising Works," *Journal of Advertising Research*, 1: 57–66.

12 Creating a Partnership between Marketing and Finance

James Meier

Introduction

Let us acknowledge that in many organizations, marketing and finance have different definitions of success, goals for how to get there, and standards of measurement by which they judge when those goals have been achieved. That being the case, it may seem virtually impossible to synthesize the two sets of goals and values, especially for marketing and finance professionals contemplating one another from across the figurative divide.

Before we can offer recommendations for how this partnership might occur, it is important to understand where specifically the trouble lies in creating it and what roadblocks organizations can expect to face as they undertake the challenge. In part, as a way of overcoming the barriers to creating this partnership, it can be helpful to recognize what an organization will get out of strong cooperation and aligning interests to create mutually desirable goals, which lead to enterprise success. To better illustrate this point, we will offer a series of hypothetical and real situations to illustrate what happens when an organization's marketing and finance departments eschew all relationship, but also what is possible when they decide to work together.

Before we get there, however, we will offer a brief overview of the history behind American organizational structure in general and the impacts this has had on marketing and finance in particular.

The Historical Relationship between Marketing and Finance in Corporate America

At its most basic, a corporation is a group of individuals with the legal right to operate as a single entity, to present a single face to the world. It is perhaps ironic, then, that once one crosses the threshold of many corporations, one finds fragmentation, lack of communication, and prolific individuality. Of course, individuals with the ability to act autonomously are a crucial part of a healthy organization, but the other traits are not so desirable; neither does this pattern exist solely in the domain of large, publicly held corporations; privately held companies may suffer from the same problems. The main point here is that the structures of many organizations are functionally siloed, resulting in departments fragmented from one another and without good channels through which to connect, or reliable methods of establishing common interests.

Enter the matrix organization. The classic matrix model pairs two different "organizing dimensions" of a company in a grid, one set of parameters or divisions running along the top of the grid and another down the side. For instance, an organization might choose to establish different departmental teams—operations, sales, marketing, and finance—each with a different product focus. So there might be an operations team for each of products A, B, and C, a sales team for products A, B, and C, a marketing team for products A, B, and C, and a finance team for products A, B, and C. Sy and D'Annunzio call this the balanced matrix.[1] Another common structure is the functional matrix, in which departments remain functionally distinct, but the organization institutes means by which they are to communicate and collaborate. Lastly, in the project matrix, "employees move between functional departments and projects and respectively retain membership with those units during the same period," and there is a strong emphasis on the project as defining paradigm.[2] Of course, matrix organizations can become very complicated or reflect subtle variations, but these are the typical foundational models.

The most compelling upside of the matrix model is that business strategies and activities are informed, executed, and evaluated from all relevant functional perspectives rather than a myopic siloed viewpoint that may in fact not align with the goals of the broad enterprise. However, matrices have their downsides, too. A matrix may complicate the issue of who should bear responsibility, and it complicates the employee's job by requiring that they report to multiple bosses and interact with multiple departments—whose expectations, goals, and standards may not always be explicitly aligned. It "can create ambiguity and conflict" as well as increased costs from additional management and administration, and can increase "likelihood of resistance to change as employees may attribute the matrix with loss of status, authority, and control over traditional domain." Plus, when organizations try to institute matrixed relationships to employees who are used to more traditional roles, employees' refusal to give up these siloed roles can cause problems with the root functionality of the matrix.[3]

Whether or not companies always "get it" when they move toward a matrix approach is the subject of some debate. Organizational theorist, Jay R. Galbraith, contends that while many companies fail to meet the objectives that spurred them to adopt a matrix model in the first place, and consequently abandon or grow frustrated with the model, some of the largest companies in the world use them with staggering success. He offers as examples Nokia, IBM, Procter & Gamble, and Toyota.[4] What are these companies doing right that others are missing? Galbraith contends that successful companies: (1) institute leaders "who grew up on both sides of the matrix, manage conflict, work as a team, create clear roles and understand power balancing"; (2) use a star model, which integrates organization design criteria, people, structure, rewards, and processes; and (3) manage change effectively, keeping lines of communication open and honoring the team-based roots of matrix design.[5]

What is clear is that organizations today are moving away from traditional organizational structures with siloed functions to models that bring departments together, meld them and their goals, provide broader cross-functional roles for employees and managers, and open the lines of communication. In these organizations, support functions such as human resources (HR) or finance continue to exist unto themselves, but then matrix in very closely with the outwardly facing, business-driving functions such as operations, sales, and marketing.

However, even organizations with a deeply embedded cross-functional mindset are siloed to some degree. There are good reasons for this, especially in the largest of companies. For example, it would be hard to run an efficient company with HR teams scattered across the organization, operating with entirely different hiring requirements or HR protocols. Equally, it would not work for finance people to enforce entirely dissimilar compliance practices or to use inconsistent accounting standards and principles. Rather, one of the main efforts of HR is to ensure fairness and equality, applying the same criteria for what constitutes a good employee to the entire enterprise. Similarly, the finance function is there to ensure that everyone in the company follows the same standards and criteria when making financial decisions.

Even when organizations *do* adopt standards that permeate an organization, it is not uncommon for these standards to have little meaning or value-adding impact outside the source department. In a traditional siloed organization, for example, finance individuals might operate strictly as accountants—closing the books, cranking out spreadsheets, and producing monthly reports that do little to provide any insight to the actual decision-makers. The problem is, others in the organization might have desperately needed and willingly welcomed that insight. Financial metrics can help, for instance, illuminate whether a new product or new supplier relationship is proving profitable. In extremely siloed organizations, the finance function may have little or shallow contact with business-driving departments of the company such as operations, sales, or marketing. What information finance does supply may be limited, providing only trivial insights, with very little in terms of options and recommendations. In these circumstances, finance has done little on its own to earn a seat at the table, which in turn limits the ability of the organization as a whole to change its behavior in such a way as to generate improved business and financial results. That is a problem.

Marketing may also be isolated, though in a different way. Partially since traditional siloed organizations do not require other departments to understand their true function or how they work, marketing may be left to their own devices, possibly making decisions based on feel or whim. So long as they stay within their overall annual budget, the company likely will not question marketing's decisions, but neither does it offer ongoing support or incremental investment. Rather, marketing in traditional siloed organizations can be viewed and treated as a cost center, ripe for spending reductions when financial results turn sour. To understand the typical mindset at the top, we need look no further than quotations from CEOs regarding marketing, gathered by Cranfield School of Management, Professor Malcolm MacDonald: "Like other departments, Marketing always requests more budgets from me, but without the metrics in place to demonstrate the impact marketing has in financial terms to our external stakeholders," says one CEO. Another CEO explains:

> Marketing has a tendency to be more activity based—focusing on the number of campaigns it runs or how many people it needs to employ, rather than justifying the impact of marketing on the bottom-line and cash flow. One of the reasons for this attitude is the relative lack of hard measurement that demonstrates the contribution of Marketing to revenue and corporate strategy.

Adds a third:

> My organization has, until recently, worked on measuring marketing spend and determining the effectiveness of it, but we are now looking at how to measure these intangibles. It is my job to accurately account for this business and its success—and marketing measurements definitely have a role to play. *My key issue is that I don't have a framework in place for this yet* (emphasis added).

A fourth asks a question most CEOs have probably posed about their marketing departments, and their financial approaches overall: "Why is it that brand equity measurement is performed as an integral part of due diligence when a company is bought and sold but not always included as part of annual reporting?"[6]

In other words, marketing in these specific situations is not *cutting the mustard financially*, which points to the significant need for marketing to align with finance. Other departments have done this already. Historically, operations got there first. Considering there is a fairly natural harmony and predictability in tying operations metrics to financial results, this is no surprise. Both operations and finance are predominantly quantifiable and objective. Whether a process is better or worse depends on whether it is resulting in more profits or fewer, is using resources more efficiently or not, and so on. Because sales is also highly quantifiable and objective, it too has had an easier time of aligning to finance.

We might also consider the fact that driving forces such as Six Sigma have stepped in to offer insight into operations and other organizational aspects with greater efficiency, less labor, reduced energy consumption, etc. But Six Sigma, with its emphasis on striving for near perfection, is a difficult ideal to adjust to for a department such as marketing that historically bases success on less quantifiable concepts such as whether consumers buy in, recognize brand, or respond favorably to this campaign or that. As a general rule, marketing has a much harder time making a case for the effectiveness of many of its activities. Some are redefining marketing's role in Six Sigma away from proving its lean effectiveness and more toward acting as the lens by which to focus the organizational sights. Marketing, in this view, identifies competitive arenas and conveys an understanding of what constitutes value, as it is defined by the market, to the rest of the organization. In this way, marketing may play a more useful role—and more importantly, be *acknowledged* as more useful by other departments.[7]

For the most part, however, marketing has not adopted this role, nor have organizations and the "non-marketers" changed their views on what marketing is and does. Instead, the department is viewed with confusion and perhaps even a little suspicion, and other departments assume it is still subjective, murky, and sometimes even fluffy. To return to the opinions of the CEOs quoted previously, marketing may routinely and consistently fail to demonstrate its own worth and effectiveness, and does not carry with it a framework by which to measure its success. That does not, however, mean that the marketing budget goes untouched, especially when an organization falls on hard times (which are presumably the times when it could use a public image boost or improved brand adoption by consumers). This, in fact, constitutes one of the main barriers between marketing and finance: that finance's lack of understanding of what marketing "does" leads it to envision the department as ripe (and presumably ready!) for budget cuts when the need arises.

That and other sources of acrimony have led to a historic absence of collaboration between the two functions. We now turn our attention to these barriers to collaboration, how they arise, and the differences in approach and educational background between these two core disciplines.

Barriers to Collaboration between Marketing and Finance

From the very start, one of the imposing barriers to collaboration from a finance perspective is their perception of marketing as being fraught with subjectivity, murkiness, and fluffiness. In the siloed mind, would any serious finance person put their neck on the line for a cutesy TV ad with children singing? How about an ad based on humor, slapstick, talking animals, tugging on the heartstrings, or inventive cartoons? It is unlikely. These things were not taught in Accounting 101, or 401, after all. While such "fun" ads might have sensory appeal, they contain little in the way of a quantifiable financial guarantee (and, as we shall later see, the inherent non-seriousness of them may also pose a problem for finance-trained brains). On the other hand, why would marketers want to allow the budget cutters of finance into their secret esoteric realm? Allowing them to see the wizard behind the curtain would most likely only embolden finance to cut the funding related to what marketing considers valuable elements in the equation. Simply put, there can easily be a broad gulf between the ways the two functions understand the world. Consider the following example of what we might call *marketing speak*, as offered by a well-known Canadian economist and marketing professor, Markus Giesler:

> Stop looking at needs. Stop looking at the psychologically oriented idea of what the consumer wants. That's almost Freudian. Start developing a more sociologically oriented understanding of how cultures change and how new energies can be captured and turned into economic capital.[8]

To a finance person, this phrase might very well constitute a horror show. In one short paragraph, it contains the phrases: "psychologically oriented idea," "Freudian," "sociologically oriented understanding," "cultures change," and "new energies can be captured." The entire quote would seem to revolve around fuzzy measurements ("*more* sociologically oriented") and a fundamental undermining of historical modes of business ("Stop looking at . . . consumer wants"). No need even to start on Freud.

What is a finance individual to make of this? While the reasoning might be sound and indeed might make a great deal of sense to the enterprise, a finance person is going to have trouble signing on to an approach that lacks clear metrics and up-ends traditional approaches. Only at the very end of the last sentence do we hear something even close to what a finance person might be looking for and, even then, there is no clear path laid out that clarifies how this so-called "economic capital" is to be measured or harvested (read as: delivered to the bottom line). Granted, this is just a short quote from an interview with Professor Giesler, but it very effectively illustrates the discomfort finance may feel around marketing ideas.

Of course, marketing has its own distinct take, in which the uneasiness of finance is attributed to a lack of understanding of what truly matters, an unwillingness to take risks, and an inability to deal gracefully with the softer sciences. Marketing is in some sense right to point out that: "Not everything that can be counted counts and not everything that counts can be counted." This turn of phrase, coined by William Bruce Cameron (and often erroneously attributed to Albert Einstein), reads in its entirety:

> It would be nice if all of the data which sociologists require could be enumerated because then we could run them through IBM machines and draw charts as the economists do. However, not everything that can be counted counts, and not everything that counts can be counted.

Cameron might well have been referring to the divide between marketing and finance when he said this. Take unaided brand awareness, for example. Ask any member of an organization, from the lowliest employee to the most high-powered CEO, from a marketing guru to a finance savant, whether brand awareness matters, and you will probably hear a resounding "Yes!" The jury is in: brand awareness most certainly does count. However, it is a qualitative thing. Sure, you can find a few metrics by which to quantify and measure it, but what does it really mean, and how does it translate to financial results? Instinctively, you might think that a higher brand awareness number means you are better off, but it is difficult to tell if brand awareness actually translates to someone heading to the store to pick up a box of cereal or a 12-pack of beer. Moreover, what if you are Target, and your brand awareness just went up because your credit card database got hacked? That is brand awareness alright, but not of the kind any organization would seek to earn.

A simple Google search for "how to measure brand awareness" makes this point quite eloquently by returning very little in the way of useful information. This is telling. No doubt any company, large or small, would love to get their hands on the secret formula for measuring brand awareness. So, if it *did* exist, the world's largest search engine would probably turn up references considerably more valuable on the topic. That is not to say, of course, that it is impossible: just that at best, for now, there is no widely agreed-upon approach that people would bet their paycheck on. At worst, considering that "high brand awareness" can be achieved in not the most desirable of circumstances, or by companies such as Blockbuster that were bankrupted by disruptive technologies, it might not be all that useful a metric anyway.

Now consider a slightly more effective brand measurement strategy, the net promoter score. The net promoter score is commonly used in marketing efforts and is based on some variation of the question: "On a scale of 0–10, how likely are you to recommend us to a friend or colleague?" Customers who answer 9 or 10 are the golden egg, producing referrals and trumpeting the brand all over town. Responses in the 7 and 8 range indicate customers who are satisfied, but not thrilled enough to actually promote, while answers in the 0–6 range are a red flag: These unhappy customers often try their best to ruin the brand through negative press and word of mouth. At first glance, it has a little more of what finance is looking for. They are numbers, anyway. It is a verifiable system that is proven to translate to the effect customers will have on the brand and that is used by such corporate notables as John Deere, Liberty Mutual, Petco, American Express, eBay, Netgear, and the Walt Disney Company. But . . . what does it actually mean financially? How does satisfaction or the lack thereof actually translate to a company's bottom line?

The point here is not that the net promoter score—or any other standard of measurement commonly used in marketing efforts—is a useless statistic. By all accounts it is in fact useful. However, the trail goes cold before it reaches a true financial destination, and this is a problem for serious efforts to align the marketing and finance functions. In order to truly provide valuable insight, organizations must take this score and turn it into a useful, actionable strategy for improving their brand (and more to the point, their products and services) in the future.

In the article "Why Can't We Be Friends? Five Steps to Better Relations between CFOs and CMOs," Jonathan Gordon, Jean-Hugues Monier, and Phil Ogren point out that a big part of the problem is an inability to focus on metrics that actually matter *to both functions*. So many metrics that each function uses are in one way or another nontransferable (or hard to transfer) to the other realm, and marketers often look in the wrong place for measurements that will matter at all to finance:

> Ideally, the relationship between the CFO and the CMO needs to function more like a partnership, in which the two explore together the performance that drives shareholder returns. That means CMOs will need to focus on the metrics that are most aligned with corporate business goals, which CFOs can help identify. Typically, these will not be brand awareness, share of voice in the market, or the number of 'likes' on Facebook—areas where many currently focus—unless those numbers can be tied to profit. CMOs must demonstrate and track marketing's impact by focusing on those key performance indicators (KPIs) that are most important for shareholder value such as return on investment, net present value, and operating margins.[9]

Adding to the problem is that marketing has historically had a hard time with, quite simply, the math. Says Wes Nichols in his article "Good Quant, Bad Quant" for *Analytics Magazine*:

> [m]arketing and math haven't always meshed. Marketing was considered a creative endeavor somehow divorced from the rigor and transparency of science-based business process. The very definition of analytics—"the scientific process of transforming data into insight for making better decisions"—caused tension in marketing-dom. For many, 'marketing science' was an oxymoron.[10]

Nichols explains that math—really, truly useful math, not fuzzy jabs at it as were formerly perpetrated by marketing departments across states, countries, and business models—is necessary to bring marketing into the twenty-first century and full usefulness. He hammers home the point that analytics are nothing without the right math:

> The cornerstone of today's successful marketing analytics technology—or what I call 'Analytics 2.0'—is the math. If you don't have the math right, by definition your attribution will be wrong, and by extension your allocations and attempts to optimize your investments will also be wrong. It's critical to understand that effective marketing resource allocation depends on accurate attribution of revenue to different marketing investments online as well as offline and at point of purchase. The 1.0 version of marketing analytics includes traditional forms of measurement that we've had for decades, such as media mix models, agent-based models, digital attribution and simple correlations using Excel spreadsheets.[11]

Certain of these models, he continues, have largely been discredited and, by smart organizations, abandoned. The related "metrics" simply have not worked historically, and the lag time in realizing this has often stemmed from marketing departments that do not *want* to realize it, perhaps because for a long time they felt there was not anything to replace it with. That is no longer the case, according to Nichols, who now posits that: "Analytics 2.0 taps today's perfect storm of big data, technology, predictive analytics and other marketing science to help companies reallocate billions of advertising dollars while realizing double-digit sales lifts with zero additional spend."[12]

This is all well and good, but clearly the problem still remains. As indicated by the quotes from dissatisfied or confused CEOs, marketing is still often unable to offer essential metrics that can align closely enough with finance to point toward solutions and meaningful innovation for the future.

Of course, sometimes marketers do strive to engage more closely with the financial realm. However, as Ambler and Roberts point out: "Marketers rarely mean ROI when they say ROI."[13] To this point, Dominique Hanssens, professor of marketing at UCLA Anderson School of Management, a co-founder of MarketShare and a member of MASB points out that the notion of return on investment (ROI) is not evil. Linking marketing to financial performance is absolutely critical. It's just that most people who use ROI *in a marketing context* probably are not applying it correctly, or really mean something else. Hanssens observes that ROI's roots are in evaluating one-time capital projects, but marketing is not a one-time capital project. We might talk about marketing "investments," but marketing expenditures are technically an expense, as opposed to an investment. In finance-speak, marketing costs are a P&L item, *not* a balance sheet item.[14]

One of the practical difficulties in applying the principles of ROI, internal rate of return (IRR), or net present value (NPV) to marketing is that these metrics are very much rooted in operations (production), and more specifically, in capital spending. Take, for example, a capital expenditure project intended to improve usage metrics (e.g., labor, utilities), which can be financially justified with relative ease and with a relatively low risk of forecast variance. Put yourself in the shoes of a CFO. The VP of Production and his financial controller arrive in the CFO's office proposing a $5m capital expenditure. "We've talked to other companies that have installed this piece of equipment," they explain. "We've done all the math. We can save $1.4m per year when we install this. It's $600,000 of utility savings and $800,000 of labor savings. Oh, and the equipment will be depreciated over 15 years. We will not miss those estimates by more than plus or minus 5 percent. And another thing, if you assume that energy and labor costs will rise in the future, we'll realize an even greater benefit." The CFO says that sounds like a good idea! Now the CMO and his financial controller arrive to deliver their pitch for the same amount of money. "We would like to invest an additional $5m in network sports television media, and at best it will probably return an equivalent amount of incremental margin, though that is directional. It's now November, so we will get some of that return in November and December, but some of the return probably falls in January and February." So, all of the $5m of expense hits the bottom line when the media runs, and the return aspect is uncertain as to amount and timing. The company has a December 31 year end, and the CFO needs to deliver a certain bottom line. Hmm . . . where the first story makes for an obvious ROI, the second does not, at least not to the same degree of quantification and certainty. In fact, with a year-end bottom line to watch out for, this media proposal is a risky investment indeed. Even if it does work out, due to lack of easily quantifiable metrics, it might *still* be hard for the CFO to make a case for the worthiness of the investment to whomever he reports to (the CEO or the Board).

Here is another thought experiment in the form of the following statement: "My mobile campaign has a great ROI because I tripled the number of likes on my brand's Facebook site." This might be true, but if that same brand's sales volumes are down 7 percent, what are we to make of this? The "R" in ROI does stand for "return," after all, yet some people consistently fail to target the correct place to look for proof that an ROI is occurring at all. Sure, the company might have more likes on Facebook, but if that does not translate to incremental sales and bottom-line profits, what is the point? Just as brand awareness can be bad (Target), brand awareness can also be just plain empty. Gordon, Monier, and Ogren offer an interesting example:

> Consider one food brand, for example. Marketing managers decided to connect with customers using Facebook advertising bolstered by contests, relevant sponsored blogs, photo-sharing incentives, and shopping-list applications. The approach delivered sales results similar to traditional marketing, including TV advertising and print promotions, at a fraction of the cost. Brand managers, therefore, considered massive cuts to their TV- and print-advertising budgets in favor of spending more on social media channels. However, when they included long-term effects in their calculations, they realized that the contribution of TV advertising significantly out-paced online displays and social media at delivering the emotional connection needed to build brand equity.[15]

The lesson? Even if two activities seem to be returning the same initial advantages, that may not be the case upon deeper inspection. This idea of singling out what exactly you are looking for in terms of return—in this case, the necessary emotional connection with prospective customers needed to build a brand that would remain stable over time—is crucial, otherwise you might end up chasing metrics that initially seem promising, but in the long run prove relatively meaningless or even destructive.

Of course, there are plenty of ways to measure marketing success. According to Adam Gaskill and Hume Winzar, these are both financial metrics (including ROI, along with revenue per customer, or marketing expenditure percentage of revenue) and non-financial metrics, such as unprompted and prompted brand awareness, market share (value and volume), website traffic (unique visitors), or number of new customers. When taken into account along with control variables (i.e., CEO background and whether the company is B2B or B2C) and plugged into the equation of marketing accountability, these numbers can return valuable insights into the benefit *to* the marketing function (credibility, additional resources, approvals) and *of* the marketing function, or business performance (customer satisfaction, profitability, market share).[16] Although figuring out how to glean these metrics from a raft of available data and apply them specifically to marketing endeavors may be tricky, it is theoretically possible.

Even if marketers do manage to correlate a marketing activity to a financial return, they may then run into that frightening question from the CFO, CEO, or the Board: "Is that causation or coincidence?" While the first means that the marketing activity actually resulted in the financial return and is therefore a beneficial and hopefully repeatable action, coincidence is something quite different. Unfortunately, it is sometimes hard to know which it is. That is not anyone's fault, but it becomes an impediment for finance to want to keep funding an activity, the worth of which no one seems able to prove. For example, explains David Stewart:

> It's well known in the beer industry that when MillerCoors altered the packaging design on Miller Lite cans in early 2014 from primarily blue to primarily white, there was an almost immediate volume trend change. Intellectually, I had no issue whatsoever calling that causation.[17]

In other words, the packaging design change from blue to white directly caused a change in sales. However, Stewart adds: "I can cite many other marketing or selling activities where it's not as clear."[18]

It is also important to think in terms of the fundamental motivations of CFOs and CMOs. Does a CMO get fired because they spend a little too much money on marketing or because they develop bad ad campaigns? Probably the latter; marketing is responsible for getting the word out in the best way possible. Do you think a CFO gets fired because they do not hit bottom-line expectations, or because they receive bad employee engagement scores? Probably the former; while both are important, a CFO is not hired to become friends with everyone, but rather to ensure the delivery of hard-hitting financial outcomes. So there is a little bit of a conflict here. A CMO might want to spend a little bit more money because their job is on the line if they fail to produce a great ad campaign; a CFO, on the other hand, could lose their job for not curtailing such spending, no matter what the motivation.

There's also a knowledge, or education, gap that creates a barrier between marketing and finance. We talked earlier about the traditional siloed corporation. But what about siloed educational curriculums? How many marketing classes does the typical undergraduate finance or accounting student take? They may barely remember "the five Ps." The opposite is also the case, with marketers frequently having minimal educational background in financial principles. Says David Stewart:

> I see very high variability among marketers in terms of financial acumen. Though, frankly, I could say the same thing about Sales, Human Resources, Operations, whatever. That said, I cannot throw too many stones, because I've run past many accountants and finance professionals who have difficulties working cross-functionally with non-finance people. (Personal communication)

These differences are bred into marketing and finance from the time they exit high school and hit the college scene. It is indeed a thorny problem to figure out how to forge common ground now after all of this early indoctrination. The problem, however, is quite real.

Even nonprofits such as the Food and Agriculture Organization of the United Nations have cottoned on, providing materials meant to train government officials in marketing and financial areas to better help them assist the farmers and policymakers they work with. What is interesting is not that the United Nations saw a need to tie marketing and finance together—many others have noted the necessity—but rather that they seek to do so in a combined curriculum "to enable marketers to be aware of the financial implications of decision making."[19] There are several items to note here: (1) that the text is speaking directly to marketers, indicating widespread belief that it is marketers who must get closer to financial accountability, rather than finance individuals who need marketing help (though the latter is undoubtedly true as well); (2) that marketing decision-making has financial repercussions; and (3) that with the right educational principles to call on, one can theoretically predict those repercussions with some reliability before making a decision, and thereby protect a firm's bottom line much more effectively.

Arguably, there is also a fundamental difference in how finance and marketing people are most comfortable thinking about things, which creates another barrier. While finance types generally are analytical and structured in their thinking, the marketing crowd tends to veer toward the conceptual and social. A brief skim of the relevant bookshelves makes the point nicely: Marketing has to its name titles such as: "Psychology of Sales: From Average to Rainmaker," "BrainScripts for Sales Success: 21 Hidden Principles of Consumer Psychology for Winning New Customers," and "Empathetic Marketing: How to Satisfy the 6 Core Emotional Needs of Your Customers." Finance, on the other hand, reads as dusty and jargon-filled as they come, with headers like "The Necessity of Finance: An Overview of the Science of Management of Wealth for an Individual, a Group, or an Organization," and "Corporate Divestiture Management: Organizational Techniques for Proactive Divestiture Decision-Making." Of course, these titles are only examples, but they are illustrative of incongruent concern, focus, and language that marketing and finance, respectively, employ. Furthermore, while group hugs are not necessarily the desired outcome, what in these titles encourages any degree of affinity between the two disciplines?

To sum up this section, marketing and finance bring different perspectives to their jobs, have different ideas of what "matters" and what constitutes success, have different uses of (and for) math and language, and come from widely contrasting educational backgrounds. All of these factors make it difficult for them to converge toward metrics that matter to both, and use them to inform the next steps of a successful, profitable company. It is no longer acceptable to simply put up with (at best) or ignore one another (at worst) as in the good old days of functionally siloed organizations. Rather, it is increasingly crucial that both find a way to relate to one another in order to collaborate in a way that leads to greater enterprise success.

A Growing Need for Collaboration

Having just illustrated how and why marketing and finance may not see eye to eye, we find ourselves at a crossroads. The good news, though, is that there is a win–win here for marketing and finance, which we will explore.

In today's competitive and global marketplace, it is simply a fact that cross-functional interaction is essential to ensure that business decisions are appropriately informed and made based on any number of inputs. These functions include marketing, sales, finance, operations/manufacturing, and others. In companies today, in fact, most project stage-gate protocols include representation from nearly all functional units rather than just a few of the "key players," recognizing that *all* players are key in the modern organization, and that those individuals or departments formerly siloed away while the big decisions happened now have a seat at the table.

Stage-gate protocols may actually have a lot to teach us about the necessary collaboration between marketing and finance. These protocols, whatever their specific form or application, cover the product life cycle from initial idea through market launch to after-action review, and it is not hard to see why finance would be involved at every step of the way: tallying costs and resource availability, forecasting revenues, assessing risk, and so on. Also, clearly, marketing can offer valuable insight on whether a product (or service) will succeed or fail, whether the idea should be modified to suit a wider cross-section of the potential audience, how to position the product to entice the widest possible customer base, and more. The big upside in this scenario is that marketing has a chance to prove their worth to the organization, and in doing so could also earn a larger budget allocation.

Put another way, the question is one of perceived value to the company. Does a CMO really just want marketing to be viewed as a cost center? Or as the "value generation division?" On the other hand, does the CFO simply want to take pride in cost cutting, and call it a day? Or does that CFO want to be a strategic leader of the business who is willing to take informed risks where there is ambiguity? In the long run, a finance department that is successful in the latter capacity earns more trust, adds more value to the organization, and to some extent shrugs off the yoke of the traditional image: bean counter and cold-hearted budget slasher. Of course, much of marketing's value will still flow from interfacing with the public, and creating brand awareness and demand. Similarly, primary roles of finance will always include compliance with policies and standards and delivering the bottom line. But these traditional roles are too narrow and, by partnering up, marketing and finance can both safely expand what they do, when they do it, and how they do it, to the benefit of each function individually and the company as a whole.

In order to achieve such a thorough collaborative model, however, several facets of many organizations need to change. The concept of finance as providing monthly reports with opaque columns and rows of numbers is very old school and does little to reflect the broad-sweeping nature of the roles performed by finance. Here, for instance, is Goldman Sachs' description of what their finance department does:

> The finance teams manage the firm's liquidity, capital and risk, and provide the overall financial control and reporting function. Their responsibilities include managing liquidity risk, long-term debt issuance and share repurchases and dividends; assessing the creditworthiness of the firm's counterparties; monitoring market risks associated with the firm's trading activities; designing and operating systems to support financial management, planning and forecasting; building risk models to support new businesses and derivatives analysis; managing the firm's relationships with regulators, rating agencies and creditors; and providing broad analytical and regulatory compliance support across all our businesses. The finance division is organized into discrete groups that cover these responsibilities.[20]

This definition is very intentional, and most organizations could learn a lot from it. Covered in this short paragraph is: (1) the broad list of functions performed by finance, *of which budgeting is but one*; (2) the fact that they "design and operate systems to support financial management, planning and forecasting," presumably for other functions as well as their own; and (3) an organizational structure that segments finance into smaller "discrete" groups that can presumably matrix with other departments more easily. Of course, as an investment company, Goldman Sachs no doubt has a particularly robust finance department, but it still offers an excellent model of greater transparency and diversification of duties that can help liberate finance from the old school spreadsheet-spitting stereotype.

On the other hand, marketing spending to budget with minimal financial input or insight is clearly suboptimal and barely ante to the game. When marketing fences off its domain in an attempt to keep finance out, obeying the letter of the law (by not going over budget) without using metrics to ensure that money is well spent, they do themselves few favors and only encourage *their* stereotype of devil-may-care, feel-good types who stake thousands or millions of dollars on hunches and whims. But, let us not be too harsh on marketing. While there is little benefit in assigning blame, in companies where this occurs, generally *both* finance *and* marketing are to blame. Marketing should instead work to increase its perceived value by cultivating both insight into how it actually spends money and what those expenditures accomplish, and by accepting input from finance. As Gordon, Monier, and Ogren remark: "Creating transparency into operations is the starting point for marketing to help CFOs understand where and how value is being gained or lost." The main problem with this, they explain, is that:

> CMOs often find it hard to say how much they actually spend—by product, market, or strategic intent, for example, or by activity—on IT, different parts of the purchase funnel, digital and social media, or non-advertising activities such as sponsorships, promotions, and trade events.

Complicating matters is the fact that "different regions may allocate the same spending to different categories. A trade-fair expenditure might fall into short-term spending in one market, for instance, but long-term brand-building spending in another."[21] This, they posit, is in part due to the fact that "Marketing departments are often reluctant to look beyond their own fiefdoms; it's also time-consuming to align spending categories accurately—and a major task to communicate the value of doing so." However, if marketing is to emerge from its current stereotype as an esoteric smoke-and-mirrors outfit that may or may not benefit the company, it is crucial that it align itself in every way possible: across activities, across regions, across campaigns, and perhaps most importantly for our purpose, *to* finance.

The authors offer as example an automotive company that made a conscientious effort—a dozen workshops in six months—to instill the value of analytics into the marketing team:

> The company used this process to develop a common approach for answering the seemingly basic question of *why it was spending marketing dollars* [emphasis added]. For example, was it trying to promote the brand or draw customers into the showroom? Drawing such distinctions makes it easier for any CMO to answer basic questions about where and how marketing dollars are spent—and makes budgeting discussions much more productive.[22]

This example is particularly illuminating. Here it becomes clear that the necessity of aligning marketing and finance stems not so much from breaking down the walls or halting the constant bickering between the two functions, but rather from *a deepening of marketing's own understanding of itself*. In other words, by appreciating the rigor and objectivity of finance, marketing cannot only earn itself a more reputable place in the company and enable the kind of matrixing that top companies use to incredible advantage, but they can within their own "fiefdom" become much more effective.

Here we return to the idea of marketing accountability, as defined by MASB, which we discussed earlier in this book. Recall that the MASB's goal in life is to help marketers "master and apply the science of measurement and process management to the art of marketing," which will result in benefits such as: "consistent growth, with improved methods for measuring, forecasting and improving the effectiveness of marketing activities and a narrowing of the gap between marketing efforts and financial outcomes."[23] It is very important that marketing understands its alignment to finance as a way to make itself better, more efficient and more valuable, rather than as simply a means of appeasing other functions or higher-ups. If it does not, then business will continue as usual, with marketing departments spending their budgets (nothing more, nothing less) on campaigns that are poorly measured, differ across regions and activities, and have trouble evolving to better satisfy consumer demands and desires, which will in turn result in suspicion and aversion to approving marketing dollars from the rest of the organization, particularly finance.

Consider one scenario within an enterprise which would see marketing asking for money for a poorly defined project whose outcomes may or may not arrive in time to satisfy year-end requirements (recall the example of the marketer hoping to get funding for network sports television spots), and finance reacting to this suggestion with suspicion and likely disapproval. Now imagine a different scenario: a brand director and the marketing financial controller standing together in front of the senior executive team and saying "We executed a packaging design change on Brand A which cost us $1.4m. Since its rollout, Brand A's sales volume trend has improved by 5 percent. On an annual basis, that translates into $5m of incremental gross margin to the company." Here we have quantifiable, time-bound metrics that matter to the organization, competent marketing individuals explaining their importance, with finance validating the results. What a fine setup for further requests from marketing, with achievements such as this proving its competence in ways that would be unheard of in a traditional siloed organization.

This is the vision put forth by passion projects such as the MASB, and with attention to good metrics, the right questions ("Why are we spending marketing dollars?"; "What are we hoping to achieve?"; "How will we know?") and a working partnership with finance, could become the norm for companies across the globe. Furthermore, it is quite possible that those organizations who cannot adapt to this new working relationship will be left behind.

How This Is Being Practically Applied at MillerCoors

MillerCoors offers an excellent window into what a good working relationship between marketing and finance might look like, what roles individuals might assume within the matrixed functions, the points and values that are important to understand within such a model, and the potential results. In the interests of eliminating organizational barriers, financial support for marketing at MillerCoors is headed up by Jim Meier. He holds the title of Senior Director, Marketing Finance, a title chosen intentionally for its ability to represent both functions without a built-in bias to either. This position reports directly to the CFO, but with dotted-line reporting to the CMO. Meier sits on both the senior finance leadership team and the senior marketing leadership team. His managers and analysts also matrix into the marketing division, which goes as far as financial analysts sitting with the brand teams rather than in a segregated "finance department."

If you go to the MillerCoors Chicago office and ask where the finance department is, you cannot get an answer because they are everywhere. These analysts are effectively "mini-CFOs," working as closely with marketing as with finance to ensure adherence to financial goals, measurement of inputs and outcomes, and the use of analytics in decision-making processes.

As an example, finance participates very closely in annual brand planning and resource allocation. Traditionally, in many companies, resource allocation has a lot of historical inertia. Finance might ask: "How much did they get last year?" and respond with a glib, "Give them the same for next year; or we'll be generous and give them that plus 2 percent." Why, after all, base the budget on metrics when marketing itself has historically been loath to do so? At MillerCoors, the partnership between marketing and finance has turned such arcane thinking on its head. In fact, the partnership extends well beyond just these two functions, also including strategy and sales, among others. A few years ago, in an approach called "the Tournament of Ideas," a portion of marketing dollars was awarded based on portfolio positioning and other factors, leaving remaining marketing dollars open to competition. In an effort to win a slice of the pie, brands came in and pitched various ideas, which were then judged by the senior executive team. This approach helped to overcome the historical inertia in which brands received essentially the same amounts over and over again, regardless of prior successes and failures, or innovative ideas. It stands to reason, moreover, that brands that assume they will receive a budget similar to the year before (and the year before that, and the year before that) have less incentive to truly innovate. Again, here we see an example of how partnership with finance not only makes better use of marketing dollars and the budget enterprise-wide but also encourages marketing, to borrow a cliché: "to be its best self."

In addition to forcing innovation and helping MillerCoors break free of a historical bind, this also helped the organization to understand that resources are limited. While finance should never say that resources are "scarce"—the implication being finance is not giving marketing (or any other department, really) enough money—encouraging departments to think of resources as limited is helpful. It not only inspires innovation and helps marketing work toward "earning" resources but also aids in bringing down traditional barriers to finance as merely soulless budget cutters who neither see the big picture nor particularly care about it. This is a semantic difference, but an important one. Taken to a world-class level, one can even imagine a CFO sourcing money from elsewhere in the enterprise and passing it to marketing to fuel the profit engine.

A helpful way to think about spending is to remember that as soon as budgets are done, they are wrong. Companies should not necessarily be spending to budget, but rather should be spending more on ideas and campaigns that are working and *not* spending on those that are not. Here we see the difference between results management versus budget management. Budget management, which requires adhering to the costs and expenditures as initially laid out when planning the budget, can hogtie an organization by insisting on following the letter of the law instead of doing more of what works when it is working. Results management does away with this mechanical adherence to a budget that was likely developed when not all facts were known and focuses on the real, measurable results that stem from any particular action or approach. Although various sources offer many possible interpretations of results management, a particularly good definition comes from the Asian Development Bank (ADB):

Results management is simultaneously (i) a management approach and (ii) a set of tools for strategic planning, monitoring and evaluating performance, reporting, and organizational improvement and learning. Results management improves organizational performance by applying traditional tools such as strategic planning, results framework, monitoring, and program evaluation in the modern context of decentralization, networking, flexibility, participatory processes, and accountability.[24]

Results management, in other words, offers a raft of benefits to the matrixed organization hoping to hitch marketing to the finance wagon. It not only provides the wider framework in which to manage and collaborate but it also offers the tools by which to accomplish specific objectives. Moreover, it uses traditional tools, but in a whole new context, thereby improving an organization's efficacy without requiring that management learn an entire new rulebook. Best of all, results management operates within decentralized, participatory organizations such as those using matrix models, which put an emphasis on networking, collaboration, and flexibility, and use accountability as the main standard of measurement for individual functions and departments as a whole. In any attempt to merge finance and marketing, a results management approach is certainly better than a more stagnant budget management one.

Because of an organization's inability to control or predict all outcomes, it becomes necessary to be more flexible about the budget, so as to catch sources of waste and opportunities more often, and leverage them to the company's benefit. You might think of this as managing tradeoffs. At MillerCoors, this happens via its "sources and uses" monthly routine. When MillerCoors closes the books each month, they sit down and comb over the budget, asking questions such as: "Where are we versus our plans?"; "Where did we budget money that we're just not spending?"; and "Where might we want to spend more?" Doing so enables marketing to find extra dollars that are currently not being leveraged to better the company, catch unrealistic spending before it becomes a problem, and consider repurposing available funds to deliver profitable company results.

Results management offers several benefits that apply specifically to building the relationship between marketing and finance. First, it removes finance's burden of having to oversee huge organization-wide goals at the expense of the smaller, more independent objectives that operate beneath the top level. Second, it allows marketing to assess its progress, achievements, challenges, and dollar usage more often, *without* the pressure of huge annual budget decisions and *with* a seat at the table. Such a sources and uses routine removes pressure from both functions to each blindly pursue its own objectives, instead offering common ground and incentivizing the relationship. Marketing gets a fair bit of control over its own budget, while finance gets the security of overseeing the process and knowing expenditures are being monitored.

Many organizations use marketing mix modeling to assess the impacts of their current combination of marketing efforts on sales and objectives, and then use the results to better sculpt their future efforts with the goal of maximizing profit. This could equally be called "demand mix modeling," in which a detailed model uses a huge variety of factors to try to determine what mix of activities will generate demand for a particular product. MillerCoors runs very detailed algorithms considering over 200 variables—including unemployment rate, weather, and sales metrics such as display and features. The model also incorporates pricing and all media activities, as well as many other non-media marketing activities. It looks back historically to try to understand what is working and what is not, offering a sophisticated and informed way to help the organization make better decisions. While it may not offer an absolute or precise answer, such a model substantially improves the organization's odds of making the right choice at any given time. It can help answer big questions, such as whether spending the same amount of money on a particular type of media could potentially get a better return, if other factors were modified. Sometimes it is not even media that needs adjustment, but rather some other factor, like points of distribution. In the end, such a model can bring much-needed objectivity to marketing.

MillerCoors is also exploring the possibility of periodically estimating brand values. Such information might enable marketing and finance to improve their resource allocation, taking into account the potential worth of the brand rather than entirely being driven by volume or P&L metrics. While this type of intangible asset is harder to value than a more physical one, such as inventory or a building, it is nevertheless a critical one to understand, and moreover one which *can* translate to tangible metrics if they are applied in the right way. Moreover, the brand asset value is subject to accretion *or* impairment—not in a strict accounting sense, but in a practical way as a decision-making tool. This idea also encourages partnership between marketing and finance as they work in unison to leverage brands for the benefit of the company. It is pretty powerful stuff, made even more powerful by the fact that a CFO is bound to understand it and embrace it . . . and a CMO would certainly like the credit for it! Imagine an enterprise that functions through the lens that: operations can purchase and maintain an asset, marketing can create and grow one.

Not too long ago, MillerCoors created a new position. The title? Director of Marketing Return Optimization. "Optimization" is a very critical word here. It is intentionally not "maximization." Theoretically, one could maximize short-term financial results simply by cutting all marketing, but that will hardly have a good long-term impact. In fact, the negative impacts may arrive sooner than one might think. Instead, the important idea is to optimize spending, so that each dollar spent drives an optimal result for the organization as a whole. While part of the approach to marketing spending optimization is outright expense reduction—cutting the fat, so to speak— more of it relates to the effectiveness of marketing activities as measured by tangible metrics. That being the case, the Director of Marketing Return Optimization reports to finance, and in most companies would likely reside in either finance or strategy. The idea is to hold marketing accountable for results, without taking the slash-and-burn approach of old, which only increases the level of mistrust between marketing and finance. While it requires a lot of collaboration, it is a worthwhile position for the autonomy it offers marketing, the accountability it offers finance, and the strong collaborative spirit it both requires and enables between the two. This is essentially another way of thinking about the governance umbrella. Without an organizational structure to marry the two functions, you are instead left with force feeding an imposed partnership to the organization and can kiss continuous and sustainable improvement goodbye.

A governing principle to seriously consider when savings or efficiencies turn up in these types of processes is that they do not immediately get dropped to the bottom line. Instead, marketing is allowed to reinvest this money. This not only removes the incentive to spend every last dollar lest it later be found and taken away but it adds incentive for people to hold themselves accountable and spend money more wisely. If they do, they may find themselves in the long run with a larger and more impactful budget than they thought they had, without ever having to make a pitch to increase it.

This does necessitate that the organization take steps to "financialize the marketers," but not to an extreme in which they are converted into de facto accountants. As discussed in this chapter and throughout this book, financial acumen among marketers within any organization can be extremely variable. The organization, to some degree, must attempt to both level the playing field and raise the bar, providing all members of the marketing department with the capability to understand and appreciate financial concepts. At MillerCoors, with the assistance of the Learning and Development department, they now offer a series of two- to four-minute videos about basic financial topics. Now, when marketing employees have questions about a financial topic, they can head to an internal website, log in, and find basic information on a wide variety of relevant financial topics. Each video comes with a learning guide and a contact person for questions. These resources are not just available to marketing but are instituted broadly across the entire organization.

So, relevant learning resources are accessible, making use of the powerful concept of self-directed learning, in which employees are more motivated to assimilate new knowledge if they can choose when, where, how, and even *why* they wish to learn it. Self-directed learning not only creates the desire to learn but also helps employees retain that important knowledge, because they learn it in a way that is engaging and useful to them. Additionally, because they seek out the new knowledge for a specific reason or for an answer to a specific question, they usually have the opportunity to apply it immediately, reinforcing learning. This encourages both short-term fluency with the material as well as long-term retention.

Let us also note the importance of cross-functional acumen to a wide variety of functions. As stated previously, there is no intent here to turn marketers into accountants. Marketing serves its own purpose and does not need to take over the role of finance. Instead, an organization needs marketers that have at least some understanding of finances, or they will have a hard time making choices that align to financial goals, and the partnership between the two functions may therefore be in jeopardy of breaking down. Further, just as marketing people should educate themselves about finances, finance individuals should also educate themselves about marketing. Both sides require a decent understanding of the root principles and processes that rule the other discipline, or they will fall right back into the old model of prioritizing only their own realms and ignoring or trampling the other's domain out of just plain ignorance.

At MillerCoors, finance people are also taught to empathize with marketers in terms of communication style and format. Simply understanding that spreadsheets are for calculating, not communicating, is a laudable first step. In the stale traditional organization, finance has felt free to send spreadsheets to convey a particular point, but while they might understand exactly why they are sending the spreadsheet and the meaning the recipient is supposed to glean from it, it is often not nearly as clear on the other end. Instead of these "data dumps," MillerCoors finance individuals are trained to make a concerted effort to use a minimum of numbers, to present ideas simply, and to drill down data to a manageable and meaningful point. The MillerCoors finance department, for instance, tends to do a lot of its presentations with simple headlines conveying the main point. The use of easy-to-read charts and other visual images augments understanding, and avoiding excessive numbers and words wherever possible dodges the confusion that can often accompany even a simple idea when it is dressed up in jargon, impenetrable metrics, and unreadable font sizes.

To cement the relationship between marketing and finance, incentive plans often prove to be the great unifier. It is good to have the CFO and the CMO on the same incentive plan, because then they are working toward common goals instead of viewing one another as the enemy. By constantly reminding both officers of their shared objectives, they get people on the same track and everybody gets the year-end payoff. Let us return a final time to Gordon, Monier, and Ogren, and their insightful ideas for unifying CFOs and CMOs, who explain that:

> In our work with clients in dozens of sectors over more than five years, we have found that the strongest CMO–CFO partnerships develop when both parties take five actions: open their books to scrutiny, focus on the metrics that matter, balance short- and long-term value creation, consider savings as well as spending, and seek opportunities to collaborate.[25]

They add that doing so results in not insignificant boons for the organization as a whole: "In our experience, companies that adopt this marketing-analytics approach can unlock 10 to 20 percent of their marketing budget to either reinvest in marketing or return to the bottom line." These approaches are made even more powerful by ancillary steps that seek to enable and add value to each action. For instance, opening the books of each department for the other to read is a good-faith action and, for that alone, probably valuable at any point. However, think of how much more enriching this action is when both parties have a working knowledge of what is actually *in* those books. Hence the massive contribution offered by the MillerCoors Learning and Development department's short instructional videos. These not only offer valuable insight into what might otherwise seem an opaque realm of number crunching but enable understanding, which in turn enables true partnership. Furthermore, these videos are presented by members of the senior finance team, not some faceless consultant with a soothing radio voice.

Lastly, it is worth noting that building a solid relationship between marketing and finance may sometimes be as simple as merely endeavoring to do so. "As obvious as it may seem, one way to improve the CMO–CFO relationship is for both parties to recognize that they're on the same team," opine Gordon, Monier, and Ogren. This is different to simply incentivizing a relationship between the two functions. While this is a commendable step, CMOs and CFOs who intentionally take it upon themselves to broaden their understanding of one another's purviews, merely by spending time together, will make the largest strides toward an accountable marketing department and a supportive finance division. "CMOs should invite finance to participate in marketing's planning process to build bridges but also to benefit from financial expertise," they say, adding: "Taking the time to speak with the CFO about the shape of the company and any shifting priorities will allow CMOs to be more attuned to the business and to move more quickly to make adjustments as necessary."

Getting involved in outside organizations can also help to broaden the horizons of individuals from both marketing and finance, helping them see exactly what is at stake in making marketing accountable, and offering innovative ideas on how to do so. MillerCoors, for example, is actively involved with outside organizations such as MASB and the Marketing Science Institute (MSI). Membership in both groups provides the opportunity to interact with peers and to be exposed to the latest and "best" thinking regarding accountability in marketing. The MASB, for example, offers membership to the following entities: marketers, business schools, measurement (modeling and software) providers, media providers, media and advertising agencies, industry associations, and independent consultants.[26] This goes to show how broad their conception is of whom, exactly, has a stake in how marketing accountability winds up. (In a word: everyone.) Similarly, the MSI "is a nonprofit, membership-based organization dedicated to bridging the gap between academic marketing theory and business practice," whose "mission is to bring the best of science to the complex world of marketing."[27]

While the ways in which MillerCoors has attempted to bridge the divide between marketing and finance undoubtedly will not work for every organization in every industry, we can clearly draw some lessons from their story. First, finance is far more effective when it breaks free of traditional siloing and emerges into a fully functional cross-divisional presence across the organization. These "mini-CFOs" offer much-needed financial acumen to marketing while simultaneously encouraging autonomy and self-governance through melded titles such as the Senior Director, Marketing Finance and the Director of Marketing Return Optimization. Second, moving away from the traditional "last year plus 2 percent" model is a good idea in an organization that wants to encourage innovation and fiscal responsibility in its marketing department. Third, using results management offers budgeting flexibility and enables an organization, on the department level, to effectively "manage tradeoffs" so that the budget is always being optimally utilized. Periodic review of the marketing budget, on a basis more often than that of the annual reallocation, will also help marketing to self-police and will instill a deeper understanding of the value of each dollar. Fourth, offering employees resources by which to learn more about functions outside their own is both a powerful tool for consensus building and a powerful enabler of learning new and sometimes scary ideas. Fifth, financial "data dumps" are not communication, and the exchange of ideas should take place in headlines and visuals rather than dense technobabble and numbers. Finally, a direct relationship between the CMO and CFO will result in a relationship between the two departments as a whole that will benefit the entire organization.

A company that hopes to create a partnership between marketing and finance to instill accountability in marketing, protect the marketing dollar against waste, wantonness, and whimsy, and use the power of analytics and measurement to create a substantially more effective and appropriately funded marketing function could do worse than follow this example.

Conclusion

As we have mentioned, the realization of a need for marketing accountability has had poor timing, coming as it has at the same time that the digital revolution has flooded organizations with never-before-seen amounts of data. The process of wading through this data has been burdensome to every department of the modern organization, siloed or matrixed, centralized or decentralized. The result, in some ways, has been to point out a problem that many companies are afraid to try and fix.

Hopefully this chapter makes a persuasive case for the necessity of a partnership between marketing and finance, and the role that such collaboration could play in making sense of this "big data" sandstorm. Without one, even companies that take pains to break free of the old siloed model toward matrix functions will find themselves hard-pressed to bring accountability to marketing and align its goals with finance and the broader enterprise. With such a partnership, however, organizations can approach market analyses, budget issues, campaign ideas, etc., with the confidence that everyone whose voice matters has a seat at the table, and that those voices will be respected when it is their turn to be heard.

References

1 Thomas Sy and Laura Sue D'Annunzio, 2005, "Challenge and Strategies of Matrix Organizations: Top-Level and Mid-Level Managers' Perspectives," *Human Resource Planning*, 28(1): 40.
2 Thomas Sy and Laura Sue D'Annunzio, 2005, "Challenge and Strategies of Matrix Organizations: Top-Level and Mid-Level Managers' Perspectives," *Human Resource Planning*, 28(1): 40.
3 Thomas Sy and Laura Sue D'Annunzio, 2005, "Challenge and Strategies of Matrix Organizations: Top-Level and Mid-Level Managers' Perspectives," *Human Resource Planning*, 28(1): 40.
4 Jay A. Galbraith, *Designing Matrix Organizations That Actually Work: How IBM, Procter & Gamble and Others Design for Success*, 2008, New York: Wiley.
5 Jay A. Galbraith, *Designing Matrix Organizations That Actually Work: How IBM, Procter & Gamble and Others Design for Success*, 2008, New York: Wiley.
6 Malcolm McDonald, "A Brief Review of Marketing Accountability, and a Research Agenda By Emeritus Professor Malcolm McDonald," *Institute for the Study of Business Markets*, last modified February 2012, http://isbm.smeal.psu.edu/resources/articles-use/a-brief-review-of-marketing-accountability.
7 R. Eric Reidenbach and Reginald Goeke, "Marketing Function Is Different in a Six Sigma World," *iSixSigma*, accessed June 9, 2015, http://www.isixsigma.com/operations/marketing-and-sales/marketing-function-different-six-sigma-world/.
8 Rebecca Harris, "How Sociology Trumps Economics in Marketing," *Marketing Mag*, April 7, 2014, http://www.marketingmag.ca/brands/the-sociological-approach-bids-marketers-dig-deeper-for-success-106528.
9 Jonathan Gordon, Jean-Hugues Monier, and Phil Ogren, "Why Can't We Be Friends? Five Steps to Better Relations between CFOs and CMOs," *McKinsey & Company*, December 2013, http://www.mckinsey.com/insights/corporate_finance/why_cant_we_be_friends_five_steps_to_better_relations_between_cfos_and_cmos.
10 Wes Nichols, "Good Quant, Bad Quant," *Analytics Magazine*, accessed June 10, 2015, http://viewer.zmags.com/publication/e0d5d66f#/e0d5d66f/8.
11 Wes Nichols, "Good Quant, Bad Quant," *Analytics Magazine*, accessed June 10, 2015, http://viewer.zmags.com/publication/e0d5d66f#/e0d5d66f/8.
12 Wes Nichols, "Good Quant, Bad Quant," *Analytics Magazine*, accessed June 10, 2015, http://viewer.zmags.com/publication/e0d5d66f#/e0d5d66f/8.

13 Tim Ambler and John Roberts, 2006, "Beware the Silver Metric: Marketing Performance Measurement Has to Be Multidimensional, Marketing Science Institute Report," Cambridge, MA: Marketing Science Institute, available at http://www.msi.org/reports/beware-the-silver-metric-marketing-performance-measurement-has-to-be-multid/.
14 http://www.forbes.com/sites/forbesinsights/2013/07/09/why-roi-is-often-wrong-for-measuring-marketing-impact/.
15 Jonathan Gordon, Jean-Hugues Monier, and Phil Ogren, "Why Can't We Be Friends? Five Steps to Better Relations between CFOs and CMOs," *McKinsey & Company*, December 2013, http://www.mckinsey.com/insights/corporate_finance/why_cant_we_be_friends_five_steps_to_better_relations_between_cfos_and_cmos.
16 Adam Gaskill and Hume Winzar, "Marketing Metrics That Contribute to Marketing Accountability in the Technology Sector," *Sage Journals*, September 23, 2013, http://sgo.sagepub.com/content/3/3/2158244013501332.figures-only.
17 David W. Stewart, personal communication.
18 David W. Stewart, personal communication.
19 "Marketing Training," *Food and Agriculture Organization of the United Nations*, accessed June 9, 2015, http://www.fao.org/ag/ags/agricultural-marketing-linkages/marketing-training/en/.
20 "Our Divisions: Finance," *Goldman Sachs*, accessed June 11, 2015, http://www.goldmansachs.com/careers/why-goldman-sachs/our-divisions/finance/.
21 Jonathan Gordon, Jean-Hugues Monier, and Phil Ogren, "Why Can't We Be Friends? Five Steps to Better Relations between CFOs and CMOs," *McKinsey & Company*, December 2013, http://www.mckinsey.com/insights/corporate_finance/why_cant_we_be_friends_five_steps_to_better_relations_between_cfos_and_cmos.
22 Jonathan Gordon, Jean-Hugues Monier, and Phil Ogren, "Why Can't We Be Friends? Five Steps to Better Relations between CFOs and CMOs," *McKinsey & Company*, December 2013, http://www.mckinsey.com/insights/corporate_finance/why_cant_we_be_friends_five_steps_to_better_relations_between_cfos_and_cmos.
23 *The Marketing Accountability Standards Board*, accessed June 10, 2015, http://www.themasb.org/.
24 "An Introduction to Results Management: Principles, Implications, and Applications," *Asian Development Bank*, 2006, http://www.adb.org/sites/default/files/institutional-document/32577/files/introduction-results-management.pdf.
25 Jonathan Gordon, Jean-Hugues Monier, and Phil Ogren, "Why Can't We Be Friends? Five Steps to Better Relations between CFOs and CMOs," *McKinsey & Company*, December 2013, http://www.mckinsey.com/insights/corporate_finance/why_cant_we_be_friends_five_steps_to_better_relations_between_cfos_and_cmos.
26 http://themasb.org.
27 "About the Marketing Science Institute," *Marketing Science Institute*, 2015, http://www.msi.org/about-msi/.

13 Reporting on Brands

Roger Sinclair

A Historical Context

For a period of time in the 1980s brands were on the balance sheet. This was not because brands were identified as assets by the accountants according to accounting standards, but because skilled financial operators were using them to raise capital and to boost company value. The practice ended sharply in 1989 in the United Kingdom with the regulatory accounting body issuing a "cease and desist" order to its members.

News Corporation's Rupert Murdoch was probably the first to understand that when he bought a publishing title the reason he paid a price that exceeded the net asset value, was because the masthead drew readers and advertising. In 1984 he had his accountants value the brands (mastheads) he had bought and include them in the financial statements as assets. This boosted the balance sheet value of the company allowing him to raise the funds he needed for his global expansion.

The rise in the overall market to book ratio during the 1980s and 1990s and sustained even after the dot.com collapse indicates the value being placed by the investment community on intangibles. The most famous examples of value attributed to brands in the 1980s are the huge transactions by: R.J. Reynolds, which bought Nabisco; Procter & Gamble, which acquired Richardson Vicks; and Grand Metropolitan in the UK (now Diageo), which bought Pillsbury. The latter, at US$5.5 billion was massive by contemporary standards.

It was argued at the time that investors gained valuable knowledge from being shown the value of acquired and self-generated brands because, while brands generate future economic benefits for the firm, historically, this value had not been acknowledged. When brands, as intangibles, are added to tangible assets on the balance sheet they provide a clearer picture of the true worth of the enterprise. They provide management and shareholders with a more realistic basis on which to evaluate the company's economic performance. Furthermore, brands on the balance sheet forge a financial link between the company's growth or decline and its marketing activities.

The approach to brands as intangible assets by these financial adventurers could best be described as creative accounting, but there was no regulation at the time to prevent it. The "cease and desist" order mentioned above was issued in the UK by the Institute of Chartered Accountants of England and Wales. Its purpose was to allow time for a commission headed by marketing professor, Patrick (Paddy) Barwise of the London Business School, to conduct an investigation into what had become the "brands as assets" controversy. At the end of an intense three-month study he and his colleagues concluded that brands could not meet the definition of an asset and should not therefore be considered as such.[1] It might have remained that way except for the seemingly inexorable rise in the value that investors continued to place on listed companies on all the world's stock markets. Figure 13.1 shows the split between tangible and intangible assets of companies on the S&P 500 between 1975 and 2010.

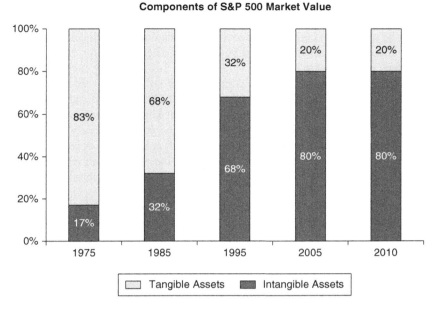

Figure 13.1 Components of S&P 500 Market Value.
Source: Ocean Tomo.

You simply cannot ignore the 80 percent represented by intangibles from 2005 onwards. Phillip Kotler, the renowned marketing academic and author, has claimed in several talks he gives around the world that "The modern balance sheet is a lie."[2] He is referring to this margin, which continues to go unexplained. He uses the example of Coca Cola to make the point. It is patently clear to even non-financial people that the reason for the Coca Cola Company earning the profits it does (US$9.0 billion in 2012) is, in very large part, due to the cash flows generated by its venerable brand. Yet accounting standards prohibit investors from knowing what the brand is worth. They should be able to look at the balance sheet to see this. Instead they have to rely on top brand tables of which there are several and which rarely agree with each other.

Fortunately, this growing gap did not go unnoticed. Robert A. Bayless, chief accountant in the Division of Corporation Finance at the Securities Exchange Commission (SEC), told a meeting of the Certified Financial Analysts (CFA) in March 2001: "Wide variations between a company's stock price and its underlying book value per share frequently are attributed to the failure of the current accounting model to recognize a company's internally generated intangibles."[3]

His comments were serendipitous, because in that same year the Financial Accounting Standards Board (FASB) issued SFAS 141 *Business Combinations* (now ASC 805). For the first time, brands could officially be called assets, because the standard required a post-transaction estimate of the costs that make up any market premium paid. In the explanatory notes the standard is unambiguous in stating that trademarks, known by marketers as brands, will qualify.

Four years later the International Accounting Standards Board (IASB) issued a similar standard: International Financial Reporting Standard (IFRS) 3 *Business Combinations*. In an accompanying document to the newly released standard, the authors state:

> [t]he FASB and IASB both observed that intangible assets make up an increasing proportion of the assets of many if not most entities. The boards also observed that intangible assets acquired in a business combination were often included in the amount recognized as goodwill.[4]

What Do These Standards Say ... and Not Say?

In order that investors and other users of financial accounts have a common basis by which company performance can be judged and compared, accounting standards are developed and issued that guide companies in how their accounts should be prepared. These standards cover a wide range of topics, but a few are relevant to brands.

Two bodies issue these standards: the FASB, which applies only in the United States of America, and the IASB, which applies to most countries outside the USA. FASB and IASB have a close working relationship and in terms of a Memorandum of Understanding, signed some years ago and updated in 2008, are working on what they describe as convergence. In essence, this is to ensure that FASB and IASB standards are comparable. It is likely that at some stage in the future there will be one set of global standards, but that point has not yet been reached.

The accounting standards that FASB and IASB issue are based on a conceptual framework, which is being developed as a joint project between the two bodies. In 2010, the IASB announced completion of the first phase of this development, which will be fully updated in the next few years. The framework sets out a number of objectives, but the theme that flows through them all is to "[p]rovide financial information about the reporting entity that is useful to existing and potential investors, lenders and other creditors in making decisions about providing resource to the entity."[5]

The need to provide "useful" information is why the accounting profession adopted methods of asset measurement that veered from its centuries-old approach. Traditionally, assets have been valued at the cost at which they were bought. This amount is then depreciated over a number of years. The number of years is based on the useful life of the asset. This approach confounded the usefulness of the accounts, because an asset might be carried in the books at a written down value when in fact it could fetch a high price on the open market. The company was therefore undervalued.

The conceptual framework lists four approaches for measuring the value of assets:

1 **historical cost**—the original cost of acquiring the asset, depreciated over a set period;
2 **current cost**—the cost that would have to be paid to acquire the asset currently;
3 **realizable or settlement value**—the amount that could be obtained if the asset were to be sold in an orderly market;
4 **present value**—the present discounted value of estimated future cash inflows.

(A more complete explanation of each of these will be found in section 4.55 of the 1989 *Conceptual Framework* text, which is in the process of being updated.)[6]

It is up to the entity itself to decide which of these approaches is most appropriate to the nature of the organization and the information needs of the users of its financial statements. The rapid growth of intangibles brought about the need for specialized accounting standards and, as we shall see, the nature of intangibles made it necessary for the available measurement approaches to be expanded.

Some assets require a fifth measurement approach: fair value. While this method could be applied to any asset, it is mostly associated with the pricing of financial instruments and intangibles. What distinguishes it from the four above is that all four are entity-specific, whereas fair value is market-based, as its definition makes clear: "[f]air value [is defined] as the price that would be received to sell an asset or paid to transfer a liability in an orderly transaction between market participants at the measurement date (i.e. an exit price)."[7]

It is important to note this approach, because the standards that deal with intangible assets specify this method. Furthermore, fair value is so new to accounting that it required a specially developed guideline to explain the process.[8]

When Brands *Are* Assets

FASB introduced SFAS 141 *Business Combinations* (ASC 805) in 2001. The IASB followed suit four years later with IFRS 3 *Business Combinations*. There are differences between the two, but insofar as brands are concerned each version achieves the same result.

At the outset, IFRS 3 states in paragraph 13: "[this recognition principle] . . . may result in recognizing some assets and liabilities that the acquiree had not previously recognized in its financial statements. For example . . . acquired intangible assets, such as a brand name." This is a key statement, because it is the first formal confirmation by the accounting profession that brands may be described as assets. The reason for this is captured by the observation mentioned above that identifiable intangible assets are "included in the amount recognized as goodwill." The intention is to provide more useful information to investors and others as to what makes up the purchase consideration and the margin between net asset value and price paid. Any amount that cannot be explained by identifiable intangibles (the residual) remains as goodwill.

This begs the question as to what process leads to the identification of acquired intangibles. If company A buys company B which is in the business of shipping, the core of the purchase is for the fleet of ships. Each vessel has an original purchase price and its current book value depends on the age of the ship and rate of depreciation. If the target company is a travel agency, the circumstances are very different. The business comprises the locations of its offices, desks, computers, and trained staff. Its value lies almost entirely in intangibles: the size of its customer lists, its online presence, its website, its relationships with travel wholesalers and carriers, its network of contacts in destinations, and, of course, awareness by customers within its target market of its brand name and the associations existing, past, and potential travelers hold of it in their memories. These are all intangibles, which together generate the cash flows that underlie the value of the business.

The standards (ASC 805 and IFRS 3) require post-transaction accounting to identify as many of these intangibles as is possible, to measure the value of each one and to detail them in the notes to the accounts. The aggregate of the intangibles is then posted to the balance sheet under the appropriate heading (intangible assets or goodwill). Table 13.1 shows a summary of the main post-transaction accounts in the year following Procter & Gamble's (P&G) purchase of The Gillette Company in 2005. The purchase price was US$54 billion.

This example shows clearly why this standard is needed. The goodwill and intangible asset amounts overwhelm the net assets. In the notes it is stated that the Gillette brand was valued at US$24 billion. At a little under half the purchase consideration the introduction of a standard such as this would appear to be justified.

Table 13.1 Summary of Main Post-Transaction Accounts—P&G's Purchase of The Gillette Company in 2005

	US$ bn
Current assets	5.553
Property, plant and equipment	3.673
Goodwill	34.943
Intangible assets	29.736
Other non-current assets	0.773
Total assets	*74.676*
Current liabilities	5.000
Other non-current liabilities	16.241
Total liabilities	*21.250*
Net assets	**53.426**

Source: Created by the author.

But Is it Always Clear What the Underlying Intangibles Are?

By their very nature, intangible assets are illusory. There is no definitive set of intangible assets to explain why an enterprise justifies a value that exceeds its cost of capital. This surplus is in the mind of the investor or interested party. It might be obvious that the Gillette brand is the power behind the US$54 billion that P&G paid for the company, but this is not inevitably the case.

Consider Google, for example. If Microsoft bought the search engine, the brand would be a major reason, but there are other intangibles at play there too. The exclusive ownership of the URL would feature, as would the complex and ever-evolving software that makes Google so fast and effective. The company's extraordinary ability to innovate new ideas and to write the codes that transform them into operational reality is a prize worth paying for. Which of these intangibles would Microsoft be buying (there might be others such as outstanding leadership), and what is the relative importance of each in driving cash flows? To guide those whose task is to prepare the post-transaction accounts, the standard setters have devised a shopping list of possible intangible assets (IAs) (Table 13.2).

Five segments divided into 28 sub-points making about 60 options overall should cover most probable intangibles, but there are more: carbon footprint; URL ownership; and research and development are a few. So the list is by no means definitive.

It is significant that the standard setters chose "marketing-related IAs" as the first heading and trademarks, with its notable brand qualification, as the very first item, because an examination of a collection of balance sheets prepared according to ASC 805 and IFRS 3 indicate that brands arguably are the most frequently nominated intangible assets for balance sheet inclusion. For example, the European Securities and Markets' Authority (ESMA), in an examination of post-transaction financial reports, found that the most frequently identified intangible asset was "customer-related" (58 percent) followed closely by "brands" (54 percent).

Do Brands Need Special Treatment?

ASC 805 and IFRS 3 *Business Combinations* are designed to interpret components of mergers and acquisition at the time of the transaction. Their purpose is to break down the amount that would have been allocated to goodwill to expose the identifiable intangibles that brought about the premium paid. (Formally, this is known as Purchase Price Allocation, PPA.) What happens next should, in the case of brands, be contentious. It is not.

The cost of the intangible asset that arises from this identification, recognition, and measurement is carried on the balance sheet at its post-transaction value. Each year the company must carry out a test of impairment to see if the current value remains at the level at which the asset is being carried. As the term implies, impairment is solely concerned with loss of value. If the value drops in any year, the amount by which it falls short of its carrying amount is considered to be an impairment loss. This loss is transferred to the income statement and reduces the company's profits. (If this is redolent of debate after the 2008 financial crisis, it is because some believe that write-downs arising from marking assets to market were a root cause of the meltdown.)

Marketers introduce brands for the long term. Keller[9] shows that of the top 25 brands in 1923, 20 still remain today in the top 25 table. In accounting terms, this longevity has been acknowledged in the way the accounting standards deal with the useful economic life of an asset. An asset has either a finite useful life or its life is indefinite. Note that, in the accounting sense, the antonym of finite is not infinite. This is to make clear that no asset is expected to live forever, but that in many cases, and this is especially so for brands, their life span cannot be predicted. If an asset is shown to have a finite life, its value is depreciated over its finite life span. An asset with an undetermined, indefinite life is carried in the books and tested for impairment.

Not only do marketers launch brands for the long term, they expect them to grow each year. If they do not, they are withdrawn from the market. If a firm's marketing investment is successful,

Table 13.2 Intangible Assets

Marketing-related IAs	Customer-related IAs	Artistic-related IAs	Technology-based IAs	Contract-based IAs
1 Trademarks, trade names, service marks, collective marks, certification marks*	6 Customer lists	Plays, operas, ballets	Patented technology	Licensing, royalty, and standstill agreements
2 Trade dress	7 Order or production backlogs	Books, magazines, newspapers, and other literary works	Computer software and mask works	Advertising, construction, management, service, or supply contracts
3 Newspaper mastheads	8 Customer contracts and related customer relationships	Musical works such as compositions, song lyrics, and advertising jingles	Unpatented technology	Lease agreements
4 Internet domain names	9 Non-contractual customer relationships	Pictures and photographs	Databases including title plants	Construction permits
5 Non-competition agreements		Video and audiovisual material, including motion pictures or films, music videos, and TV programs	Trade secrets, such as secret formulas, processes, and recipes	Franchise agreements
*The explanatory text in IFRS 3 states that marketers use brand and brand name as synonyms for trademarks and other marks.				Operating and broadcast rights
				Service contracts such as mortgage and servicing contracts
				Employment contracts
				Use rights (drilling, water, air, timber, and routes)

Source: Created by the author.

it will achieve its goals of increasing the number of customers who buy the brand, improve the volume they buy and the price they pay for it, and the brand asset should consequently improve in its proportional contribution to the value of the enterprise. If financial accounts in subsequent years do not recognize this, the accounts will show a diminishing relative value for the brand and an increase in the amount allocated to goodwill; the very reason for introducing these new standards in the first place.

Accountants have an available term that means asset growth, but they prefer not to use it. The term is *accretion* and is the opposite of *impairment*. If the balance sheet is to be true to the objectives in the conceptual framework and be of use to investors, it must be constantly updated to show assets that lose as well as gain value. The vibrant nature of brands demands this. We will look more closely at this shortly.

Returning to the example of the P&G purchase of Gillette, the value shown for the world famous brand remains at the 2005 purchase value. Even though the brand has kept pace with trends in its market category, has extended its range of products and variants, and has maintained its market leadership, relative to the market worth of its parent, it is falling in value (in 2006 Gillette represented 16 percent of P&G's market capitalization. In 2013 it had dropped to 12 percent). See Sinclair and Keller (2016).[10]

Clearly, the accounting authorities should recognize that brands are expected to have long lives, that they are a vital link in earning the firm its cash flows, and that if the firm is successful with its marketing investment, the brand asset will increase in value each year. The term accretion should be introduced into accounting for intangibles so that periodic tests of the carrying amount are shown not just by their impaired amount but also by the amount of value they have added. How this is treated in the accounts is a matter for the accounting technicians, but there are precedents for dealing with this type of gain (e.g., IFRS 3: 34–36 dealing with Bargain Purchases).

When Brands Are *Not* Assets

A different standard deals with intangible assets (as opposed to intangible assets acquired in a business combination as discussed above). The FASB version was called SFAS 142 *Goodwill and Other Intangible Assets*. In FASB's new codification this standard is ASC 350. The IASB version is International Accounting Standard (IAS) 38 *Intangible Assets*. It is IAS as opposed to IFRS, because it has not yet been amended and converted to an IFRS. In its current form, IAS 38 *Intangible Assets* specifically disallows brands from being identified and recognized as intangible assets (IAS 38–63/64). ASC 350 is not quite as specific, but its paragraphs that deal with brands (25-3) have the same effect.

At the time of writing, the standard setters (FASB and IASB) do not see the need to change this apparent contradiction (brands acquired in a business combination are assets; brands that are internally developed are not) as a priority and until they do, internally generated brands, as opposed to those acquired as discussed above, will be denied a place on the balance sheet. In this section we make the case for change and trust that during the currency of this book that will take place.

The standard setters identify many instances where entities "expend resources, or incur liabilities on the acquisition, development, maintenance or enhancement of intangible resources" (IAS 38–9). These are items such as computer software, patents, copyright, motion-picture films, fishing license rights, and others such as trademarks (including brand names). This list is immediately qualified to make it clear that "not all these items meet the definition on an intangible asset" (IAS 38–10).

The cause of this can be traced back to the time when historical cost was the foundation of accounts. The change from *historical* to *current* cost and the more recent adoption of the notion of *fair value* should have brought change to this conflict as well. The reason why it has not is found in the section of IAS 38 that deals with the identification and recognition of intangible assets. When specifying which assets will be recognized, IAS 38–21a states: "It is probable that the expected future economic benefits that are attributable to the asset will flow to the entity," and IAS 38–21b: "the cost of the asset can be measured reliably." It then states: "An intangible asset shall be measured initially at cost," (IAS 38–24). It concludes: "Expenditure on internally generated brands . . . cannot be distinguished from the cost of developing the business as a whole." Therefore: "internally generated brands . . . shall not be recognized as intangible assets" (IAS 38–63/64).

This standard was issued in the late 1990s before the standard setters recognized the role that intangible assets play in the value of enterprises. When FASB announced SFAS 141 and IASB followed suit with IFRS 3, they introduced the concept of *fair value*, which is the polar extreme of historical cost. So significant is the difference that FASB wrote and issued SFAS 157 (now ASC 820) *Fair Value Measurement* and IASB issued IFRS 13 *Fair Value Measurement*. These are almost identical explanations of how fair value is measured. If the standards that deal with intangible assets were updated to change the language from cost to fair value, brands would immediately become assets.

While there is little logic in perpetuating the conflict, the logic for change is clear and straightforward. Brands are assets when they are identified and recognized following a business combination. So certain are the standard setters about this that "marketing-based intangible assets" is the first of the five segments that are listed as intangibles that will be identified, and trademarks (with its brand synonym) is the first entry (see Table 13.2). The difference between the specific allowance in the business combination standard and the older one that deals with intangible assets is terminology. Valuation at fair value is acceptable, measurement at initial cost is not.

Accountants have always believed that the only way to establish a value is by reference to what the asset cost. Six hundred years of preparing accounts makes that tradition hard to jettison. In the case of a business combination, the argument is that the price paid establishes the cost. If the component ascribable to net tangible assets is removed, what remains is the intangible portion. Except that is not what happens. The subtraction of net assets from purchase consideration leaves a margin that was allocated to *goodwill*. The new standards require goodwill to be broken down to expose its identifiable components, among which will be trademarks or brands. The standard setters and the prime users of the standards are happy that a measurement technique based on the principles in *Fair Value Measurement* (ASC 820 and IFRS 13) produces an acceptable value. This same approach is not thought suitable to measure intangibles, such as brands, which have been internally generated. As a result, as the P&G example above illustrates, users of the accounts are not given complete information. Only intangibles that have been acquired are listed in the balance sheet; those that have driven a company such as P&G for more than 150 years are kept hidden.

There can be no justification for not changing the standard so that intangibles in both *business combinations* and *intangible assets* feature the same identification and measurement method. The reason it has not been changed so far is probably more to do with the resistance of tradition and a degree of inertia. It is a change that must be made if the accounting standards are to remain true to their central objective of being "[u]seful to existing and potential investors, lenders and other creditors in making decisions about providing resource to the entity" (IASB: OB2).[11]

Testing the Water

Both FASB and IASB have conducted what they call Post Implementation Reviews (PIR) of their respective *Business Combination* standards. FASB was in 2013 and IAS in 2014. This is accomplished by a formal Request for Information (RFI), which results in interested parties submitting letters about their experience of the standard. The aim is to discover if the standard is "performing as intended." The Marketing Accountability Standards Board (MASB) Improving Financial Reporting (IFR) task team submitted letters to each.

The author of this chapter analyzed the 90 letters that had been submitted to the IASB by the closing date of May 31, 2014 and presented his findings at the Winter MASB Summit in Chicago.[12] He identified six main themes, but the most frequently mentioned problem was "complexity." The respondents felt that while the standards generated useful information, the process of following the fair value measurement guidelines was: time-consuming, complex, and expensive, because external experts had to be employed. In the summaries published so far by the two accounting bodies, this theme has also been noted:

> The FASB also acknowledged the PIR findings related to the cost and complexity of applying the fair value measurement guidance in FASB Statement No. 157, *Fair Value Measurements*, to certain types of assets and liabilities acquired in a business combination. The FASB said it would review the findings of the forthcoming PIR on Statement 157, and will coordinate with the IASB once the review of IFRS 3 is complete, before deciding whether to undertake any standard-setting action.[13]

In the IASB summary, the same theme is noted: "Many preparers think that the calculations are often difficult to prepare, taking a significant amount of time and often require the engagement of independent valuation specialists, which makes the exercise costly."[14]

This is a serious challenge to the valuation industry and the range of methods offered. In an *Economist* article (August 30, 2014) on brands and their measurement, Senior Technical Director at the IASB, Allan Teixeira, said: "Brand values vary wildly." The absence of a robust, universally accepted valuation methodology acceptable by those who prepare accounts and report on assets that companies acquire or own and by those who use these documents, could bring to an end the quest for brands being identified and recognized as assets. In a global investment environment in which intangible premiums are as much as 80 percent of total value and in which brands make up over 50 percent of intangibles identified in business combinations, this would be a tragedy.

The MASB Brand Investment and Valuation Project (BIV) described in Chapter 14 is working toward this goal. It might be a question of what happens first: completion of the BIV project or a decision by the accounting standard setters to eliminate the complexity. The next year or so will determine the fate of brands as assets.

Methods of Measurement

In this section we look at the main valuation methods available. There are a plethora of measurement methods. Gabriela Salinas suggested that there were at least "39 proprietary brand valuation models," when she wrote her book in 2009.[15] The market for product brand valuation[16] is dominated by three firms and a technique. The technique is *relief from royalty*, a simple approach that is favored by the major accounting firms, trade mark lawyers, and the banks that conduct mergers and acquisitions. The three firms are London-based Interbrand, and Brand Finance and Millward Brown based in the USA.

Relief from royalty is based on the notion that a company would have to pay a royalty to a third party for use of the trademark if the company did not own it. The value of the trademark must be the capitalized present value of the future economic benefits saved by not having to pay the royalties, because the company owns it.

The measurement is conducted over whatever period the life dictates, normally between five and ten years, because the kind of intangible assets that have historically been measured have finite lives. In many jurisdictions, the amortized amount is allowable as a tax deductible expense and therefore tax not paid is a saving. This is known as the tax amortization benefit or TAB. Most brands will have indefinite lives and TAB does not therefore apply. In this case an annuity is sometimes used to take account of the long life. There are two major problems with this approach:

1. **royalty rate**—there is no universally accepted way to calculate the appropriate royalty rate. Some companies in the United States claim to research rates and make them available to valuators. The source of their information is primarily what they pick up in the business pages of the media. By definition this is incomplete, because not every licensing deal is reported in the media. Also the rates quoted for a category will have been assembled over time, so some will be recent and others could be from years back. Finally, one rate tends to be used for all trademarks in a category; only by applying subjective adjustments can the rate be made specific to the asset being valued. An approach to calculating the rate is sometimes used. It is called the "25 percent rule" and is based on the idea that there should be a fair division of profits between the licensee and licensor and that should be 25 percent of the ratio between sales and operating profit. This is quite a crude device and, while it is specific to the trademark being valued, it is also subject to the fluctuations of financial performance.
2. **use of an annuity for indefinitely long-lived assets**—to use the relief from royalty method, the valuator needs to make assumptions about future growth rates and discount rates. In particular, account must be taken of the indefinite life of the asset. An annuity is used for this.

Table 13.3 shows an example of relief from royalty, based on a 4 percent royalty rate, a growth rate of 5 percent per annum for six years and a discount rate of 8 percent. The capitalized present value of the first five years is 12,613. An annuity is then calculated on the sixth year after a discount factor has been allowed (six years at 8 percent = 0.63). Apart from the need to have well considered and justified growth rates and a properly calculated discount rate, the simple division of the discounted sixth year by the discount rate to provide an allowance for the asset's indefinite long life is at best tenuous and yet it accounts for two-thirds of the total value.

It is probably true to say that the majority of valuations for use in business combination post-transaction accounting are conducted by the relief from royalty method. In the notes to the balance sheet it is rare for any of the three firms noted above to be mentioned. A reason for this might be found in the disparity of values demonstrated in Table 13.4. This depicts the values calculated by each of the three firms for their annual top brand tables. These are the 2013 values.

The extent of disparity in both order and quantum (and direction over time) presumably disqualifies any of the three from being used for accounting purposes. If relief from royalty is unreliable and the top valuation companies are erratic, how should brands be valued?

A Matter of Principle

In the IFRS Conceptual Framework currently (July, 2013) being issued as a discussion paper it states: "A single measurement basis for all assets and liabilities may not provide the most relevant information for users of financial statements" (IASB-DP, 2013, Section 6b). This establishes the notion that there is unlikely to be a single valuation methodology that can be used for

Table 13.3 Relief from Royalty Example

	y1	y2	y3	y4	y5	y6
Sales	100,000	105,000	110,250	115,763	121,551	127,628
Rate @ 4%	4,000	4,200	4,410	4,631	4,862	5,105
less tax (28%)	2,880	3,024	3,175	3,334	3,501	3,676
PV (y1-y5)	12,613				discount factor	0.63
Annuity	28,946					2,316
Value	**148,439**					

Source: Created by the author.

Table 13.4 Disparity of Values among the Top Ten Brands

	Interbrand	US$ bn	Millward Brown	US$ bn	Brand Finance	US$ bn
1	Apple	98.3	Apple	185.0	Apple	87.3
2	Google	93.3	Google	113.7	Samsung	58.8
3	Coca Cola	79.2	IBM	112.5	Google	52.3
4	IBM	78.8	McDonald's	90.2	Microsoft	45.5
5	Microsoft	59.5	Coca Cola	78.4	Walmart	42.3
6	GE	46.9	AT&T	75.5	IBM	37.2
7	McDonald's	42.0	Microsoft	69.9	GE	37.2
8	Samsung	39.6	Marlboro	69.4	Amazon	36.8
9	Intel	37.3	Visa	56.0	Coca Cola	34.2
10	Toyota	35.3	China Mobile	55.4	Verizon	31.0

Source: Created by the author.

all brand measurements. As has been observed earlier, Salinas has counted close to 40 brand valuation methodologies that are commercially available. None of these could possibly aspire to be the single method of choice for all valuations; there has to be scope for employment of the one most suited to the task. At the same time, the necessity for reliability is not served if the resulting values differ as radically as those shown in Table 13.4.

One solution would be for there to be a set of guiding principles that could be used universally to judge the suitability of a valuation scheme. This would limit the approach used to those that comply with the principles, and this in turn would ensure that the values the approaches generate would fall within a relatively narrow range.

Alternatively, as we have already mentioned, a measurement technique that is uncomplicated, easy to use, and inexpensive to apply could become the de facto global standard. In the interests of marketing and brands, it is a challenge worth the effort it would take.

How Would Brands Appear on the Balance Sheet?

The modern balance sheet has two line items to allow for the requirements of ASC 805 *Business Combinations* and IFRS 3 *Business Combinations*: "Goodwill" and "Intangible assets." These both deal with assets acquired in a business combination. The values are the immediate post-transaction valuations calculated according to the principles laid out in ASC 820 and IFRS 13 *Fair Value Measurement*.

Goodwill and intangible assets are each tested regularly (not necessarily annually) for impairment. That is accounting language for loss in value. If it should occur that the carrying amount (the value of the asset at the time of the test) is greater than the newly estimated value, an impairment loss is declared and the amount of the loss is treated as an expense in the income statement. This has the effect of depressing profits by an amount that is not a real expense. The detail behind the calculations is explained in the "notes to the accounts" and elsewhere in the narrative part of the accounts.

If the internally generated intangible asset strictures in ASC 350 and IFRS 3 were to be changed, a further line item would likely be included to allow for Intangible assets (internally generated). Against this title would be a single number, which is the aggregate of all the intangible assets identified and measured. The detail would be in the "notes to the accounts" and elsewhere in the narrative part of the report.

If a brand were to lose value and be impaired, it would be because the brand's cash flows had slipped or it was losing its consumer support. The reaction of a company whose brands were in decline would be either to invest additional funds to support the brands or withdraw them from the market. Since the usual practice is to withdraw marketing support from an irredeemably fading brand, milk its profits, and ultimately remove it, the brand would remain within the portfolio until it was deemed to have failed entirely.

If, however, the firm invested marketing funds in the brand and it recovered its position due to an innovative formulation change or new look, this would not be reflected in the accounts, because there is no accounting mechanism to show a gain in asset value as opposed to a loss. Even the great Coca Cola has lost value over the years due to an ill-considered change in formulation and an unfounded scare in one European market that the beverage was tainted with poison. It has undoubtedly recovered from these temporary setbacks and remains one of the most valuable brand assets the world has known.

The accounting standards partially deal with the unique nature of this class of intangible asset in that the business combination standards allow for assets that are finite in economic useful life or which have indefinite long lives. In the case of a finite life, the asset is amortized over the period. Assets that are deemed to have indefinite lives (as will be the case with most brands) are carried in the balance sheet at their initial cost (a fair value measurement conducted at the time of the transaction) and tested annually for impairment.

But, as the above discussion shows, this is insufficient. The growth in brand value is a function of marketing activity, and the goal of this activity is to increase the cash flows that the brand generates either by accelerating the collection of these cash flows or enhancing the forecast trajectory. If brands are subject to occasional declines, they are at least as likely to register increases in the contribution they make to enterprise revenues and profit. For this a new unit of account is needed and, as we discussed earlier, this calls for the introduction of the available account term: accretion.

The Integrated Report

Integrated reporting (IR)[17] is a relatively new approach for businesses to communicate with investors. It recognizes that enterprise value is more complex than a company's financial records indicate. In 2013, the London-based International Integrated Report Committee (IIRC) issued a draft framework for the integrated report and called for comment. Over 350 responses were received from individuals and bodies across the globe and, in December 2013, the IIRC issued the framework that will guide companies during a test period. Once the test is completed it is hoped the IR concept will be adopted worldwide. During the test period some 100 companies will use the framework.

The integrated report brings together information on a comprehensive range of activities within the business that between them underpin the company's strategy for growth and records its performance. Central to the idea are "five interrelated capitals," which drive the business.

The model in Figure 13.2 summarizes the process and adds a sixth form of capital, intellectual, to the traditional five of financial, manufactured, human, social, and natural. At the heart of the approach is the business model, which encompasses the entire process and ethos that guides the business in creating value for investors. It draws on the five traditional capitals, and the outcomes of its various processes are measured by these five capitals.

An IR will be between 30 and 40 pages in length, but because it is based on such concise elements it will very quickly provide readers with a comprehensive understanding of the company and how it operates. More importantly will be metrics that explain performance and achievement.

Brands and marketing feature prominently in the framework. Under the heading of Social and Reputational Capital the framework includes this line: "Intangibles associated with the brand and reputation that an organization has developed." Elsewhere in the text the report mentions segmentation, market share, customer loyalty, and other terms that are used by marketers to describe their activities.

Regardless of whether the accounting changes referred to above come about, it would seem that brands will be fully covered in the integrated report which looks set to be adopted by many companies around the world.

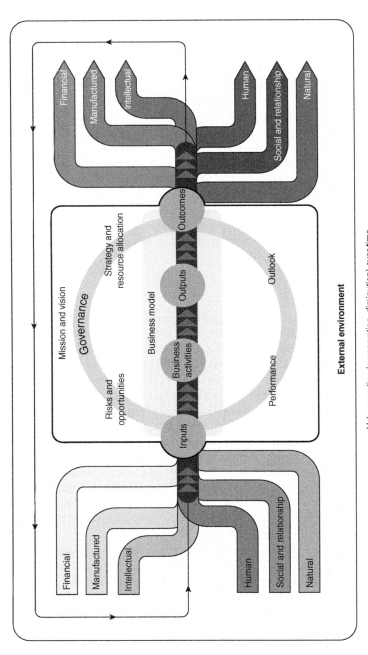

Figure 13.2 External Environment.

Source: The International <IR> Framework.

Summary, and Management and Marketing Implications

According to Thomson Reuters, in the full year of 2014 there were 40,000 business combination deals worth just over US$3.75 trillion. This is down on previous years, but taking that number as an annual average there will have been roughly 400,000 deals over the 10 years since the business combination accounting standards have been operative. If brands are identified and recognized in 54 percent of deals, there are over 200,000 financial statements in which brands are listed as assets. These are just instances where one company has bought another. No brands that have been "internally generated" are recognized as assets by accountants. If the standards were to be changed to rectify this omission, not only would the number run to millions, but a large proportion of the 80 percent premium between market value and net assets would be explained. Furthermore, the explanation analysts and investors would examine would be brands. Two main implications arise from this:

1. Accounting standards are designed to make "useful" information available to investors, shareholder, and lenders. If brands represent 50 percent of enterprise intangible value, nothing could be more useful or important.
2. Marketers have for generations sought a way to report on their activities to the board that is relevant and linked to enterprise wealth. Reporting marketing expenditure as a return on a major asset achieves this goal and elevates marketing to a vital and measureable business operation.

During the currency of this book, the obstacles confronted by the business combination standards will be resolved by the standard setters. The direction they take will have a decisive impact on the status of brands. Marketers will have little say in this matter and can do no more than watch from the sidelines.

References

1. Barwise, P., Higson, C., Likierman, A., and Marsh, P., *Accounting for Brands*, 1989, London Business School and the Institute of Chartered Accountants in England and Wales.
2. For example see: http://www.marsdd.com/articles/intangible-assets-kotler-on-marketing/.
3. http://www.cfainstitute.org/ethics/ASCs/Pages/comprehensive_business_reporting_model.aspx.
4. IASB: IFRS 3 Business Combinations, basis for conclusions BC 157.
5. http://www.ifrs.org/Current-Projects/IASB-Projects/Conceptual-Framework/Pages/Conceptual-Framework-Summary.aspx.
6. http://www.ifrs.org/Current-Projects/IASB-Projects/Conceptual-Framework/Pages/Conceptual-Framework-Summary.aspx.
7. IFRS 13. IN8 (ASC 820–20).
8. IFRS 13; ASC 820, was SFAS 157.
9. Keller, K. L., *Strategic Brand Management: Building, Measuring and Managing Brand Equity*. 3rd edition, 2008, Upper Saddle River, NJ: Pearson-Prentice-Hall, p. 30.
10. Sinclair, R. N. and Keller, K. L., 2016, "The Moribund Effect: How Brands Suffer from an Unintended Consequence of Accounting Standard IFRS3 Business Combination," MASB Working Paper. Available on request from info@themasb.org.
11. Sinclair and Keller have argued this case fully in: http://www.themasb.org/themasb.org/wp-content/uploads/2008/12/JOBM_actual_2014.pdf.
12. http://www.themasb.org/themasb.org/wp-content/uploads/2014/08/H.-BrandsAsAssets-Sinclair.8.14F.pdf.
13. http://www.fasb.org/jsp/FASB/FASBContent_C/NewsPage&cid=1176162711427.
14. http://www.ifrs.org/Meetings/MeetingDocs/IASB/2014/September/AP12F-IFRS%20IC%20Issues-PIR%20IFRS%203.pdf.
15. Salinas, G., *The International Brand Valuation Manual*, 2009, New York: Wiley.
16. Corporate brand valuation is distinct from product brand valuation in that it places a value on the company's reputation. Corebrand is the leading purveyor of corporate brand valuations in the USA. See Chapter 14 of this book.
17. http://www.theiirc.org/.

14 Brand Valuation in Accordance with GAAP and Legal Requirements

Marc Fischer

Purposes of Brand Valuation

With growing evidence of its long-term impact on firm value, brand equity represents an important market-based asset for many firms.[38, 45] Top managers, shareholders, and other stakeholders are increasingly demanding higher transparency of the financial impact of investments by marketing managers (e.g., Ambler 2000),[34] resulting in a number of important contributions to the marketing literature in recent years.

The necessity to disclose the value of intangible assets such as brands in financial reports has been called for and discussed since the 2000s.[3, 13, 31, 46] For many companies, intangible assets contribute significantly to their value. Empirical capital markets research underlines the value relevance of intangible assets. For example, analysts seem to prefer dealing with companies that dispose of important intangible assets.[4] A study among Australian firms reveals that revaluations of long-lived intangible assets, which is allowed under Australian generally accepted accounting principles (GAAP), are positively correlated with share prices, whereas the findings are inconsistent with regard to tangible assets such as property, plant, and equipment.[3] Kallapur and Kwan[26] find that brand assets recognized by UK firms are highly value relevant. However, market capitalization rates of brands differ among firms, leading the authors to conclude that the applied brand valuation procedures do not produce consistent results. This finding emphasizes the need to develop a valuation standard that yields reliable estimates.

In recognition of the increased importance of intangible assets to investors and credit grantors, the Financial Accounting Standards Board (FASB) revised its rules regarding the treatment of intangible assets in financial reports in 2001.[16, 17, 18] Due to this revision, the demand for financial brand values in financial reports will rise further in the future. First, the revised standards require that in a business acquisition or merger, identifiable intangible assets other than goodwill be recognized at fair value. Second, intangible assets deemed to have indefinite lives will not be amortized, but instead be tested for impairment at least annually. Since brands are reckoned to be identifiable long-lived assets, these rules apply and require the continued application of a brand valuation method.[31, 46] Internally generated brands still cannot be capitalized.[17] However, in response to public discussion on this issue, FASB[19] initiated a project on disclosure of self-generated intangible assets, e.g., in voluntary explanatory notes to the annual report. Note that Scandinavian firms such as Celemi or Skandia have already been using such supplementary statements to the annual report for many years.[7, 42]

Recognizing the brand value[a] and annual impairment testing under the new rules are not the only brand value applications for which the measure should adhere to GAAP. Among other applications are reports to tax authorities, purchase price allocations in acquisitions, mergers, and sales of businesses, communications to investors, litigation and insolvency proceedings, and securitized borrowing. All these valuations target external stakeholders who might only accept measures that meet generally accepted accounting standards.

Another major group of brand value applications targets internal stakeholders or partners in the value chain, e.g., top and senior management, employees, and retailers. This group includes valuations for management purposes. These are decisions on the long-term brand strategy, brand portfolio management, or marketing budget allocation, for example. Here, the absolute value might play a minor role, because it is rather essential that the metric reflects differential effects of brand decisions in a consistent and valid way. Without doubt, a measure consistent with GAAP also serves this purpose, underlining the importance of aligning characteristics of the brand valuation method with GAAP.

The financial value of a brand reflects the incremental discounted future cash flows accruing from the brand name. It is intangible by nature. Unfortunately, the true value cannot be observed. Consequently, several methods have been suggested since the start of the brand valuation era in the late 1980s. Salinas[39] identified 65 models. A quick look at today's prominent brand ranking tables by Interbrand,[23] Millward Brown,[32] or Brand Finance[6] reveals that valuation results differ to a great extent, which raises serious concerns about the validity of these methods. Hence, it is crucial that marketers agree on a generally accepted valuation method that produces valid results and makes marketing accountable. Following our earlier discussion, it would be extremely useful to have brand valuation standards that adhere to accounting standards to expand acceptance among external financial and other stakeholders.

The two main objectives of this chapter are: (1) to develop a common understanding of what is required to perform brand valuation in accordance with GAAP; and (2) to present a valuation approach that meets these requirements. I will discuss the process of brand value generation and deduce a catalog of criteria relevant for an accounting measure of brand value. I will briefly discuss the three basic philosophies underlying brand valuation models. Finally, I will delineate a brand value method that is in accordance with GAAP and therefore with the Marketing Accountability Standards Board's (MASB's) Marketing Metric Audit Protocol (MMAP) characteristics of an ideal metric. I demonstrate empirical evidence of its validity and reliability and conclude with an outlook on brand valuation.

Understanding the Process of Brand Value Creation

Before addressing the requirements for brand valuation that derive from GAAP, it is important to understand how brand value is generated. Consistent with the notion of financial brand equity in the literature,[2, 40, 41] I define brand value as the *discounted incremental future cash flows accruing from products and services bearing the brand name compared with a (fictitious) situation in which the firm offerings had no brand name*. This definition reflects the bottom-line impact of branding that is eventually relevant to senior management and external stakeholders such as shareholders, creditors, and tax authorities. Figure 14.1 adopts the idea of a brand value chain by Keller and Lehmann[29] and exhibits the process of brand value creation that underlies brand value measurement.

The process of brand value creation starts with marketing program investments that impact customers in various ways. Customers perceive a company's performance in the marketing mix and translate this performance into benefits. In addition, marketing activities build brand knowledge that affects future customer response in a direct and indirect way. Brand knowledge is central to the established concept of customer-based brand equity by Keller,[28] which he defines as: *"the differential effect of brand knowledge on consumer response to the marketing of the brand"* (italics in the original, p. 8). Note that customer-based brand equity is an antecedent of financial brand equity and is measured on a psychometric scale not a dollar scale. Brand knowledge is defined in terms of brand awareness and brand image. Customer response to marketing refers to customer perceptions, preferences, and behavior such as brand choice arising

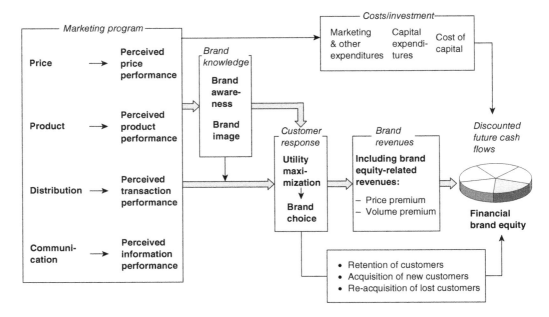

Figure 14.1 The Process of Brand Valuation Creation.

Source: Created by the author.

from marketing mix activity.[28] Hence, a measurement approach that integrates Keller's model should emphasize the effects of the marketing mix program that are mediated and moderated by brand knowledge. A powerful surrogate measure for predicting actual brand choice is the brand preference measure that is covered in detail in Chapter 4.

Brand choice can easily be transformed into quantities of economic relevance such as brand revenues or cash flows. Since brand equity affects not only current brand choice but also future brand choice (e.g., via brand repurchases), future brand cash flows can also be related to brand equity. The present value of future cash flows accruing from customer-based brand equity establishes the value of a brand in financial terms. The corporate valuation literature[9] discusses DCF valuation approaches and their practical applications at length. Recent contributions in marketing advocate the use of customer-level data to explicitly model customer acquisition, retention, defection, and possible return over time, which can be used to predict future cash flows attached to the brand (see Chapters 6 and 7 of this volume).

Criteria for an Accounting Measure of Brand Value

The FASB presents a hierarchy of qualitative characteristics of accounting information in its *Statement of Financial Accounting Concepts No. 2* (FASB 1980) (see the first column of Table 14.1). Any measure of brand value claiming broad acceptance among diverse external and internal stakeholders should demonstrate that it is in line with these requirements. A brand value measure typically yields a single dollar value reflecting the monetary benefits due to brand equity. The FASB emphasizes relevance and reliability as primary qualities for establishing a useful accounting measure. An accounting measure is considered relevant if it makes a difference in the decision-making of the addressees of financial reports by helping them to form predictions or verify prior expectations. It is future-oriented and uses information from the past as a basis for

Table 14.1 FASB Accounting Qualities and Derived Critical Brand Asset Valuation Criteria

General accounting qualities and their definition (FASB 1980, pp. 9–11)	Components of general accounting qualities (FASB 1980)	Relevant issues in brand asset valuation	Derived critical criteria for models of brand asset valuation
Relevance: The capacity of information to make a difference in a decision by helping users to form predictions about the outcomes of past, present, and future events or to confirm or correct prior expectations	• Predictive value • Feedback value • Timeliness	– Consideration of future cash flows	• Future orientation
Reliability: The quality of information that assures that information is reasonably free from error and bias, and faithfully represents what it purports to represent	• Verifiability • Representational faithfulness • Neutrality	– Objectivity in data collection and processing – Completeness of model, in particular consideration of price and volume premium – Theory-based model development	• Objectivity • Completeness
Comparability: The quality of information that enables users to identify similarities in and differences between two sets of economic phenomena	• Consistency over analysis units • Consistency over time	– Applicability of model across companies/industries – Consistency in model application over time – Relative stability of model results over time	• Comparability
Understandability: The quality of information that enables users to perceive its significance		– Parsimonious model development – Capability of non-experts to calibrate the model (e.g., absence of econometric techniques)	• Simplicity
Benefits > Costs		– Usage of existing secondary data – Limited need to collect new data (e.g., with parsimonious market research)	• Cost-effectiveness
Conservatism:[1] A prudent reaction to uncertainty to try to ensure that uncertainty and risks inherent in business situations are adequately considered		– Prevention from valuation of non-exercised brand options (e.g., brand extension, co-branding)	

Source: Created by the author.

Note
1 This is not considered an accounting quality per se, but rather a rule on how to use and combine information in the process of valuation.

predictions. As a consequence, a measure of brand assets should take into account future cash flows. In this context, the FASB recently emphasized the importance of discounted cash flow techniques for accounting measures (SFAC No. 7; FASB 2000).[15]

The reliability of a measure rests on its representational faithfulness and verifiability. Representational faithfulness (or validity) refers to the correspondence between the measure and the phenomenon it contends to represent. The separation of the brand effect from other effects is crucial and should emanate from a strong theoretical basis. A brand value measure should also be complete, i.e., be capable of capturing a price as well as a volume premium. Measures that, for example, focus on a price premium alone cannot determine the value of discount brands such as Southwest Airlines or Walmart. Verifiability demands that independent measurers using the same method should arrive at the same result. A prerequisite is the independence and accessibility of relevant information. Many commercial offerings[23] do not satisfy these requirements since they rely on proprietary, subjective expert knowledge.

As a result of the preceding discussion, I emphasize three critical criteria that a brand value measure should fulfill to establish relevance and reliability: *future orientation*, *completeness*, and *verifiability*.

Comparability is a further important quality of accounting information. Comparability implies that the method can be consistently applied across industries and time, so that investors can truly compare the results for different brands or companies over several years. Most brand value measures depend on specific types of data, making an industry-wide application impossible. Comparability refers also to the relative stability of results over time.

Finally, the FASB mentions two important constraints that need to be considered. First, a measure is only useful to decision-makers who can understand it. Many measures suggested in the academic literature impress by their brilliant methodology, but require a marketing science knowledge even most marketing executives, not to mention their counterparts from finance and accounting, do not have. Simple models that rely only on a few pieces of input information also reduce the number of potential sources of error. Second, the benefits of an accounting measure should be greater than its costs. Cost-effectiveness is easier to achieve if secondary information can be used that is already collected for the preparation of the annual report. Primary data collection should be reduced to a minimum. Most of the existing brand value models do not permit a continuous cost-effective application over multiple years. Critical brand valuation criteria that derive from the aforementioned issues are *comparability*, *simplicity*, and *cost-effectiveness*.

The six brand valuation criteria derived from accounting qualities are also fully in line with the MMAP characteristics of an ideal measure (see Chapter 17 for details on the MMAP process). The MMAP process builds on the notion that there is a conceptual link between marketing activities and intermediate outcome metrics and measures of financial return. The process involves the validation and causality audit based on the ten characteristics of an ideal metric. In the words of MMAP, the ideal metric is relevant, predictive, objective, calibrated, reliable, sensitive, simple, causal, transparent, and quality assured. All these criteria are reflected in the aforementioned general accounting qualities. In addition, MMAP requires a metric to be causal and quality assured. Causality implies that brand valuation includes and connects intermediate outcome measures such as brand preference, brand image, etc. to financial outcome measures as conceptualized by the brand value chain in Figure 14.1. Quality can be attested by a formal and independent external audit.

While many brand valuation models have been suggested in the past, only little attempts have been made to validate the models against these or related criteria. In fact, many (commercial) models are presented in a way that means the model and its results should stand alone and be convincing based on face validity alone. Additional validity tests are not performed. Surprisingly, rigorous tests of model validity are also very limited in the academic literature.

Three Fundamental Approaches to Brand Valuation

Salinas[41] provides a complete summary of 39 proprietary financial brand valuation methods. I do not attempt to repeat the details of this excellent review. The main purpose of this section is to delineate the ideas behind the three major brand valuation philosophies that emerge from the literature.[24, 39] These philosophies are: *cost-based*, *market-based*, and *income/DCF-based* approaches.

Cost-Based Approach

This approach determines the brand value in terms of prior investments into developing and building the brand. A straightforward method is to measure the *historical cost* of creation by accumulating all expenditures on the brand until the period of valuation.[5] A more realistic approach is to follow the idea of an *advertising stock* where brand expenditures build up the stock that decays at a constant rate over time.[35] While cost-based measures are attractive due to the objective and easy collection of data, they are heavily criticized for their theoretical weaknesses. Prior brand expenditures measure past efforts for brand building but not future outcomes, such as excess profits, that accrue from the brand (Salinas: 60ff.).[39]

Market-Based Approach

Following the efficient market hypothesis,[12] the market price for an asset represents the fair value for that asset, provided that all investors have the same amount of information available and engage in many transactions. Unfortunately, there does not exist a liquid market for brand transactions, i.e., transaction prices are not readily available. But given that a brand is part of the firm value, its value is implicitly included in the market value of a company. The idea of a market-based approach, such as the CoreBrand model (see also Chapter 13) or the model by Simon and Sullivan,[41] is to separate the brand value from the observed market capitalization of the firm. The major advantage of this approach is its consistency with capital asset pricing theory and fair valuation principles. But there is no general agreement about the right approach to isolate the brand value from the company's market value and applications are limited to publicly listed firms.[20]

Income/DCF-Based Approach

The income/DCF-based approach attempts to project the (future) stream of profits or cash flows, respectively, due to the brand.[20, 39] In theory, the present value of this stream equals the market price of the brand. There are multiple ways to arrive at the estimate for the present value of brand-generated cash flows, such as the relief-from-royalty method (Brand Finance), income split method,[20, 23, 32] or incremental income method. I also consider the revenue premium model by Ailawadi *et al.*[2] as a current-period income-based method as it can easily be used to determine the incremental cash flow that is attributable to the brand. The major advantage of these models is that they are consistent with the basic principles of fair asset valuation that is inherent in DCF models. Major concerns exist about the subjectivity and uncertainty that is often associated with the forecast and separation of expected brand cash flows.[2]

A Cost-Effective and Easy-to-Implement Brand Valuation Model

In this section, I introduce a brand value measure that is consistent with GAAP and MMAP qualities. Specifically, it meets the aforementioned requirements of future orientation, objectivity, completeness, comparability, simplicity, and cost-effectiveness. The method offers significant benefits to practitioners: it models directly the goal that practitioners have in mind when they think about separating the brand asset from other assets. Further, it permits the application of established valuation routines that often preexist in companies, i.e., it can easily be adapted to organization-specific conditions of planning and reporting. Most importantly, it incorporates actual brand perceptions of existing and potential customers in a very efficient way that reduces market research costs to a minimum.

The methodology has been rigorously tested in empirical applications in three different product categories. Moreover, it has been successfully implemented in several companies to value multiple brands covering diverse industries across many countries. A major impetus for its adoption was its cost-effectiveness and compatibility with existing company planning and reporting procedures. In addition, the method has demonstrated its application value in litigation and insolvency cases, and in mergers and acquisition transactions.

I shall outline the basic idea of the model, the measurement of the model's components, its empirical validation, and practical application. I will not cover the theoretical development of the model and details of its methodology and econometric estimation. For more information on these aspects, I refer to Fischer.[20]

Basic Formula for Determining the Brand Value

Recall that the financial value of a brand reflects the incremental discounted future cash flows accruing from the brand name. By definition, the incremental cash flows due to brand equity are fully incorporated into the total cash flows of the underlying branded business. A straightforward top-down approach would be to separate the problem into two parts: the measurement of the brand's discounted cash flows and the measurement of the share that belongs to brand equity. Let $BR_{kl,t}$ denote brand k's net revenues in product market l and period t, and $m_{kl,t}$ denote a percentage margin that accounts for all cash expenses (e.g., out-of-pocket cost of goods sold, selling, general and administrative expenses, tax payments, and capital expenditures), excluding payments to investors. Discounting cash flows at a rate of r will satisfy their return expectations. Then, the financial value of brand k in product market l is:

$$Brand\ Value_{kl} = Brand\ Equity\ Share_{kl}\ [\text{in }\%] \times \sum_{t=0}^{\infty} \frac{(1-m_{kl,t})BR_{kl,t}}{(1+r_{kl})^t}$$

Aggregation across product markets, which may represent different geographic markets and/or product categories, yields the total financial value of brand k. Note that brand revenues are part of the brand's discounted cash flows and implicitly contain any volume or price premium attributable to brand equity.[2] US GAAP emphasizes the use of discounted cash flow techniques to determine the fair value of an asset such as the brand if quoted market prices are not available (SFAC No. 7 in FASB 2000).[15] The theory of corporate valuation provides the basis for calculating the discounted cash flow of the brand.[9] Experts in finance and accounting are usually very familiar with the application of corporate valuation methods. Since these methods are discussed at length in the finance literature I do not focus on the calculation of the discounted cash flow of the brand, but refer the reader to the relevant literature.[9] Most importantly, the valuator can simply use the input from the existing valuation procedure used in the specific organization.

What Does Brand Equity Share Mean?

Fischer[20] shows how the brand value measure in Equation (14.1) formally derives from the theory of customer utility maximization and brand choice. The brand equity share is a direct outcome of the development of the brand valuation formula in Equation (14.1). It measures the utility due to brand image or brand reputation, respectively, as a proportion of the total utility that arises from the firm's present and past marketing activities. In the brand choice framework, a rise in perceived utility by the product increases the brand choice probability, which in turn leads to higher unit sales. For expositional convenience, I use "product" as a synonym for products and services.

The increase in utility may be due to several reasons. The underlying product is superior, the product is offered at a more attractive price, customers are better informed about the product, and/or the firm has achieved a greater distribution with the product increasing the transaction utility. In addition, the brand may also enjoy a more favorable brand image than other brands. Only brand image can be claimed as resulting from brand equity.[36] The brand image offers additional intangible benefits that are not explained by other characteristics. On the one hand, such benefits may arise from the signaling function of brands in the market.[10, 11] The brand signal may reduce the customer's perceived risk and lower their information costs.[20, 21, 27] Lower perceived risk and information costs increase the likelihood of considering and purchasing the brand.[10, 22, 37] On the other hand, the brand may also provide direct benefits to the customer, for example, by its symbolic value (e.g., Harley Davidson) or its prestige value (e.g., Mercedes).[8, 20, 21, 28]

How to Measure the Brand Equity Share

Following the preceding arguments, I propose to measure the brand equity share with the following two metrics (Equation 14.2):

$$\textit{Brand Equity Share}_{kl} [\text{in \%}] = \textit{Brand Relevance}_l \text{ in Category } [\text{in \%}] \times \textit{Brand Image}_{kl}$$

where k refers to the brand and l to the product market or category, respectively.

Fischer et al.[20, 21] introduced the *brand relevance* concept into the literature. They define brand relevance in category (BRiC) as the extent to which customer decision-making is influenced by the brand compared to other decision criteria, e.g., purchase convenience, price, etc. Hence, BRiC varies across categories, but not across brands within a category. The construct has much in common with the utility weight of brand image that is part of a preference or brand choice model. The brand's strength in terms of image is captured by *brand image* that measures the perceived image of a brand relative to the average competitor. Table 14.2 summarizes the scale definitions to measure the brand equity share.[b] In an empirical application, attention should be spent on the aggregation of the brand equity share that is available from each respondent. It seems reasonable to weight for customer characteristics such as purchase intensity when computing the average brand equity share across respondents. Heavy customers contribute more to firm performance, which should be reflected in their weight for the aggregate, market-level brand equity share in Equation (14.2).

Measuring Brand Relevance

In the style of Srinivasan and Park,[44] I propose to measure the brand relevance weight with a constant-sum procedure by asking respondents to allocate 100 points across the 4 brand performance dimensions and the brand name (see the appendix for the exact procedure used in the automobile questionnaire). This task is easy to understand and provides reliable estimates of the weight a customer assigns to marketing mix purchase factors such as price, quality, etc. as well as the brand name. Fischer et al.[21] demonstrate that the metric correlates strongly with their proposed multi-item brand relevance scale.

Table 14.2 Overview of Measures Used to Compute the Brand Equity Share

Measure	Purpose	Scale definition	Transformation into relative scale
Brand relevance	Measurement of the relevance of the brand name as a purchase criterion relative to other criteria in a specific product category	Constant-sum measurement of the purchase weights of brand name, price, quality, distribution (purchase convenience), and information	$\frac{\text{No. of points allocated to brand name}}{100}$
Brand image	Composite measurement of brand associations held in customer memory	Formative index composed of four brand image dimensions	Weighted sum of relative brand image dimensions
Brand affect	Holistic measurement of customers' emotional ties with the brand	Likert-type scale that rates a brand's likeability relative to the average competitor (Range: $-3, \ldots, 0, \ldots, +3$)	$\frac{\text{Rating score} + 4}{4}$
Brand quality	Holistic measurement of customers' quality associations with the brand	Cf. definition of "brand affect" scale	$\frac{\text{Rating score} + 4}{4}$
Brand uniqueness	Holistic measurement of customers' perceived uniqueness of the brand	Cf. definition of "brand affect" scale	$\frac{\text{Rating score} + 4}{4}$
Brand trust	Holistic measurement of customers' trust in the brand	Cf. definition of "brand affect" scale	$\frac{\text{Rating score} + 4}{4}$

Source: Created by the author.

Note
K = No. of brands evaluated.

Measuring Brand Image

I also propose an easy measurement of brand image. Specifically, I suggest asking respondents for the perceived image of a brand within four dimensions. The marketing literature does not offer a generally accepted definition of brand image. Note that for use as an accounting measure, the scale must be *reasonably* free from error and bias (FASB 1980: 9)[14] and permit a *cost-effective* application. A synthesis of the literature reveals four image dimensions that have been consistently used by researchers and commercial vendors.[1, 28] These four dimensions are *brand quality*, *brand uniqueness*, *brand affect*, and *brand trust*. For example, brand quality and brand uniqueness are part of Aaker's Brand Equity Ten[1] and can be found in most other conceptualizations.[10, 27, 28, 30] Brand affect is an important dimension reflecting the emotional ties of customers with their brands.[8] Brand trust arises from consumption experiences over time and describes the willingness of the customer to rely on promises made by the brand.[8, 10, 33] Both dimensions fit well into the emerging theory of brand commitment in relationship marketing.[33] The appendix provides the exact survey items for the scale that can be applied across industries.

I conceptualize brand image as a formative indicator scale. A reflective indicator scale would not be appropriate since it assumes that changes in one image dimension also involve changes in the other dimensions.[25] However, one may find, as an example, equally strong brands that are predominantly driven by quality perceptions and less by emotional ties (e.g., high-tech brands such as Intel and IBM), and vice versa (e.g., McDonald's and Red Bull).

Weighting the Brand Image Dimensions

A natural question arises as to how the brand image dimensions should be weighted. Fischer[20] investigated this issue with representative data from three different product categories of consumer durables, packaged goods, and services. The study provides strong empirical evidence that the four dimensions are indeed relevant to the formation of a brand image index. Moreover, the analysis reveals a remarkable consistency of the dimensions' relative contribution to the index across the three markets: 50 percent for brand affect, 25 percent for brand uniqueness, and 12.5 percent each for brand quality and brand trust.

Does Brand Awareness Impact Brand Value?

Apparently, only people who are aware of the brand can derive utility from it. Hence, awareness does not influence the brand equity share. However, this observation does not imply that brand awareness is irrelevant to brand value. Quite the opposite: it is a fundamental source of brand equity that, all things being equal, scales up (down) the expected future amount of brand choices. In the brand valuation formula (14.1), the impact of awareness materializes in brand revenues, $BR_{kl,t}$.[c]

Validity of the Measurement Approach

The suggested approach to measure the brand equity share is the simplified version of a more complex but also more rigorous approach. Consistent with the theoretical conceptualization of the brand value measure, Fischer[20] obtains brand equity shares for various brands in three product markets from a choice model. Here, brand equity shares are estimated in an econometric fashion from observed actual brand choices of a representative sample of customers. Table 14.3 illustrates the brand equity shares obtained by both measurements in the analyzed markets for automobiles, cosmetics, and grocery stores. There is strong empirical evidence that the simpler approach is indeed able to replicate the results of the choice model. Discrepancies between brand

Table 14.3 Comparison of Choice Model and Heuristic Method Brand Equity Shares across Different Industries

	Automobiles[1]				Cosmetics				Groceries			
	Estimated brand equity share in %		Difference test[2]		Estimated brand equity share in %		Difference test		Estimated brand equity share in %		Difference test	
Brands[3]	Choice model [95% interval]	Heuristic method [95% interval]	p-value	N	Choice model [95% interval]	Heuristic method [95% interval]	p-value	N	Choice model [95% interval]	Heuristic method [95% interval]	p-value	N
Brand 1	20.5 [19.2, 21.8]	21.0 [18.6, 23.4]	.738	282	27.3 [26.4, 28.2]	24.0 [21.6, 26.3]	.010	385	12.2 [11.7, 12.8]	11.2 [9.8, 12.6]	.202	423
Brand 2	15.8 [14.6, 17.0]	15.8 [14.1, 17.5]	.987	307	21.7 [20.9, 22.5]	21.9 [20.2, 23.6]	.820	341	13.2 [12.4, 14.1]	10.8 [9.5, 12.2]	.005	381
Brand 3	21.5 [20.1, 22.8]	21.6 [19.3, 23.9]	.917	213	21.5 [20.5, 22.4]	21.0 [19.1, 23.0]	.704	312	12.1 [11.3, 12.9]	12.4 [10.5, 14.3]	.760	403
Brand 4	25.4 [24.0, 26.7]	25.0 [22.4, 27.5]	.796	222	20.3 [19.4, 21.2]	19.9 [18.2, 21.7]	.749	329	10.8 [10.1, 11.5]	11.0 [8.7, 13.3]	.836	354
Brand 5	19.7 [18.4, 21.1]	19.3 [17.2, 21.3]	.697	304	19.5 [18.6, 20.4]	19.7 [18.3, 21.1]	.798	352	12.1 [11.4, 12.9]	9.0 [7.7, 10.3]	.000	318

Source: Created by the author.

Notes

1 Results for the pooled categories are informative since pooling is allowed according to the formal pooling test.
2 Difference test is based on a paired-samples t-test since choice model and heuristic brand equity shares are obtained from the same group of respondents.
3 Brands 1–5 appear in the following order: VW, Opel, Mercedes, BMW, Ford (Automobiles); Nivea, L'Oréal, Dove, Gillette, Fa (Cosmetics); Aldi, Edeka, Lidl, Penny, Rewe (Groceries).

equity shares are due to sampling errors and do not reflect systematic differences between the two methods. For the vast majority of brands in Table 14.3, the paired samples t-test could not be rejected. Note that the test results are rather conservative, because the choice model shares do not take into account the uncertainty in parameter estimates. Thus, their variance is likely to be underestimated, which makes it harder to detect non-significant differences. Hence, it can be concluded that the cost-effective simpler measurement performs equally well in predicting brand equity shares as the choice model. This important finding is relevant across the categories.

Robustness, Convergent Validity, and Stability of the Brand Value Measure

As for any other brand value measure, its convergent validity and relative stability over time should be shown.[2] Additionally, it would be helpful to apply the method to a wide range of brands from different industries to corroborate its claimed robustness and cost-effectiveness. For this purpose, I apply the method to a broad sample of 34 national and international brands. Due to space limitations, I do not document the valuation steps in detail.

Data Collection and Valuation Approach

I calculate the brand value with respect to the *German market* not the global market. The chosen 34 brands reflect a broad range of industry sectors covering durable goods, non-durable goods, services, and retailers. Most of the brands belong to companies listed on the DAX, the leading German stock market index. Adopting the proposed measurement approach, market research data were collected by a market research firm via representative computer-aided telephone surveys among German customers during summer 2003 (500 respondents per wave). The formulation of survey items (e.g., screening questions, brand relevance questions) was adapted to appropriately reflect customers' perceptions of the purchase process.

For the computation of discounted brand cash flows, I used the definitions and data sources as summarized in Table 14.4. Cost and investment data are based on industry averages since an external investor would not consider cost differences that are specific to the firm, but unrelated to the brand. I adopt the common financial perpetuity formula (Equation 14.3) for deriving the discounted cash flow of the brand:[9]

$$\text{DCF-Brand}_k = \frac{BR_k(EBITDA_k - IR_k)(1 - tax_k)}{r_k - g}, \text{with } r_k - g > 0$$

where $EBITDA_k$ is the earnings margin before interest, tax, depreciation, and amortization; IR_k denotes the investment rate for replacement expenditures; tax_k is the corporate cash tax rate; and g refers to the expected long-term inflation rate in Germany. *EBITDA* and *IR* are percentage figures with respect to brand revenues.

Implicit to the valuation approach is the assumption that the current level of cash flows will be maintained in the future, i.e., except for inflation I assume no growth in revenues. Therefore, only replacement investments that are required to maintain the tangible asset base for a certain revenue level are relevant. In most cases, this assumption will lead to rather conservative estimates. According to FASB, conservatism is the rule to follow if better information is not available.

I am fully aware that the Equation (14.3) is a simplified procedure to compute DCF-brand that serves the purpose of illustrating the application of the brand valuation method. I do *not* advocate that this is the way to obtain the present value of brand cash flows. It may be substituted by more elaborated approaches of DCF computation. In particular, if an organization has already established a preferred model, then this should be the model to use.

Table 14.4 Overview of Variable Definitions and Data Sources for the Calculations of Brand Value in Table 14.5

Variable	Label	Definition	Time period	Data source	Comments
Brand revenues	BR	Net brand revenues available to company	Average of past three years	Annual reports, press releases, company executives	1 Longer time period (10 years) is used if industry depends strongly on business cycles or capital market 2 Definition of revenue is adapted to industry specifics (e.g., financial institutions)
EBITDA	EBITDA	Earnings before interest, taxes, depreciation, and amortization in % of net brand revenues	Average of past three years	Bloomberg	1 Average of international top 15 players in industry 2 Longer time period (10 years) is used if industry depends strongly on business cycles or capital market
Investment rate	IR	Investment rate for replacement expenditures in % of net brand revenues	Average of past five years	Bloomberg	Cf. EBITDA
Weighted average cost of capital	r	Mixture of cost of private equity and debt according to target capital structure	Valuation year	McKinsey & Co. Corporate Finance Practice	1 Average of international top 15 players in industry 2 For financial institutions, only private equity costs apply 3 Annual rates are transformed into continuous rates by taking logarithm of (1 + annual rate)
Corporate cash tax rate	tax	Effectively paid taxes in Germany as % of cash profits	Valuation year	Center for European Economic Research	
Expected long-term rate of inflation	g	Expected long-term rate of inflation	20 years ahead	World Market Monitor	Annual rates are transformed into continuous rates by taking logarithm of (1 + annual rate)
Brand relevance		Percentage multiplier (cf. Table 14.3)	Valuation year	INRA Research	Questionnaire items are adapted to consumers' perception of purchase process in the respective category
Brand image		Composite index measure relative to average competitor (cf. Table 14.3)	Valuation year	INRA Research	Cf. Brand relevance

Source: Created by the author.

Table 14.5 Financial Value of Selected Brands in the German Market as of 2003

Brand	Company	Industry	Estimated DCF-brand (EUR millions)	Estimated brand value (EUR millions)	Estimated B2C-share in brand value (%)[1]
Adidas	Adidas-Salomon	Apparel	1,483	305	100
Aldi	Aldi	Groceries	12,079	1,281	100
Allianz	Allianz-Dresdner	Insurance	17,934	2,189	96
Audi	Volkswagen	Automotive	8,078	1,973	100[2]
Beck's	Interbrew	Beverages	426	84	100
Bild	Axel Springer	Publishing	2,410	210	100
BMW	BMW	Automotive	12,764	3,191	100[2]
Boss	Hugo Boss	Apparel	689	130	100
Citibank	Citibank	Banking	1,823	679	30
Deutsche Bank	Deutsche Bank	Banking	7,757	1,590	58
Deutsche Post	Deutsche Post	Logistics	3,687	1,067	47
Deutsche Telekom	Deutsche Telekom	Telecom	75,551	10,252	98
E.ON	E.ON	Energy	2,664	780	40
H&M	Hennes & Mauritz	Apparel	2,897	487	100
Hypo-Vereinsbank	Hypo-Vereinsbank	Banking	2,903	420	80
Karstadt	Karstadt-Quelle	Retail	5,060	544	100
Lufthansa	Lufthansa	Airlines	2,604	538	25
Media Markt	Metro	Retail	2,394	279	100
Mercedes	DaimlerChrysler	Automotive	25,656	5,852	95[2]
Nivea	Beiersdorf	Cosmetics	1,899	425	100
Nokia	Nokia	Electronics	751	201	78
Persil	Henkel	Home Care	1,144	188	100
Porsche	Porsche	Automotive	1,471	358	100[2]
Postbank	Deutsche Post	Banking	2,067	246	100
Red Bull	Red Bull	Beverages	437	61	100
RWEAvanza	RWE	Energy	1,686	514	40
Saturn	Metro	Retail	1,014	116	100
Schwarzkopf	Henkel	Cosmetics	1,169	222	100
Siemens Mobile	Siemens	Electronics	499	103	100
T-Mobile	Deutsche Telekom	Telecom	22,683	1,978	100[3]
TUI	TUI	Tourism	1,101	161	100
VW	Volkswagen	Automotive	16,501	3,465	100[2]
Warsteiner	Warsteiner Brauerei	Beverages	940	206	100
Wella	Procter & Gamble	Cosmetics	816	330	48

Source: Created by the author.

Notes
1 B2C share does not reflect the share in revenues but in brand value since estimated brand relevance figures differ between B2C and B2B customers.
2 For simplicity, the business with company cars is captured under B2C since the buying process is very similar to consumer markets.
3 No data on B2B sales were available.

196 *Marc Fischer*

Robustness of the Method

Table 14.5 summarizes the valuation results. Recall that the brand value estimates refer to the *German market* in 2003 not the global market. Since a few brands also have significant B2B businesses it was meaningful to complement their B2C value. For this purpose, industry experts estimated a B2B-specific brand relevance weight that was assumed to be lower than the B2C-specific weight. Note that the need for expert judgments arises from a lack of B2B survey data, not because of limitations of the proposed method. Most importantly, none of the following conclusions changes if only B2C brand values are considered or brands with B2B businesses are excluded from the sample.

Interviewers did not report any problems with the survey. They completed the interview on average within ten minutes, because respondents had to answer only five questions per brand. Hence, the survey approach appears to be very cost-effective and robust in application across industries. Most importantly, today, the survey will be administered via online media, which in fact further reduces the market research cost.

Convergent Validity

Convergent validity of the measure can be shown by its correlation with other measures.[2] I use the publicly available annual brand value list published by Semion, a German-based brand consulting firm specializing in financial brand valuation. Semion's brand value model is close in spirit to the Interbrand model (for details, see their website at www.semion.de). In contrast to Interbrand, Semion determines the international value of many national brands, among them 19 brands from the list in Table 14.5. Since I do not have data from international market research, I extrapolate the German brand value to the international value proportional to the ratio of national to international sales.

The correlation of the two measures is very high with a value of .73. However, this result is based on a small sample. To increase sample size to 57 cases, I also use values from the years 2001 and 2002. For these years, I base cash flow predictions only on annual data instead of three-year averages. Note that these changes increase the error variance of the estimates, making the association test more conservative. The correlation between the two measures in this sample is still very high with a value of .70 and significant ($p < .01$).

Stability over Time

Ailawadi *et al.*[2] use the correlation of their brand value measure with its one year-lagged value to assess the stability over time. I follow their approach and calculate the value for each brand in 2001, 2002, and 2003 according to the procedure described above. Recall that the error variance of estimates should increase, making the association test more conservative. The new method proves to provide stable estimates over time. The measure's correlation with its lagged value is highly significant ($p < .01$) and amounts to .98 for 2003/02 and to .96 for 2002/01, respectively.

Conclusion

Assigning a dollar value to a brand—an ill-defined task at best—is necessary these days. A 2001 revision of FASB's rules for the treatment of intangible assets such as brands in financial reports included a requirement to recognize intangible assets at fair value, under several conditions. This change greatly increases the visibility and accountability of a firm's marketing efforts to investors, creditors, and the government, as well as within the firm itself.

Under these rules, intangibles like brands with indefinite lives must be valued at least annually and compared to the previous year's value. This means that managers need a reliable and cost-effective method of valuing brands.

Existing brand valuation methods are largely impractical for these and other purposes, falling short of the relevance, reliability, comparability, understandability, and cost-effectiveness requirements outlined by FASB. Some existing measures fail to take future cash flows into account; other approaches are applicable to only certain types of brands. Furthermore, hiring a branding consultancy to value a brand means paying a lot of money for a valuation that is based on proprietary expert knowledge and analysis.

I presented a new method of financial brand valuation that is practical for use in financial reporting, purchase price allocations in acquisitions, mergers, and sales of businesses, communications to investors, litigation and insolvency proceedings, and other applications that require consistency with generally accepted accounting standards. Because the method is adaptable to organization-specific conditions of planning and reporting, it does not require companies to perform extensive additional research or analysis.

The suggested measure of brand value is simple and intuitive. In fact, it models directly the goal practitioners have in mind when they think about separating the brand asset from other assets. Consistent with the requirements derived from US GAAP (see again Table 14.1), the metric qualifies as an accounting measure of brand value. It is future-oriented because it is based on discounted future cash flows. It is objective because a third independent party can easily verify all input information. The measure is also sufficiently complete. Any volume and price premiums are implicitly contained in brand cash flows. The integration of the theories of corporate valuation and brand choice provides a solid theoretical basis for the measure. Since the metric relies on only a few pieces of information that are combined in a straightforward manner, it is simple to calculate and understand. The underlying logic is intuitive and should facilitate the adoption by users without a deeper marketing knowledge. Most of the information has to be collected during the auditing process anyway. Hence, the computation of the brand value does not incur extra costs.

The only costs arise from market research to calibrate the brand equity share. The use of cross-sectional surveys has its shortcomings due to measurement errors and potential causality issues. However, these issues should be of less concern here since measurement errors tend to cancel out in aggregation and the underlying theory of brand choice is very strong. Indeed, previous research has shown that cross-sectional surveys can be successfully applied to brand equity or related measurement problems.[36, 38, 43] Most importantly, the survey approach appears to be the only alternative to measure brand equity shares in a cost-effective way that can be consistently replicated over industries and time. In fact, data collection cost in today's digital world tends to become irrelevant.

Appendix

This is an example of survey items that were used in the automobile category (translated from German). It is not a full documentation of the computer-aided telephone survey.

Brand Image Scale and Brand Performance Scales (Choice Model Measures)

1 "You answered that you are aware of the following makes [. . .]. Please, compare now the makes and tell me what your overall image of these makes is. For this task you have a total of 100 points available. The better your image is of a make, the more points you should assign to this make. It is not necessary that you have bought the make in the past or would ever consider buying the make in the future."

2 "I shall now read a few statements about selected makes. Please tell me how strongly you agree or disagree with each statement. All statements refer to one make that you should compare to all other makes you are aware of, including those I have not mentioned so far." (+3 = strongly agree, 0 = no difference to other brands, −3 = strongly disagree.)

- The prices and maintenance costs of Make A are on average lower than for other makes.
- Cars by Make A meet my quality demands better than cars of other makes.
- The purchase of a car by Make A is easier and more convenient for me than for other makes.
- Compared with other makes, I notice commercials and other kinds of information about Make A more often.

Brand Relevance Weight and Brand Image Scale (Heuristic Method Measures)

1 "Now I would like to talk about criteria that may be important to you when buying a new car. These criteria are: (1) the price of the car and its maintenance costs; (2) the quality of the car; (3) the convenience of buying the car (e.g., closeness to the dealer, support by the dealer); (4) information about the car and the make by the manufacturer (e.g., advertisement on TV, radio, newspapers, at the dealer, product brochures); and (5) make of the car. How relevant is each of these criteria to you when you have to make a decision about buying or not buying the car? You can allocate a total of 100 points. The more important a criterion is to you, the more points you should assign to this criterion."

2 "I shall now read a few statements about selected makes. Please tell me how strongly you agree or disagree with each statement. All statements refer to one make that you should compare to all other makes you are aware of, including those I have not mentioned so far." (+3 = strongly agree, 0 = no difference to other brands, −3 = strongly disagree.)

- I like Make A more than other makes.
- Make A stands more for quality than other makes.
- Make A stands out from the crowd in a favorable manner.
- You can trust Make A more than other makes.

Notes

a Throughout the chapter, I use *brand value* as a synonym for *financial brand equity* to avoid confusion with other types of brand equity measures.
b I acknowledge that in theory the brand equity share may exceed 100 percent. However, simulation results and empirical application to several dozens of brands show that this scenario virtually does not occur. Specifying Equation (14.2) in a fully robust way is possible, but increases the mathematical complexity and therefore unnecessarily raises acceptance barriers for practitioners.
c A formal proof of the argument is available from the author upon request.

References

1 Aaker, David A., *Building Strong Brands*, 1996, New York: The Free Press.
2 Ailawadi, Kusum L., Donald R. Lehmann, and Scott A. Neslin, 2003, "Revenue Premium as an Outcome Measure of Brand Equity," *Journal of Marketing*, 67(October): 1–17.
3 Barth, Mary E. and Greg Clinch, 1998, "Revalued Financial, Tangible, and Intangible Assets: Associations with Share Prices and Non-Market-Based Value Estimates," *Journal of Accounting Research*, 30(Supplement 1998): 199–233.
4 Barth, Mary E., Ron Kasznik, and Maureen F. McNichols, 2001, "Analyst Coverage and Intangible Assets," *Journal of Accounting Research*, 39(1): 1–35.

5 Barwise, Patrick, Christopher Higson, Andrew Likierman, and Paul Marsh, *Accounting for Brands*, 1989, London, UK: London Business School.
6 Brand Finance, 2013, "Methodology," accessed August 24, 2013, available at http://brandirectory.com/methodology.
7 Celemi, 2003, *Annual Report 2002 Celemi Group*, Celemi Group.
8 Chaudhuri, Arjun and Morris B. Holbrook, 2001, "The Chain of Effects from Brand Trust and Brand Affect to Brand Performance: The Role of Brand Loyalty," *Journal of Marketing*, 65(April): 81–93.
9 Copeland, Thomas E., Tim Koller, and Jack Murrin, *Valuation, Measuring and Managing the Value of Companies*, 2000, 3rd edition, New York: John Wiley & Sons.
10 Erdem, Tülin and Joffre Swait, 2004, "Brand Credibility, Brand Consideration and Choice," *Journal of Consumer Research*, 31(1): 191–198.
11 Erdem, Tülin, Joffre Swait, and Ana Valenzuela, 2006, "Brands as Signals: A Cross-Country Validation Study," *Journal of Marketing*, 70(January): 34–49.
12 Fama Eugene F. and Kenneth R. French, 2006, "The Value Premium and the CAPM," *Journal of Finance*, 61(5): 2163–2185.
13 Farquhar, Peter, John Han, and Yuji Ijiri, 1992, "Brands on the Balance Sheets," *Marketing Management*, 1(Winter): 16–22.
14 FASB, *Statement of Financial Accounting Concepts No. 2: Qualitative Characteristics and Accounting Information*, 1980, Stamford, CT: FASB.
15 FASB, *Statement of Financial Accounting Concepts No. 7: Using Cash Flow Information and Present Value in Accounting Measurements*, 2000, Stamford, CT: FASB.
16 FASB, *Statement of Financial Accounting Standards No. 141: Business Combinations*, 2001, Stamford, CT: FASB.
17 FASB, *Statement of Financial Accounting Standards No. 142: Goodwill and Other Intangible Assets*, 2001, Stamford, CT: FASB.
18 FASB, *Statement of Financial Accounting Standards No. 144: Accounting for the Impairment or Disposal of Long-Lived Assets*, 2001, Stamford, CT: FASB.
19 FASB, *Proposal for a New Agenda Project: Disclosure of Information About Intangible Assets not Recognized in Financial Statements*, 2001, Stamford, CT: FASB.
20 Fischer, Marc, 2007, "Valuing Brand Assets: A Cost-Effective and Easy-to-Implement Measurement Approach," *Marketing Science Institute Working Paper Series*, Report No. 07–002, pp. 23–50.
21 Fischer, Marc, Franziska Völckner, and Henrik Sattler, 2010, "How Important Are Brands? A Cross-Category, Cross-Country Study," *Journal of Marketing Research*, 47(5): 823–839.
22 Hauser, John and Birger Wernerfelt, 1990, "An Evaluation Cost Model of Consideration Sets," *Journal of Consumer Research*, 16(March): 393–408.
23 Interbrand, 2012, *Methodology*, accessed August 24, 2013, available at http://www.interbrand.com/de/best-global-brands/2012/best-global-brands-methodology.aspx.
24 ISO, 2010, ISO10668: 2010, *"Brand Valuation—Requirements for Monetary Brand Valuation,"* accessed January 15, 2015, available at http://www.iso.org/iso/catalogue_detail?csnumber=46032.
25 Jarvis, Cheryl Burke, Scott Mackenzie, and Philip M. Podsakoff, 2003, "A Critical Review of Construct Indicators and Measurement Model Misspecification in Marketing and Consumer Research," *Journal of Consumer Research*, 30(2): 199–218.
26 Kallapur, Sanjay and Sabrina Y. S. Kwan, 2004, "The Value Relevance and Reliability of Brand Assets Recognized by U.K. Firms," *The Accounting Review*, 79(1): 151–172.
27 Kapferer, Jean-Noël, *Strategic Brand Management, Creating and Sustaining Brand Equity Long Term*, 1997, London, UK: Kogan Page.
28 Keller, Kevin L., 1993, "Conceptualizing, Measuring, and Managing Customer-Based Brand Equity," *Journal of Marketing*, 57(January): 1–22.
29 Keller, Kevin L. and Donald R. Lehmann, 2003, "The Brand Value Chain: Optimizing Strategic and Financial Brand Performance," *Marketing Management*, (May/June): 26–31.
30 Krishnan, H. S., 1996, "Characteristics of Memory Associations: A Consumer-Based Brand Equity Perspective," *International Journal of Research in Marketing*, 13(4): 389–405.
31 Lev, Baruch, *Intangibles, Management, Measurement, and Reporting*, 2001, Washington, DC: Brooking Institution Press.

32 Millward Brown, 2013, *Methodology*, accessed August 24, 2013, available at http://www.millwardbrown.com/BrandZ/Top_100_Global_Brands/Methodology.aspx.
33 Moorman, Christine, Zaltman, Gerald, and Rohit Deshpande, 1992, "Relationships between Providers and Users of Market Research: The Dynamics of Trust within and between Organizations," *Journal of Marketing Research*, 29(3): 314–328.
34 Tim Ambler, *Marketing and the Bottom Line*, 2nd edition, 2004, Upper Saddle River, NJ: FT Press.
35 Nerlove, Marc and Kenneth J. Arrow, 1962, "Optimal Advertising Policy under Dynamic Conditions," *Economica*, 29(114): 129–142.
36 Park, Chan Su and V. Srinivasan, 1994, "A Survey-Based Method for Measuring and Understanding Brand Equity and its Extendibility," *Journal of Marketing Research*, 31(May): 271–288.
37 Roberts, John and Glen L. Urban, 1988, "Modeling Multiattribute Utility, Risk, and Belief Dynamics for New Consumer Durable Brand Choice," *Management Science*, 34(2): 167–185.
38 Rust, Roland T., Katherine N. Lemon, and Valarie A. Zeithaml, 2004, "Return on Marketing: Using Customer Equity to Focus Marketing Strategy," *Journal of Marketing*, 68(January): 109–127.
39 Salinas, Gabriela, *The International Brand Valuation Manual*, 2009, Chichester, UK: Wiley.
40 Shocker, Allan and Bart Weitz, 1988, "A Perspective on Brand Equity: Principles and Issue," in *Defining, Measuring, and Managing Brand Equity: Conference Summary*, Leuthesser, Lance (ed.), Marketing Science Report No. 88–104, Cambridge, MA: Marketing Science Institute.
41 Simon, Carol J. and Mary W. Sullivan, 1993, "The Measurement and Determination of Brand Equity: A Financial Approach," *Marketing Science*, 12(1): 28–52.
42 Skandia, 1995, *Visualizing Intellectual Capital in Skandia, Supplement to Skandia's 1994 Annual Report*. Skandia AB.
43 Srinivasan, V. and Chan Su Park, 1997, "Surprising Robustness of the Self-Explicated Approach to Customer Preference Structure Measurement," *Journal of Marketing Research*, 34(May): 286–291.
44 Srinivasan, V., Chan Su Park, and Dae Ryun Chang, 2005, "An Approach to the Measurement, Analysis, and Prediction of Brand Equity and Its Sources," *Management Science*, 51(9): 1433–1448.
45 Srivastava, Rajendra K., Tasaduq A. Shervani, and Liam Fahey, 1998, "Market-Based Assets and Shareholder Value: A Framework for Analysis," *Journal of Marketing*, 62(January): 2–18.
46 Tollington, Tony, *Brand Assets*, 2002, New York: John Wiley & Sons.

15 Measuring the Value of Corporate Brands
Translating Corporate Brand Strategy into Financial Results

James R. Gregory

Introduction

The corporate brand can be one of a company's most valuable assets. In some cases, it may be the most valuable asset. Indeed, to many outsiders, it *is* the company, a distillation of factors such as name recognition, reputation, and economic value that determine whether individuals will invest in the company, buy its products, and recognize and repeat its name. Since the corporate brand can be measured and valued, it can be shaped and managed. The proliferation of products and services often creates a confusing array of competing offerings and marketing messages to consumers and business customers alike. They rely increasingly on corporate brands to guide their buying and investment choices.

The corporate brand is a business asset, which can—and should—be managed over time in the same manner as any other business asset. Because no two companies are exactly alike, it is important to develop a standard set of research metrics and reporting methodologies to determine the financial value of the company brand and identify specific strategies, including budget allocation, to increase what is known as "corporate brand power"—a key factor that ultimately leads to corporate brand equity value. Since marketing is crucial to corporate success, marketing accountability must be reliable with consistent financial metrics that tie marketing performance to growth and value creation. Understanding the significant financial value related to the management of the corporate brand, as well as a systematic method to evaluate improvements in perception, should result in improved financial performance across the enterprise. A generic methodology, along with specific metrics, will be covered later in the chapter.

The corporate brand is the result of managing all communications and messages emanating from a corporate entity. These communications may be intended, such as advertising, product packaging, signage, public relations, investor relations, and employee relations. Alternatively, the communications may be unintended, such as an executive making an unguarded remark on an open microphone, or an employee being caught on video delivering an expensive TV by launching it over a fence. Corporate branding includes every aspect of the corporate persona and can grow or decline in prestige at the slightest infraction. Our definition is: *The corporate brand is everything you say and do*. Understanding the corporate brand, the tremendous value that it contributes to the company, and how to manage it, are the subjects of this chapter.

There are many aspects of building and managing a corporate brand. Most important is understanding how the process of brand building works. Think about the signals that corporations send out every day. Most of them are unintended, but they create subliminal impressions, which add up over time. They happen all the time, every day. If you have ever received an incorrect invoice from a company, the way it is handled creates an immediate and lasting impression about the integrity of a company and the quality of its customer service. Another example is attending a meeting in a conference room where coffee cups from the previous meeting have not been

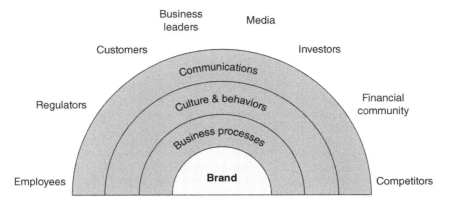

Figure 15.1 The Brand Experience.
Source: CoreBrand.

removed. The impression is "sloppiness." Another incident could be an employee speaking ill of another. The impression here could be an "unhappy environment." The opposite would be an employee heaping praise on another. The impression here is a "positive/productive environment," where gratitude prevails. These examples, and many others, are the power of a corporate brand at work. Positive impressions can also be spontaneous, for instance, a flight attendant helping an inexperienced traveler to find their proper seat, and doing it with genuine kindness. Is this training, experience, courtesy, or branding? The answer is that it is all of them. Every instance of a brand impression being created is called a "trust point."

These trust points are the basic building blocks we call "the brand experience," in which the constituent (customer, shareholder, employee, or other key audience) sees the brand through a series of filters. These filters are manageable touch points in brand building. They include the company's business processes, culture, and behavior, and communications in all forms (see Figure 15.1).

The Brand Experience

Brands are built through touch points that are linked in different ways with the corporation. Every key audience will see the brand through their own perspective. The employee is concerned about the corporation as an employer, and the main concerns are the benefits of the employer, how the company treats employees, and the working environment. For a customer, the touch points are different. A customer is interested in the quality of the product or service, along with pricing and reliability. Every key constituency looks at the corporate brand with their own self-interest. The way these constituencies view the brand is through a series of lenses. These lenses are the trust points in building relationships and they happen throughout the company. How a receptionist answers the phone is a trust point—an outsider's first glimpse into the "culture" of the company. This trust point is also a pure form of "communication," indicating how a single interaction can be an important opportunity to create a brand impression.

Sometimes a brand impression can be created even when it is unintended. A delivery truck that has not been washed in a long time, or is in obvious disrepair creates an immediate impression. This impression may be subliminal in nature or more obvious. Understanding that every trust point creates either positive or negative brand impressions establishes the awareness, which is necessary effectively to manage those impressions. The number of key constituencies will vary widely depending on the company and the industry. Nearly all companies share the key constituencies shown above, but the types of customers and influencers change from company to company. Determining which audiences are critical to your success is an important step in managing the brand.

The next step is to measure those audiences who are most important to the success of the corporate brand. Those deemed to be the most important should be diligently researched on an ongoing basis. This type of benchmark tracking system will provide insight into the trends of each audience and help identify variations of the norm before problems arise. Consistent quantitative benchmark tracking of key audiences and peer companies provides a fundamental ingredient into building corporate brand value. Benchmarking also allows for the use of model building to determine the cause and effect of changes to the trust points (e.g., how will increased advertising impact my revenue?).

The Corporate Brand "Perspective"

If the corporate brand is everything the company says and does, then managing the trust points with every key constituency is of paramount importance. The well-managed corporate brand is a holistic balancing of all the trust points of key constituencies (those who have the biggest potential impact on success or failure). Manageable trust points include corporate identity, signage, advertising, employee communications, training, speeches, investor relations, community relations, media interaction, and responsiveness (also known as public relations). It also includes all those subliminal signals being sent by the corporation every day. Thus, the maintenance staff should be trained as to their role in brand building. The delivery staff need to understand that they are often the front line of a brand impression. Thinking about a corporate brand from this perspective will help everyone understand its long-term impact.

Understanding the Brand

Understanding the strengths and weaknesses of a corporate brand and how to manage it requires continuous research of those key constituencies that are important to reaching long-term strategic goals. The process of building a corporate brand requires a systematic review of inputs from company employees and intimate observers to delineate "who we are" and "what we believe." The information is crafted into a distinguishing message and positioning, which can be tested for accuracy and credibility in the marketplace. Reflecting these findings, a comprehensive communications program is designed to reflect the findings in order to impart a specific impression on a target audience. The program can be benchmarked and models created for understanding both the qualitative and quantitative impact on the image of the company and ultimately the financial performance.

Defining the Corporate Brand

Corporate branding needs to make a persuasive statement to customers, investors, the media, and, most importantly, employees. The brand provides everyone in the organization with a common goal. It also benefits the corporation by communicating the subtext: "You can believe in our company and in our products." Corporate branding is a valuable investment in the company's future, because it buoys the company's divisions and product brands through increased awareness and opportunities for improved cross selling. Visionary, targeted, controlled, and cost-effective, corporate branding is a dynamic concept—a corporate communication tool whose time has come.

Managing the Complete Corporate Experience

To express the essence of the whole corporation, a corporate branding program must influence all forms of corporate communications: corporate advertising, brand advertising, media relations, investor relations, customer service, employee communications, and more. Corporate branding is a carefully planned, integrated program that shapes desired opinions and prompts positive behavioral responses from targeted audiences—a thorough marketing-oriented approach that can contribute to the corporation's marketing success and value-creating financial performance. Corporate branding manages the various manifestations of identity in service of the brand, including the company's name, symbols and logotype, and nomenclature system. In addition, the corporate brand may be reflected in the company's societal concerns or by the style of its architecture and decor, if these are intended to create a specific impression.

Corporate branding is the complete corporate ethos and experience summed up in the company's reputation and consciously projected to select audiences. By linking the corporate name closely with such favorable attributes as quality value, dependability, innovation, community-mindedness, good management, environmental consciousness, and so on, corporate branding builds a special relationship with target audiences. It can change behavior toward the company. With respect to the competition, all other things being equal, corporate branding can be the tiebreaker that motivates people to invest in the corporation, buy its products, recommend it to others, or seek employment with the company.

Leading Edge of Corporate Strategy

Just about everyone has their own idea about how best to build a corporate brand. CEOs and CFOs, marketing and communications officers, agency and media executives—they all have opinions on the subject. The reason is that brand building has many possible objectives for a large number of target audiences; thus, it is viewed from a wide range of perspectives. If you are a CEO, you probably regard corporate branding primarily as a critical weapon in the arsenal to mold the corporation in your vision. If you are the director of corporate communications, you may be more interested in its immediate successes. If you are the CFO, you may be primarily focused on the return on investment and stock price impact. Whatever the perspective, corporate branding can help propel the corporation dramatically toward its corporate goals and objectives. It can be the leading edge of corporate strategy and is essential to positioning a company for profitable growth.

Perception Is Reality

Corporate reputation is the public's perception of a company—the preconceived ideas and prejudices that customers form over time. Their perceptions may not always accurately reflect a corporation's true profile, but to the public it is reality. Therefore, one of the CEO's major responsibilities is to ensure that initial public impressions about the company are molded into a positive force—one that enhances the corporation's business prospects. Communicating the corporate brand is not a new strategy. It began almost a century ago, with the first image ads concentrating on the great changes then taking place in the American lifestyle. As new inventions such as the automobile, telephone, airplane, and radio were evolving into major industries, the public needed to be educated about the reliability of the new corporations that manufactured and offered them. Although the major portion of advertising budget dollars is still allocated to product branding or product promotion, corporate image communications is a valuable tool that helps make it easier to sell products while building the corporate brand. When a company's corporate brand becomes dated or invalid, its customers, shareholders, employees, and other constituencies may begin to wonder not only about the company's products but also about its overall profits, direction, and future viability. Clearly, key public stakeholders need to understand the dynamics, extent, and consequences of the changes. A corporation undergoing important changes must communicate its new reality to its publics and create a new context for up-to-date perception.

Benefits of Corporate Branding

There are nine major benefits for communicating the corporate brand. Properly conceived and implemented, corporate branding can be the leading edge of corporate strategy, helping to do the following:

1. build public awareness and acceptance, thus establishing a more favorable market position;
2. redefine your company after a merger, takeover, acquisition, divestiture, change of management, name change, or change in strategy;
3. presell target markets to support your product marketing;
4. influence your shareholders and the financial community;
5. establish your company's position on timely issues;
6. assist in managing a crisis situation;
7. attract and hold quality employees;
8. create a cooperative environment in local communities;
9. indicate the company's involvement in corporate social responsibility.

In order to achieve these benefits, corporate branding should be market driven, aiming toward strategic goals and objectives. For example, a campaign to announce a company name change can increase public awareness of the corporation and its strengths, stimulate interest in company brands, convey important information to the financial community, and influence potential employees. The point is that a seemingly minor endeavor can have positive results if approached with a strategic outlook.

The Benefits of Measuring the Corporate Brand

The corporate brand is a business asset, which can—and should—be managed over time in the same manner as any other business asset. While no two companies are exactly alike, it is important to develop a standard set of metrics and reporting methodologies to determine the financial value of the company's brand. To quote a well-worn phrase: "people manage what is measured." Establishing a set of metrics that link to specific strategies sets the stage for budget preparations and takes the mystery out of resource allocation and organizational responsibility. When this alignment of strategic goals/objectives, value-based measurements, and resource allocation is in place, the company is on a path to increase what is known as "brand power"—a key indicator of brand equity value. Allocating resources to business and brand strategies is consistent with managing shareholder value creation. In this regard, treat the corporate brand as an intangible asset that:

- can be accurately and consistently measured and valued;
- can be compared to competitive companies and industries;
- can be budgeted for and managed similar to other assets;
- can grow or lose value over time;
- can be evaluated on a return on investment and value creation basis;
- can be used as a company-wide communication tool;
- can be an indicator of future cash flow.

Since 1990, CoreBrand has conducted quantitative benchmark tracking research and developed regression models (collectively called the CoreBrand Index®),[1] which provides continuous data and insights into the stock side of the total value equation for over 1,000 companies, across 50 industries. CoreBrand's research proves the average corporate brand accounts for 5 to 7 percent of market capitalization (common stock value). The corporate brand's contribution can vary significantly by industry and general economic conditions, and within the database there are some companies that get nothing for their brand, while others get as much as 21 percent. For some industries, like building materials, the brand has a relatively low impact, with only a 2 percent average impact on market capitalization. However, in the beverage industry, the corporate brand plays a major role, showing an 11 percent on average impact on market capitalization. Understanding the brand equity of a specific company in the context of its industry provides valuable insight into the current position of the corporate brand. Evaluating a company's brand equity growth compared to the performance of the industry provides immediate insight into the effectiveness of the management team and the investment in marketing efforts. Comparing a firm's quarterly value against its peer group is a perfect dashboard measure of the health, vitality, and value of the corporate brand.

In the following example, the client company already had an advantage over their peer group, but wanted to expand that competitive advantage. A $24 million communications campaign was budgeted to build the corporate brand. Over the period tested, there was a brand equity improvement of 2.2 percent of the market capitalization over the competition (Table 15.1).

Integrating Communications to Reach Corporate Goals

Corporate branding combines all corporate communications programs into a coordinated marketing plan with specific targeted goals. It is a total communications program, internal as well as external, presenting a single, unified message—one that says clearly in one voice: *This is who we are and how we work. You can believe in our products and in our company.* Corporate branding is, therefore, a carefully planned and directed strategy to leverage all communications budgets for greater efficiency and effectiveness.

Our Corporation Is Our Brand

Unified by a compelling vision, the corporate brand can actually function as a bond between a company and its customers. A common theme spanning across a company's advertising establishes a contract—a promise the company holds out to its customers. That promise rallies all the employees to a common purpose. Customers identify with slogans, using them to compliment companies when they are happy with the product and/or service, and complain when that product/service does not meet expectations. Driven by a common set of business objectives and strategies, a company's corporate and product/service advertising, along with

Table 15.1 Client's Brand Equity vs. Peer Group Brand Equity

	Q1	Q2	Q3	Q4	Q5	Q6
Peer Average Brand Equity %	6.8	6.6	6.4	6.1	5.5	5.4
Client Brand Equity %	8.1	8.2	8.4	8.8	8.9	8.9
Client Brand Equity Improvement %	0.0	0.3	0.7	1.4	2.1	2.2
Communications Budget ($millions)	0.0	5.0	8.0	9.0	2.0	0.0

Source: Created by the author.

its total communications effort, serves to embody their brand promise to establish the corporation itself as a meaningful brand. The smartest marketers know that done correctly and with commitment, corporate branding works to increase market share and actually sell products. The best corporate branding speaks with one voice, long term. It is tied to the products of the corporation, creating an environment of trust and familiarity. Conversely, good product brand advertising reflects positively on the image of the parent company. Both product and corporate branding should work hand-in-hand to achieve maximum value.

A Covenant between Company and Consumer

A quality brand has to be more than a quality product. A quality product or service must be marketed in a quality manner. Quality must be deeply involved with every aspect of every consumer contact. The product, its advertising and promotion, the purchase experience, product service, customer information, customer relations, and the follow-up marketing should all reflect that quality. An important point to remember when building a convincing corporate brand is that all forms of corporate communications are needed to assure an enduring and successful reputation in the marketplace. The synergistic effect of advertising, web presence, internal branding, promotion, and public relations is very powerful. They must work in concert, not in conflict, to build a profitable, dominant brand. The companies that do this best usually have a clear, concise, and consistent brand and state it very simply (e.g., Apple equates to being "cool").

In a corporate culture, we understand brand stewardship not so much as an issue of decentralization versus centralization but as a commitment to establishing a common brand-based language throughout an entire organization. This means the integration of marketing, communications, and design. It also means the entire company, from finance to legal, makes decisions based on a brand-first mindset. Because the brand is generally recognized as a company's most valuable asset, the corporate role is actively to encourage integration and consistency in brand communication. This ensures that consistency of expression is grounded in the core values and promise of the brand. Even when a company has had long experience with corporate branding, fine-tuning may still be required in order to establish the global brand, or even a totally different approach, especially in developing markets.

Aflac—the Two Sides of Brand Value—"Revenue" and "Stock"

Most will recall seeing those crazy ads on television starring the Aflac duck. Suddenly, supplemental insurance was propelled to the forefront of our insurance consciousness. The ingenious campaign pioneered a new trend in the insurance industry and most importantly generated increased revenue for the sponsoring firm. The increase in revenue that it created is called "premium income per share (PIPS)."

The campaign also had an important secondary impact. It created far greater awareness of the Aflac corporate brand, which, in turn, created improvements in the stock price beyond the expected performance. This is called "corporate brand equity" and is identified through a continuous quantitative benchmark tracking survey called the Corporate Branding Index®, which has been conducted by brand consultancy CoreBrand on 1,000 companies across 50 industries since 1990.

Aflac[2] is one of the companies tracked in the CoreBrand Index, which allows them to examine the results of a successful campaign and the impact on both the "revenue" and "stock" performance of the company. We will now examine the history of Aflac's corporate brand.

208 *James R. Gregory*

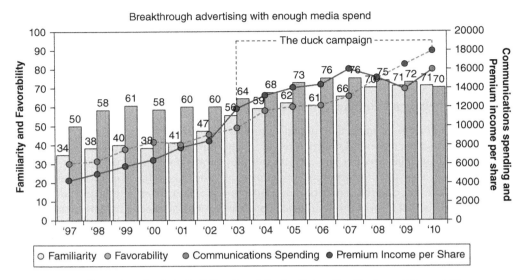

Figure 15.2 Aflac—Case Study in Building Brand Equity Value. Familiarity and Favorability.

Source: CoreBrand Index®.

Aflac was improving in "familiarity" throughout the time period studied. The light gray columns represent "familiarity" and they increased at a fairly steady pace from 34 in 1997 until it reached 47 in 2002. Familiarity then surged ahead as a result of the surge in spending for the duck campaign in 2003, until reaching a score of 71 in 2010. Favorability also improved from 50 to 60 from 1997 until 2002. Then favorability surged from 60 to a high of 76 in 2007.

Advertising was the primary driver of these improvements. Not only did Aflac have a differentiating breakthrough campaign but they were also spending enough to break through the clutter of mass media to get and hold the consumers' attention. Aflac had been spending more each year prior to the launch of the duck campaign in 2003, but spending grew significantly for the launch of the new campaign. Spending grew from $24 million in 1997 to $42 million in 2002, then increased dramatically to $60 million in 2003 for the launch of the duck campaign and peaked at $80 million in 2007.

Aflac revenue is measured by the value called PIPS. There was a direct correlation between the success of the campaign and the resulting impact on revenue. PIPS improved from $6,000 to $8,000 from 1997 to 2002 and then improved dramatically after the launch of the duck campaign, reaching $18,000 in 2010 (Figure 15.2).

The CoreBrand Index also measures three attributes of favorability. These are shown in Figure 15.3 as three lines:

- gray squares—Overall Reputation;
- gray triangles—Perception of Management;
- gray circles—Investment Potential.

The three attributes correlate to the same time period as in Figure 15.2: 1997–2010. The gray squares, triangles and circles are for Aflac and the white squares, triangles and circles in the background represent the average of their industry peers.

Measuring the Value of Corporate Brands 209

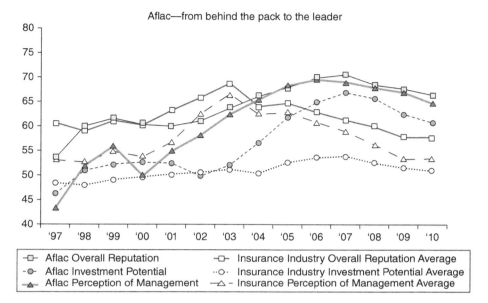

Figure 15.3 Aflac—Case Study in Building Brand Equity Value. Favorability Attributes.
Source: CoreBrand Index®.

In 1997, all three attributes for Aflac not only lagged behind the industry, but they were dead last. From 1997 to 2002 Aflac improved somewhat, but they were still lagging behind the average. From 2003 until 2007, after the onset of the duck campaign, they surged ahead and captured the lead of the industry—this is a remarkable growth of attributes in an extremely short time. Interestingly, in the financial industry meltdown that started in 2008, Aflac was able to maintain its lead even though attributes declined for them and the industry.

The impact of Aflac's duck campaign on corporate brand equity value is in addition to the effect that the campaign had on increased revenue and improved cash flow. The impact identified by corporate brand equity is that portion of the stock that relates to future expected cash flow. As such, it is an excellent dashboard measure of the health and vitality of the reputation of the corporation and the value associated with the corporate brand.

In 2002, just prior to the launch of the duck campaign, Aflac's brand equity percent (percent of total market capitalization) stood at 6.4 percent, while the industry average was at 4.8 percent (Figure 15.4). So, going into the campaign, Aflac already enjoyed a premium to the average competitor, but what happened after the release of the duck campaign created real separation. In 2005, mid-way into the duck campaign, the industry brand equity percent had barely moved—increasing to only 4.9 percent. Aflac, however, soared to 10.6 percent. By 2010, the Aflac advantage grew, with the measure reaching 12.8 percent, which doubled their brand equity from the starting point in 2002. Meanwhile, the industry in 2010 had declined to 3.8 percent, a full percent decline from their starting point in 2002. This huge advantage for Aflac is one that would be very difficult to see in the overall "noise" of Wall Street if it were not for continuous quantitative research and models that tie into market capitalization.

The financial value of the improvements in market capitalization is equally impressive. The 6.4 percent brand equity as a percent of market cap was worth $0.94 billion in 2002. In 2010,

	2002 BEV%	2002 BEV$
Aflac	6.4%	$940 Million
Industry Average	4.8%	$630 Million
	2005 BEV%	2005 BEV$
Aflac	10.6%	$2.58 Billion
Industry Average	4.9%	$1.22 Billion
	2010 BEV%	2010 BEV$
Aflac	12.8%	$3.36 Billion
Industry Average	3.8%	$800 Million

Figure 15.4 Aflac—Case Study in Building Brand Equity Value. CoreBrand Equity Value.
Source: CoreBrand Directory of Brand Equity.

that figure had grown to 12.8 percent, or $3.36 billion. That is an improvement of $2.42 billion for the investment in the duck campaign and is over and above the value created on the revenue side of the equation.

An Overview of Corebrand's Methodology for Determining Brand Strength and Value

What Is the CoreBrand Index?

- CoreBrand's proprietary database contains the financial information, advertising spending, and a continuous quantitative brand image survey of over 1,000 companies across 50 industries and 10 sectors of the economy.
- These companies represent some of the world's best corporate brands.
- Financial information and advertising spending are acquired from public sources including ValueLine, Bloomberg and Thomson Financial.
- Brand image ratings (brand power, familiarity, favorability) are derived from CoreBrand's annual survey of more than 10,000 "opinion elites" and business decision-makers from the top 20 percent of U.S. businesses.

Survey Audience

The opinion elites' audience is made up of senior business audience (VP level and above) and represents the investment community, potential business partners, and business customers across 50 key industries. Every year there are 10,000 completed interviews, and each year an entirely new audience is interviewed. The survey is conducted by telephone, ensuring we have the right person on the call. Each participant is asked to evaluate 40 corporate brands from 40 different industries. This survey method prevents vertical industry bias seen in other surveys. It also allows for comparison of corporate brands across industries if required (e.g., a comparison of the corporate brands of Target and Ford Motor Company can be made if desired). The individuals in the survey audience impact corporate brands from two important perspectives:

Business Decision-Makers

- executives at companies with sales revenue greater than $50 million;
- 80 percent involved in B2B purchase decisions;
- 90 percent determine purchase needs;
- 72 percent select specific companies' partners;
- 68 percent authorize purchases.

High-Level Consumers

- valuable demographics;
- 72 percent ages 35+;
- 83 percent HH size 2 or more;
- 87 percent college degrees;
- 74 percent above $75K HHI.

Measuring the Power of a Corporate Brand

Brand power is a measure of size (familiarity) and quality (favorability):

Familiarity

- a weighted percentage of survey respondents who are familiar with the brand being evaluated; rated on a five-point scale, respondents are considered to be familiar with a brand if they state that they know more than the company name only.

Favorability

- those familiar with a corporation are then asked favorability dimensions, overall reputation, perception of management, and investment potential;
- favorability attributes are evaluated on a four-point scale.

Familiarity and favorability are then combined into a single brand power score. Brand power rankings compare the size and quality of a brand to all other brands in the Corporate Branding Index:

- The brand power rankings provide a market-view evaluation of brand strength regardless of industry affiliation.
- Brand power data from the Corporate Branding Index are updated quarterly.

Determining CoreBrand Equity

The corporate brand is an asset that can contribute many millions or even billions of dollars to a company's stock price and market valuation. Understanding your corporate brand's value is the first step toward managing this fundamental asset. Brand strength ratings and each company's financial data are used in CoreBrand's statistical model to determine the percentage of market capitalization that is directly derived from the corporate brand. Once that percentage is calculated, a dollar value is assigned.

An expected base level of brand power will be achieved based on a company's size in revenue and shareholder value alone. Any level of brand power above that base level is generated by a

212 *James R. Gregory*

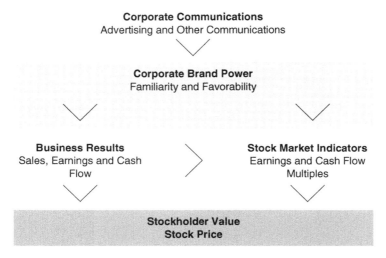

Figure 15.5 The Two Dimensions of Corporate Brand Power.
Source: CoreBrand.

company's brand (either intentionally or accidentally). To analyze and illustrate the notion that corporate brand building directly impacts stock price performance, a stock price model will be presented that is built upon the following foundations:

- consistent quantitative research from business decision-makers collected over time;
- modeling that includes comparative analysis of a specific company versus industry peers and the overall stock market;
- factors that influence brand power—a determinant in the corporate brand's impact on stock price;
- algorithms that evaluate the impact of improving brand equity on shareholder value (and vice versa).

There are some important relationships that link advertising, corporate image (or brand power), and shareholder value. At the core of these relationships is corporate brand communications, which includes all forms of communications, but specifically measureable are corporate, brand, and trade advertising carrying the corporate name. Corporate brand communications have been quantitatively proven to impact corporate brand power, based on a number of variables that will be presented. Corporate brand power has two dimensions—familiarity and favorability—and is a factor that impacts business financial performance and, ultimately, a company's stock price. These linkages are illustrated in Figure 15.5.

Concepts and Definitions

The following are important terms in a financial discussion and equity valuation/stock price analysis related to corporate brands:

- **brand image**—the sum total of all the accumulated perceptions across the broad spectrum of audiences shaped by many factors, which can be controlled;
- **brand power**—a measure of the size of a company's audience and their disposition toward the company, encompassing:

a **familiarity**—how well known is the company, and
b **favorability**—what is the overall reputation, perception of management and investment potential of the company.

Familiarity and favorability scores, which help indicate the strength of a company's image and reputation, can be utilized to understand how brand helps to drive business results (revenue) and financial performance (stock price). The following sections cover important terms used in a financial discussion and equity valuation/stock price analysis—whether related to corporate brands or any other element of a business that can contribute to shareholder value.

Managing the "Brand Experience"

The brand experience can be managed in three ways: through business processes, culture and behavior, and communications. By ensuring that these are consistent, companies can build their brand image in a predictable way. Brand experience is what a company does, including its business processes, and what it makes in terms of products and services. Brand experience also encompasses how a company behaves and acts toward its stakeholders, employees, communities, customers, partners, and investors. In other words, what is the culture of the company? What a company says about itself regarding its intentions, deliverables, and actions is also part of the consumer brand experience. The collective stakeholder audience experiences what a company does and says, and the sum of these experiences is the "brand" (some also refer to it as "reputation"). In understanding how brand contributes to value, the biggest hurdle lies in establishing a quantitative view of the size and quality of corporate reputation. The first real step toward developing this involves determining familiarity and favorability scores. The familiarity score provides a quantitative view on how well known a given company is, i.e., the size of a company's reputation. The favorability score provides a quantitative measure of how positively predisposed a familiar audience is toward a given company. Because these measures are quantitative, i.e., robust, they can be used in predictive financial modeling.

The familiarity and favorability scores, which help indicate the strength of a company's image and reputation, can be utilized to understand how brand helps to drive top-line business results (revenue and market share) and financial performance (profitability and stock price). A company's single favorability score is a combination of three attribute measures: respondents' ratings on a company's:

1 overall reputation;
2 perception of management;
3 investment potential.

These scores can be used as quantitative variables in models similar to the way financial variables are used. Marketers can develop quantitative research by measuring a neutral, business savvy audience of business decision-makers. The advantage of using a neutral audience such as business decision-makers (as opposed to customers) means that these measures are not subject to any vertical industry bias (i.e., the unique operating characteristics shared by a specific industry) and can be utilized in predictive financial modeling, because of their objectivity. Customer research is also incorporated when evaluating the impact of the brand on revenue.

Foundation for a Brand Communications ROI Model

The first challenge facing a brand valuation model is how to define and capture the measures that ultimately provide the corporate brand's contribution to stock price. These measures must be:

- **robust**—examine the meaningful attributes that drive category and company performance;
- **objective**—provide an unbiased report on reputation and financial performance;
- **predictive**—identify the opportunities and brand leverage available;
- **repeatable**—track progress and provide accountability.

Any metric must meet the above criteria in order to be included in a brand measurement model. Financial factors for modeling a brand's impact on market capitalization are based upon the actual factors that drive stock performance for a specific industry. Cash flow (actual and expected), earnings growth, dividends, and underlying financial strength make up about 80 percent of what drives stock price. The remaining 20 percent has traditionally been "unknown." Through regression modeling, CoreBrand has discovered that the corporate brand makes up a portion (about 5 to 7 percent on average across all companies in an extensive database) of the total stock price; thus 25 to 33 percent of that "unknown" number is non-financial factors such as quality of management and business strategy. Image attributes and financial factors should be constantly analyzed. Each element's importance can be measured by using an algorithm. When there is significant market change, such as the recent steep market declines, the models should be recalibrated according to current market conditions.

The extent of a company's opportunity to improve its economics by strengthening its brand varies widely, depending on the industry and the existing level of strength within a company's brand. Unrealized value might be available based on the company's brand strength and market dynamics. By understanding how much value is available and defining how much it costs to realize that value, equations can be generated on a case-by-case basis for individual companies. This methodical process takes the emotion out of the brand budgeting and planning process and puts it into a business context. Brand value is dependent on the strength of four areas:

1. familiarity and coherence of the brand;
2. reputation of the company;
3. respect that external audiences extend to corporate leadership and brand ambassadors (employees);
4. confidence that financial audiences hold for the company's stock performance.

The model that will be presented and discussed has the following attributes related to its database:

- tracking of 1,000 leading U.S. corporate brands across 50 industries;
- consistent and reliable historical data (back to 1990);
- survey of 10,000 VP level and higher executives in the top 20 percent of U.S. businesses each year to measure familiarity and favorability with corporate brands;
    - a interviews are conducted continuously throughout the year;
    - b 400 different respondents rate each company each year;
    - c 1,000 companies are measured each year.
- financial data collected from sources such as Value Line, Bloomberg and others, covering both financial fundamentals and analyst rankings;
- advertising spending data collected from Kantar Media Intelligence to track brand investments.

The brand communications ROI model has two key regression equations:

1. The first measures the factors that drive changes in brand power (familiarity and favorability);
2. the second measures the factors that drive changes in stock price.

Measuring the Value of Corporate Brands 215

In the first model, brand power is the dependent variable, and independent variables are advertising investment, corporate size, dividend, stock price growth, and earnings volatility. Approximately 78 percent of brand power variance is explained by this equation. The dependent variable in the second model is stock price. Independent variables are cash flow, earnings, dividend, expected future cash flow growth, company size, financial strength, and brand power. Between 85 and 90 percent of stock price variance is explained by this equation.

Elements for a Brand Communications ROI Model

The factors impacting corporate brand power are advertising investment, corporate size, earnings volatility, stock price growth, and dividend payout, along with other factors such as public relations, corporate communications, and investor relations. These factors are illustrated in Figure 15.6.

Advertising in all measurable forms is still the biggest factor that builds image. In recent years, advertising as a driver of brand image has been under attack for losing its potency. We have not seen advertising diminish despite all the claims of its demise. The next biggest factor is company size—simply by size alone a company builds corporate brand image. The larger the company the more employees it is likely to have, the more investors, the more buildings for signage, the more vehicles with mobile signage, and the more communities in which they are likely to be located. Other communications—public relations, investor relations, employee relations, website, internet, and social media—all of these harder-to-measure forms of communication contribute significantly to the image of a company.

Dividends are an important contributor to a company's image. Dividends provide a zone of comfort and can be a significant driver of image in certain industries where the corporate brand plays less of a differentiating role—the electric utilities industry, for example. Stock price growth (aka "momentum") is a contributor to brand. People like a winner, and a brand that has momentum creates a halo of optimism that impacts brand image in a positive way. Alternatively, a company that loses momentum has a negative impact on the brand, which we call "drag." Earnings volatility is an indicator that a company has the opportunity for rapid growth.

The factors impacting corporate stock price are current earnings, dividends and cash flow, expected cash flow growth, financial strength, corporate size, recent stock price momentum, brand power, and other non-financial factors. These factors are illustrated in Figure 15.7.

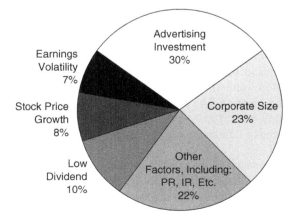

Figure 15.6 Factors Impacting Corporate Brand Power.

Source: CoreBrand.

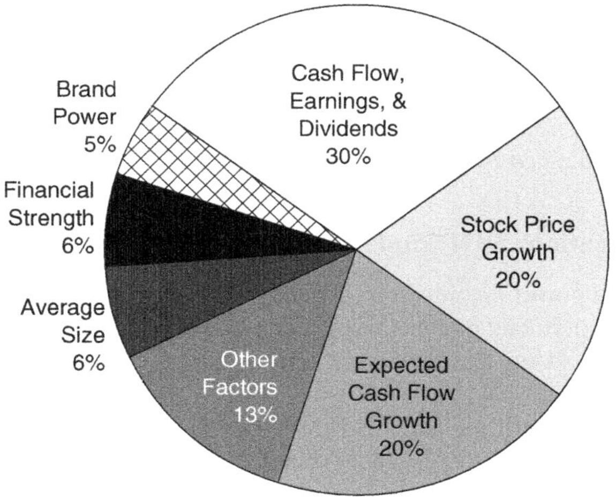

216 James R. Gregory

Figure 15.7 Factors Impacting Corporate Stock Price.
Source: CoreBrand.

The brand communications ROI model is used to identify the return in increased market capitalization for increased communications investment. The model assigns weights to the factors that cause change in both brand power and stock price. Once weights are assigned to each of the variables, the model can measure the impact that changes in advertising investment can have on brand power and, in turn, stock price. The model holds all other variables (mostly financial) constant in order to isolate the impact that spending will have, and measure its return in terms of market capitalization. Thus, the analysis is focused on the sensitivity of a company's stock price to changes in communications investment. This level of sensitivity is called the benefit-to-cost ratio (B/C ratio)—the change in shareholder value divided by the cost of advertising. This B/C ratio is the result of quantitatively evaluating the relationships cited earlier—corporate brand communications, corporate brand power, and shareholder value—based on studies of hundreds of actual companies. The results of the brand communications ROI model are expressed as marginal revenue versus marginal cost analysis. In Figure 15.8 the straight line indicates incremental increases or decreases in the advertising spending level, and the curved line represents the corresponding expected impact on market capitalization for each spending level. This "valuation" line is curved, because there are both increasing and diminishing marginal return relationships between advertising investment and stock price impact. The key objective of the model is to identify, statistically, at which advertising budget level shareholder value increase exceeds investment by the greatest amount. In other words, at what point is the positive "spread" the greatest. The model also reveals the breakthrough point (that is, where increased market value occurs), the point of diminishing returns (positive, but a decreasing rate), and the point of negative returns (where additional investment is counterproductive and results in decreased value).

This approach is judged to be optimal for analyzing corporate advertising and communication spending as it is consistent with the concept of evaluating ROI on the basis of their "spread" versus either the weighted average cost of capital or cost of equity capital, and then using this "spread" as a predictor of how the market price of total or equity capital relates to the book value (of total or equity capital). This ratio is the M/B (market-to-book) ratio. Thus, the brand equity model is consistent with

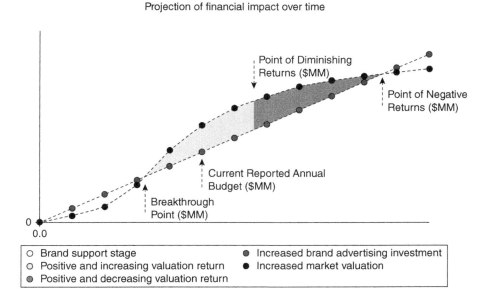

Figure 15.8 Communication ROI. Projection of Financial Impact over Time.
Source: CoreBrand.

accepted financial theory and practice. Another aspect of consistency is that existing and expected cash flows are key inputs to the model. Figure 15.8 provides a graphic illustration of this concept of increasing and decreasing marginal returns, taking into account the statistics that have been gathered and analyzed to show the impact of changes in advertising spending on market capitalization.

Brand Communications ROI—Illustration

Applying the learning from the brand communications ROI model about the impact of the corporate brand on future market capitalization, we have developed a model to measure the current value of the corporate brand. This model determines the expected minimum level of brand power that a company would have based on its size in revenue and market capitalization. The technique employed is one of analyzing a scatter diagram of all the companies in the database and fitting a trend-line to the lowest level of brand power for companies of a given size. The model identifies the impact of the difference between the expected minimum brand power based on the size of the company and the actual brand power of the company.

Notes

1. CoreBrand®, Corporate Branding Index®, are registered trademarks owned by Brandlogic Corp., DBA Tenet Partners. All exhibits, research methods, and models referring to use of CoreBrand are the property of Brandlogic Corp., 122 West 27th Street, New York, NY 10001.
2. Aflac is not a client of CoreBrand. The data is an example of the type of research in the CoreBrand Index. The use of this case study is not implied as an endorsement by Aflac of CoreBrand's methods or models.

16 Tax Implications of the Treatment of Marketing Expenses

Michael L. Moore

Introduction

There has been significant concern by the marketing community regarding recent proposals from Congress that advertising expenditures be changed from a long-standing treatment of immediate deduction of these expenditures to one that stretches these deductions out over a longer period of time. Such expenditures, for the most part, have been immediately deducted for taxation and financial accounting under the theory that there are significant doubts that future economic benefits will be derived from the expenditures and thus an asset is not created. On the other hand, it is difficult to argue that no future benefit is derived from marketing expenditures since many companies have internally developed marketing assets such as product brands and corporate brands that represent significant value for an entity, but are not on the balance sheet.

There are current ongoing discussions to recognize the value of brands in the financial statements, on the balance sheet or otherwise disclosed in notes, or in the Management Discussion and Analysis section of annual reports. Such discussions have been ongoing by the Marketing Accountability Standards Board (MASB). These discussions have raised many questions including how taxes for a business might be affected if the current tax treatment of brands is modified, and what might be the tax consequences if the recognition of the value of brands for financial accounting purposes is implemented.

This chapter will discuss the treatment of advertising and marketing costs, and proposals for changes in the treatment. Also discussed is the author's view of the tax and financial accounting implications of including the value of brands on a company's balance sheet.

Background—Tax Treatment of Advertising and Marketing Expenditures

For Federal income tax purposes, advertising and marketing expenses are generally deductible on a current basis as an ordinary and necessary business expense (IRC Section 162(a)). This treatment is prescribed because advertising expenditures are recurring in nature, or because the benefit does not extend beyond the tax year. Regulation 1.162–20(a)(2) goes on to provide, in part, that expenditures for institutional or goodwill advertising, which keeps the taxpayer's name before the public, are generally deductible as ordinary and necessary business expenditures, provided the expenditures are related to patronage the taxpayer might reasonably expect in the future.

As to capitalizing rather than expensing, Section 263 and Section 263A of the Code provide that no deduction is allowed for any amount paid out for permanent improvements or betterments made to increase the value of any property. For example, package design costs generally have useful lives of greater than one year and are generally capitalized under Section 263.[1]

The IRS position is that package design costs more closely resemble nonrecurring promotional or advertising expenditures that result in benefits to the taxpayer that extend beyond the year the expense was incurred.

Package design costs do not include coupon insets and refund offers, nor does it include costs that are unrelated to the package design itself, such as a change in ingredients.[2] On the other hand, in RJR Nabisco,[3] package designs were held to be expenses since future benefits were deemed not to arise significantly beyond those traditionally associated with institutional goodwill advertising.

In some other marketing expenditure areas, such as free samples, new channels of distribution, and catalogs, the deductibility or capitalization decisions by the courts generally hinged on the question of future benefits. Decisions were for each treatment.[4]

Current law and interpretations favor deductions rather than capitalization for advertising costs. The decision in Indopco[5] held that for capitalization, a significant long-term benefit must result from the expenditure. In the case of advertising it has been quite challenging to measure a significant long-term benefit. In Rev. Rul. 1992–80[6] the IRS stated that the Indopco decision does not affect the treatment of advertising as a business expense, which is generally deductible under Section 162 of the Code. This means the expenditures for institutional or goodwill advertising, which keep the taxpayer's name before the public, are generally deductible as ordinary and necessary business expenditures, provided the expenditures are related to patronage the taxpayer might reasonably expect in the future, as mentioned previously.

The tax laws in other countries, for example the UK, Germany, France, and Japan, permit the deduction of advertising and marketing costs. Canada, in general, permits the deduction, but does have some restriction on deductibility of some advertising expenses for non-Canadian directed advertising. China allows the deduction of advertising costs, but limits the deduction to 15 or 30 percent of sales revenue, depending on the product being advertised.

The Link to Financial Accounting

It should be noted that income subject to taxation in the United States and most other countries must be computed under the method of accounting on the basis of which the taxpayer regularly computes his income in keeping his books, as long as the books clearly reflect income.[7] There are exceptions reflected in the law when the government attempts to encourage or discourage social, economic, behavioral, or other government policy objectives. In these cases, financial accounting treatment of an item of income or an expenditure may differ. The tax treatment of advertising and other marketing expenditures for the most part conforms to the required treatment under generally accepted accounting principles (GAAP) and coincidentally to the treatment under International Accounting Standards (IAS) as reflected in International Financial Reporting Standards (IFRS). For accounting purposes, it is held that advertising costs incurred in anticipation of future probable economic benefits are usually expensed currently, because the benefit period is presumed to be short or the periods in which economic benefits might be received or the amount of economic benefit cannot be determined easily and objectively (FASB 720–35–05–3).

In Statement of Position 93–7[8] the Accounting Standards Executive Committee (AcSEC) provides a framework for expensing or capitalizing advertising costs, i.e., creating an intangible asset. The framework divides advertising into two alternative treatments: expense or capitalization. The general rule is that the costs of advertising should be expensed either as incurred or the first time the advertising takes place. This general rule is subject to the exceptions of direct-response advertising and expenditures for advertising costs that are made subsequent to recognizing revenue related to those costs.

The costs of direct-response advertising are capitalized if two conditions are met.[9] First, the primary purpose of the advertising must be to elicit sales to customers who in the past have responded specifically to the advertising, and second, the direct-response advertising results in probable future benefits. In order to conclude that advertising elicits sales to customers who responded specifically to the advertising, there must be a means of documenting that response, including a record that can identify the name of the customer and the advertising that elicited the direct response. Demonstrating that direct-response advertising will result in future benefits requires persuasive evidence that its effects will be similar to the effects of responses to past direct-response advertising that resulted in future benefits. The attributes to consider in determining whether the response is similar include the demographics of the audience, the method of advertising, the product, and the economic conditions.

In the absence of a specific entity's operating history, industry statistics are not considered objective evidence that advertising will result in future benefits. If the entity does not have operating histories for other new products or services, statistics for the other products or services may be used if it can be demonstrated that the statistics for other products or services are likely to be highly correlated to the statistics of the particular product or service being evaluated. Direct-response costs that cannot be demonstrated to result in future benefits are expensed.

Other amounts spent for tangible assets are capitalized and amortized. Examples include billboards and blimps. Tangible assets are not created when costs are incurred to produce film, or audio tape used to communicate advertising. Brochures and catalogs may be accounted for as prepaid advertising, and these costs would be treated as advertising expense or capitalized depending on whether these are direct-response advertising or not.

In summary, both for financial accounting and taxation, current expenditures for advertising and marketing are generally presumed not to create assets. An asset will be recorded in the books if it can be demonstrated that economic value is created. In addition, for tax purposes, if a customer-based intangible asset was created, it could not be amortized. From a pure economic perspective, current tax deductions generally have more value than deductions in the future. On the other hand, for financial reporting, firms might prefer to report higher current earnings by forgoing current deductions even if creation of assets were a possibility. Accounting rules generally preclude creating intangible assets unless it can be shown that future economic value is inherent in these expenditures.

Proposals to Change the Historical Treatment of Advertising Expenses

Over the years, the deductibility of advertising expenses has been an agenda item before Congress, but these proposals were for social and economic reasons rather than to raise revenue. In the 1950s, Congress debated using the deductibility of advertising costs as an economic stabilizer during a period of high demand and inflation, in order to restrain increased consumption. Congress also discussed targeting drug ads, alcohol and tobacco ads, and, more recently, ads for unhealthy food products for children.

A major threat to the immediate deductibility of advertising costs was a proposal under consideration in the Tax Reform Act of 1986 to disallow 20 percent of advertising costs. The advertising industry mounted a furious lobbying effort and was able to exert enough influence such that this proposal was not part of the final legislation. Congress was not deterred from this issue along with many other revenue enhancing proposals.

A proposal to change the tax treatment of advertising expenditures primarily to raise government revenues was put forth in a Joint Committee on Taxation report in 1987.[10] The possible proposals would require that all or a specific portion of advertising costs paid or incurred during a taxable year be amortized over some period, rather than deducted currently. The possible proposals would also deny the deduction for advertising for, or promotion of, alcohol and/or tobacco products. Aside from the alcohol and tobacco product arguments, there were four accounting or economic arguments for these proposals and five arguments against, three related to accounting, one policy issue, and one a consumer choice issue. The four principle arguments for the proposal were as follows:

1 The benefit of amounts paid for advertising extends beyond the year of the expenditure. Requiring some portion of advertising costs to be deferred to a later year thus results in a more proper matching of the expenses with the income generated by them.
2 Advertising expenditures do not lend to increase competitiveness; they merely shift consumer buying practices. Thus, there is no justification for a tax subsidy for these expenditures.
3 Permitting a current deduction for advertising costs creates a preference for businesses that invest in advertising over businesses that invest in tangible assets or other intangible assets, the costs of which must be depreciated or amortized.
4 Since it is difficult to determine precisely what portion of advertising costs benefit a particular year, it is appropriate to provide an assumed allocation of the benefit of such costs by statute.

The five principle arguments against the proposal were as follows:

1 Advertising costs are costs of selling a product in the current taxable year, and do not create a separate and distinct asset having a life that extends beyond the end of the year. Accordingly, they should be fully deductible in the year incurred.
2 Severe definitional and administrative problems will result in trying to differentiate between advertising and promotional expenses on the one hand, and fully deductible selling expenses on the other.
3 Even if some portion of advertising costs theoretically benefits future taxable years, it is only a de minimis amount. In any event, it is impossible to verify the degree of proper allocation of the benefits to future years.
4 It is not appropriate tax policy to restrict the deductibility of advertising expenses, while retaining expensing for similar expenditures such as research and development.
5 Advertising provides a valuable service by providing information about prices and product quality that helps consumers make more informed choices.

The advertising industry was stunned in late 2013 by draft proposals to be introduced as part of tax reform legislation by Representative, Dave Camp (R-Mich), chairman of the House Ways and Means Committee, and Max Baucus (D-Mont), chairman of the Senate Finance Committee, to limit deductions for advertising. The House Ways and Means Committee provision would allow advertisers to deduct only 50 percent of all advertising expenses in the first year and amortize the remaining 50 percent over the following 10 years. The Senate Finance Committee proposal would allow a business to deduct 50 percent of its advertising costs in the first tax year and amortize the remaining 50 percent over 5 years.

These latest proposals were immediately attacked by the Association of National Advertisers, the American Advertising Federation and the Advertising Coalition, among others. The objections warn of dire consequences to the U.S. economy. In addition it is pointed out that Congress appears to be more concerned with raising revenue in order to reduce the corporate tax rate to 25 percent than the dynamic impact the advertising industry has on the economy. Data from the advertising media community show that almost 15 percent of U.S. jobs are connected with advertising and $6 trillion of the U.S. economy is generated by advertising. As at the time of writing, it remains to be seen whether a proposal such as this will become law.

Recognizing Brands on the Balance Sheet

The current regimes in accounting and taxation do not support reporting on the balance sheet internally developed (self-created) assets. Under the historical cost method of accounting, marketing activities are treated as expenses and, even though there is a chance that assets might be created by marketing activities, such assets will not be shown on the financial statements. As to *internally developed* intangible assets, for GAAP purposes, costs of internally developing, maintaining, or restoring intangible assets (including goodwill) that are not specifically identifiable, that have indeterminate lives, or that are inherent in a continuing business and related to an entity as a whole, are recognized as an expense when incurred.[11] Assuming it could be shown that these costs created an economic benefit beyond the current year, such costs would be capitalized and shown on the balance sheet at historical cost and not at fair value.

IAS 38 prescribes the accounting treatment for intangible assets. It describes an intangible that is a resource controlled by an entity as a result of past events, such as by purchase or self-creation and from which future economic benefits are expected. Under IAS 31 an entity recognizes an intangible asset, whether purchased or self-created (at cost), if it is probable that the future economic benefits that are attributable to the asset will flow to the entity and the cost of the asset can be measured reliably. However, IAS does not hold that certain marketing expenditures pass these tests. Brands, mastheads, publishing titles, customer lists, and items similar in substance that are internally generated should not be recognized as assets.[12] This standard also requires that expenditures for advertising and promotional costs, including mail order catalogs must be treated as an expense when incurred.[13] As such, these expenditures will not create intangible assets. The IAS does provide that some intangible assets, which are initially valued at cost, may subsequently be treated under either a cost model or a revaluation model. Under the cost model, the intangible asset is carried on the balance sheet at cost less any amortization or impairment losses. Under the revaluation model approach, intangible assets may be carried at fair value less any subsequent amortization and impairment losses only if fair value can be determined by reference to an active market.[14] The IAS expects that active markets may be uncommon for intangible assets and cites as examples possible active markets for production quotas, fishing licenses, and taxi licenses.[15]

For intangibles *acquired* in a business combination, FASB 805 requires an acquiring entity to allocate the purchase price of the acquired entity to the assets acquired and liabilities assumed. Intangible assets are subject to two tests to determine whether they are recognized as assets apart from goodwill. The first test is whether it arises from contractual or other legal rights—regardless of whether those rights are transferrable or separable from the acquired entity, or from other rights or obligations. If an intangible asset does not arise from contractual or other legal rights, then the second test as to whether it should be recognized as an asset apart from goodwill is whether it is separable, that is, capable of being separated or divided from the acquired entity. This means that the asset must be capable of being sold, transferred, licensed, rented, or exchanged regardless of whether there is any intent to do so.[16] Examples of marketing-related intangibles include trademarks, trade names, service marks, collective marks, certification marks, trade dress (unique color, shape, and package design), internet domain names, noncompetition agreements, customer lists, books, and advertising contracts.[17]

Under IAS, there is a presumption that in a business combination the fair values of identifiable assets and liabilities are measured at their fair value at the acquisition date. Intangible assets must always be recognized at fair value. An intangible asset is identifiable if it meets either the separability criterion or the contractual-legal criterion. An intangible asset that meets the contractual-legal criterion is identifiable even if the asset is not transferable or separable from the acquiree, or from other rights and obligations. Examples of these types of intangible assets include a non-transferable lease, a nuclear power plant license, and a patent and license of that patent that is restricted to a certain market.[18] The separability criterion means that an acquired intangible asset is capable of being separated or divided from the acquiree and sold, transferred, licensed, rented, or exchanged, either individually or together with a related contract, identifiable asset, or liability, even if the acquirer does not intend to sell, license, or otherwise exchange it.[19] SFAS 141 (2001) (now FASB 805) and IFRS 3 (2005) changed the status of brands in the context of accounting for mergers and acquisitions. Prior to the issuance of these statements, brands were not considered to meet the recognition criteria for inclusion on the balance sheet as assets. Hence, there arose a need to value brands in acquisitions.

For tax purposes, the acquirer allocates the purchase price to classes of assets. After allocations are made to cash, fixed assets, investments, and inventory, the next allocation priority is to what are described as Section 197 intangibles.[20] Among those listed as Section 197 intangibles are goodwill, going concern value, workplace in force, and customer-based intangibles.[21] Therefore, in an acquisition, any identifiable customer-based intangibles, such as branding, may be recorded on the balance sheet at market value, assuming the acquisition price includes the value of such intangibles. For tax purposes these are amortized over a 15-year period.[22]

With respect to branding and other marketing intangibles, one cannot fail to notice the inconsistencies between the treatment of purchased intangibles and internally developed intangibles. Purchased intangibles are recorded on the balance sheet of the acquirer at their market value, while internally developed intangibles are usually not included on the balance sheet of the seller at all. Also, one cannot help but notice the great hurdles to clear to satisfy the GAAP and IAS rule-making bodies. Criticism of these current reporting requirements by marketing professionals appears to be building. That the balance sheet does not reflect the fair value of an asset or even reflect the existence of an asset is felt to fall short of information necessary for the evaluation of areas such as marketing effectiveness, investment and portfolio optimization, asset management, and benchmarking.

This current debate revolving around whether or not intangible assets, such as branding, can be recorded on the balance sheet in situations where economic value was created as a result of prior expenditures, must be resolved by GAAP and IFRS policy. Recording assets at fair value on GAAP or IAS financial statements is generally limited to marketable securities.

The second part of the debate regarding consideration of whether or not intangibles can be recorded on the balance sheet is the other accounting side of the write-up. If an asset is written up, then there is an entry to the equity. The most likely candidate for this side of the transaction is *Other Comprehensive Income*. Other comprehensive income contains all changes in equity that are not permitted to be included in profit and loss. This account is helpful in understanding changes in the fair value of a company's assets. The items typically included in other comprehensive income include value changes for available-for-sale securities, cash flow hedge derivative instruments gains and losses, certain foreign currency gains and losses, and certain transactions involving pensions or post-retirement benefit plans.

Taxation Issues of Recognizing Brands on the Balance Sheet

There are a few instances under current tax laws where write-ups or write-downs have an effect for income tax purposes. In general, the rules for taxation require a transaction in order to recognize a gain or loss. Exceptions to the transaction requirement are economic benefits that accrue to the taxpayer, such as forgiveness of debt, and for economic losses such as a casualty, a bad debt, a worthless security, or a deemed sale transaction. Additionally, write-downs to market (but not write-ups) are permitted in accounting for inventory, and an expense is recognized for tax purposes.

Those instances where a transaction is not required for tax recognition of gain or loss include certain futures contracts called Section 1256 contracts, which are written up or down to market resulting in gain or loss recognition for tax purposes. There is a well-organized market for regulated futures contracts and the mark-to-market rule corresponds to the daily cash settlement, mark-to-market system employed by commodity futures exchanges in the United States for determining margin requirements. In addition, Section 475 of the Internal Revenue Code requires that inventory in the hands of a securities' dealer must be included in inventory at fair market value and any security which is not inventory that is held at the close of the taxable year must recognize gain as if the security were sold for fair market value, with the gain or loss taken into account. All property of certain expatriates is treated as sold for fair market value as of the expatriation date, and gain or loss must be recognized. Also, under the passive foreign investment rules, there is an election under Section 1256 to mark-to-market marketable stock and recognize gains or losses. Except in the case of expatriates, the properties in question are financial assets that are relatively easy to value. A reliable market such as this for brands is certainly not in the foreseeable future.

Another impediment to recognizing taxable income deals with the wherewithal to pay the taxes. There are many provisions in tax law where there is no recognition of gain when the taxpayer's economic position has not significantly changed. Examples are exchanges of assets that are held in a different form, such as formation of a corporation or partnership, deferred tax exchanges of certain assets, and corporate acquisitions. A very strong argument for not recognizing taxable income upon the write-up of internally developed brands is that the owner of the brand is not in a different economic position, owning the same asset as was owned before the write-up.

Conclusion

In conclusion, following the reasoning above, the mere recognition of brands as assets on the balance sheet should have no tax effect on the company. However, from a political perspective, unless the policy makers are convinced that the creation of intangible assets cannot be traced to annual advertising expenditures, further attacks on the deductibility of advertising can be expected.

References

1. See Alabama Coca-Cola Bottling Company, TCM 1969–123.
2. Rev. Rul. 89–23, 1989 C.B. 85.
3. RJR Nabisco, Inc. 76 TCM 71 (1998).
4. Free samples were expensed in Northwestern Yeast, 5 BTA 232 and capitalized in Marko Durovic, 542 F. 2d 1328 (1976); new channels of distribution were held to be expenses in Briarcliff Candy Corp, 475 F. 775, CA–2 (1973), but the lower court in the same case held such expenditures should be capitalized (Briarcliff Candy Corp, 31 TCM 171 (1972)). Costs of catalogs were expenses in E.H. Shelton & Co. 214 F2d 655 (1954), and capitalized in Best Lock Corp. 31 T.C. 1217 (1959). Revenue Ruling 68–360, 1968–2 C.B. 197 also required capitalization of catalog costs.
5. 503 U.S. 79.
6. 1992–2 C.B. 57.
7. IRC Section 446.
8. Statement of Position 93–7, Reporting on Advertising Costs, AICPA Technical Practice Aids, December 29, 1993, codified by FASB 340–20–25.
9. FASB 340–20–25.
10. Joint Committee on Taxation, *Description of Possible Options to Increase Revenues Prepared for the Committee on Ways and Means*, 1987, U.S. Government Printing Office, pp. 138–139.
11. SFAS 142, 10.
12. IAS 38.43.
13. IAS 38.69.
14. IAS 38.75.
15. IAS 38.78.

16 FASB 805–20–25 Identifiable.
17 FASB 805–20–25–14.
18 IFRS 3, B32.
19 IFRS 3, B3.
20 Treas. Reg. sec. 1.338–6 provides for allocation based on fair market value to seven classes of assets beginning with Class I assets and proceeding through the classes in number sequence. Class I assets are cash and general deposit accounts; Class II assets are actively traded personal property; Class III assets are mark-to-market assets and debt instruments; Class IV assets are inventory; Class V assets are assets other than those in Classes I–VII; Class VI assets are Section 197 intangibles other than goodwill and going concern value; Class VII assets are goodwill and going concern value.
21 For tax purposes, a customer-based intangible is any composition of market, market share, or other value resulting from the future provision of goods and services pursuant to contractual or other relationships in the ordinary course of business with customers (Treas. Reg. Section 1.197–2(b)(6)).
22 IRC Section 197(a).

17 The Marketing Metric Audit Protocol

David W. Stewart, Margaret Henderson Blair, and Allan R. Kuse

Background

As described in the first chapter of this book, *The Boardroom Project* recognized an increasing demand for accountability and justification of expenditures in the marketing discipline and the imperative for standards to evaluate metrics used in measuring the contributions and outcomes associated with marketing activities. Measurement standards are essential to the efficient functioning of a marketing-driven company, because decisions about the allocation of resources rely heavily on credible and understandable information.

The 2005 white paper[1] discussed the need for these standards and identified specific standards that link marketing metrics to financial outcomes and objectives. A set of characteristics for an "ideal metric" based on best practices in marketing measurement, and a set of guidelines for measures of return on marketing investment, also were presented. The Marketing Metric Audit Protocol (MMAP) assessment process grew from this work.[2, 3]

The Boardroom Project members suggested that an "ideal measure" be identified to exemplify how to evaluate marketing measures according to the MMAP. A measure of television ad pretesting was chosen and became the first measure assessed with the process.[4, 5]

Need for the MMAP Audit Process

Although there are hundreds, if not thousands, of measures, metrics, and models in marketing literature and practice, few have been linked to financial metrics associated with brand profitability or cash flow. Why cash flow? Both short term and over time, cash flow is the ultimate metric to which all activities of a business should be linked to facilitate resource allocation and achieve a desired return. But, in fact, although historical performance may be linked to financial outcomes, some of the most costly marketing activities have no outcome metrics that reliably *predict* "return" (e.g., advertising and store/channel activities).

Unlike in the 1980s,[6] most of the publicly available information provided by research vendors focuses on integrated suites of products and services with little technical information or descriptions for specific measures. It is often the case that measures of the same or similar name are quite different from one vendor to another. Without comparable information about measures and methods, research buyers have no factual basis on which to distinguish high quality from low quality, or to choose the metric that will best meet their needs and inform them about expected financial returns from the measured marketing activity.

The MMAP process was developed to enable research buyers to make informed purchase decisions, and research providers to distinguish their offerings from those of competitors.

Conceptual Basis of the MMAP

The MMAP is a formal process that first defines the linkages between intermediate marketing outcome metrics, marketing outcomes, and short-term or long-term cash flow drivers (see Figure 17.1a).

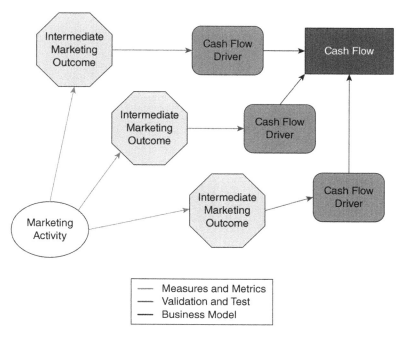

Figure 17.1a Conceptual Basis of the MMAP.

Source: MASB.

The first step is to *identify the cash flow driver(s)* that the metric is intended to predict. There will be at least one source of cash and one business model underlying the linkage. In many businesses there is a dominant source and dominant model that is of most importance to the marketer. For instance, the business model, or how the firm generates cash, might be *margin* (selling price minus costs), *velocity* (the rate of sales), *leverage* (the potential for new or expanded markets), or some combination of these. The marketing source of cash flow might be *sales volume, price premium*, or *market share* (see Figure 17.1b).[7]

The second step in the process is to *identify the metrics or measures of intermediate marketing outcomes* that will be presented for the audit. This is intended to distinguish between measures of efficiency, like CPM and cost per lead, and measures of effectiveness, like redemption rate for coupons and market share. The intent of the Marketing Accountability Standards Board (MASB) is to focus first on measures of effectiveness.

The third step, perhaps the most challenging, is to *identify the conceptual links between the marketing activity and the marketing outcome metric*. Every measure of a marketing action should have an identified outcome metric in order to establish the validity of that measure. If there is no logical link between an outcome predicted by a marketing measure and a cash flow driver, one might question the need for measuring that marketing activity, or question the utility of the measure employed.

The final step is to *identify which are the causal links*. When there is uncertainty about the causal link between a marketing outcome and one or more cash flow drivers, validation or testing the relationship is appropriate, especially if the costs of the marketing activity are high.

Figure 17.2 shows the conceptual linkages from the first MMAP audit conducted in 2008, which was updated in 2012.[8] Three of the ten conceptual linkages were demonstrated to be causal linkages in the MMAP audit: the link between a specific marketing activity (TV ads) to a pre-market measure (APM Facts, a measure of customer brand preference); and the links

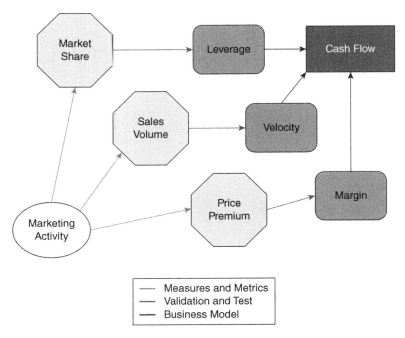

Figure 17.1b Conceptual Basis of the MMAP.

Source: MASB.

between the pre-market measure and two intermediate market outcome measures (market share and volume). The link between the APM Facts measure and price premium was anecdotally observed, but not documented by the measurement provider, so could not be considered as demonstrated during the audit.

Information Provided for an Audit

Once the conceptual linkages have been established, a description of the marketing metric, data sources, derivations, applications, strengths, and limitations are documented. Next, the metric is examined relative to the "ten characteristics of an ideal metric":[9]

1 *relevant*—the metric's results address specific, pending decisions and actions;
2 *predictive*—the metric provides information about the future, accurately predicts the outcome of pending action, and is able to quantify future outcomes;
3 *objective*—the metric provides facts, explanations, and information that are meaningful and not subject to personal interpretation or distortion by personal feelings or prejudices;
4 *calibrated*—the metric means the same thing across conditions, products, markets, and cultures;
5 *reliable*—the metric is dependable and stable over time and conditions;
6 *sensitive*—the metric identifies and differentiates meaningful differences in outcomes and actions;
7 *simple*—the metric is readily available, uncomplicated and easy to use; its meaning and implications are clear; and it is empowering, because it can be adopted and acted upon easily;
8 *causal*—the metric is used to choose a course of action that leads to improvement; that is, it identifies the cause or reason for a given outcome, suggests specific intervention(s) for change, and includes a means for assessing that the intervention has had the desired effect;

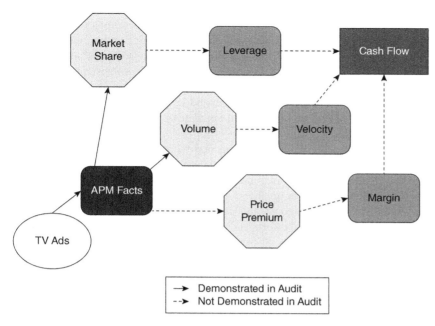

Figure 17.2 APM Facts: Marketing Activity, Metrics and Financial Links.
Source: MASB.

9 *transparent*—claims of specific properties or capabilities for the metric are substantiated and open to independent verification;
10 *quality assured*—the metric is subject to ongoing quality assurance and improvement; that is, there exist formal processes for assuring the reliability, validity, and sensitivity of the measure and for making the measure better and more useful.

Guidelines for Measures of Return on Marketing Investment

Every intermediate marketing outcome metric should be validated to a short-term or long-term cash flow driver, drivers of cash flow drivers, or to cash flow. The final step in the MMAP process is to assess how the metric aligns with a set of guidelines for measures of short-term and long-term marketing productivity. Measures of return on marketing investment should:

1 provide a specific link to financial performance—no measure or measurement system is complete without one. To be a credible contributor to the strategic success of the firm, marketing must translate the outcomes of its activities into economic metrics that are consistent with the way in which the firm reports its results;
2 reflect standard financial concepts of return, risk, time value of money and cost of capital—alternative marketing actions cannot be compared without consideration of risk, return, and the time over which the return is received by the firm. Returns realized in future periods should reflect the firm's cost of capital; a dollar today is worth more than a dollar tomorrow;
3 provide information for guiding future decisions by predicting future economic outcomes and also provide retrospective evidence of the impact of marketing actions—while retrospective analysis is useful and may provide evidence of the efficacy of marketing actions it does not specifically inform future decision-making or provide a means for forecasting future

outcomes. Measures of return should provide a reliable and robust means for forecasting the likely outcomes of marketing actions and a basis for making decisions regarding non-comparable marketing actions (such as a decision between advertising and promotion);

4 recognize both immediate, short-term effects of actions and longer-term outcomes, and the fact that short-term and long-term effects need not be directionally consistent—marketing actions may have multiple effects. These effects may be immediate and short-lived or they may be more gradual and persistent. Such short-term and long-term measures of marketing actions are most amenable to the development of standardized measurement systems that might be shared across firms;

5 recognize the difference between total return and incremental return on investment—knowledge of the total return on marketing investment, while useful, may be less helpful in many circumstances than knowledge of the return on incremental investment. Many marketing decisions take the form of determining whether an incremental investment in one action produces a superior return relative to an incremental investment in some other action. Measures of return on marketing investment should inform such decisions as well as provide information that suggests the point at which additional investment in a particular action is no longer justified by the expected return;

6 recognize that different products and markets produce different rates of return—products and markets differ with respect to their size, rate of growth, profit margins, and relative competitive positions of firms, among other things. Measures of return on marketing investment should recognize these differences and their implications for the financial performance of the firm;

7 distinguish between measures of outcome and measures of effort—many measures employed in marketing are measures of effort (e.g., number of sales calls), or efficiency (e.g., CPM), or productivity (e.g., average cost per sale). Measures of return on marketing investment should include indications of outcome(s) in addition to effort, efficiency, and productivity;

8 provide information that is meaningful and comparable across products, markets and firms—only in this way can a firm make decisions that maximize return on investment across the firm's portfolio of products and markets. It is also important that shareholders be able to meaningfully compare the marketing performance of firms. There is a place for measures that are specific to a particular product, market, or firm, but these do not substitute for metrics that are robust across products, markets, and firms;

9 identify clearly the purpose, form and scope of measurement—there is no single all-purpose metric for return on marketing investment. As in finance, where different metrics provide different insights into performance and inform different kinds of decisions, there is a role for multiple measures of return on marketing investment. Some measures, such as market share, may provide a direct link to economic performance. Others, such as measures of brand equity, may be more indirect or derived through statistical estimation. The functional relationship of indirect and derived measures to financial performance should be defined and validated;

10 be documented in sufficient detail to allow a knowledgeable user to understand utility and make comparisons among alternative measures—claims of the utility and validity of measures should be verifiable and subject to independent audit. Independent verification of claims by individual firms is less efficient and less robust than validation that is transparent and publicly accessible. At a minimum, providers of marketing metrics should provide sufficient information about the measurement properties and validation of their measures to provide a reasonable basis for comparison of alternative measures with respect to their cost, timeliness, and predictive validity;

11 be assessed relative to generally accepted standards of measurement development and validation—there exist well-established standards for the conduct of marketing research and the development and validation of measures and metrics. Measures of return on marketing investment should adhere to these standards and exhibit characteristics that reflect best practices in measurement development and validation (these are part of the MMAP process);

12 be recognized as a necessary investment for assuring sound decision-making, accountability, continuous improvement, and transparency for all stakeholders—there are ample reasons to believe that the development and use of effective measures of return on marketing investment can produce greater returns for the firm while reducing total current marketing costs. The returns and cost savings obtained by firms that have successfully embraced the continuous quality improvement movement give us confidence that similar attention to the role of marketing in contributing to the financial performance of the firm will also produce significant returns.

Why Should Measurement Vendors Undergo the Audit?

The independent, objective, and industry-credible MMAP process allows measurement vendors to move beyond the "adverse selection" problem of buyers not being able to distinguish high-quality from low-quality metrics. Without such differentiation, price can too often be the primary driving factor of vendor selection. It gives participating vendors immediate awareness among MASB members (top tier marketers, leading industry associations, and top business school faculty) and their industry contact networks. The audit also provides a highly credible resource for public relations and sales promotion. In addition, participation in the audit process provides a new perspective on strengths and limitations and may uncover recommendations for improvement of the metric or the measurement process.

How Are the Audits Conducted?

MMAP audits are conducted by qualified auditors from the MMAP Center, who report to the MASB Board and work closely with the Metrics Catalogue Project[10] sponsored by MASB. An audit is initiated with the signing of a non-disclosure agreement between the auditor and the vendor to ensure confidentiality for proprietary intellectual property and an open exchange of information.

The audit is conducted primarily by phone and email. There is one "site visit" by the auditor to the vendor's offices. The information collected for the audit is summarized in Table 17.1. Factual claims are included when documentation for the claims is made available to the auditor. If an analysis can be performed to support a claim (e.g., a reliability claim), it will be performed and the results made available. At the conclusion of the audit, the pertinent information is collated and summarized.

Although the audit summary undergoes an approval process involving the MAF president and MASB chair, and is reviewed by the MASB Catalogue Project team, any proprietary supporting

Table 17.1 Information in a MMAP Audit Summary

- The name of the metric provider
- A brief definition or description of the metric
- The source of data—how and where data are collected
- How the metric is derived or calculated
- How the metric is used and for which marketing activities
- Any notable strengths of the metric
- Any notable limitations of the metric
- General relationship of metric results to specific financial metrics
- How the metric aligns with the characteristics of "ideal metrics"[1]
- How it fits the guidelines for measures of marketing productivity[1]
- Source documents used to document information in the audit
- Other references

Source: Created by the authors.

1 Described in the chapter.

documentation is only shared with the auditor. With the agreement of the vendor, the summary of the audit is included in the MASB Metrics Catalogue on the MASB website, which is available to all MASB members. A specific metric entry is also available to the provider to enable sharing of the information with customers and potential customers.

Discussion

The MMAP process was developed to enable research buyers to make informed purchase decisions, and for research providers to distinguish their offerings from those of competitors. Although this goal has been embraced by research buyers, until recently, it has not been as readily accepted by providers of research metrics. Encouragingly, as this chapter is being written, a number of providers, including two of the largest in the world, have expressed interest in having a "lead" product audited. As more metrics are audited and included in the MASB Metrics Catalogue, the value to the seller of an independent, factual differentiation of the metric from competitors' claims, and the value for buyers to have this information readily available will become evident.

An outcome envisioned by The Boardroom Project was a catalog of all metrics offered by research suppliers that could be accessed by research buyers to choose the metric most appropriate to their specific needs. Although convincing providers of current metrics to undertake an audit may be a slow and arduous task, it is a much more attractive, and relatively inexpensive, way to promote new marketing measurements. While working to include currently provided metrics, the MMAP audit process will become a normal step in the introduction of new marketing metrics and the reintroduction of improved or enhanced metrics. Eventually all marketing metrics offered will be in the Metrics Catalogue and easily compared to allow informed buyer decisions.

References

1. David W. Stewart, Mitch Barnes, Margaret H. Blair, Michael Duffy, Wade Holmes, Dwight Riskey, and Kate Sirkin, July 2005, "Contributing to the Bottom Line: Marketing Productivity, Effectiveness and Accountability," *The Boardroom Project*, available at www.themasb.org.
2. Roy A. Young, Allen M. Weiss, and David W. Stewart, *Marketing Champions*, 2006, Hoboken, NJ: John Wiley & Sons, Inc.
3. David W. Stewart, 2008, "How Marketing Contributes to the Bottom Line." *Journal of Advertising Research*, 48(March): 94–105.
4. Margaret H. Blair, 2008, *Measuring and Improving the Return from TV Advertising—An Example*, available at www.themasb.org.
5. *Marketing Metric Audit Protocol (MMAP)*, 2009, available at www.themasb.org.
6. David W. Stewart, D. H. Furse, and R. Kozak, 1983, "A Guide to Commercial Copytesting Services," *Current Issues and Research in Advertising*, 6: 1–44.
7. *Common Language in Marketing, The Global Resource for Defining Marketing Terms and Metrics*, an online compilation of definitions of marketing terms approved and sponsored by a consortium of marketing industry associations including MASB, AMA, ANA, and MSI, available at www.marketing-dictionary.org.
8. Margaret H. Blair, 2008, *Measuring and Improving the Return from TV Advertising—An Example*, available at www.themasb.org.
9. *Marketing Metric Audit Protocol (MMAP)*, 2009, available at www.themasb.org.
10. "MMAP Marketing Metrics Catalogue." In MASB Projects, *Overview of All MASB Projects*, available at www.themasb.org.

Section IV
Organizational Dimensions of Marketing Accountability

18 Navigating Barriers, Opportunity, and Change on the Marketing Accountability Journey, or Road to ROMI

Margaret Henderson Blair and Pamela Hoover Forbus

Introduction

As the era of "financial engineering" for shareholder value winds down,[1, 2, 3] and in response to mounting pressure from corporate boardrooms for accountability,[4] marketing professionals are stepping up, beginning to master and apply the science of measurement and process management to the art of marketing.[5, 6] This fundamental change will usher in a new era of marketing accountability that will drive consistent growth, with improved methods for measuring, forecasting, and improving the effectiveness of marketing activities and a narrowing of the gap between marketing efforts and financial outcomes.

The era of "marketing engineering" will involve both "science" and "governance," with the role of marketing measurement central, integrated with other metrics along the value chain, all tied to overall financial analyses, and institutionalized across the business enterprise, where the "science" of *improvement* includes:[7]

1 measurement development;
2 integrated data bases;
3 research-on-research (analytics);
4 knowledge;
5 better practice (process management);
6 forecasting models.

And "governance" for *continuous improvement* involves enterprise engineering:[7]

1 cross-functional teams (e.g., marketing, finance, sales, R&D);
2 continuous improvement orientation;
3 common purpose;
4 common rewards;
5 central funding;
6 thresholds.

Governance is the umbrella for continuous improvement over time and personnel such that the key marketing metrics and processes stay in place and continual improvement can be achieved. It has been observed that when a CMO leaves their position, the new one brings in their preferred (more comfortable) metrics and processes, thus disturbing the continuous improvement process.[8]

On the other hand, when a CFO leaves a firm, their key financial metrics and processes stay in place, because the key metrics for accounting and financial reporting are standard across all businesses, having been set by the SEC and their Financial Accounting Standards Board (FASB).

Setting measurement standards in marketing, tied to the key financial metrics and analyses across the value chain, will be equally important for a marketing-driven business, because decisions about the allocation of resources and assessment of results will rely similarly on credible, valid, transparent, and understandable information that applies across internal investment opportunities and across firms.

The Marketing Accountability Standards Board (MASB) is serving in this capacity as the independent, cross-industry forum where marketing and finance professionals are setting measurement and accountability standards for creating value in the twenty-first century.

Since the late 1990s, the "science" involved in improvement initiatives has been applied by visionary marketing scientists here and there; and while their work has generally been ahead of its time, it has not been lost. Vast amounts of knowledge have been gained and many barriers and opportunities identified. As the time for marketing accountability has finally come, and practitioners begin their journeys, it may be helpful to understand and address those barriers, opportunities, and changes that will be encountered along the way.

Barriers

Perhaps the most important barrier to confront and overcome at the onset of the journey is *fear of change*, and there will be plenty of it, especially with regard to marketing communications. By definition, the road to improvement in any context, including marketing communications, is all about measurement and process management, both of which are foreign and uncomfortable concepts to the profession.[9] The 50-year-old habits, practices, and belief systems of marketing management and their ad agencies cannot be transformed overnight, but they must be dealt with head-on . . . in cross-functional and cross-disciplined teams for support, with empirical and replicated findings as the roadmap, and with innovative thinking as well as new, more user-friendly business solutions to help bridge the gaps between the unaccounted-for past, and the accountable future.

While measurement and process management are the only way to a return on marketing investment (ROMI), one of the most deeply rooted barriers is the belief that marketing communication is *art not science* . . . that it therefore cannot be measured, and that treating it as a process will kill the art.[10] While the first part of this belief system is true (developing great marketing campaigns and advertising *is* art), measuring its business impact and improving the track record is science (a truth for all business activities). The interesting aspect of this dilemma is that often, the process changes indicated by the science of improvement will actually unleash creativity, relative to traditional habits and processes. For instance, in one empirically-derived improved process, the 50-year-old tradition of "copy-testing" is being deemed obsolete, because over 90 percent of all ads produced are worthy of airing. This occurs because moving to the "creative" process only after getting the more strategic value proposition (or reason to buy) right, leads to over 70 percent success later on, and then connecting with consumers both rationally and emotionally at the creative stage leads to over 90 percent success. In this particular ad development and ad management process redesign, all ads go to air without being cut or held up at a "copy-testing" stage, and media weight is placed behind them according to the forecasted business return of each one in the portfolio. Some get more weight than others.[11]

The movie industry might serve as an analogy to this campaign management (media optimization) in terms of deciding how much to invest behind specific ads. The large movie houses understand that at any one point in time they will have a portfolio of a few big winners, a few losers, and many films in the middle. Once the movie is in hand, the movie companies manage their marketing and distribution expenditures wisely. The winners get advertised and promoted heavily for optimal return from the box office through to the end of the chain. The losers proceed quickly to video stores and on-demand, and the ones in the middle get varying amounts of marketing support relative to their appeal levels and forecasted business returns. In like manner, media dollars will be allocated behind ads, based on the forecasted business value of each one in the portfolio, avoiding conflict with the creative process, and giving marketing management increased flexibility to meet portfolio business objectives, quarter on quarter.

So, while the art of marketing communications will find new freedoms, the issue of *long-term versus short-term* effects is the next barrier to be addressed. Many practitioners feel that even if advertising does not work to produce sales in the short term, it will work to build "the brand" long term, or that some advertising that works to move sales short term will backfire on the brand's health long term. With the right methodologies, it is possible to measure and forecast both the short- and long-term business impact with the same metrics. These authors and others in the marketing community are beginning to land on common ground with respect to the overall purpose of marketing communications and thus the appropriate metrics: the purpose of marketing is to create preference for a brand in the hearts and minds of consumers, in a manner that leads to sales, margin, market share, market value, and cash flow both short term and over time.[12] With a generally accepted definition for the goal of building brand preference, the appropriate metrics become clear as well: for the messages (consumer brand preference/choice, along with the rational and emotional underpinnings of brand choice), the media (effective reach from moment-by-moment ratings among targets), the message and the medium combined (brand preference points delivered),[13] and the market (distribution, price, sales, share, baseline, etc.).

The next barrier to remove is the misunderstanding and misuse of *survey research versus behavioral measurement*. Most marketers lean on the direction indicated and stories are told about "the brand" from survey research professionals and methods. This traditional part of the marketing communications process by itself has not led to improvement in the outcomes.[14] Overall, survey research methods are best utilized for gaining insights and hypotheses (to test), but behavioral measurement methods and development are a must for the ROMI future of forecasting and improving financial return. While measurement development and standards have long been established for media (e.g., GRPs) and for market impact (e.g., market share), they have not been considered with respect to the message, even though all major studies regarding how advertising works have demonstrated that the power of the message far outweighs the media (weight).[13, 15, 16, 17, 18]

If measurement development and standards are not established, and the industry moves forward with a basketful of survey research methods to address the message part of ROMI, cause and effect will appear to be what they are not, and the advertiser and agency will waste time and money trying to improve on dimensions that in the end do not improve the market impact and financial results consistently across time and borders.

For example, common techniques for screening ads include classes of survey research questions and answers to get at consumer recall, intent to buy, emotion, and other attitudes and reactions . . . often conducted through different research agencies and/or slightly different methods with the same agency. If a standard measurement (say brand preference/choice) and measurement standards (reliability, relevance, validity, calibration, etc.) have not been developed and maintained across the world, it is likely that recall might be found to be most important, say, in China, emotion the most important dimension in Chile, and so on; when in fact these findings are the result of the questions and methods employed versus real differences in consumer behavior. Clearly, there is a pressing need to adopt *measurement standards* for intermediate outcomes of all marketing activities in the hearts, minds, and hands (choices) of consumers across the world, and with metrics that have been tied directly to the market impact and financial performance of the brand and the firm, both short term and over time.

Opportunity

While progress has been made in improving the return from pricing and promotional activities, the foundational opportunity for progress with regard to marketing communications lies in the *integration of media, message, and market measurement standards* into a single data stream and warehouse. Heretofore, the syndicated market measurement providers such as Nielsen, IRI, IMS, Polk, Crest, etc., have delivered standard facts about price and promotion, along with the facts about the market impact, but no information about the media or the message. Consequently, the advertiser has not been able to easily observe, understand, and improve advertising's impact on market results over time. Furthermore, there has been little demand for integrating this data, given the belief systems in the advertising community. These authors, devoted to advertising measurement and improvement for decades, have heard the following statements from the lead marketing researchers of some of the world's largest advertisers: "Tell someone who cares about improvement"; "I refuse to confront the brands and agencies with an improvement message"; "This missionary work is not worth the pain and suffering"; "They hate you in particular because you're the most quantitative." Until now, most marketing scientists have chosen to avoid the political battles that have erupted on the advertising side of marketing measurement and improvement, in order to protect their careers.

This phenomenon is analogous to the experiences of W. Edwards Deming with manufacturing and operations management in the US (versus Japan). Deming and his scientific methods were at first rejected by the U.S. electronics and automobile manufacturers. He went to Japan (sponsored by the US Government) to help rebuild Japan after WWII. He taught them how to manufacture a quality product, at a lower cost. Eventually, his time and methods became standard operating procedure in the US (in the form of TQM) once it was discovered why the Japanese auto builders were taking significant market share.[19] Furthermore, while it will take courage, so too has the call for ROMI set the opportunity stage for the *marketing, or demand, scientist* to practice the scientific methods of measurement and process management for improved return from marketing activities . . . and without fear of losing their employment.

There is a well of opportunity for moving from ROMI talk to ROMI action in the body of *empirical knowledge* already discovered, replicated, forward validated, and documented in the marketing and advertising journals. While most of this knowledge relates to TV activities, what better place to start than where both the largest costs and greatest opportunities for improved return lie. The following handful of major discoveries have been made and documented by JP Jones, ARS/rsc, IRI and others, and are summarized in the *Journal of Advertising Research*.[11,18,20]

1   When measured competently, changes in consumer brand preference/choice are highly predictive of subsequent changes in sales, market share, and market value.
2   Today, TV is still the most leverageable element in the marketing mix (although its form and costs are in motion).
3   Ads work quickly (and predictably) to impact market/business results and wear out just as quickly (and predictably) in the process.
4   The effectiveness of the ad itself outweighs the media investment placed behind its advertising impact.

Change

The empirical findings summarized above offer straightforward insight regarding process reengineering and organizational change for ROMI action and improvement, as shown in Figure 18.1:

1   Choose a measurement partner with proven and documented competencies in measuring consumer brand preference/choice and forecasting the business implications (partner with behavioral measurement experts).
2   Start the ROMI journey with the marketing communications activity having the greatest costs and return potential (master the TV process first).

3   Identify a strong value proposition (reason to buy) with the same predictively precise behavioral measurement of consumer brand preference/choice before moving to creative . . . spend a little more upstream in the process and far less downstream, in classic Deming fashion (improve/reengineer the ad development process).
4   At the creative stage, add a behavioral measure of consumer emotion to ensure the ads are on target and to learn how to connect with consumers more often and more consistently (continue the reengineering of the ad development process).
5   Account for wear out at the "shoot" so that there is enough footage to refresh ads with others when they will no longer impact market behavior at desirable levels (enhance the ad production process).
6   Begin managing the media and the messages based on forecasted returns from the combination (combine ad trafficking and media processes—ad management).
7   Measure the business values of all ads as they go to air, making final forecasts for the advertised product, line, and halos, and adjust media allocations behind each in order to meet overall market and financial objectives across the portfolio, quarter on quarter (add flexibility to the marketing management process).

One final note regarding these scientific approaches and opportunities for improvement—they are not merely hypothetical. Practitioners have piloted them with dramatic improvements in return—to some, even unbelievable improvement in ROI—and in all cases, far more than enough to offset the rising costs of the medium; some have also published their experiences,[14, 21, 22, 23, 24, 25, 26, 27] but these pioneers were two to ten years before the ROMI mandate from the boardrooms, before the need for change was recognized, and during a period in time that one day might be referred to as the marketing science *counterrevolution*. They were all a bit ahead of their time, just as Deming was ahead of his time in the U.S. manufacturing segment of the business, although his principles are now standard operating procedures across the world.

Last but not least, without an umbrella of "governance" (management control or stewardship) over the "science" (measurement and process or better practice, where better practice is defined as a *documented method of operating that yields a higher level of performance than other operating behaviors*)[7] to institutionalize at the enterprise level, there will be improvement for a time, but likely not continuous improvement over a long period of time, given that marketing measurement and processes are currently set and controlled by the ever changing CMO. Again, using the Deming analogy, Nelson Fraiman, Graduate School of Business Columbia University, and Director W. Edwards, Deming Center for Quality, said recently: "TQM may be defined as managing the entire organization so that it excels on all dimensions of products and services that are important to the external and internal customer."[28] General management at the enterprise level must cross silos and form cross-functional teams including representatives from all the operating stakeholder silos (marketing, finance, sales, operations, R&D, etc.) to reengineer measurement and processes across the value chain. The cross-functional teams will employ change agents, or motivators, such as defining a common purpose (i.e., continuous improvement in return, embodied by specific goals or KPIs), common reward structure (e.g., bonuses on profitable growth being predicted and achieved over set periods of rolling times over time), central funding (so that investments or resources can be allocated across similar or dissimilar activities that will provide the best return both short and longer term), and investment hurdles (levels of predicted return that warrant less or more investment).

Summary and Overview

While marketing scientists here and there have been applying the science of measurement, knowledge, and process management to the art of marketing for improvement in financial return, they

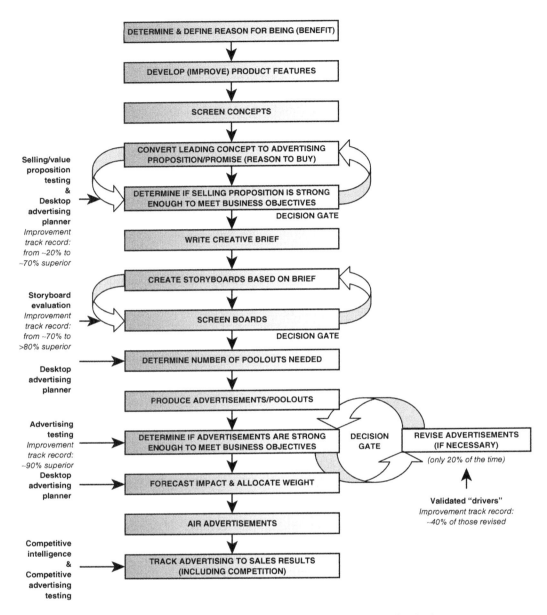

Figure 18.1 Reengineered Ad Development and Management Process w/Vendor Tools.

Source: Blair, Margaret H. and Allan R. Kuse, 2009, "Better Practices in Advertising Can Change a *Cost of Doing Business* to *Wise Investments in the Business*," *Journal of Advertising Research*, 44(1): 71–89.

have generally been ahead of their time, given the belief systems of their marketing colleagues and the control points in their firms (particularly with regard to marketing communications or advertising). Their time and work has not been lost, however, because much of the knowledge gained along the way has been documented in various marketing journals and on industry association podiums, and major barriers as well as opportunities have been identified. Thus, there is a solid foundation to begin the marketing accountability journey, or road to ROMI, now that its time has come.

While most of the empirical knowledge accumulated so far (and opportunity for ROMI improvement) relates to the TV medium, other channels of communications as well as the holistic impact of all marketing activities (including "campaigns") can be approached in a similar fashion: media, message, market, and financial metrics developed and standardized across brands, conditions, and cultures; integration into data warehouses and accessible to all in nearly real time; investment in basic research-on-research or analytics (to gain knowledge or understanding of the connections and provide insight for improvement); and better practice/process reengineering (for improved return on the activities investments).

Adding the elements of enterprise "governance" to the elements of the "science" will enable marketing professionals to deliver to the call for accountability and continuous improvement in return from marketing activities. This will elevate the CMO and marketing function, and enable the CFO and financial function to move seamlessly from the more recently risky "financial engineering for shareholder value" to "marketing engineering for creating value." In partnership, they will also reclassify marketing activities from discretionary "expense" (control costs) to wise "investments" in the business (creating and offering products and services that customers want to buy short term and over time). As Jim Meier, Senior Director of Marketing Finance at MillerCoors, noted during the MASB 2015 Winter Summit: "Manufacturing (with Finance) can construct and maintain an asset, Marketing can create and grow an asset."

Also, in the context of scientific revolutions, Thomas S. Kuhn (1970) wrote:

> Though a generation is sometimes required to effect the change . . . communities have again and again been converted to new paradigms . . . Conversions will occur a few at a time until, after the last holdouts have died, the whole profession will again be practicing under a single, but now a different, paradigm.

Practitioners who champion the science and governance of measurement and process reengineering will continue to be the marketing leaders of the twenty-first century.

References

1 Zorn, Dirk M., 2004, "Here a Chief, There a Chief: The Rise of the CFO in the American Firm," *American Sociological Review*, 69(June): 345–364.
2 Zorn, Dirk M. and Frank Dobbin, "Too Many Chiefs? How Financial Markets Reshaped the American Firm," prepared for Constance Conference on *Social Studies of Finance: Inside Financial Markets*. Organized by Karin Knorr Cetina and Alexandru Preda. University of Constance, May 2003.
3 Fligstein, Neil, "The End of (Shareholder Value) Ideology?," Department of Sociology University of California, August 2004.
4 Tharpe, Arthur, "Top Concerns: Recent ANA Survey Findings (Marketing & Procurement)," presented at the MASB 2013 Summer Summit (August 8, 2013, Boston, MA).
5 Meier, Jim and Bill Berg, "Finance and Marketing Working Together to Create Value," presented at ANA Advertising Financial Management Conference (May 5, 2014, Naples, FL).
6 Forbus, Pam and Scott Davis, "Where Marketing and Finance Agree on Measurement for Creating Value," presented at The Advertising Research Foundation *re:think* Conference (March 26, 2014, New York).
7 Forbus, Pam and Scott Davis, "The CMOs Role in the Accountability Journey," presented at the 2015 MASB Winter Summit (February 12, 2015, San Antonio, TX).
8 Banks, Greg, "Where We Stand on Measurement and Process Management for Continuous Improvement and What We Might Learn from TQM," presented at the 2014 MASB Summer Summit (August 14, 2014, Chicago, IL).
9 ANA, *Total Accountability: Before and Beyond Dashboard*, draft, January 30, 2007.
10 ANA, *ANA Marketing Accountability Task Force Findings*, October 2005.

11 Blair, Margaret H. and Allan R. Kuse, 2004, "Better Practices in Advertising Can Change a *Cost of Doing Business* to *Wise Investments in the Business*," *Journal of Advertising Research*, 44(1): 71–89.
12 Stewart, David W., Frank Findley, and Jonathan Short, "Brand Investment & Valuation (BIV) Project Review & Status," 2015 MASB Winter Summit (February 12, 2015, San Antonio, TX).
13 Blair, Margaret H., "ROMI Branding Future: Integrated Measurement Systems for Market Mix Forecasting, Portfolio Management, and Improving Return from Marketing Communications Activities," presentation at *Institute for International Research*, ROMI Conference, February 7, 2006.
14 Shirley, Dan, 1999, "From Copy Testing and Diagnostics to Process-Driven Improvement: A Paradigm Shift in Advertising Development," *ANA/The Advertiser*, April/May.
15 Lodish, L. M., "Key Findings from the 'How Advertising Works' Study," in *Transcript Proceedings of the ARF Marketplace Advertising Research Workshop*, 1991, New York: Advertising Research Foundation.
16 Jones, John Philip, 1995, "Does Advertising Produce Sales Today or Tomorrow?," *Journal of Marketing Communications*, 1(1): 1–11.
17 Blair, Margaret H., 1987, "An Empirical Investigation of Advertising Wearin and Wearout." *Journal of Advertising Research*, 27(6): 45–50.
18 Blair, Margaret H. and Michael J. Rabuck, 1998, "Advertising Wearin and Wearout: Ten Years Later, More Empirical Evidence and Successful Practice," *Journal of Advertising Research*, 38(5): 7–18.
19 Blair, Margaret H., "The ROMI-Ready World and Process Approach: Deming Training Session," rsc The Quality Measurement Company (February 6, 2006).
20 Jones, John Philip and Margaret H. Blair, 1996, "Examining 'Conventional Wisdoms' About Advertising Effects with Evidence from Independent Sources," *Journal of Advertising Research*, 36(6): 37–59.
21 Conlin, Ronald P., 1994, "Goodyear Advertising Research: Past, Present, and Future," *Journal of Advertising Research*, 34(3).
22 Bean, Bill, "Oscar Meyer Lunchables: The In-Market Effects of Advertising," in *Transcript Proceedings of rsc T.Q. Advertising Success Forum I*, 1995, Evansville, IN: The ARS Group.
23 Cox, Doug, "The Citrucel Case Study," in *Transcript Proceedings of rsc T.Q. Advertising Success Forum I*, 1995, Evansville, IN: The ARS Group.
24 Mondello, Mike, 1996, "Turning Research into Return-on-Investment," *Journal of Advertising Research*, 36(4).
25 Adams, A. J., "Advertising Research," in *Dartnell's Advertising Manager's Handbook*, 4th edition, David Bushko (ed.), 1997, Chicago, IL: The Dartnell Corporation.
26 Masterson, Peggy, 1999, "The Wearout Phenomenon," *Marketing Research*, 11(3): 26–31.
27 Shepard, Barry and Susan R. Ashley, "Developing and Managing Advertising with a More Positive Return on Investment," presented at the ARF Annual Conference, April 2002.
28 Fraiman, Nelson, "Lessons Learned from TQM," presented at the 2014 MASB Winter Summit (February 20, 2014).

19 Marketing Organization and Accountability

David W. Stewart and Robert D. Winsor

Introduction

As a collection of necessary tools, strategies, and systems for managing demand, increasing sales, and efficiently distributing goods, the marketing function has long been recognized to be an important, if not indispensable, factor contributing to business success. As this function developed, marketing departments rightly earned their place in firms decades ago. Only since the 1990s, however, have boards and executives across the country begun to realize that truly functional marketing departments must offer accountability for their actions and display a willingness to align to company strategy. This realization stems from awareness that marketing expenditures often make up as much as a quarter of a firm's total outlays, and that operational efficiencies in other areas of the firm have greatly eclipsed those of the marketing function.

The operational aspects of businesses have been successfully scrutinized and fine-tuned from both scientific and financial perspectives since the 1970s, because minimal opportunities for further gains in these areas are perceived as being readily exploitable. Marketing has somehow avoided much of this attention, because it is justifiably perceived as lagging behind other areas of business. As such, many see marketing as the least understood and perhaps the least efficient function in business. As one CFO recently remarked: "I've squeezed all the cost I can from operations; now it's time to look at marketing."[1] As a result, the marketing function is now under increasing scrutiny to justify its costs and increasing pressure to yield cost-effective results. These require, broadly speaking, linking marketing to a firm's financial performance and determining strong reliable metrics with which to measure this link.

With this realization, however, comes an attendant need to recognize that the role of marketing varies widely by firm. While in some firms marketing crosses functional boundaries and roots deeply in the organization's approach to all aspects of its business, in other firms it plays a more specialized and less-widely distributed role. This variability has implications for how the contribution of marketing should be measured and how marketing should be accountable to the larger organization and its stakeholders. Beyond the implications for organizational operation, management, control, and internal governance, issues of marketing boundaries and accountability may affect the overall structure of industries and perhaps the business itself. The evolution of marketing practice, marketing data, and the ability to link marketing activities with financial outcomes have, at numerous points in history, substantially altered the balance of power between manufacturers, wholesalers, and retailers. For example, the vast trove of data provided by supermarket barcode scanners has radically altered the balance of power and influence in the marketing channel in favor of retailers and at the expense of manufacturers.[2]

In trying to determine the best ways to align marketing responsibilities with marketing accountability, this chapter will first look at what marketing is, how it evolved as a discipline, what role it generally plays within firms, and how it influences the firm overall. Next, the chapter will turn to an examination of differences in the way the marketing function is deployed in organizations and

What Is Marketing?

Traditionally and from the layperson's perspective, marketing has been viewed as a set of actions aimed at getting a consumer to buy something from an organization. To many business people, marketing is simply selling at a larger scale.[3] This narrow view of marketing has occurred due to the inaccurate and unfortunate conflation between sales and marketing, an occurrence that has traditionally allowed both lay and executive people to discount the role and the importance of marketing within the organization. Consistent with this observation, this conflation between sales activities and the larger domain of marketing has tended to result in what Steiner called the "prejudice against marketing."[4] Steiner noted that, from a macroeconomic standpoint, marketing activities like advertising have been viewed as contributing little in the way of overall productivity to the economic system.[5] From both consumer and macroeconomic perspectives, marketing has been typically portrayed as a value-depleting rather than a value-enhancing activity. Therefore, there can be little wonder that business executives have also been inclined to feel that the marketing function contributes little operational utility beyond a temporary boost in consumer demand.

More recently, however, organizations have begun to realize that marketing is more a way of building relationships that extend across all brand and product processes, far beyond the narrow domain existing between seller and buyer. More importantly, these relationships have long-term value, which is essential to organizational success, and which, at the same time, is difficult to measure or appraise. As both a process and a range of strategic possibilities, marketing is thus more difficult to summarily pigeonhole than popular usage of the term would indicate. As defined by the American Marketing Association (AMA) and approved in June 2013: "Marketing is the activity, set of institutions and processes for creating, communicating, delivering and exchanging offerings that have value for customers, clients, partners and society at large."[6]

Yet this evolution in marketing thought has been a slow one. In 1955, Peter F. Drucker wrote:

> The economic revolution of the American economy since 1900 has in large part been a marketing revolution caused by the assumption of responsibility for creative, aggressive, pioneering marketing by American management. Fifty years ago, the typical attitude of the American businessman toward marketing was still "The sales department will sell whatever the plant produces." Today it is increasingly: "It is our job to produce what the market needs." (p. 38)[7]

Some offer a more in-depth description, wedding marketing to the decision-making processes that drive a company. They define marketing expertise as "the ability to make better marketing decisions," and in turn "argue that marketing expertise creates better decisions by providing interpreted market data."[8] More recently, many firms have adopted the mindset that marketing cannot be extricated from its relationship with business strategy, and that without paying heed to a firm's strategic direction, marketing has little chance of success.[9]

Evolution of Marketing Accountability

The earliest writings concerning what would now be considered as marketing were largely limited to understanding this function as practiced by merchant middlemen and retailers.[10] Typically, notions of "accountability" as applied to these endeavors were undertaken from the perspective of customers or the larger society.[11] As essential movers of "supply" such as agricultural commodities and industrial materials, from the fields, quarries, and seaports to the rapidly evolving "demand" of the cities, merchants were understood to play a critical role in the economic cycle and, as such, their specific contributions began to be carefully analyzed and measured.[12]

Whereas historical writings on the topic of merchant trade focused on the public good and ethics, certainly the individuals and groups who engaged in business were focused on profitability. Early on, assessments of risk were necessarily balanced with computations of potential profit that could be derived from particular supply and demand characteristics. As individual and familial merchants gave way to chartered merchant companies, and as the organizational objectives of these companies substantially broadened, the metrics of the merchant trade (based on risk and potential profit) became more sophisticated in order to satisfy the more diverse and complex demands of investors, shareholders, and sponsoring governments.

The early evolution of marketing accountability, as considered from a promotion vantage point, paralleled the evolution in branded consumer products in the United States. As U.S. manufacturers attempted to achieve independence from merchant wholesalers in the late 1800s, it became obvious that creating independent consumer demand for their branded products would require substantial investments in promotion. In part, these requisite investments were necessary because the manufacturers were then engaged in a battle for control over consumers with retailers and wholesalers. Whereas manufacturers formerly competed among rivals on the basis of price to secure distribution for their output, efforts to appeal directly to consumers required new tactics to establish brand preference and loyalty. As a result, both the primary purchasers of advertising and the messages of these advertisements exhibited a dramatic transformation at this time.[13] As a result of these changes in the late 1800s, the popular conceptualization of marketing began to broaden and, in many cases, came to be wholly engulfed by the rapidly evolving field of advertising. As such, perceptions of the field during the nineteenth and twentieth centuries often conflated marketing with advertising.

Directly related to this shift in power from independent wholesalers to manufacturers were the unparalleled growth opportunities available to manufacturers by the late 1800s. A large portion of the early push for accountability in marketing can be attributed to these new opportunities and the competitive urgency they created. Due to a unique convergence of newly emerging technologies (mass production, efficient transportation, more effective packaging, and mass media), producers in many industries had the ability to serve nearly limitless markets. This munificence in the market brought with it the need for tools to manage such complexity and for determining which markets and activities provided the optimal return on the firm's resources. This need led firms to adopt various "scientific methods," especially in operations and labor management, which identified significant cost savings and efficiencies.[14]

These highly successful applications of scientific methods and accountability in manufacturing led to the focus upon marketing and advertising as comparatively "unscientific" by nature. Widely understood as an endeavor characterized by a significant proportion of waste and uncertainty, advertising was easily acknowledged as a field that was ripe for improvement. As a result, the application of scientific or numerical approaches to marketing was seen as a natural extension to the trends in other areas of business at the time. As an example of this disciplinary synthesis, Herbert Casson immediately championed the advertising application of Frederick Winslow Taylor's principles of scientific management in the same year that Taylor published his theories (1911).[15] Casson advocated using experimentation and other scientific techniques to reduce the waste of ineffective advertising, and the utilization of careful research and record keeping to facilitate the process of incremental improvement and demonstrate efficacy.

The increasing desire of advertising agencies to establish a role as uniquely capable intermediaries between manufacturers and consumers required greater evidence of the efficacy of this mediation. As Pamela Walker Laird notes, growing consumer products manufacturers had larger budgets to allocate to the marketing function, and: "as the costs and marketing consequences of conducting advertising programs rose, making decisions about them became more complex and risky."[16] Because of this, concerns began to emerge about the effectiveness of advertising and how budgets for promotion should best be spent. Advertising agencies were eager to fan the flames of these concerns, because they could use these apprehensions to cement their emerging role as necessary experts in securing consumer demand.

Part of this evolution was motivated by the agencies' desires to move away from their general role as negotiators of discounted media rates, because this role limited their own profits and perceived authority.[17] In these efforts, advertising agents attempted to reframe their role away from the merely "clerical" tasks of media buying and toward that of highly specialized "professionals," which were uniquely (and indispensably) capable of performing critical tasks related to the analysis and manipulation of consumer demand. This transition required two things: (1) the validation of advertising specialists as experts uniquely capable of understanding and thus influencing consumers; and (2) the wresting of control over the message from the company founders.

Throughout the nineteenth century in the United States and even into the early twentieth century, advertising was considered the "voice" of company founders, and these men (or occasionally women) considered themselves uniquely qualified to champion their products.[18] Moreover, it was widely assumed among this group that consumers viewed "personal" messages from these business leaders as more credible and authoritative, and thus more convincing. As a result, the advertising messages of even the largest consumer product manufacturers were often personally crafted by the founders of these firms. Therefore, the first and foremost task of the advertising agencies was to seize control of the message and process of promotion away from the company directors. This takeover could only occur if agencies could convince company directors (both logically and empirically) that results would be superior under the guidance of experts and specialists.[19] These goals of wresting advertising away from internal corporate or founder control and establishing agency intermediaries as vitally important professionals, called for "scientific" assertions as to the unique effectiveness (and thus authority) of these advertising experts. Thus, the initial efforts to make advertising "scientific" and accountable represented an effort to force manufacturers of branded consumer products to acknowledge the expertise, and thus the indispensability, of advertising intermediaries (agencies). In short, accountability was pursued as the most effective path toward legitimacy.

During this period, the primary efforts to demonstrate accountability took the form of market research studies. The goal of these efforts was to implicitly suggest that research-based understanding of consumers resulted in cost-effective advertising by eliminating unproductive expenditures. Many advertising agencies established extensive market research departments at this time to demonstrate this "data-driven" approach and expertise.[20] Formalized market research became the *avant-garde* tool for adopting scientific principles to the marketing or sales management side of business in the early twentieth century. When Earnest Elmo Calkins and Ralph Holden published *Modern Advertising* in 1905, they cited many examples of manufacturers and advertising agencies that utilized market demographic studies, conducted tests on advertising copy, and tabulated coupon redemptions using codes to represent different copy or different magazines.[21]

In 1929, William J. Reilly authored a formal analysis of survey research methodology entitled *Marketing Investigations*, and in 1931, Percival White's *Marketing Research Techniques* was published.[22] By 1937, the AMA had formally recognized the field of market research by hosting a conference on market research, and textbooks on the topic were commonly used in colleges across America.[23] Thus, it became common business practice to acquire "hard data" and then leverage this data into "scientific" marketing strategies.[24] However, as Samuel noted, despite the goal of bringing science to the practice of selling, many of these early market research efforts were primitive and deeply flawed. As a result, they were often ineffective and thus failed to gain the widespread acceptance of business executives and even advertising practitioners.[25]

In contrast, the adoption of techniques such as motivation research methods in later decades represented an attempt to use "scientific" methods to more fully understand consumers in an effort to better anticipate and serve their needs.[26] This focus on using market research for product design and overall strategy, as opposed to merely sharpening the edge of sales and promotion, became more compelling to business executives as production began to significantly outpace demand in the middle of the twentieth century. Thus, while scientific methods were first introduced into marketing for the purposes of crafting more effective promotional efforts, later uses of scientific tools were focused on better alignment of the firm's offerings with customer needs in a competitive marketplace.

Varied Roles and Responsibilities of Marketing

As previously noted, marketing was for many years seen simply as a tool (and a rather blunt tool at that) to push a brand or product onto the masses. When done well, marketing does have the effect of increasing demand for a specific product or service and improving a company's bottom line. Increasingly, however, firms began to realize that to be most effective, marketing should be involved at every stage of the process, not just post-production advertising. According to Mehmet Pasa and Steven M. Shugan, in their study "The Value of Marketing Expertise," marketing's role has evolved from simply enhancing demand for the factory's current output to being a critical part of the strategic planning process. Using market information, defining market segments, and target marketing are now crucial components of the business plan. Marketing expertise helps a firm make better marketing decisions that can improve the performance and profitability of the firm.[27] Ironically, even as marketing's role grew and it generated even more data, skepticism of the value of marketing persisted. This skepticism continues to manifest itself in the very different ways the marketing function is deployed among firms and also in the continuing view among some that marketing remains a "soft" (non-quantitative) discipline without clear direction.

While most executives agree that marketing expertise is a valuable asset to any firm, organizations vary considerably in the weight they place on marketing's importance. Pasa and Shugan offer as an example the contrasting strategies of Ford and Boeing, both hugely successful companies that respectively prize marketing expertise versus production expertise.[28] Moreover, they report a survey that offers conflicting results as to whether marketing or production expertise should take top priority. Kohli and Jaworski found that marketing is more valuable in industries with greater competition. However, greater competition also requires cost cutting and more efficient manufacturing, which makes production more valuable. Without a compelling theoretical model, they argue, it remains difficult to sort out the many factors and reconcile the different views.[29]

Based on this dilemma, Kohli and Jaworski aim to provide such a theoretical model, providing guidelines as to when paying for marketing expertise is most helpful and when it brings diminishing returns. In this effort, they defined marketing expertise as: "the ability to make better marketing decisions." Their study concluded that firms will benefit from marketing expertise most in times of market instability and when they have greater market presence (for marketing research spending). On the other hand, "higher organization instability, larger organization size and competition decrease the value of marketing expertise."[30] Their study concluded that marketing expertise may not always be the best type of expertise or the most valuable use of a firm's financial resources.

Christine Moorman and Roland T. Rust explained in the introduction to their study "The Role of Marketing" that, during the past ten years, there has been a movement toward thinking about marketing less as a business function and more as a set of values and processes that all functions participate in implementing. In this view, marketing becomes everybody's job, which potentially diffuses the marketing function's role, but increases marketing's influence. As marketing gains increasing prominence as a set of processes that all functions participate in deploying, a critical issue that arises is the specific contributions of the marketing function.[31]

In trying to define marketing and its roles, Moorman and Rust argued that marketing can be both a market orientation, as well as a function within the firm, and that these roles should coexist rather than one supplanting the other. In so doing, "the marketing function facilitates the link between the customer and various key processes within the firm."[32]

They began with teasing apart the definitions of a marketing organization's structural approach. They defined a functional marketing organization as: a "concentration of the responsibility for marketing activities (knowledge and skills) within a group of specialists in the organization"; whereas a marketing process organization "refers to the dispersion of marketing activities (knowledge and skills) across non-specialists in the organization." The first organization type tends to prioritize the marketing function, while the second places more emphasis on a market orientation.

These researchers pointed to one research angle, which underlines the "cross-functional dispersion of marketing or the process marketing organization." They noted that: "integrated knowledge and skills have been linked to reduced conflict . . . and increased communication in organizations. Stronger functional orientations, conversely, have been found to reduce information sharing within firms." In this view, spreading a marketing process orientation and associated skills across the firm will likely benefit a firm, whereas maintaining a strict emphasis on functional compartmentalization is more likely to reduce a firm's effectiveness than it is to boost it.[33] This view of marketing as a business philosophy raises the question of who is accountable and by what metrics. It also creates a tension between two quite different perspectives on the role of marketing in the firm: a tension between (1) the market orientation, which proposes that firms spread a marketing mindset and the activities that complement that mindset across departments; and (2) the marketing function, which suggests a specialized role for marketing and its expertise. With such conflict between these two divergent views of marketing's role within a firm, it is understandable why so many organizations have trouble deciding what to expect from marketing and how to align both responsibilities and accountability for marketing and strategy within the firm. As a common result, marketing processes and market orientation may both be undervalued and thus underutilized for the overall strategic benefit of the firm.

In an effort to reduce this tension, Moorman and Rust offered the view that both an organizational marketing orientation and the specialized expertise resident in the marketing function are important contributors to organizational performance. In contrast to an increasing belief in the functionality of a dispersed marketing function, they demonstrated that a firm will likely benefit from a marketing function with a strong knowledge of the customer–product connection, the customer service delivery connection, and the customer-financial accountability connection. Following this, they showed that the more the marketing function develops knowledge and skills related to managing these three customer connections, the more it will contribute to the: (a) financial performance; (b) customer relationship performance; and (c) new product performance of the firm *beyond the contribution of an organization-wide market orientation* [emphasis added].[34]

For this chapter's purposes, the most interesting conclusion of Moorman and Rust is that significant organizational underpinnings already exist for each of the connections:

> If the marketing function were organized into a subgroup for each connection, it would probably appear as follows: The customer-product subgroup would be similar to the existing marketing group . . . The customer-service delivery subgroup would be similar to a typical customer satisfaction/retention group . . . The customer-financial accountability subgroup would be similar to the customer information system and database management group at a modern financial services company.[35]

Respectively, these groups would oversee: (1) setting prices, planning promotions, and designing products; (2) tracking customer satisfaction and heading customer loyalty initiatives; and

(3) "collecting and storing information related to customer profitability and the effect of the firm's product and service delivery initiatives on that profitability."[36] Adopting this mindset would offer firms an interesting opportunity to preserve both a strict marketing function and a market orientation. The result would be a consistent marketing approach across all functional groups, while leveraging the specialty knowledge that marketing experts bring to the table.

It becomes valuable to revisit the notion that a firm with an operational marketing *function*, even one that heavily prioritizes that marketing function, may be quite different from a firm with a market *orientation* (sometimes referred to as a marketing orientation). While this difference might appear to be one that is either nuanced or semantic, it is an important distinction. The marketing function represents the staff and processes essential for the execution of product, price, promotion, and distribution tactics in the management of market demand. A market orientation refers to an overarching company philosophy or mindset based on the primacy of customers as essential to the long-term success of the organization in reaching its goals. Thus, a market orientation is one in which a marketing mindset pervades every aspect of the organization regardless of function or SBU, and thus drives many of the strategic goal development and decision-making processes of the organization. This approach suggests the need for organization-wide measures of accountability. For this breadth of accountability, the marketing function alone cannot be held responsible for implementing such a pervasive philosophy of business. This raises the question of what measures of accountability are appropriate for the marketing function.

Accountability and the Role of Marketing

The measures for the evaluation of performance of the marketing function must depend on what marketing is expected to do for the organization, the responsibilities of the function, and what it is empowered to do, e.g., what resources and decision rights the function possesses. The responsibilities and empowerment of the marketing function differ widely across organizations, as has been demonstrated in empirical research that has examined how marketing is deployed. Two studies illustrate these differences.

Association of National Advertisers/Booz Allen Classification

Booz Allen Hamilton, a national management consulting firm, collaborated with the Association of National Advertisers to determine the differences in how marketing is deployed in firms. This study used four key elements (or "building blocks") to classify marketing organizations. These building blocks are scope, decision rights, capabilities, and organizational linkages. While "scope" is *where* a marketing organization operates, "decision rights" refers to *how* it is allowed to exercise its authority. "Capabilities" covers *what* the marketing organization may do and "organizational linkages" looks at *who* the marketing organization forms relationships with and in what capacity they carry out those relationships.[37] Using these building blocks they identified six broad types of marketing organizations, as defined in "The DNA of Marketing" by Andrew Tipping et al.:

1. *Growth champion*: "Recognized and valued for its contribution to revenues, the growth champion helps set the company's priorities, leading product innovation and new business development." With a growth champion profile, the marketing function is as important as sales, finance, and other major departments and plays a major role in defining a company's strategy and direction. It also takes a hand in category management.
2. *Senior counselor*: "The senior counselor offers the Chief Executive Officer and individual businesses guidance on marketing strategy and leads advertising, promotion and public relations initiatives," but unlike the growth champion, is not a leader in the company's strategy. Instead, a senior counselor marketing profile has separate marketing subunits:

"with central marketing offering advice on strategic issues and local marketing doing the same for operative issues."

3   *Brand builder*: "Among the most important support organizations in the company, the brand builder provides such marketing services as a communications strategy, creative output and campaign execution." The brand builder profile manages agency relations and provides brand direction as well as "guidance to geographically organized business units."

4   *Marketing master*: "Equipped with the authority and the skills to lead company-wide marketing efforts and to set business priorities, the marketing master coordinates with sales, product development and other functions." Although marketing masters do play a role in overall company strategizing, they do not execute leadership duties and have limited decision-making capabilities.

5   *Best practices advisor*: "The goal is to help individual businesses be effective and efficient marketers, so the best practices advisor provides guidance on internal and external marketing best practices. This type of marketing organization plays the role of an internal process-focused consultant," but generally provides an outside perspective and lends specialty services to an organization in need of them.

6   *Service provider*: Like the best practices advisor, the service provider actually handles the "advertising, promotion, public relations and other marketing services to brand and product teams." Unlike the other classifications, the service provider is not an integral part of the organization but is instead brought in at the last stages of the marketing process to help with "tactical execution."[38]

Landry *et al.* were careful to clarify that none of these models is generally "right" or generally "wrong." Neither do they represent a hierarchy or an evolutionary ladder. They are right or wrong only when they do or do not fit the particular market position, competitive challenge, and growth strategy of a given organization. However, it is critically important that a company has the marketing profile that best suits its needs and that this profile is consistent with whatever metrics are used to evaluate performance."[39]

However, if any one of these categories could be characterized as sitting at the top of the "evolutionary ladder," it is the growth champion. As explained by Bob Liodice of the Association of National Advertisers (ANA), this study found that growth champions own their companies' key growth-support functions, whether or not those functions fit into conventional definitions of the marketing practice. For example, growth champions are not only responsible for traditional tasks, such as introducing new products and expanding the market for mature ones but they also drive the entire product development and innovation function, and significantly contribute to decisions about entering new markets and acquiring new businesses.[40]

In other words, growth champions do epitomize effective marketing. This offers a particularly interesting idea to ponder, in that the best marketing structures may not look a whole lot like traditional marketing anymore. In addition to traditional marketing responsibilities, growth champions demonstrate how "marketers have learned to stretch their discipline's traditional boundaries to encompass activities many companies don't even think of as marketing," in order to drive growth.[41]

Because of their unique boundary-spanning abilities, growth champions are characterized by traits that make them particularly useful in any attempt to find a prototype that can help organizations align marketing responsibilities with marketing accountability. Perhaps most importantly, they "can clearly identify their contributions to revenue growth, giving them added organizational credibility and authority." Moreover, since they "are perceived by other executives, especially in C-suite offices, as contributors to and leaders of the growth agenda," they have little trouble in helping drive the organization's growth and direction.[42] They also:

"possess a broad range of analytic, financial and creative capabilities." Growth champions, in other words, pull their skills from a range of traditional roles and seamlessly combine them to direct marketing efforts through the organization in a credible and authoritative manner.

All of this helps to alleviate some of the stressors and frictions common in organizations with a more traditional arrangement, where marketing is expected to inform company strategy, build brand, and drive profit, but lacks the leadership capabilities and overall knowledge of business strategy that would make this possible. In this sense, growth champions are an example of Moorman and Rust's idealized marketing structure, offering a diffused marketing presence throughout the organization as well as a highly localized marketing center that focuses on specialty skills.

Unfortunately, organizations that are confused about either their business strategy or their marketing approach often have a difficult time aligning the two. Even when these organizations are clear on one or the other, they may have a difficult time matching one department's skill set and approach to that of another. Technology sometimes plays a role as well, for it has effectively eradicated organizations' abilities to "develop mass products for mass audiences, market them over mass channels, maintain technological differentiation for years at a time and sustain prices without undue threat from disruptive or otherwise advantaged competitors."[43] Firms now struggle to keep up with the new role of the internet in marketing as opposed to older methods of communication in building brand awareness and enticing customers, creating an even stronger need for leadership.[44]

Landry *et al*. argued that it is important for the firm to be clear about the role and responsibilities of marketing. Strategy& (formerly known as Booz & Company, a spinoff of Booz Allen) seeks to do just that, offering a diagnostic tool that further determines an organization's structure, classifying it as passive-aggressive, fits-and-starts, outgrown, over managed, just-in-time, military precision, or resilient. The answers to their short survey help an organization discover which type of marketing approach it ought to take.[45]

The idea that marketing strategy should be aligned with the way the organization is organized is not a new idea, but it is not clear whether many firms have been explicit about aligning marketing responsibilities and accountability.

Slater and Olson Classification

Stanley F. Slater and Eric M. Olson offered a somewhat different classification of the structure of marketing organizations. While the Booz Allen classification implicitly suggests that the "growth champion" type of organization is best, the Slater and Olson classification does not identify a best type of organization. Rather, it simply suggests that there is a need for alignment between marketing style, organization, and business strategy.

Critical to the alignment of marketing responsibilities and accountability is assurance that the type of marketing organization matches the business model used by a firm. A major disjuncture between the two is likely to result in less effective marketing efforts. Vorhies and Morgan observed: "the more similar a business's marketing organization profile is to that of the ideal marketing organization for its strategic type, the greater is its marketing effectiveness." Slater and Olson deduced a similar importance between aligning business strategy with marketing style in their study "Marketing's Contribution to the Implementation of Business Strategy: An Empirical Analysis."[46]

In contrast to the Booz Allen approach, which is based on characteristics of marketing organizations, Slater and Olson begin by defining four broad types of business strategies: prospectors, analyzers, low-cost defenders (who participate in established markets but offer low-cost goods and compete on price) and differentiated defenders (who also operate in well-established markets but provide high-cost, quality goods and services):

1   *Prospectors*: These strategies are highly informal and adaptive with few formal procedures, where important decisions are made at relatively low levels, and where there are high degrees of specialization.
2   *Analyzers*: These strategies are moderately informal and highly decentralized with some marketing specialization, with more formal decision-making than prospector types, but considerable delegation to specialists.
3   *Low-cost defenders*: These strategies are moderately informal and highly decentralized with a large majority of generalists (low specialization).
4   *Differentiated defenders*: These strategies are moderately informal with decentralized decision-making and a moderate number of marketing specialists. This "significantly greater reliance on marketing specialists" is the single most important distinguishing factor between low-cost defenders and differentiated defenders.[47]

They surveyed senior marketing managers about their marketing organizations including questions about market research, segmentation/targeting, product line breadth, product innovation, product quality, customer service, premium pricing, selective distribution, advertising, internal sales force, and support to promotion process. Based on responses to these questions, they grouped respondents' marketing organizations into four clusters that reflect four distinct marketing styles: aggressive marketers, mass marketers, marketing minimizers and value marketers.[48] They developed a detailed description of each type of marketing style:

- *aggressive marketers*: "target the segment of buyers that value high quality, innovative products, and that are willing to pay premium prices. Typically, these products are perceived by these buyers to provide an advantage in competitive markets";
- *mass marketers:* "offer a broad product line of largely undifferentiated products. They utilize an intensive distribution strategy and charge low prices";
- *marketing minimizers:* make fairly little effort toward marketing whatsoever: "Their limited product line, lack of investment in marketing or innovation and low prices indicate that marketing is not a key element in their value chains";
- *value marketers:* "utilize selective distribution to provide high-quality, innovative products but at significantly lower prices than Aggressive Marketers."[49]

These four marketing styles were then compared to business strategy in an effort to determine which marketing style is optimal for any particular business strategy. Their results indicated that the optimal form of marketing organization is indeed dependent on the general business strategy employed by the firm. Thus, while prospectors achieved superior performance when they utilized an aggressive marketing strategy, analyzers benefited most from a mass-marketing strategy, low-cost defenders from a marketing minimizer strategy, and differentiated defenders from a value marketing strategy.[50]

The researchers noted that the results are "consistent with the proposition that a particular marketing strategy would predominate within a business strategy type. That is, marketing strategy is not simply a reflection of business strategy."[51] They also noted that: "there is no significant difference among the business strategy types with regard to either profitability or market performance (relative to objectives and competitors) when marketing strategy type is appropriately matched to business strategy type."[52]

A related study demonstrated that overall firm performance is influenced by how well the marketing organization's structural characteristics (i.e., formalization, centralization, and specialization) and strategic behavior emphasis (i.e., customer, competitor, innovation, and cost control) complement alternative business strategies (i.e., prospector, analyzer, low-cost defender, and differentiated defender).[53]

These results suggest that organizations should adopt marketing strategies, styles, and organizations that support their business strategy and should not assume that their marketing style will automatically derive from their business approach. These results also provide compelling evidence that the marketing organization needs to carefully align particular business types with business strategy to most effectively achieve business goals. An important implication of these results is that the responsibilities of marketing, and the measures by which the performance of the marketing function is evaluated, must be aligned with the broader business strategies of the firm.

Marketing Metrics: Drowning in Data

The empirical research is clear: a firm that successfully aligns its business strategy with its style of marketing organization increases the likelihood of higher performance. This is conceptually simple, but is difficult in practice. This is because it requires clarity of purpose by the organization as well as a set of metrics that reflect both the achievement of the organization's objectives and marketing's contribution to achieving those objectives. In the digital age, there is no shortage of data or measures. More than ever before, organizations are swimming in data that could potentially help them make sense of their marketing efforts, but only if they can link those measures to the performance metrics of the firm, including financial performance. Few firms have the types of processes in place, similar to those described in Chapter 17, which provide clear linkages from marketing actions to the financial performance, growth objectives, and other goals of the firm.

The ANA has described a "metric development and embedment process" for any firm looking to make sense of their data. The steps are as follows:

1   create a cross-functional team;
2   identify marketing's strategic intent and deliverables;
3   select metrics;
4   develop data strategy;
5   set targets for each metric;
6   review metrics and targets with stakeholders;
7   calculate current values;
8   share with organization via dashboards;
9   review and revise process (ongoing).[54]

Note that this metrics development process does not presuppose the existence of any specific type of data, but rather offers a relatively flexible approach to targeting, delineating, and embedding metrics with attention to the needs and opinions of stakeholders and other functions within the organization. Therefore, it will work for organizations across industries and, presumably, even for many different types of firms and marketing styles. The MMAP process described in Chapter 17 provides examples of how these steps might be implemented.

The ANA suggests that creating a permanent marketing metrics model requires attention to "four major axes." Each of these axes observes a sliding scale of behavior that exists in organizations today: at one end, inattention to the factor; and at the other, superlative efforts to realize it. In summary, these axes are:

- *Data*: "Accountability implies quantification and quantification implies data, most desirably time series data, permitting sophisticated analytics." On the one hand, some companies exhibit a lack of data "directly connecting marketing expenditure to a shift in attitudes or behavior." On the other, some organizations have huge amounts of available, useful data.
- *Analytics*: "The confluence of masses of time series data, powerful computer hardware and agile software has enabled a revolution in analytical sophistication." Here one sees a range

of analysis abilities, from those whose marketing efforts still rely too heavily on "virtually useless input data" to companies with "market mix analytics embedded in real-time marketing spending models permitting rapid changes in marketing spending by target consumer and marketing element."

- *Culture*: Organizational approaches to accountability vary widely, from those "in which marketers not only expect to be measured but demand it" to those in which "metrics becomes part of a game aimed at avoiding serious accountability." In the middle are "organizations who struggle to establish fair and sustainable metrics understood as such by all the key departments across all SBUs."
- *Process embedment*: "A key to creating a culture of accountability is a process that enrolls key members of the organization to develop fair measures which can be sustained over time." Underdeveloped or young organizations are likely to exhibit no such processes and:

> create measures without attaining the organizational input from experts in finance, IT, operations, and market research who are often critical to the development of a serious metrics effort. At the other end of the spectrum are mature organizations [that] have a robust metrics process that involves key stakeholders and takes pains to integrate marketing metrics into an overall balanced corporate scorecard approach, which gets wide visibility across all SBUs and functions. A critical objective of the process is to provide marketing metrics with the same credibility that is accorded metrics in operations, finance and manufacturing.[55]

Complexities from the Competitive and Evolutionary Nature of Marketing

Marketing performance, by its very nature, is defined in a competitive context. The outcomes of marketing activities are influenced both by what the individual firms do and what their competitors do. In some ways, this reality differs from the perspective required within the finance discipline (where metrics must often fall within parameters stipulated by regulatory bodies or ratings agencies). This competitive element implies four important characteristics that tend to confound the utility of any given metric for a particular firm, and thus the marketing discipline in general.

First, marketing strategies tend to be implemented in complex environments where both market conditions and the size and ambitions of direct and indirect competitors can conceivably fall within a very wide range. The consequences of this diversity are that any given marketing activity or strategy will be difficult to measure or quantitatively assess in isolation of the external (competitive and environmental) milieu characterizing its application. For example, imagine a promotional campaign that increases sales for a brand by 5 percent. Can this be considered a "successful" strategy? Clearly, the answer to that question must be contingent upon the competitive context or environment within which the campaign is executed. In saturated markets, or where the brand already possesses a majority market share, this 5 percent would likely be considered a remarkable achievement. Conversely, in a fast growing market or for a small-share brand, this same 5 percent growth would easily be deemed a relative failure that could conceivably lead to catastrophic outcomes.

Second, the competitive nature of marketing implies that the success or failure of a marketing action must generally be interpreted as a relative outcome, rather than an absolute one. What this means is that for many aspects of business strategy, financial outcomes must be conceptualized as being relative to the outcomes for competitors, rather than by evaluating them on some absolute measure of success. In other words, because marketing is typically executed in a "zero-sum" competitive context, the success of any given firm (measured by any number of metrics) will typically result in a largely negative impact upon its competitors (on those same metrics). Again, this means that even in a specific market environment, a 5 percent growth in sales would generally be difficult to qualify as absolutely "good," or "great," or "bad," but would usually best be understood in comparison to the sales of competitors. Thus if the 5 percent growth is higher than the rate of all competitors, that would likely qualify the firm's performance on that particular metric as "good," in contrast to the scenario where all the competitors are growing at greater than 10 percent.

Third, the competitive nature of markets implies an evolutionary rather than a static interpretation of success. It is obvious that to compete in virtually any area of business (technology-based or otherwise), dated strategies, techniques, or investments will put a firm at a disadvantage. Competition forces firms to battle at ever-increasing levels of commitment and sophistication. In evolutionary biology, this notion is known as Van Valen's "Red Queen Hypothesis," after Lewis Carroll's character in *Through the Looking-Glass* who describes the dilemma that occurs in "Looking-Glass Land."[56] (When questioned by Alice about why the Queen appears to be running in the same place without making any progress, the Red Queen replies: "Now, here, you see, it takes all the running you can do, to keep in the same place.") In competitive business environments, this Red Queen argument can be used to describe the competitive "arms race" that typically exists in which new strategies and financial commitments must be continuously allocated to a brand merely to maintain market share or position, let alone expand it.

Ultimately, for business, the Red Queen hypothesis condemns any given marketing activity or strategy to a limited life span over which it can be efficaciously leveraged. This is because marketing strategy evolves with ever-increasing velocity and complexity within nearly every industry. As previously noted, when one firm achieves a market success, the impact of this achievement upon competitors is typically negative by definition. Immediately, these competitors will seek to nullify the market advantages of that firm's original strategy and concomitantly seek to develop both defensive actions to that strategy as well as unique offensive strategies of their own to stage a "counter-attack." Because of this marketing "arms race," a strategy that is wildly successful today is unlikely to be as successful tomorrow. In a corollary fashion, what may be acknowledged as a relatively effective marketing strategy for one company must ultimately be considered as possibly (or even probably) ineffective for a rival (or even for another firm in an unrelated industry).

As a result of this Red Queen dilemma, and often unlike the situation faced in the fields of accounting, manufacturing operations, human resource management, or even some portions of finance, it is largely unrealistic to seek standardized solutions or "best practices" in marketing strategy. In marketing, definitions of competitive success must be bounded within highly unique contexts and are typically based upon transitory, evolving, and relative strategies.

Finally, marketing accountability and the analytics necessary for establishing this accountability tend to be somewhat complicated by interactions between conflicting goals that may exist within the management of a given firm or brand. The comparisons among firms that are necessary to establish the criteria for relative success (as previously noted) will always be confounded by internal differences that exist between these firms in terms of costs, strategic goals, and financial characteristics such as debt or tolerance for risk. Thus, interactions between the various metrics will make performance on any given metric a subjective interpretation. Again, using the prior example, 5 percent sales growth may greatly exceed the rates of the competitors, but if overall profits decline as a result (as might happen from lowering prices or from excessive promotional expenditures), then it is likely that 5 percent would no longer be considered an overall success.

The implications of these four features of competitive marketing environments for analytics and accountability are that static, uniform, and absolute measures of performance tend to be of less utility in marketing than they might be within the fields of, for example, finance or quality control. Thus, there is a need to focus more on measurement processes rather than on any specific measure.

Aligning Organizations with Measures of Accountability

Assuming that effective marketing processes must account for some method of financial measurement, this chapter turns to determining what those metrics might be. In their book *Marketing Metrics: The Definitive Guide to Measuring Marketing Performance*, Paul Farris *et al.* made a case for linking marketing efforts to financial results and offered several solid approaches to getting started.

They advised that marketers, especially those that are new to the whole "accountability" idea, begin by familiarizing themselves with a few key terms because "understanding how the metrics are constructed and used by finance to rank various projects will make it easier to develop marketing plans that meet the appropriate criteria."[57] Among the suggested terms are rate of return, return on sales, return on investment, residual income, net present value, internal rate of return, and others.[58] While a thorough recapping of each of these terms is beyond the scope of this chapter at this point, it is important to note the underlying assumption, which is that *marketing departments can adapt their accountability measures from preexisting financial metrics*. In a sense, this option is liberating, enabling marketing organizations to learn and co-opt measures of success rather than having to develop them from scratch.

Of course, this is not to say that marketing metrics must be identical to those used in the finance function. Instead, the point is that by developing marketing-oriented measures based on previously existing and well-documented financial measures, marketing departments can benefit from already defined measurement processes and thereby increase their chances of remaining accountable to the overall business strategy. However, many marketing metrics will be specifically configured to take into account the marketing function. Farris *et al.* offer as examples the market size in units, company unit share, unit sales, premium brand units, discount brand units, and advertising and promotion spend.[59]

They contend that with the combination of these metrics with financial metrics, an organization will be able to determine whether their marketing efforts are paying off. Although a complete discussion of which marketing metrics provide the best chance of financial accountability is impossible, the authors concluded with the statement that a huge array of metrics exist for potential use:

> We do not believe it is generally possible to provide unambiguous advice on which metrics are most important or which management decisions are contingent on the values and trends of certain metrics. These recommendations would have to be of the "if, then" form, such as "If the relative share is greater than 1.0 and the market growth is higher than change in GDP, then invest more in advertising.[60]

This reflects that marketing metrics are not simply a measure by which an organization has met a certain goal or not, but a part of a robust and flexible system for use in making marketing decisions.

Next Stage in the Evolution of Marketing: Orientation and Accountability

Does the alignment of marketing accountability with marketing responsibilities harmonize with the alignment between company processes and market needs? As previously noted, marketers have long called for both a broader and deeper influence within the firm. As the central component of this crusade, marketers have argued for the importance of adopting a comprehensive "market orientation" at every level of the organization, such that all sectors and functions are coordinated around the common goal of effectively identifying and serving customer needs. In other words, marketers have justifiably argued that organizational effectiveness can be significantly improved by the coordinated alignment of company functions and processes with market preferences and needs.

Commonly, the push for the adoption of a company-wide market orientation is argued from the position of *centralizing* marketing planning (within the marketing department), while broadly *decentralizing* marketing execution and a market-oriented mindset. This is because a market orientation often implies a mutually shared, coordinated implementation of an organized and singular strategy. Of course, this coordination and organization would seem to imply a broader and more robust influence of the marketing function on other areas of the organization. For this reason, it is not uncommon that the insistent call for embracing a company-wide market orientation is often accompanied by efforts to reinforce the authority and power of the marketing executives. Consequently, these efforts at developing a market orientation are likely to be viewed with skepticism by executives of other departments of the organization, who may infer power-oriented motives. Thus, whether legitimate or self-serving, marketers' efforts to organize and align company processes with market needs may meet with resistance from other executives due to perceptions that these efforts represent "empire building" on the part of the marketing department. This is unfortunate, because the potential benefits of a market orientation and/or alignment efforts have been demonstrated with considerable consistency.

These efforts to implement a market orientation or enhance alignment between marketing and the other functional areas of an organization, and the often corresponding endeavors (whether real or merely perceived) to enhance the power and influence of the marketing group within an organization, have significant relevance to the important task of increasing the accountability of the marketing function. Authority without accountability tends to be wielded recklessly and imprudently. Whereas the marketing function (whether housed in internal departments or external agencies) has long tended to petition for greater authority over organizational goals and strategies, this authority (whenever it has been attained) has less commonly been accompanied by increased accountability. This expanding decoupling of authority from accountability has led marketing to the state where its effectiveness is often questioned. As a result, just as organizations need to be realigned with markets through the application of a united market orientation, the authority of the marketing function is in need of realignment with financial and operational accountability.

Accountability necessarily requires both consequences and transparency. Ultimately, marketing accountability implies holding the performance of marketing accountable to standards that have been established a priori according to the strategic goals of the organization. This means marketing activities that do not meet these standards or advance these goals must change. Accountability means that immediate and substantive actions will be taken when standards are not met. Similarly, accountability requires transparency, and transparency means being able to acknowledge your failures to other functional departments within the firm that are dependent upon marketing.

True acceptance and embrace of the paradigm of accountability implies that marketing must emerge from the shadows and draw back the veil, or perhaps the myth, of secret knowledge. Accountability requires the use of metrics and standards that are both visible and comprehensible to all executives of the company, regardless of functional expertise or authority. As noted above, this requirement reinforces the advantages of employing measurements consistent with, or at least compatible with, those already used by finance. Whereas a market orientation requires that all areas of the organization adopt an understanding and concern for consumer needs, marketing accountability requires that all of these same areas of the organization be able to easily observe, assess, and compare the outcomes of marketing processes and functions against pre-established standards. In other words, marketing accountability means that all areas of the firm can easily monitor and scrutinize the methods and, most importantly, the results of marketing (both successes and failures).

This level of transparency is, of course, somewhat threatening or even terrifying to marketers. This is because transparency results in vulnerability. Yet vulnerability must be accepted, and even embraced, if marketing is to be truly accountable. As Peter Drucker (1954)[61] noted, marketing is perhaps the key essential function within business. Yet despite this essentiality, marketing without accountability cannot effectively serve the strategic objectives of the firm.

Conclusions

Due to the blossoming of the digital age, a widespread acceptance of the importance of marketing accountability is now colliding with a torrent of available data. Just as firms are beginning to realize the need for aligning marketing metrics with their organizations' overall goals, they are flooded with almost more information than they can handle. Whether this convergence is interpreted as fortuitous or merely a case of poor timing is likely to depend upon how effectively organizations respond to this opportunity. At a minimum, firms have two options: (1) to become immobilized, effectively resigning the organization to competitive oblivion; or (2) to accept the necessity of adopting a slow, steady, ever-evolving, and unrelenting planning and measurement process. That latter option requires not only dictating responsibilities but also undergoing a serious effort to determine the firm's characteristics and goals and then choosing an effective marketing approach.

Without the alignment of business strategy and the marketing organization, there can be no effective alignment of marketing responsibility with marketing accountability. Only after these factors are determined can a firm move forward, delineating what it expects of its marketing function, and matching those expectations with measures of accountability to determine that the marketing function is serving and fulfilling its highest and best purpose.

References

1. David W. Stewart, 2009, "Marketing Accountability: Linking Marketing Actions to Financial Results," *Journal of Business Research*, 62: 636–643.
2. Nicholas Varchaver, "Scanning the Globe. The Humble Bar Code Began As an Object of Suspicion and Grew Into a Cultural Icon. Today It's Deep in the Heart of the FORTUNE 500," *Fortune*, May 31, 2004.
3. "What is Marketing?," *Forbes*, last updated August 9, 2012, http://www.forbes.com/sites/sap/2012/08/09/what-is-marketing/.
4. Ralph Steiner, 1976, "The Prejudice against Marketing," *Journal of Marketing*, 40(3): 2–9.
5. Ralph Steiner, 1976, "The Prejudice against Marketing," *Journal of Marketing*, 40(3): 2–9.
6. "About AMA: Definition of Marketing," *American Marketing Association*, accessed November 23, 2014, https://www.ama.org/AboutAMA/Pages/Definition-of-Marketing.aspx.
7. Peter F. Drucker, *The Practice of Management*, 1955, London, UK: Heinemann.
8. Mehmet Pasa and Steven M. Shugan, 1996, "The Value of Marketing Expertise," *Management Science*, 42(3): 370–388.
9. Douglas W. Vorhies and Neil A. Morgan, 2003, "A Configuration Theory Assessment of Marketing Organization Fit with Business Strategy and Its Relationship with Marketing Performance," *Journal of Marketing*, 67(1): 100–115.
10. D. G. Brian Jones and Eric H. Shaw, "A History of Marketing Thought," in *Handbook of Marketing*, Barton A. Weitz and Robin Wensley (eds), 2002, Thousand Oaks, CA: Sage Publications, Inc., p. 39.
11. William T. Kelly, 1956, "The Development of Early Thought in Marketing and Promotion," *Journal of Marketing*, 21: 59–68; D. G. Brian Jones and Eric H. Shaw, "A History of Marketing Thought," in *Handbook of Marketing*, Barton A. Weitz and Robin Wensley (eds), 2002, Thousand Oaks, CA: Sage Publications, Inc., pp. 41–44.
12. William L. Wilkie and Elizabeth S. Moore, 1999, "Marketing's Contribution to Society," *Journal of Marketing*, 63(Special Issue): 198–218.
13. Susan Strasser, *Satisfaction Guaranteed: The Making of the American Mass Market*, 1989, New York: Pantheon Books, pp. 18–24.

14 Hounshell, David A., *From the American System to Mass Production, 1800–1932: The Development of Manufacturing Technology in the United States*, 1984, Baltimore, MD: Johns Hopkins University Press; Taylor, Frederick Winslow, *The Principles of Scientific Management*, 1911, New York: Harper and Brothers.
15 Herbert N. Casson, *Ads and Sales: A Study of Advertising and Selling from the Standpoint of the New Principles of Scientific Management*, 1911, Chicago, IL: A. C. McClurg.
16 Pamela Walker Laird, *Advertising Progress: American Business and the Rise of Consumer Marketing*, 1998, Baltimore, MD: The Johns Hopkins University Press, pp. 211–214.
17 Pamela Walker Laird, *Advertising Progress: American Business and the Rise of Consumer Marketing*, 1998, Baltimore, MD: The Johns Hopkins University Press, pp. 249–253, 330.
18 Pamela Walker Laird, *Advertising Progress: American Business and the Rise of Consumer Marketing*, 1998, Baltimore, MD: The Johns Hopkins University Press, pp. 105–108; Donald Davis, *Conspicuous Production: Automobiles and Elites in Detroit, 1899–1933*, 1988, Philadelphia, PA: Temple University Press.
19 Herbert N. Casson, *Ads and Sales: A Study of Advertising and Selling from the Standpoint of the New Principles of Scientific Management*, 1911, Chicago, IL: A. C. McClurg, pp. 71–73.
20 Susan Strasser, *Satisfaction Guaranteed: The Making of the American Mass Market*, 1989, New York: Pantheon Books, pp. 153–154.
21 Susan Strasser, *Satisfaction Guaranteed: The Making of the American Mass Market*, 1989, New York: Pantheon Books, pp. 146–147.
22 Lawrence R. Samuel, *Freud on Madison Avenue*, 2000, Pennsylvania, PA: University of Pennsylvania Press, p. 5.
23 Lawrence R. Samuel, *Freud on Madison Avenue*, 2000, Pennsylvania, PA: University of Pennsylvania Press, p. 5.
24 Regina Lee Blaszczyk, *American Consumer Society, 1865–2005: From Hearth to HDTV*, 2009, Wheeling, IL: Harlan-Davidson, pp. 123–125.
25 Lawrence R. Samuel, *Freud on Madison Avenue*, 2000, Pennsylvania, PA: University of Pennsylvania Press, pp. 7–9.
26 Lawrence R. Samuel, *Freud on Madison Avenue*, 2000, Pennsylvania, PA: University of Pennsylvania Press, pp. 6–18.
27 Mehmet Pasa and Steven M. Shugan, 1996, "The Value of Marketing Expertise," *Management Science*, 42(3): 370.
28 Mehmet Pasa and Steven M. Shugan, 1996, "The Value of Marketing Expertise," *Management Science*, 42(3): 370.
29 Mehmet Pasa and Steven M. Shugan, 1996, "The Value of Marketing Expertise," *Management Science*, 42(3): 371.
30 Mehmet Pasa and Steven M. Shugan, 1996, "The Value of Marketing Expertise," *Management Science*, 42(3): 386.
31 Christine Moorman and Roland T. Rust, 1999, "The Role of Marketing," *Journal of Marketing*, 63(Special Issue): 180.
32 Christine Moorman and Roland T. Rust, 1999, "The Role of Marketing," *Journal of Marketing*, 63(Special Issue): 180.
33 Christine Moorman and Roland T. Rust, 1999, "The Role of Marketing," *Journal of Marketing*, 63(Special Issue): 181.
34 Christine Moorman and Roland T. Rust, 1999, "The Role of Marketing," *Journal of Marketing*, 63(Special Issue): 185.
35 Christine Moorman and Roland T. Rust, 1999, "The Role of Marketing," *Journal of Marketing*, 63(Special Issue): 191.
36 Christine Moorman and Roland T. Rust, 1999, "The Role of Marketing," *Journal of Marketing*, 63(Special Issue): 191.
37 Edward Landry, Andrew Tipping, and Brodie Dixon, "Six Types of Marketing Organizations: Where Do You Fit In?," *Strategy + Business*, last updated October 11, 2005, http://www.strategy-business.com/article/rr00025?gko=489ba.
38 Andrew Tipping, Edward Landry, and Brodie Dixon, "The DNA of Marketing," last updated 2006, http://www.strategyand.pwc.com/media/uploads/The_DNA_of_Marketing.pdf.

39 Andrew Tipping, Edward Landry, and Brodie Dixon, "The DNA of Marketing," last updated 2006, http://www.strategyand.pwc.com/media/uploads/The_DNA_of_Marketing.pdf.
40 Bob Liodice, "CMOS Must Live Up to The Boss' Expectations," *Advertising Age*, last updated November 12, 2007, http://adage.com/article/btob/cmos-live-boss-expectations/269447/?btob=1.
41 Bob Liodice, "CMOS Must Live Up to The Boss' Expectations," *Advertising Age*, last updated November 12, 2007, http://adage.com/article/btob/cmos-live-boss-expectations/269447/?btob=1.
42 Bob Liodice, "CMOS Must Live Up to The Boss' Expectations," *Advertising Age*, last updated November 12, 2007, http://adage.com/article/btob/cmos-live-boss-expectations/269447/?btob=1.
43 Andrew Tipping, Edward Landry, and Brodie Dixon, "The DNA of Marketing," last updated 2006, http://www.strategyand.pwc.com/media/uploads/The_DNA_of_Marketing.pdf.
44 Andrew Tipping, Edward Landry, and Brodie Dixon, "The DNA of Marketing," last updated 2006, http://www.strategyand.pwc.com/media/uploads/The_DNA_of_Marketing.pdf.
45 "Org DNA Profiler Survey," accessed November 26, 2014, http://www.strategyand.pwc.com/global/home/what_we_do/services/ocl/ocl_service_areas/49036161/orgdna-profiler.
46 Stanley F. Slater and Eric M. Olson, 2001, "Marketing's Contribution to the Implementation of Business Strategy: An Empirical Analysis," *Strategic Management Journal*, 22(11): 1055–1068.
47 Eric M. Olson, Stanley F. Slater, and G. Tomas M. Hult, 2005, "The Performance Implications of Fit Amount Business Strategy, Marketing Organization Structure, and Strategic Behavior," *Journal of Marketing*, 69: 61.
48 Stanley F. Slater and Eric M. Olson, 2001, "Marketing's Contribution to the Implementation of Business Strategy: An Empirical Analysis," *Strategic Management Journal*, 22(11): 1059.
49 Stanley F. Slater and Eric M. Olson, 2001, "Marketing's Contribution to the Implementation of Business Strategy: An Empirical Analysis," *Strategic Management Journal*, 22(11): 1060.
50 Stanley F. Slater and Eric M. Olson, 2001, "Marketing's Contribution to the Implementation of Business Strategy: An Empirical Analysis," *Strategic Management Journal*, 22(11): 1061.
51 Stanley F. Slater and Eric M. Olson, 2001, "Marketing's Contribution to the Implementation of Business Strategy: An Empirical Analysis," *Strategic Management Journal*, 22(11): 1062.
52 Stanley F. Slater and Eric M. Olson, 2001, "Marketing's Contribution to the Implementation of Business Strategy: An Empirical Analysis," *Strategic Management Journal*, 22(11): 1063.
53 Eric M. Olson, Stanley F. Slater, and G. Tomas M. Hult, 2005, "The Performance Implications of Fit Amount Business Strategy, Marketing Organization Structure, and Strategic Behavior," *Journal of Marketing*, 69: 49.
54 "ANA Marketing Accountability Task Force Findings," *Association of National Advertisers*, last updated October 8, 2005, http://www.bim.bz/emm_1/docs/ANA%20White%20Paper.pdf.
55 "ANA Marketing Accountability Task Force Findings," *Association of National Advertisers*, last updated October 8, 2005, http://www.bim.bz/emm_1/docs/ANA%20White%20Paper.pdf.
56 Leigh Van Valen, 1973, "A New Evolutionary Law," *Evolutionary Theory*, 1: 1–30.
57 Paul W. Farris, Neil T. Bendle, Phillip E. Pfeifer, and David J. Reibstein, *Marketing Metrics: The Definitive Guide to Measuring Marketing Performance*, 2010, Upper Saddle River, NJ: Pearson FT Press, p. 337.
58 Paul W. Farris, Neil T. Bendle, Phillip E. Pfeifer, and David J. Reibstein, *Marketing Metrics: The Definitive Guide to Measuring Marketing Performance*, 2010, Upper Saddle River, NJ: Pearson FT Press, pp. 337–338.
59 Paul W. Farris, Neil T. Bendle, Phillip E. Pfeifer, and David J. Reibstein, *Marketing Metrics: The Definitive Guide to Measuring Marketing Performance*, 2010, Upper Saddle River, NJ: Pearson FT Press, p. 364.
60 Paul W. Farris, Neil T. Bendle, Phillip E. Pfeifer, and David J. Reibstein, *Marketing Metrics: The Definitive Guide to Measuring Marketing Performance*, 2010, Upper Saddle River, NJ: Pearson FT Press, p. 367.
61 Peter Drucker, *The Practice of Management*, 1954, New York: Harper and Row.

20 Epilogue

Craig T. Gugel and David W. Stewart

Introduction

It was John D. Rockefeller, Jr. who once said: "The secret of success is to do the common thing uncommonly well."[1] American marketers have long been known for their brand-building prowess, their ability to take common everyday products and turn them into marquee brands. However, as the U.S. product marketplace and the global brand forum have consolidated, the complexity of the marketing function has rapidly escalated. It is no longer adequate to implement a marketing campaign without concrete metrics to measure its success. The American Marketing Association (AMA) has said that: "In the current hyper competitive business environment, it is crucial for marketers to understand how all aspects of their marketing activities perform and how that performance links to the organization's financial outcomes."[2] The AMA goes on to say that: "Brands must be managed as critical financial assets, requiring a relationship of trust and transparency between marketing and finance. Marketers should have strong financial acumen and speak the language of finance along with being the champion of the customer."[3]

The Boardroom Project, the Marketing Accountability Foundation (MAF) and the Marketing Accountability Standards Board (MASB)

As brand marketing accountability becomes the rule rather than the exception at most consumer goods manufacturers, the need to harmonize metrics, metric definitions, and measurement standards has become paramount. In an effort to formally move the industry in this direction, The Boardroom Project launched MAF, which established its standard setting group, MASB, in 2007. MASB was charged with creating, compiling, and adopting "generally accepted standards for the measurement of marketing outcomes that are explicitly linked to the financial performance of the firm in predictable ways" (p. 16).[4]

MASB believes that standard setting is not a singular event. It is iterative, grounded in the corporate business model, and "aligned with the company's financial reporting and business decision making processes" (p. 4).[5] MASB members also assert "that every marketing activity leads to an intermediate marketing outcome which ultimately drives cash flow" (p. 4).[6]

Historically, documenting marketing's impact on a brand's bottom line has been a rather disjointed process. Lack of meaningful metrics was one of the primary reasons why marketing was often looked upon skeptically by corporate financial management. While MASB recognized that change was needed, the question became: "Where to start?" After conducting an extensive review of pertinent literature, evaluating numerous presentations from industry financial experts, and analyzing extensive fast-moving consumer goods (FMCG) datasets, it became apparent that MASB could best move forward by studying and applying the precepts of the twentieth century's manufacturing quality movement. Many corporations that have undertaken implementation of quality movement standards have recognized that they were able to transform inefficient production processes and operations into vastly streamlined systems of manufacturing (p. 18).[7]

MASB members agree that: "For a company to be successful in today's fiercely competitive global economy, marketing must be excellent" (p. 38).[8] Or, as might be inferred from John D. Rockefeller Jr.'s statement above, brand success is likely to result from brand promotion performed "uncommonly well." In so doing, MASB members believe that:

> [marketers] must adhere to strict standards that are based not on opinions, hunches, nostalgia, or history but rather on statistics that pave the way for a control process. Only then can marketing departments guarantee their results, confidently build brand, protect market share, and propel the companies they represent into the future. (p. 38)[9]

Common Language Database

Part of moving companies into the future also involves creating a common language for database business analytics and measurement standards that are likely to be used cross industry. Implementation of harmonized metrics and metric definitions will help to increase marketing efficiency and will help in paving the way for general acceptance and credibility on the part of financial management. MASB members believe that we will be able to improve both intra- and inter-company communications if we all operate from the same metric-standard script (p. 46).[10] Included in this metric-standard script will be terms such as: brand preference, brand valuation, return on investment (ROI), customer lifetime value (CLV), brand awareness, discounted cash flow, brand strength, perceived value, and net present value among many others.

Brand: Preference, Strength, Awareness, Perceived Value and Discounted Cash Flow

MASB believes in the importance of the brand preference metric as it "can be used to anticipate the success of marketing activities and to assess the financial performance of brands" (p. 58).[11] However, prior to this occurring, brand preference must be linked in tandem to basic brand awareness and financial measures. Through implementation of its Marketing Metrics Audit Protocol (MMAP), MASB is able to conceptually link "marketing activities to intermediate outcome metrics [and then] to measures of financial return, [using] a validation and causality audit based on [ideal metric characteristics] and guidelines for measures of return on marketing investments" (pp. 226–227).[12]

During their investigation, MASB members uncovered three pertinent metrics that needed to be integrated into what has come to be called its brand valuation model. These metrics include: perceived value, discounted cash flow, and brand strength. MASB posits that perceived value, an empirically validated metric based on economic theory, is likely to be an ideal measure to link "marketing metrics such as attitudes and intentions to financial metrics such as contribution and cash flow" (pp. 226–227).[13] MASB members also believe that discounted cash flow, rather than the royalty relief method, is more efficacious, and that brand strength which is driven by competitive conditions, marketing effectiveness, and other external environmental factors is a significant risk predictor that can help determine the probability that future cash flows will result from marketing activity over a particular time period (pp. 67–68).[14] Whether it is through use of behavior-based measures such as brand awareness, attitudinal surveys, or conjoint analyses, MASB members are on the forefront of linking brand preference metrics to financial performance (p. 57).[15]

CLV

Buyers of consumer package goods continue to be a fast-moving target. Given diminishing levels of consumer loyalty, i.e., with customer turnover averaging about 40 percent a year, understanding product purchasers and their allegiance to one brand or another can be problematic. One metric that MASB has found to be effective in helping to measure customer loyalty is CLV. Customer relationship management programs typically use CLV as a net present value measure to determine potential profits that may be gleaned from various existing or new customer strata over a given time frame (p. 83–84).[16]

In analyzing several FMCG datasets over the past several years, MASB members have found that "the CLV metric is a more stable, slow-moving metric that can be predictive of future business results" (p. 84).[17] The MASB study indicated that couponing and price discounts were solely short-term sales drivers, while increased advertising messaging drove both CLV and short-term sales. These findings suggest that marketers can make smarter brand decisions by analyzing advertising's impact on CLV (p. 84).[18]

Long-Term Outcomes of Marketing Actions

Throughout its work, and as is clearly reflected in this book, MASB has recognized that the effects of marketing actions take place in both the short term and the longer term. Longer-term effects have historically been more difficult to quantify, but there is no doubt that such effects are real. The market effects and economic value of brands and customer satisfaction often persist long after the marketing actions that created them have been completed. The contributions of marketing and the returns on investments in marketing activities will be underestimated if these longer-term outcomes are ignored. Attention to these longer-term outcomes are also what makes marketing a strategic discipline.

ROI

As marketing accountability becomes more prevalent cross industry, use of the key performance indicator ROI will take on greater relevance. Marketing activities and metrics, such as brand preference and customer equity, that can be linked directly to ROI and thus through to brand financial performance, are likely to see a significant increase in use in the coming years (p. 58).[19] There are significant challenges to realizing this goal. Organizations will need to improve, and in some cases create, linkages between marketing activities and financial performance. This will require effort and resources. However, if done well the return on investing in a better understanding of these linkages will be large, as it was in the quality movement.

Another challenge will be related to financial reporting. Brands and customer equity are undeniably important assets of the firm. Yet, as described in several chapters in this book, these assets are not well represented in the financial reporting of the firm.

It's a Process

An important lesson embedded within this book is that marketing accountability is not fundamentally about measures and measurement. Measures are important and necessary, of course. However, measures alone are insufficient for assuring accountability. Rather, there must be processes in place which guide the selection and use of measures, facilitate the identification of better or worse actions and associated outcomes both in advance and following those actions, and aid organizational learning. This is a lesson first learned by the quality movement, but which must be applied in a marketing context. Just as the quality movement ultimately demonstrated that quality was an organizational issue that could not be left to the operations functions, so too will marketing accountability require the engagement of the whole organization.

Concluding Comments

The American Association of Advertising Agencies recently commented:

> It is encouraging to note that marketers are recognizing that persistent messaging of all kinds at reasonable spend levels will measurably improve brand value. Most importantly, persistent messaging targeted against brand loyalists will increase short-term cash flow because these customers require less promotion spending which is [a variable that] improves a brand's short-term cash flow. This should be music to the ears of CFOs and procurement officers.[20]

The Advertising Research Foundation (ARF) recently concurred and stated that: "Defining the relationship of marketing to financial performance is a critical part of these initiatives, and has particular relevance for comparing investments across media channels." The ARF goes on to state that:

> This is a time of transformation for marketing, research, insights and analytics functions worldwide, with silos being broken down and new roles established. The importance of MASB's work in all of these contexts, in terms of driving growth for the C-suite through accurate and comparable measurement of all marketing efforts, establishing accountability standards, and building CMO/CFO alignment, cannot be understated.[21]

Finally, the Association of National Advertisers (ANA) reasons that accountable marketing is crucial in an age of media fragmentation and product proliferation. "The ANA believes that MASB's work in setting industry-wide metrics, standards, and a common understanding of marketing accountability best practices plays an important role in that process." As Bob Liodice, President and CEO of the ANA, commented several months ago: "There is one group exclusively devoted to marketing measurement [that is] predictive of financial return, and all marketers who are serious about meeting the accountability mandate should get involved."[22]

References

1 Demers, J., (June 13, 2015), *Quotes to Inspire Success in Your Life and Business*, www.inc.com, retrieved from http://www.inc.com/jayson-demers/51-quotes-to-inspire-success-in-your-life-and-business.html.
2 Costopulos, N., 2015, *American Marketing Association Commentary*. Unpublished.
3 Costopulos, N., 2015, *American Marketing Association Commentary*. Unpublished.
4 Blair, M. H., Barns, M., Sirkin, K., and Stewart, D. W., "Delivering to the Marketing Accountability Mandate," in D. W. Stewart and C. T. Gugel (eds), *Accountable Marketing: Linking Marketing Actions to Financial Performance*, 2016, New York: Routledge/Taylor & Francis, pp. 3–17.
5 Blair, M. H., Barns, M., Sirkin, K., and Stewart, D. W., "Delivering to the Marketing Accountability Mandate," in D. W. Stewart and C. T. Gugel (eds), *Accountable Marketing: Linking Marketing Actions to Financial Performance*, 2016, New York: Routledge/Taylor & Francis, pp. 3–17.
6 Blair, M. H., Barns, M., Sirkin, K., and Stewart, D. W., "Delivering to the Marketing Accountability Mandate," in D. W. Stewart and C. T. Gugel (eds), *Accountable Marketing: Linking Marketing Actions to Financial Performance*, 2016, New York: Routledge/Taylor & Francis, pp. 3–17.
7 Stewart, D. W., "Lessons from the Quality Movement," in D. W. Stewart and C. T. Gugel (eds), *Accountable Marketing: Linking Marketing Actions to Financial Performance*, 2016, New York: Routledge/Taylor & Francis, pp. 18–42.
8 Stewart, D. W., "Lessons from the Quality Movement," in D. W. Stewart and C. T. Gugel (eds), *Accountable Marketing: Linking Marketing Actions to Financial Performance*, 2016, New York: Routledge/Taylor & Francis, pp. 18–42.
9 Stewart, D. W., "Lessons from the Quality Movement," in D. W. Stewart and C. T. Gugel (eds), *Accountable Marketing: Linking Marketing Actions to Financial Performance*, 2016, New York: Routledge/Taylor & Francis, pp. 18–42.

10 Farris, P., Reibstein, D., and Scheller, K., "Marketing's Search for a Common Language," in D. W. Stewart and C. T. Gugel (eds), *Accountable Marketing: Linking Marketing Actions to Financial Performance*, 2016, New York: Routledge/Taylor & Francis, pp. 45–51.
11 Hess, M. and Kuse, A. R., "Measuring Brand Preference," in D. W. Stewart and C. T. Gugel (eds), *Accountable Marketing: Linking Marketing Actions to Financial Performance*, 2016, New York: Routledge/Taylor & Francis, pp. 52–59.
12 Hess, M. and Kuse, A. R., "Measuring Brand Preference," in D. W. Stewart and C. T. Gugel (eds), *Accountable Marketing: Linking Marketing Actions to Financial Performance*, 2016, New York: Routledge/Taylor & Francis, pp. 226–232.
13 Sinclair, R., "Reporting on Brands," in D. W. Stewart and C. T. Gugel (eds), *Accountable Marketing: Linking Marketing Actions to Financial Performance*, 2016, New York: Routledge/Taylor & Francis, pp. 226–232.
14 Findley, F., "Measuring Return on Brand Investment," in D. W. Stewart and C. T. Gugel (eds), *Accountable Marketing: Linking Marketing Actions to Financial Performance*, 2016, New York: Routledge/Taylor & Francis, pp. 60–68.
15 Hess, M. and Kuse, A. R., "Measuring Brand Preference," in D. W. Stewart and C. T. Gugel (eds), *Accountable Marketing: Linking Marketing Actions to Financial Performance*, 2016, New York: Routledge/Taylor & Francis, pp. 52–59.
16 Abens, R. and Parcheta, D., "Customer Lifetime Value in the Packaged Goods Industry," in D. W. Stewart and C. T. Gugel (eds), *Accountable Marketing: Linking Marketing Actions to Financial Performance*, 2016, New York: Routledge/Taylor & Francis, pp. 83–95.
17 Abens, R. and Parcheta, D., "Customer Lifetime Value in the Packaged Goods Industry," in D. W. Stewart and C. T. Gugel (eds), *Accountable Marketing: Linking Marketing Actions to Financial Performance*, 2016, New York: Routledge/Taylor & Francis, pp. 83–95.
18 Abens, R. and Parcheta, D., "Customer Lifetime Value in the Packaged Goods Industry," in D. W. Stewart and C. T. Gugel (eds), *Accountable Marketing: Linking Marketing Actions to Financial Performance*, 2016, New York: Routledge/Taylor & Francis, pp. 83–95.
19 Hess, M. and Kuse, A. R., "Measuring Brand Preference," in D. W. Stewart and C. T. Gugel (eds), *Accountable Marketing: Linking Marketing Actions to Financial Performance*, 2016, New York: Routledge/Taylor & Francis, pp. 52–59.
20 Donahue, M., 2015, *American Association of Advertising Agencies Commentary*. Unpublished.
21 Snyder, J., 2015, *Advertising Research Foundation Commentary*. Unpublished.
22 Liodice, R., 2015, *Association of National Advertisers Commentary*. Unpublished.

Index

A/B testing 34
Aaker, David A. 191
Abens, Rick 83–95
accountability 16, 31, 156, 243; ANA/Booz Allen classification 249–251; competitive nature of marketing 254–255; corporate branding 214; data 253; evolution of 244–247; financial 157, 256; FMCG brands 85–86; importance of 258; market orientation 256–257; Marketing Metric Audit Protocol 231; MASB 14–15, 160, 165, 236, 264; MillerCoors 163; need for 166; organizational culture 254; pressure for 235; processes 263; results management 162; return on marketing investment 10; transparency 257–258
accounting: brand valuation 182–183, 184–186, 197; reporting on brands 169–181; tax implications of marketing expenses 219–220, 222–224
accretion 174, 179
acquisition 31, 77, 89–90, 91, 94, 184
active buyers 86–87
ADB *see* Asian Development Bank
adverse selection 7, 15, 231
advertising: advertisement attributes 57, 58; Aflac duck campaign 207–210; agencies 15; brand communications ROI model 215; brand equity 123, 124; brand preference 52, 53, 55, 245; consumer response 96, 97–102, 112, 115, 117–118; copy testing 56–57; corporate behavior 97, 102–111, 112, 115, 118; corporate branding 203, 204, 206–207; customer lifetime value 94, 263; evolution of marketing accountability 245–246; expenditure on 114, 214, 216; "fun" 152; impact on sales 84, 91–92, 119–120, 263; investment in 236–237; long-term impacts 96–113, 115, 117–121, 139, 156, 237; measurement of 115–116; need for metrics 12; reengineered ad development 240; return on investment 58, 238–239; short-term impacts 96; social media 156; tax implications 218–224

Advertising Coalition 221
Advertising Research Foundation (ARF) 124, 264
advocacy 60, 65–66, 131
Aflac duck campaign 117, 207–210
agencies: advertising 15, 246; media 16; research 237
aggressive marketers 252
Ailawadi, Kusum L. 187, 196
alcohol products 221
alignment 251, 256–257, 258
"always a share" approach 71–72
AMA *see* American Marketing Association
Amazon 178
Ambach, Greg 116–117
Ambler, Tim 66, 155
American Advertising Federation 221
American Association of Advertising Agencies 264
American Express 154
American Marketing Association (AMA) 49, 50, 122, 244, 246, 261
American Society for Quality 19, 20
amplification 130
ANA *see* Association of National Advertisers
analytics 154–155, 164, 165–166, 241, 253–254, 255; advertising 97, 98, 102, 109, 110, 118; common language 45, 262; customer lifetime value 79
analyzers 251–252
APM Facts 109, 111, 112, 118, 119; brand preference 60; conceptual links 8, 9; consumer response 98, 99, 100, 102; feedback effects 103–107; Marketing Metric Audit Protocol 227–228, 229
Apple 48, 178, 207
ARF *see* Advertising Research Foundation
"arms race" 255
ARS Persuasion 55, 56, 98, 107, 109, 112
artisans 22
Asian Development Bank (ADB) 161–162
ASSESSOR 54–55
assets 168–175, 177–179, 181, 182, 196–197, 263; corporate branding 201, 205; MillerCoors 163;

tax implications of marketing expenses 220, 222–223, 224
Association of National Advertisers (ANA) 16, 49, 138, 221, 249–251, 253, 264
AT&T 27, 178
attitudinal measures 53, 58, 63–67
authority 257
Automotive Purchasing Model 131

Barns, Mitch 3–17
Barwise, Patrick 168
BASES 54, 99
BAV 48
Bayless, Robert A. 169
behavioral measures 54–55, 66, 237, 239, 262
Bell Laboratories 23, 24, 25, 36
benchmarking 18, 46, 203, 206, 223
best practices advisors 250
Biel, Alexander L. 53
big data 155, 166
BIV *see* Brand Investment and Valuation Project
Blair, Margaret Henderson 3–17, 52, 58, 98, 102, 226–232, 235–242
Blockbuster 153
The Boardroom Project 3–4, 10–12, 37, 226, 232, 261
Boeing 247
Booz Allen Hamilton 249–251
BPIR *see* Business Performance Improvement Resource
brand: customer lifetime value 83–95; long-term marketing 114; measurement 153; MillerCoors 163; net promoter score 153–154; perceived value 141, 146; "real options" 6; reporting on brands 168–181, 263; return on investment 60–68; role of 33–34; switching 79, 86, 93, 121; total quality 21
brand affect 190, 191
brand awareness 60, 63–67, 156; Aflac 117; brand value 183, 184, 191; common language 262; long-term marketing 114; measurement of 153
brand builders 250
brand communications ROI model 213–217
brand equity 58, 85, 91, 230; brand valuation 183, 184, 188–193, 197; corporate branding 201, 205–206, 207, 209, 211–212; definitions of 48, 122; long-term marketing 114, 115, 122–124; measurement of 151; price promotions 121, 122; social media 133, 156
brand experience 202–203, 213
brand extensions 6, 56, 123, 144, 145, 185
Brand Finance 48, 176, 178, 183
brand image 183–184, 189–191, 194, 197–198, 210, 212, 215

Brand Investment and Valuation (BIV) Project 58, 68, 176
brand loyalty 65–66, 78–79
brand power 201, 205, 210, 211–212, 215, 217
brand preference 52–59, 184, 237, 238, 239, 262; advertising 124, 245; Duracell 111, 118; Marketing Metric Audit Protocol 8; return on investment 60–68
brand quality 190, 191
brand relevance 60, 65–66, 189, 190, 194, 198
brand strength 60–61, 67, 214, 262
brand trust 190, 191
brand uniqueness 190, 191
brand valuation 60, 67–68, 115, 125, 182–200, 262; brand value creation 183–184; common language 262; corporate brands 201, 210–217; criteria for accounting measure 184–186; market share 61; model of 187–193; purposes of 182–183; reporting 168, 175, 176–181; tax issues 218; three fundamental approaches to 187
BrandZ 48
budgets 18, 55, 84, 139, 152; marketing-analytics approach 164; MillerCoors 161, 162; review of 165; trade promotion 96; *see also* costs; investment
Business Performance Improvement Resource (BPIR) 29
business schools 16
business-to-business (B2B) marketing 70, 72–73, 76, 196, 211
"buy down" phenomenon 61–63

C-Suite Insider 18, 21–22, 34
Calkins, Earnest Elmo 246
Cameron, William Bruce 153
capitals, five interrelated 179, 180
Carroll, Lewis 45, 255
carryover effects 96, 97, 117–118, 119–120, 125
cash flow 8–9, 16, 139, 151, 226, 237; brand communications ROI model 216; brand preference 61; brand valuation 67, 179, 183–184, 186, 187, 188, 193, 197, 262; corporate branding 205, 214; customer lifetime value 77–78; Customer Value Added 144; expenditure on 217; Marketing Metric Audit Protocol 227, 228, 229; targeted marketing 264; total quality 31, 32
Casson, Herbert N. 245
causal links 8–9, 227
causation 156, 186
CE *see* customer equity
centralization 257
CEOs *see* chief executive officers
CFOs *see* chief finance officers

change management 30, 150
Chartered Institute of Marketing 33
Chartered Quality Institute 32
Chattopadhyay, Amitava 57
chief executive officers (CEOs) 15, 151, 204
chief finance officers (CFOs) 15, 154–155, 157–159, 161, 163–165, 204, 235, 241, 264
chief marketing officers (CMOs) 15, 132, 154–155, 157–161, 163–165, 235, 241
China Mobile 178
Citrucel 103–104, 110
CLV *see* customer lifetime value
CMOs *see* chief marketing officers
Coca Cola 123, 169, 178, 179
Code of Marketing Research Standards 32–33
collaboration: barriers to 152–158; MillerCoors 160–166; need for 158–160
Common Language Project 48–50, 52; *see also* language
communication: brand communications ROI model 213–217; brand value creation 184; corporate branding 201, 203, 204, 206–207, 212; shared vocabulary 35; total quality 20; "trust points" 202
company founders 246
company size 215, 247
competition 247, 254–255; competitive reactions to advertising 97, 109–111, 117–118; price promotions 121; standard setting 7, 8
competitive advantage 7, 15, 16, 80
competitive life cycle 141, 144–146
conceptual links 8–9, 37, 186, 227
conjoint methodology 53–54
constrained choice models 142
consumer response 96, 97–102, 112, 115, 117–118
continuous improvement 35, 46; enterprise engineering 235; Marketing Metric Audit Protocol 231; return on marketing investment 10; total quality 20, 21
contract-based assets 173
control charts 23–24, 33, 35, 36–37
copy testing 56–57, 236
CoreBrand 187, 206, 207, 208, 210–212, 214
corporate behavior 97, 112, 115, 118
corporate branding 201–217
corporate social responsibility 205
corporate valuation 188
costs: advertising 245–246; asset value 170; brand valuation 184, 186, 187, 197; competitive life cycle 145, 146; cost of capital 86, 229; customer lifetime value 71, 72; Customer Value Added 143, 144; financial metrics 155; marketing function 243; product life cycle 158; tax implications of marketing expenses 219, 220, 221, 222; total quality 21, 29; transaction 7; *see also* budgets; investment
craft guilds 22
creativity 22, 31, 37, 236
Creech, Bill 27
crisis management 35–36
CRM *see* customer relationship management
Crosby, Philip B. 25
cross-sales effect 110
customer equity (CE) 83, 84–85, 88–89, 91–93, 94, 95
customer lifetime value (CLV) 13, 69–82, 83–95, 139, 262–263; adoption of 76–78; barriers to implementation 78–79; common language 47–48, 262; concept and definition of 69–70; deterministic models 72–73; marketing impact on 91–93; MASB pilot test 87–90; measurement of 70–72; need for 74–76; purchase transaction data 93; stochastic models 73, 74
customer relationship management (CRM) 69, 70, 74, 76, 77, 84, 263
Customer Value Added (CVA) 143, 144, 146–147
customers: behavioral measures 239; brand equity 122–123, 183, 189; brand experience 202–203; consumer response to advertising 96, 97–102, 112, 115, 117–118; CoreBrand Index 211; corporate branding 206, 207; focus on 20, 31; intangible assets 173; marketing function 248–249; net promoter score 153–154; perceived value 140–143; relationships with 139; satisfaction 28, 32, 77, 132, 156, 248, 263; *see also* customer lifetime value
CVA *see* Customer Value Added
cycle of control 26–27

D'Annunzio, Laura Sue 149
data 36, 37, 46, 253, 258; big data 155, 166; brand valuation 186, 193, 197; corporate branding 214; customer lifetime value 78, 88; data warehouses 241; "hard" 246; purchase transaction data 86, 93, 117; scanner data 116–117, 122, 243; social media 130, 131; *see also* analytics; metrics
DataNet Quality Systems 19
decentralization 257
decision-making 4–6; fact-based 20; financial consequences 157; market orientation 249; Marketing Metric Audit Protocol 231; MASB 12; return on marketing investment 10
decision rules 97, 108–109, 117–118
Dekimpe, Marnik G. 117
demand curves 142, 143
demand mix modeling 162
"Deming cycle" 27, 28

Deming, William Edwards 24–26, 27, 28–30, 31, 33, 34, 35, 238, 239
Department of Defense (DOD) 29
deterministic models 72–73
Diageo 168
differentiated defenders 251–252
differentiation 46, 115, 118, 122–123
DiGiorno 90
direct-response advertising 219–220
discounted cash flow (DCF) 61, 67, 184, 186, 187, 188, 193, 195, 197, 262
Disney 33, 34, 154
distribution 63, 64, 184
dividends 215, 216
DOD see Department of Defense
Donkers, Bas 73
Drucker, Peter F. 244, 258
Dubé, Jean-Pierre 79
DuPont Corporation 46, 47
Duracell 106–107, 111, 118, 119

eBay 154
education 157
effectiveness 8, 152, 227, 235, 256–257
efficiency 8, 151, 227, 230
Ehrenberg-Bass Institute 89
employees: autonomy and pride 29; corporate branding 202, 203, 205; Japan 29; matrix organizations 150; quality 20, 21, 27, 28; self-directed learning 163–164
enterprise engineering 235
equity mix 85, 95
Eveready 106–107, 111, 118, 119
expenses 218–224

Facebook 127, 128, 130, 131, 154, 155–156
Fader, Peter S. 47, 74, 87, 88, 124–125
fair value 170, 175–176, 178–179, 188, 222, 223, 224
"fame" campaigns 124
familiarity 124, 207, 208, 210–213, 214
Farris, Paul 45–51, 256
FASB see Financial Accounting Standards Board
"fast followers" 145
fast moving consumer goods (FMCG) 83–95, 261, 263
favorability 208–209, 210–213
feedback effect 97, 102–108, 112, 117–118
Feigenbaum, Armand V. 29
Financial Accounting Standards Board (FASB) 11, 169–171, 174–176, 182, 184–186, 193, 196–197, 235
financial performance 4, 15, 243, 264; accountability 256; brand preference 57–58, 262; competitive life cycle 144–146; corporate branding 201, 213, 214; customer lifetime value 76, 77–78; DuPont Model 46, 47; finance/marketing relationship 137–148, 149–167; marketing function 248; Marketing Metric Audit Protocol 8–10, 229–230; MASB 37–38; perceived value 139–143; reporting 263; total quality 31; see also return on investment
Findley, Frank 60–68
firm value 77–78, 84
Fischer, Marc 182–200
flow metrics 76, 84
FMCG see fast moving consumer goods
Food and Agriculture Organization 157
Forbus, Pamela Hoover 235–242
Ford 27, 35, 247
forecasting 6, 12, 14, 45, 46, 229–230, 235, 238
Four Absolutes of Quality Management 25
four Ps 141
Fraiman, Nelson 239
Fram, Eugene H. 31, 32
functional marketing orientation 248
Furse, D. 66
futures contracts 223–224

GAAP see generally accepted accounting principles
Galbraith, Jay R. 150
Gaskill, Adam 156
Gaskin, Ed 18, 20, 22, 34, 35
General Electric (GE) 178
General Mills 123
General Motors (GM) 30
generally accepted accounting principles (GAAP) 182–183, 187, 188, 197, 219, 222, 223
George, Stephen 31
Germany 193–196
Giesler, Markus 152–153
Gillette 107, 171, 172, 174
goals 20, 154, 162, 205, 255, 258
Goldman Sachs 159
Gordon, Jonathan 154, 156, 159–160, 164–165
goodwill 171, 174, 175, 178, 218, 219, 222, 223
Google+ 128
Google 172, 178
governance 235, 239, 241
government standards 7
Grand Metropolitan 168
Gregory, James 67, 201–217
gross contribution margin 71–72
growth champions 249, 250–251
Gugel, Craig T. 261–265
guilds 22
Gupta, Sunil 77

Hanssens, Dominique M. 72, 76, 85, 96–113, 117, 155
Hardie, Bruce G. S. 47, 87
Harley Davidson 189
Hess, Michael 52–59, 114–126
Holden, Ralph 246
How Brands Grow study 89–90
Huawei 140, 141
human resources (HR) 150
Hume, David 45

IAS *see* International Accounting Standards
IASB *see* International Accounting Standards Board
IBM 33, 34, 73, 150, 178, 191
"ideal metric" 8, 9–10, 37, 132, 186, 226, 228–229
IIRC *see* International Integrated Report Committee
immediate consumer response 96, 97, 112, 117–118
incentive plans 164
income/DCF-based approach 187
Indopco 219
Industrial Revolution 23
industry associations 7, 16
Information Resources, Inc. (IRI) 78, 98, 101, 112, 117–118, 238
innovation 21, 35, 250
Instagram 127, 128
Institute of Chartered Accountants 168
intangible assets 168–175, 178–179, 182, 196–197; corporate branding 205; MillerCoors 163; tax implications of marketing expenses 220, 222–223, 224
integrated reporting (IR) 179–180
Intel 48, 178, 191
Interbrand 48, 176, 178, 183, 196
Internal Revenue Service (IRS) 218–219
International Accounting Standards (IAS) 174–176, 219, 222–223
International Accounting Standards Board (IASB) 11, 169, 170, 171, 174
International Financial Reporting Standards (IFRS) 169, 171, 172, 176, 177, 178, 219, 223
International Institute of Marketing Professionals 32
International Integrated Report Committee (IIRC) 179
International Standards Organization (ISO) 11, 28, 30, 32
internet 34, 80, 251; *see also* social media
investment: brand valuation 193, 194; decision-making 4–6; favorability 208, 213; investor pressures 125; *see also* return on investment

IR *see* integrated reporting
IRI *see* Information Resources, Inc.
IRS *see* Internal Revenue Service
ISO *see* International Standards Organization

Jacobson, Robert 48
Japan 25–27, 29, 238
Jaworski, Bernard J. 247
John Deere 154
Jones, John Philip 53, 98
Juran, Joseph M. 23, 25, 26–27, 29–30, 33

kaizen 46
Kallapur, Sanjay 182
Kalwani, M. U. 122
Keane, Timothy J. 73
Keller, Kevin L. 172, 183, 184
Kellogg's 124
Kimberly-Clark 77
Kohli, Ajay K. 247
Kotler, Phillip 169
Kuhn, Thomas 241
Kumar, V. 69–82
Kuse, Allan R. 52–59, 102, 226–232
Kwan, Sabrina Y. S. 182

Laborie, Jean-Louis 57
Lacoste 123
Laird, Pamela Walker 245–246
Landry, Edward 250, 251
language 35, 45–51, 262
leaders 150
learning 163–164
Lecinski, Jim 46
Lee, Vincent 52
Lehmann, Donald R. 183
Liberty Mutual 154
LinkedIn 127, 128
Liodice, Bob 250, 264
Lodish, Leonard M. 119
long-term effects 5, 114–126, 156, 237, 263; advertising 96–113, 115, 117–121, 139; brand equity 122–124; customer lifetime value 84–85; Marketing Metric Audit Protocol 230; price promotions 121–122
longitudinal research 55–56, 60
low-cost defenders 251–252
loyalty 46, 48, 91; advertising 92, 115, 118; Automotive Purchasing Model 131; brand 60, 65–66, 78–79; brand equity 123; customer lifetime value 77, 78–79, 94, 263; diminishing levels of 262; fast moving consumer goods 83; long-term marketing 114; loyalty programs 72; marketing function 248; price promotions 122

Lunchables 98, 99
luxury brands 123–124, 141

MAC *see* MASB Advisory Council
MacDonald, Malcolm 151
MAF *see* Marketing Accountability Foundation
management: quality and 27–29; results management 161–162, 165
managers 26, 138–139
manufacturing 3, 18, 238, 261; Deming's approach 25; evolution of marketing accountability 245; Industrial Revolution 23; Japan 25–26; total quality 19, 21, 24, 29
market-based approach to brand valuation 187
market capitalization 182, 187, 206, 209–210; brand communications ROI model 216, 217; corporate branding 206; P&G 174
market orientation 248, 249, 256–257
market research: accountability 246–247; brand valuation 197; longitudinal 55–56, 60; surveys versus behavioral measures 237
market share 3, 46, 75, 83, 156, 230, 237; advertising impact 100, 101, 102, 103–106, 120; brand preference 53, 54–55, 61–63, 238; copy testing 56–57; corporate branding 207; Duracell 111; Marketing Metric Audit Protocol 8, 227, 228, 229; protecting 38, 262; terminological issues 47
marketing 36–37, 243–260, 261, 264; ANA/Booz Allen classification 249–251; common language 45–51; competitive nature of 254–255; corporate brand power 201; costs 72; crisis management 35–36; customer-level 69; customer lifetime value 85, 91–93; definition of 50, 244; evolution of marketing accountability 244–247; expenditure on 108; expertise 247, 248; finance relationship 137–148, 149–167; intangible assets 173; long-term effects of 114–126; processes 34–35; reporting 181; response-based 102–103; roles and responsibilities of 247–249; Slater and Olson classification 251–253; standards 32–33; tax implications 218–224; total quality 30–32, 38
Marketing Accountability Foundation (MAF) 4, 11–12, 13, 14, 37, 261
Marketing Accountability Standards Board (MASB) 4, 10–16, 37–38, 160, 236, 261–262, 264; Brand Investment and Valuation Project 58, 68, 176; brand preference 60, 262; brand valuation 67–68, 115, 125, 218; Common Language Project 49–50, 52; customer lifetime value 87–90, 263; effectiveness 227; "ideal metric" 132; Improving Financial Reporting task team 175; long-term effects 263; Long-Term Project 96; MillerCoors 165; mission 14, 57; MMAP 133, 231–232; quantifiable methods 125; vendor selection 231
marketing masters 250
Marketing Metric Audit Protocol (MMAP) 4, 8–10, 14, 226–232, 253, 262; brand preference 56, 60; brand valuation 186; conceptual basis 226–228; social media 133
marketing minimizers 252
marketing mix 3, 162; advertising 118; brand preference 52, 58; brand value creation 183–184; customer lifetime value 77; decision rules 108–109; FMCG brands 85; short-term effects 5; standard metrics 6; television 238
Marketing Research Association (MRA) 32–33
Marketing-Schools.org 33–34
Marketing Science Institute (MSI) 49, 165
Marlboro 178
MASB *see* Marketing Accountability Standards Board
MASB Advisory Council (MAC) 11, 13
mass marketers 252
math 154
matrix organizations 149–150, 160–161, 162, 166
McDonald's 178, 191
measurement 3–4, 16, 46, 263; accountability 256; behavioral measures 54–55, 66, 237, 239, 262; brand awareness 153; brand equity 48; brand preference 53–58; brand valuation 176–178, 184–186, 189–193, 197; competitive nature of marketing 255; corporate branding 205–206; customer lifetime value 70–72; finance/marketing relationship 165–166; lack of 151; long-term effects 115–117, 125; marketing function 253–254; Marketing Metric Audit Protocol 8; MASB 14, 37; net promoter score 153–154; science of 235, 236; social measurement 130, 131–133; standards 6–8, 226, 230, 235–236, 237, 261; *see also* metrics
media 16, 128–130, 237–238, 239
Meier, James 68, 149–167, 241
Mela, Carl F. 122
Mercedes 189
mergers and acquisitions 168, 176, 181, 223
Metamucil 110
metrics 4, 5–6, 16, 46; A/B testing 34; advertising 112; brand preference 60, 262; brand success 83; brand valuation 201, 262; CLV compared to traditional 74–76; common language 48–49, 262; competitive life cycle 144–146; corporate branding 205, 214; defining 8–10; financial 137–140, 144, 146, 150–151, 154–156, 160, 235, 243, 256; harmonization of 261; "ideal metric" 8, 9–10, 37, 132, 186, 226, 228–229;

ignored by marketing executives 36, 138; long-term effects 237; marketing function 253–254; MASB 13–14, 37, 264; need for 12; perceived value 139–143, 146–147; purchase reinforcement 98; purchase transaction data 93; quality 31, 32; short-term effects 85, 237; social media 132, 133; standard 6, 7; transparency 257; *see also* customer lifetime value; Marketing Metric Audit Protocol; measurement; return on investment
Microsoft 172, 178
MillerCoors 156, 160–166, 241
Millward Brown 176, 178, 183
mission 20
MMAP *see* Marketing Metric Audit Protocol
Moe, Wendy W. 124–125
Monier, Jean-Hughes 154, 156, 159–160, 164–165
Moore, Michael L. 218–225
Moorman, Christine 247–248, 251
moral hazard 7, 15
Morgan, Neil A. 251
Motorola 30
MRA *see* Marketing Research Association
MSI *see* Marketing Science Institute
Murdoch, Rupert 168

Nabisco 168
net present value (NPV) 70, 83, 84, 86, 88, 154, 262, 263
net promoter score 153–154
Netgear 154
neuromarketing 53
The New York Times 27
Nichols, Wes 154–155
Nielsen 8, 78, 83, 88, 98, 99, 238
Nishibori, Eizaburo 26
Nokia 150
NPV *see* net present value

Objectives of Marketing Standards 4
Ogilvy, David 52
Ogren, Phil 154, 156, 159–160, 164–165
Olson, Eric M. 251–253
options 5–6, 33
organizational culture 254
organizational structure 149–151, 159, 163, 252
Oscar Mayer Lunchables 98, 99

P(Alive) model 71–72
P&G *see* Procter & Gamble
packaging 156
Parcheta, Debra 83–95
Park, Chan Su 189
Pasa, Mehmet 247

past customer value (PCV) 69–70, 75
Pauwels, Keon 122
PDCA cycle 28
perceived value 139–143, 145, 146–147, 262
persistence modeling 117, 122
persuasiveness 98–101, 107, 110, 111, 112, 118
Petco 154
Peters, Tom 30
Peterson, Robert A. 74
Phillips, Carol 56
Pillsbury 168
Pinterest 128
pioneers 144–145
Prego 99, 101–102, 104–106, 111
premium income per share (PIPS) 207, 208
price: brand equity 123–124; brand preference 63, 64; brand switching 93; brand value creation 184; discounts 84, 91–92; marketing function 248; perceived value 140–141, 142; promotions 115, 121–122, 124; vendor selection 231
price elasticity 91, 92, 114, 124
price premium 227, 228, 229
processes 20, 23–24, 34–35, 263
Procter & Gamble (P&G) 6, 27, 150, 168, 171, 172, 174, 175
product development 16, 250
product life cycle 158
Professional Marketing Standards 33
profitability 3, 156, 245; advertising impact 111; brand equity 124; customer lifetime value 70, 72–73, 76, 77; Customer Value Added 144; investment decisions 5; marketing function 249; metrics 46; perceived value 146
promotions 83, 96, 114, 115, 121–122, 124; aggregate measures 76; corporate branding 207; marketing function 248; Marketing Metric Audit Protocol 231; short-term effects 139
prospectors 251–252
public relations 203, 207, 231
purchase intent 53, 60, 65–66, 131
purchase reinforcement 96, 97–98, 99, 103, 112, 115, 117–118
purchase transaction data 86, 93, 117
purchasing behavior 54

quality 18–32, 34, 38, 261; application to marketing 30–32; brand quality 190, 191; corporate branding 207; crisis management 36; economic benefits of total quality 21–22; importance of total quality 21; Industrial Revolution 23; Japan 25–27, 29; leaders 24–25; management and 27–29; processes 23–24, 34–35, 263; roots of 22; systems approach 29–30; World War II 24

Ragu 111
"real options" 5–6, 31
recency-frequency-monetary (RFM) value 69, 75
red bead experiment 27–28
Red Bull 191
"Red Queen Hypothesis" 255
Reibstein, David 45–51
Reilly, William J. 246
Reinartz, Werner J. 74
relief from royalty 176–177, 187
reporting 168–181, 182, 184–186, 196–197, 223, 263
reputation 7, 36, 189, 201; corporate branding 204, 214; favorability 208, 213
resource allocation 4, 6, 15, 16, 205, 226; customer lifetime value 76, 77; MillerCoors 161, 163; net present value 86; standards 28, 235–236
response-based marketing 102–103
results management 161–162, 165
retailers 78, 243
retention 31, 84, 91; brand value creation 184; customer lifetime value 77–78, 94; purchase reinforcement 97–98, 118
return on investment (ROI) 3, 4, 9–10, 83, 137, 154, 236–241, 263; advertising impact 103, 105; brand communications ROI model 213–217; brand preference 58, 60–68; common language 47, 262; corporate branding 204, 205; customer lifetime value 85, 88; definition of 37; ignored by marketing managers 138; long-term marketing 115, 116; Marketing Metric Audit Protocol 229–231; MASB 12; meaning of 35; metrics 31, 46; Prego 111; quality 32; "real options" 6; short-term effects 96; social media 133; total quality 21; use of the term 155–156
revenue 151, 156; Aflac 208; brand value creation 184; corporate branding 213; perceived value 142, 143, 146; revenue premium model 187
Reynolds, Tom 56
Richardson Vicks 168
risk assessment 245
risk management 28
R.J. Reynolds 168
RJR Nabisco 219
Roberts, John 155
Rockefeller, John D. 261, 262
ROI *see* return on investment
royalties 176, 177
Rust, Roland T. 74, 247–248, 251

sales 5, 151, 156, 237; advertising impact 84, 91–92, 108, 111, 112, 119–120, 263; Aflac 117; aggregate measures 76; baseline 58; brand preference 53, 238; competitive nature of marketing 254–255; copy testing 56–57; customer lifetime value 84, 85, 88–89; Duracell 119; feedback effect 102, 107; Marketing Metric Audit Protocol 8, 227, 228, 229; metrics 46; MillerCoors 156, 161; price promotions 121; scanner data 116; terminological issues 50
Salinas, Gabriela 176, 178, 183, 187
sampling 24
Samsung 178
Samuel, Lawrence R. 246
scanner data 116–117, 122, 243
Scheller, Karen 45–51
Schmittlein, David C. 74
Schuster, Arthur 45
"scientific methods" 245, 246–247
selling expense 137
Semion 196
Senate Finance Committee 221
senior counselors 249–250
service providers 250
Sexton, Donald E. 137–148
Sexton's Contribution Law 143
Sexton's Revenue Law 143
Shah, D. 73
"shakeout" 145, 146
share of requirements (SOR) 54, 121, 123
share of wallet (SoW) 31, 69, 75, 121
shared vocabulary 35, 45; *see also* language
shareholder value 144, 154, 205, 212, 216
shareholders 182, 230; corporate branding 204–205; evolution of marketing accountability 245; total quality 21
Shewhart, Walter 23–24, 33, 35, 36
short-term effects 5, 114–115, 139, 237; fast moving consumer goods 83, 85; Marketing Metric Audit Protocol 230; price promotions 121; short-term lift 97, 112
Shugan, Steven M. 247
silos 150–151, 166, 239, 264
Silverstein, Larry 45
Simon, Carol J. 187
Sinclair, Roger 168–181
Sirkin, Kate 3–17, 127–134
Six Sigma 30, 151–152
Slater, Stanley F. 251–253
Smith, Jim L. 23–24
Snapchat 127, 128
social listening 130, 131
social measurement 130, 131–133
social media 36, 37, 72, 127–134, 144, 156
SOR *see* share of requirements
Southwest Airlines 186
SoW *see* share of wallet
SPC *see* statistical process control
spreadsheets 154, 164

SQC *see* statistical quality control
Srinivasan, V. 189
Sriram, S. 122
stage-gate protocols 158
stakeholders 10, 182, 183; brand experience 213; corporate branding 204–205; Marketing Metric Audit Protocol 231; metrics 254; total quality 21
standardization 6–7, 33, 34, 46
standards 6–8, 10–11, 28, 35, 38, 125, 226; accountability 257; accounting 170–172, 174–176, 179, 181, 182–183, 219, 222–223; brand valuation 183; common language 262; creating and teaching 32–33; harmonization of 261, 262; importance of 235–236; MASB 12, 13–14, 37, 261, 264; measurement development and validation 230, 237; siloed organizations 150; total quality 31, 32
star model 150
Starbucks 33, 34
Starkist 98–99, 103
statistical process control (SPC) 19–20, 23, 24, 28, 31
statistical quality control (SQC) 19–20, 23, 24, 25, 28
Steiner, Ralph 244
Stewart, David W. 3–17, 18–41, 66, 156, 157, 226–232, 243–260, 261–265
stochastic models 73, 74
strategy 139, 151; corporate branding 204; marketing and 244, 251–253, 255, 258; MillerCoors 161; total quality 20
Strategy& 251
Sullivan, Mary W. 187
Sunder, Sarang 69–82
surveys 55–56
Sy, Thomas 149
systems approach 29–30

tangible assets 220
tax 193, 194, 218–225
Taylor, Frederick Winslow 23, 245
technology 33, 173, 245, 251; *see also* internet; social media
Teixeira, Allan 176
television 12–13, 238; advertising impact 91–92, 98, 111, 118–121; copy testing 56–57; Duracell 107, 118; return on investment 58
tenure 75
Tipping, Andrew 249
tobacco products 221
Toshiba 26

total quality management (TQM) 15, 18–32, 34–35, 36, 38, 238, 239; *see also* quality
Toyota 150, 178
trademarks 173, 176, 177, 222
transparency 10, 182, 257–258, 261; finance 159; "ideal metric" 229; Marketing Metric Audit Protocol 231; MASB 12
trust 190, 191, 261; corporate branding 207; "trust points" 202, 203
Tumblr 128
Twitter 127, 128, 131, 132

United Nations 157
utility 188–189

Vakratsas, D. 66
value for money 65–66
value marketers 252
value, perceived 139–143, 145, 146–147, 262
Van den Berg, Sjef 48
Van Valen, Leigh 255
Venkatesan, Rajkumar 77
Verizon 178
Villanueva, Julian 72, 76, 87
Visa 178
vision 20, 21, 36, 206
VK 127
Vorhies, Douglas W. 251

Walmart 178, 186
Wang, Paul 73
Watt, James H. 48
Weibo 127
Weimerskirch, Arnold 31
Welch, Greg 77
White, Percival 246
Wiesel, Thorsten 78
willingness to pay 140, 141
Winsor, Robert D. 243–260
Winzar, Hume 156
word-of-mouth 98, 153
World War II 24

Xerox 27

Yoo, Shijin 79, 83, 84, 88
YouTube 128, 131

Zeithaml, Valerie 77
zero defects 25